STATE OF REBELLION

STATE OF REBELLION

RECONSTRUCTION IN SOUTH CAROLINA

RICHARD ZUCZEK

THE UNIVERSITY OF SOUTH CAROLINA PRESS

© 1996 University of South Carolina

Cloth edition published by the University of South Carolina Press, 1996
Paperback edition published in Columbia, South Carolina,
by the University of South Carolina Press, 2009

www.sc.edu/uscpress

Manufactured in the United States of America

18 17 16 15 14 13 12 11 10 09   10 9 8 7 6 5 4 3 2 1

The Library of Congress has cataloged the cloth edition as follows:
Zuczek, Richard, 1966–
  State of rebellion : reconstruction in South Carolina / Richard Zuczek.
    p. cm.
  Includes bibliographical references and index.
  ISBN 1-57003-105-3
  1. South Carolina—Politics and government—1865–1950. 2. Reconstruction—South Carolina. I. Title.
  F274.Z83 1996
  975.704—dc20   95—50219

ISBN: 978-1-57003-848-8 (pbk)

To my parents,
Stanley and Janet Zuczek,
who supplied the gifts,

and to my wife,
Etsuko,
who made sure I did not waste them.

CONTENTS

List of Illustrations	viii
Preface	ix
Acknowledgments	xi
Introduction	1
Chapter 1: Conservative Reconstruction	10
Chapter 2: The Battle Is Joined—Again	28
Chapter 3: "We Must Fight the Devil with Fire"	47
Chapter 4: Divide and Conquer: The Election of 1870	71
Chapter 5: "A Perfect Reign of Terror"	88
Chapter 6: Truce and Consequences: Federal Retreat and the Conservative Resurgence	118
Chapter 7: The Tide Turns: Republican Isolation and Democratic Mobilization	135
Chapter 8: "It Is in Every Sense a Military Campaign"	159
Chapter 9: The Revolution of '76	188
Conclusion	206
Bibliography	212
Index	229

ILLUSTRATIONS

Photographs

Following page 134

Benjamin F. Perry
A. P. Aldrich
Wade Hampton III
James L. Orr
Matthew C. Butler
Robert K. Scott
Alonzo Ransier
Francis L. Cardozo
Daniel H. Chamberlain
Martin Witherspoon Gary
Johnson Hagood
The Columbia State House
Hampton calming Columbia crowds, 1876

Figures

Figure 1. South Carolina during Reconstruction   2
Figure 2. Bar graph depicting frequency of Klan outrages, October 1870–July 1871   104

Table

Timing of, and evidence for, Klan outrages, taken from the *Ku Klux Klan Report*.   105

PREFACE

Of all the critiques and comments authors dread hearing, perhaps one phrase stands out, so innocent in appearance yet devastating in effect. "Another book on what?" can send the most aloof scholar into an anxiety attack. Why then do I dare to tread over a path as worn as Reconstruction?

In part, because *this* story has not been told. True, studies of Reconstruction in South Carolina first appeared in the late nineteenth century, and the interest continues. Considering the Palmetto State's integral role in both the Civil War and Reconstruction (it experienced both the longest period of Reconstruction and the largest and most dynamic federal presence), the examination of Carolina politics, personages, and society is necessary to an understanding of the era as a whole. Yet despite the bulk of scholarship, the central figures in this drama, conservative white Carolinians, have received a surprisingly small amount of attention. This group, former Confederates and planters, crackers and politicians, held the key to Reconstruction; their support, their indifference, or their opposition would have a critical impact on the present and future condition of the state. Why and how they opposed Reconstruction, and why and how their opposition succeeded, is the subject of this book.

While the focus is South Carolina, larger questions cannot escape notice. The failure of Reconstruction in general, the role of the federal government in state affairs, and the ethnic dilemma facing the postwar nation are broader issues which underlie my subject. Largely a work of Southern political history, this book also hopes to shed light on other aspects of Southern society, such as its penchant for vigilantism, its constitutional and societal conservatism, and its Machiavellian militancy. Readers will no doubt notice a distinctly "military" subtheme. Reconstruction should not be severed from the Civil War or removed from the sectional struggle of nineteenth-century America as a whole. Examining the nature of Reconstruction and its Southern opposition—the personalities, arguments, issues, and course—reveals that 1865–1877 was a continuation of

PREFACE

the struggle of 1861–1865, albeit carried on by different means. Students of military history interested in "people's war" and "low-intensity conflict" should explore this successful revolution of white Southerners against the "Black Republican" governments. Unfortunately, as is often the case in human history, it is the tragedies of the past which seem to offer the most meaningful lessons for the future.

ACKNOWLEDGMENTS

Publishing a book can be compared to achieving immortality, for the author may go on to "live" forever. But the price is high, and the debts incurred are enormous. This undertaking began at the Ohio State University, where Allan R. Millett, Michael Les Benedict, and Joan Cashin succeeded in turning a brash young student into a brash young scholar. The financial support provided by the university's history department and graduate school was priceless, as was the emotional and intellectual support that came from my fellow "Nesters." Other individuals played equally important roles. Some, like Robert McMichael, Trish Montgomery, Margaurite Ward, and Patty Ingram, provided me with lodging during my research, while Matthew Oyos supplied the means—a classic 1980 'Vette, believe it or not—to get me there.

At the archives, I was in the capable hands of the unsung heroes of research; my thanks go out to the staffs of the National Archives, the Ohio Historical Society, the South Caroliniana Library, the South Carolina Department of Archives and History (in particular Carolyn Quickmire), the Southern Historical Collection at the University of North Carolina, Chapel Hill, the Alderman Library at the University of Virginia, and the Special Collections Library of Duke University.

Two other staffs bear mention, those of the University of South Carolina Press and the Papers of Andrew Johnson at the University of Tennessee. Their patience and knowledge, and their confidence in my abilities, rendered the reinforcement I needed. As to the latter, special thanks go to Paul Bergeron and Glenna Schroeder-Lein, who, in subtle but crucial ways, helped this project reach its completion. Finally, I wish to thank my wife, Etsuko, who, while overachieving on her own, still managed to rush my notecards to safety during tornado warnings, call 911 when my appendix burst, and fund my research trips with her paycheck. I owe her greatly, and know that my debt will only continue to grow.

STATE OF REBELLION

INTRODUCTION

War by Another Means

On the evening of April 14, 1865, Laura M. Towne sat down to record the day's events in her diary. The native Pennsylvanian, who had been teaching blacks on South Carolina's Sea Islands, had not yet heard news that President Lincoln lay dying from an assassin's bullet. Instead, she wrote of something she had witnessed firsthand that spring day, an event that had caused a sensation across the Palmetto State. In Charleston Harbor, General Robert Anderson raised the United States flag over Fort Sumter, four years to the day after he had surrendered it. The assassination of President Lincoln and the raising of the Stars and Stripes presented an uncanny coincidence of closure to America's bloodiest conflict.[1]

For South Carolinians, the raising of the flag over Fort Sumter did not signify an end. True, it brought sorrow, Northern occupation, and a transformation within their society which, ironically, their desperate act of secession had been designed to avoid. But rather than bringing an end, the raising of the flag marked the beginning of a new phase in a continuing struggle by white South Carolinians to protect their state—and preserve their society—from what they perceived as the encroaching designs of a hostile Northern population. It was a struggle that opened with the century itself, a struggle that had led to a bloody civil war, a struggle which seemed lost in the face of Northern victory.

But lost it was not. The surrender of General Robert E. Lee at Appomattox and Joseph E. Johnston at Bennett's House may have ended military campaigning, but many issues of the Civil War were yet to be resolved. The awesome questions of the status of both the newly freed slaves and the late insurrectionary states lay before the new president,

1

Introduction

Andrew Johnson, and the victorious North. But the heart of the issue was *control:* who was responsible, who had the right and the authority to determine the nature of a state's society. White South Carolinians were not yet ready to surrender this power. Force of Northern arms and armies had destroyed slavery, but Carolinians were resolute in their determination not to let the nature and substance of slave society pass away.

As the president, and later Congress, put forth their respective—and competing—plans for Reconstruction, white South Carolinians embarked on their own program for dealing with the overwhelming changes. At first, whites quickly sought to reinstate their white supremacist society through a combination of government restrictions and private, community-based action. Later, with former Confederates displaced and disfranchised and a new state government established under congressional reconstruction, the struggle for control took on other forms. Fraud and terrorism appeared as conservative Carolinians sought to disrupt reconstruction programs and regain power over their state. The violent reception to Republican rule in the state did not bode well for peaceful change.

The perception of Reconstruction as a period of turmoil and confrontation is, of course, not new.[2] A century of Reconstruction historiography has produced a variety of interpretations concerning white opposition to the postwar world. Many of the earliest Reconstruction studies viewed opposition to Reconstruction as not only justified but necessary. Historians such as William Dunning, John Burgess, and Claude Bowers argued that Republican governments were corrupt and incompetent, supported only by a (wrongly) enfranchised inferior race and a tyrannical federal government. The Dunning School, as it came to be called, saw Republicans as fanatics bent on sadistically torturing a misguided—but penitent—South.[3]

As the racism and pro-Southern bias of the Dunning School passed, "revisionists" began to see Congress and the carpetbaggers in a more favorable light. With this change came a considerable loss of esteem for Andrew Johnson and the Redeemers. Soon Reconstruction lost public admiration as well, as a new wave of "neo-revisionists" questioned the accomplishments of the period altogether: black civil and political rights were illusory, the Southern Republican party had disintegrated, and the Republican hold on Washington was short-lived.[4]

A common thread among these schools is the search for "responsibility" to try to explain the failure of Reconstruction. Some historians have argued that key obstacles lay in the North. Eric McKitrick blamed the rise in Southern intransigence on Andrew Johnson's theory of "individual disloyalty" and his desire for a speedy restoration. Michael Les Benedict believed "American constitutional conservatism"—federalism, property rights, even the belief in laissez-faire—hamstrung the postwar revolution. William Gillette emphasized the inconsistency and Northern preoccupation of Ulysses S. Grant and Congress, which defeated hopes for equal rights and a Republican party in the South.[5]

Recently, historians have begun paying more attention to the South and examining more carefully the role Southerners played in Reconstruction. Michael Perman and Dan Carter have demonstrated how Southern conservatives influenced policy—directly or indirectly—at the national level. Other authors have presented important state accounts, focusing on how Southerners managed to reclaim their states from black and white Republicans. Works by Joel Williamson, Vernon Wharton, Jerrell Shofner, and Joe Gray Taylor have generated consistent findings, showing that a combination of Southern Republican mismanagement and disunity, Northern apathy, and determined conservative resistance ruined Reconstruction governments in the South.[6]

These Southern studies have provided new insights into the study of Reconstruction's failure. It is not surprising that the most frequent reaction to the new order was violent, as John Hope Franklin acknowledged as early as 1961 in *Reconstruction: After the Civil War* and Brooks Simpson—in his recent study of Ulysses S. Grant—has reaffirmed.[7] Un-

INTRODUCTION

fortunately, few authors have analyzed Southern violence in a systematic way. Allen Trelease, Otto Olsen, and George Rable argued that violence was an influential factor in overturning Republican state governments in the South.[8] However, these studies are fragmentary and discuss specific outbreaks or periods of violence without an overall understanding of the relationship between violence, other forms of resistance to Reconstruction, and the ultimate goals.

Articles by Orville Vernon Burton and Melinda Hennessey, and Lou Faulkner William's work on the Ku Klux Klan, all deal with specific cases of violence but do not attempt to place such affairs into the larger Reconstruction context.[9] Studies of short periods or single counties shed little light on an entire state's experience and fail to provide significant insights that help explain a decade of conflict. Michael Perman's 1991 essay on "counter-reconstruction" addressed many of the shortcomings of past studies and offered a thoughtful summation of white opposition to Reconstruction. He suggested that Reconstruction "amounted to a continuation of the South's campaign for autonomy, a campaign begun in defense of slavery before the war and continued after it in order to uphold the practice of white supremacy."[10]

Civil War scholars, however, often overlook the continuity between the war years and Reconstruction. To be sure, conventional campaigning was over, and much of the Old South was gone forever. But the conflict had only shifted in means and in intensity. To see *independence* as the goal of secession removes the war from the greater conflict and context of nineteenth-century American history.[11] Paul Escott has shown in *After Secession* that only Jefferson Davis was firmly committed to independence; for the planters the goal was the preservation of slavery.[12] The Confederate president's plans to abolish slavery to gain foreign recognition, to arm slaves, and to offer freedom to deserving black veterans met with meager support. Planters were committed to slavery and the society it created, not to independence or nationalism.[13] Escott correctly implies that secession and independence were only the *means* to an *end*. As Drew Gilpin Faust noted, "nationhood" itself was an offshoot of a region's "effort to protect its cherished way of life from the challenge of American national control."[14]

Many white Carolinians would continue fighting to regain this "way of life." Conventional warfare and guerrilla operations were out of the question in 1865, but there were avenues of opposition, loopholes for exploitation. Under President Johnson's provisional government, conservative reconstruction took place within a legitimate system. After the establishment of Radical rule in 1868, disorganized, locally-based resistance appeared, along with trial-and-error attempts at cooperation, abstention, fraud, and economic intimidation in an effort to weaken the state Republican machine. Over the years violence grew more coherent, political, and widespread, and so did conservative politics and political opposition. White Carolinians grew more unified and deliberate, and their resistance became more organized, directed, and effective. By 1876 resistance had evolved into war.

The standard definition of war is "organized, *socially sanctioned* armed violence." Or, as the military theorist Carl von Clausewitz wrote, "war is an act of force to compel our enemy to do our will," a "continuation of political intercourse, carried on with other means."[15] John Shy and Thomas Collier defined *revolutionary* war as "the seizure of political power by the use of armed force . . . it has other connotations: that the seizure of power is by a popular or broad-based political movement, that the seizure entails a fairly long period of armed conflict, and that power is seized in order to carry out a well-advertised political or social program. The term also implies a consciousness that a 'revolutionary' war is being fought."[16]

War is organized, coherent, and self-aware, based in force, and designed to bring about political change. "People's war" is the choice of the revolutionary underdog, and while terrorism, assassination, and intimidation are the most dramatic weapons, propaganda, fraud, and economic pressure may also play important roles.[17] A revolution may also operate *within* normal channels, using elements accessible to the revolutionaries (the judiciary, for instance) to weaken a government. In some cases, illegal means are used to gain access to the legal channels; violence carries an election, and then counter-revolutionary legislators implement their changes.[18]

This is not to say that a revolutionary insurgency sprang in its maturity from the head of Zeus. Former Confederates did not run home after the surrender and organize revolutionary cells to topple their state government. It took a decade of defeat and dissension, plus significant changes in national politics and the state Republican party, to create the climate necessary for a successful revolution. Eventually, by 1876, the resistance of Carolina whites had coalesced into "people's war," resulting in the overthrow of an "alien" government, its native collaborators, and its unacceptable social system.

Since the early nineteenth century, Carolinians had demanded "the right" to reap the rewards of a slave-labor agrarian economy, to live under white man's government, to practice aristocracy while preaching democracy, and to keep blacks subjugated in all sectors of life. In 1860, after decades of compromise and suspicion, the fear of losing these rights outweighed the advantages of union. As a result, slaveholders "launched a revolution to secure conservative ends, and they found that their means and ends were incompatible."[19] Military campaigns had failed to secure for Southerners the control they desired, the power to direct their own region, lives, and society. In addition, the crucible of war had forever altered the South, for its most precious component, African slavery, had been destroyed. But after half a century of conflict, Southerners would not give up so easily. In other words, the North stopped fighting—physically and mentally—in 1865; the South, however, did not.

Notes

1. Rupert Sargent Holland, ed., *Letters and Diary of Laura M. Towne, Written from the Sea Islands of South Carolina, 1862–1884* (Cambridge: Riverside Press, 1912; New York: Negro Universities Press, 1969), 159.

2. The richness of Reconstruction historiography has made review essays a necessity. One of the earliest is Bernard A. Weisberger, "The Dark and Bloody Ground of Reconstruction Historiography," *Journal of Southern History* 25 (November 1959): 427–47. More recently published articles are Richard O. Curry, "The Civil War and Reconstruction, 1861–1877: A Critical Overview of Recent Trends and Interpretations," *Civil War History* 20 (September 1974): 215–38; and Eric Foner, "Reconstruction Revisited," *Reviews in American History* 10 (December 1982): 82–100. Also see Foner's brief but excellent preface to his *Reconstruction 1863–1877: America's Unfinished Revolution* (New York: Harper and Row, 1988) for the latest discussion of Reconstruction historiography.

3. Some of the standard accounts of the Dunning School include William Dunning *Reconstruction, Political and Economic* (New York: American Nation Series, 1905); John W. Burgess, *Reconstruction and the Constitution, 1866–1876* (New York: Charles Scribner's Sons, 1902); Walter L. Fleming, *The Sequel of Appomattox* (New Haven: Yale University Press, 1919); and Claude G. Bowers, *The Tragic Era: The Revolution after Lincoln* (New York: Blue Ribbon Books, 1929). An argument can be made that the school persisted as late as E. Merton Coulter's, *The South during Reconstruction, 1865–1877* (Baton Rouge: Louisiana State University Press, 1947).

4. Probably all historians accept that a blend of "Northern" and "Southern" causes were responsible for the dismantling of the Reconstruction agenda. But because human nature seems always to call for a "decision" and not waffling, most historians seek to discover which of the two, the North or the South, was the more influential.

5. Eric L. McKitrick, *Andrew Johnson and Reconstruction* (Chicago: University of Chicago Press, 1960); William Gillette, *Retreat from Reconstruction, 1869–1879* (Baton Rouge: Louisiana State University Press, 1979); Michael Les Benedict, *A Compromise of Principle: Congressional Republicans and Reconstruction* (New York: W. W. Norton, 1974); Benedict, "Preserving the Constitution: The Conservative Basis for Radical Reconstruction," *Journal of American His-*

tory 61 (June 1974): 65–90; Benedict, "Equality and Expediency in the Civil War Era: A Review Essay," *Civil War History* 23 (December 1977): 322–35.

6. Scholars who focus more on the South and its role in Reconstruction plans and problems include Michael Perman, in his *Reunion without Compromise: The South and Reconstruction 1865–1868* (New York: Cambridge University Press, 1973), and his *The Road to Redemption: Southern Politics, 1869–1879* (Chapel Hill: University of North Carolina Press, 1984); and Dan T. Carter, in *When the War Was Over: The Failure of Self-Reconstruction in the South, 1865–1867* (Baton Rouge: Louisiana State University Press, 1985). Some good works which examine Reconstruction at the state level include Joel Williamson, *After Slavery: The Negro in South Carolina during Reconstruction, 1861–1877* (Chapel Hill: University of North Carolina Press, 1965); Jerrell Shofner, *Nor Is It Over Yet: Florida in the Era of Reconstruction, 1863–1877* (Gainesville: University Presses of Florida, 1974); Joe Gray Taylor, *Louisiana Reconstructed, 1863–1877* (Baton Rouge: University State University Press, 1974); and Vernon Wharton, *The Negro in Mississippi, 1865–1890* (New York: Harper and Row, 1965).

7. John Hope Franklin, *Reconstruction: After the Civil War* (Chicago: University of Chicago Press, 1961); Brooks D. Simpson, *Let Us Have Peace: Ulysses S. Grant and the Politics of War and Reconstruction* (Chapel Hill: University of North Carolina Press, 1991).

8. Allen W. Trelease, *White Terror: The Ku Klux Klan Conspiracy and Southern Reconstruction* (New York: Harper and Row, 1971); Otto H. Olsen, ed., *Reconstruction and Redemption in the South* (Baton Rouge: Louisiana State University Press, 1980); George C. Rable, *But There Was No Peace: The Role of Violence in the Politics of Reconstruction* (Athens: University of Georgia Press, 1984).

9. Melinda Meeks Hennessey, "Racial Violence during Reconstruction: The 1876 Riots in Charleston and Cainhoy," *South Carolina Historical Magazine* 86 (April 1985): 100–12; Orville Vernon Burton, "Race and Reconstruction in Edgefield County, South Carolina," *Journal of Social History* 12 (Fall 1978): 31–56, and *In My Father's House Are Many Mansions: Family and Community in Edgefield, South Carolina* (Chapel Hill: University of North Carolina Press, 1985); Lou Faulkner Williams, "The Great South Carolina Ku Klux Klan Trials, 1871–1872" (Ph.D. diss., University of Florida, 1991). More recent is Mark M. Smith's "'All Is Not Quiet in Our Hellish County': Facts, Fiction, Politics, and Race—The Ellenton Riot of 1876," *South Carolina Historical Magazine* 95 (April 1994): 142–55.

10. See Michael Perman, "Counter-Reconstruction: The Role of Violence in Southern Redemption," in *The Facts of Reconstruction: Essays in Honor of John Hope Franklin*, ed. Eric Anderson and Alfred A. Moss (Baton Rouge: Louisiana State University Press, 1991), 139.

11. Emory Thomas, for instance, is convinced that the goal was independence, pure and simple. He argues that the South "was willing to give up her 'peculiar institution' just as she had foresaken other cherished institutions, for the sake of independence." Southerners may have abolished slavery if it could have brought them independence. Once they were a separate nation, who could then

INTRODUCTION

regulate their internal affairs? Thomas misses both the significance of slavery and the fact that any system can be dismantled without destroying the spirit or practice of it entirely. His interpretation comes from relying too heavily on Jefferson Davis. The Confederate president *did* perceive independence as the ultimate goal of the war, rather than as a *means* to accomplish a goal. See Thomas, *The Confederacy as a Revolutionary Experience* (Englewood Cliffs, N.J.: Prentice-Hall, 1971), 119; and his "Reckoning with Rebels," in *The Old South and the Crucible of War*, ed. Harry P. Owens and James J. Cooke (Jackson: University Press of Mississippi, 1983), 12–13.

12. See Paul D. Escott, *After Secession: Jefferson Davis and the Failure of Confederate Nationalism* (Baton Rouge: Louisiana State University Press, 1978), 225, 228, 240–55.

13. Some scholars will point out that the Confederate Congress did pass a bill authorizing the use of slaves and offering emancipation as a reward. Davis first proposed such a measure in the fall of 1864, but it did not pass until spring 1865, when the Confederacy had all but collapsed and legislators were desperate. Even then, however, the bill only *barely* passed in each house. And, contrary to many perceptions, it did *not* grant emancipation; instead, it merely suggested to owners that they consider such a reward if slaves distinguished themselves in duty. The most complete work on this remains Robert F. Durden, *The Gray and the Black: The Confederate Debate on Emancipation* (Baton Rouge: Louisiana State University Press, 1972).

14. Drew Gilpin Faust, *The Creation of Confederate Nationalism: Ideology and Identity in the Civil War South* (Baton Rouge: Louisiana State University Press, 1988), 15. The story is all the more true for South Carolina, with antebellum leadership deeply divided over how best to protect the society—stay in the Union, or leave it? Ultimately, as Steven A. Channing argued, independence was only a means to an end. See Channing, *Crisis of Fear: Secession in South Carolina* (New York: Simon and Schuster, 1970).

15. Carl von Clausewitz, *On War*, trans. and ed. Michael Howard and Peter Paret (Princeton: Princeton University Press, 1976), 75, 87.

16. John Shy and Thomas Collier, "Revolutionary War," in *Makers of Modern Strategy: From Machiavelli to the Nuclear Age*, ed. Peter Paret (Princeton: Princeton University Press, 1986), 817; emphasis in original.

17. The concept of the Civil War as "people's war" is different from that of "guerrilla" war, which conjures up visions of gray-clad veterans roaming the countryside ambushing Union soldiers. See Emory Thomas, for example, "The Paradoxes of Confederate Historiography," in *The Southern Enigma: Essays on Race, Class and Folk Culture*, ed. Walter J. Fraser and Winfred B. Moore, Jr. (Westport, Conn.: Greenwood Press, 1983), 221; and Thomas, "Reckoning with Rebels," *The Old South and the Crucible of War*, 12–13.

18. The best introductions to the concept of revolutionary war—or "people's war"—are Gerard Chaliand, ed., *Guerrilla Strategies: An Historical Anthology from the Long March to Afghanistan* (Berkeley: University of California Press, 1982); and Shy and Collier, "Revolutionary War," in *Makers of Modern Strategy:*

From Machiavelli to the Nuclear Age. The classic work on revolution in general remains Crane Brinton, *The Anatomy of a Revolution,* 2d ed. (New York: Vintage Books, 1965). Readers will note the similarities between the former Confederates' postwar experience and Brinton's "stages of revolution." Unfortunately, space limitations prohibit here an exploration of the fascinating parallels.

19. Paul D. Escott, "The Failure of Confederate Nationalism," in *The Old South and the Crucible of War,* ed. Harry P. Owens and James J. Cooke (Jackson: University Press of Mississippi, 1983), 25.

CHAPTER ONE

CONSERVATIVE RECONSTRUCTION

> What is to be done? We know not. But let our people dismiss the idea that we are going to pass under the Yankee yoke. Nothing of the sort is going to take place. There is more going on that we wot of. "Man's extremity is God's opportunity."
>
> *Edgefield Advertiser,* April 26, 1865

I

In June of 1865, Richard Henry Dana delivered his famous "Grasp of War" speech, arguing that "a war is over when its purpose is secured. It is a fatal mistake to hold that this war is over, because the fighting has ceased. This war is not over. We are in the attitude and status of war to-day."[1] Dana's views were more accurate than he may have realized. While the North believed its purpose secured—the Union preserved and rebellion crushed—the South was neither successful nor subdued. To be sure, the North had pummeled the body of the Confederacy, and by the spring of 1865 its armies lay in tatters and its cities in ruins.

Conservative South Carolinians, largely native whites and former Democrats, soon found that the North was not content with victory but desired to reshape fundamentally the society of the South. The question of the nature of the Union had been decided; now the issues were the status of states and citizens within that Union. Results of Northern victory, and agents of Northern interests, were present throughout the Palmetto State: emancipated slaves; the Bureau of Refugees, Freedmen, and Abandoned Lands; military courts; and a federal occupying force.

But all was not lost, for conservatives soon learned that they had an unlikely ally, President Andrew Johnson. Taking advantage of Johnson's desire for a speedy restoration and his support of local political elites, state conservatives embarked on their own plan of reconstruction. Carolinians by the end of 1865, had reestablished their control over blacks, the economy, and politics, and waited for Congress to recognize them as the legitimate rulers of their state.

Congress had not been in session when Andrew Johnson became president in April 1865. As a result the legislature had no input on his plan of reconstruction, which was designed to readmit the Southern states to the Union as quickly as possible with minimal constitutional and political turmoil. Johnson's policy, grounded in the theory of *individual* disloyalty rather than *state* disloyalty, became official on May 29, 1865, with two proclamations defining the course Southerners must follow. The first, the Proclamation of Amnesty and Pardon, required participants and supporters of the rebellion to take an oath of loyalty to the Union, repudiate secession, and accept emancipation. Fourteen classes of Southerners were banned from receiving a pardon in this way, and had to appeal directly to the president. Johnson's second proclamation set forth his demands on the states. He would appoint a provisional governor, who was then responsible for calling a convention to amend the state constitution, which must meet the same requirements as individuals.[2]

Carolinians who at first complained about the severity of Johnson's plan soon realized the new chief executive was more friend than foe. The administration granted pardons liberally, even to the ex-Confederates who fell into the special classes. By September, presidential pardons were coming at over 100 a day, and within nine months of the proclamation, 14,000 had been issued; in fact, Johnson's official "Clerk of Pardons" was M. F. Pleasants, a former Confederate colonel! By September, Carolinian Henry W. Ravenel was praising the president for his "firmness and consistency—and perhaps as much clemency as it was possible for him to exercise. . . ."[3]

The leniency of Johnson's plan of Reconstruction encouraged Carolinians, who had no intention of allowing outsiders run their state and dictate racial policy. Although devastated by the fortunes of war, Carolinians were without neither means nor motivation. As Emma LeConte noted in May, "in the future can we still hope . . . [that] after years of recuperation we may be strong enough and wiser by experience to renew the struggle and throw off the hateful yoke." "The only other chance," the diarist pondered prophetically, "is that by their oppression and insolence they may drive the people to 'Guerrilla' warfare and be wearied out at last."⁴

It was not surprising then that reports from South Carolina indicated a conspicuous lack of love for the Union. Major General Carl Schurz, in the state on a fact-finding trip, reported *"an utter absence of national feeling"* and warned that Carolinians were only waiting to "rid themselves of the federal troops and obtain once more control of their own affairs."⁵ His observations were confirmed by Sidney Andrews, just one of many journalists and literary entrepreneurs who journeyed south after the war. Andrews claimed that there was "very little pretence of love for the Union" and that although the people may be following the letter of the law, "the whole current of their lives flows in direct antagonism to its spirit."⁶ John T. Trowbridge, another correspondent, claimed that he found "in South Carolina a more virulent animosity existing in the minds of the common people against the government and people of the North than in any other State I visited."⁷

II

In 1863 William Whiting, a War Department solicitor, warned that even if the Union was preserved, Southerners could "gain the right of managing their affairs according to their will and pleasure, and not according to the will and pleasure of the people of the United States." He surmised that "under the guise of submission, amnesty and restoration, they may gain . . . that which they could not achieve by feat of arms."⁸

In 1865, regardless of the desires of Washington or the spirit of honorable submission, South Carolinians began their own plan of reconstruction. At the center was Benjamin Franklin Perry, chosen by President Johnson to lead an unruly flock back into the fold. Perry, like many of Johnson's other provisional governors, was a moderate, and had been a Unionist before the war. Typical of South Carolina Unionists, Perry had opposed secession for practical reasons, believing it would endanger, rather than protect, slavery. Also like other Carolinians, he supported his state unequivocally after secession, even serving in the state government during the war.⁹

Perry was determined to pry federal fingers off South Carolina while molding order out of anarchy. Meeting with Johnson in late June to accept his appointment, Perry happily discovered that the president was committed to a hands-off policy, as he told the new governor to "write occasionally, let him know how I was getting on in reconstructing the state."¹⁰ The Carolinian quickly took control of affairs with his proclamation of July 20. This declared to be in force all laws which were operating at the time of secession, and allowed all officials holding office at the war's end to reclaim their positions upon taking Johnson's oath. Perry also called for the formation of volunteer militia companies—whites only, of course—to help "curb lawlessness."[11]

United States Army officers in the state had serious reservations about the governor's acts. General Adelbert Ames, the commander of the Military District of Western South Carolina (and future carpetbag governor of Mississippi), reported to divisional headquarters that Perry's proclamations put the state government "into the hands of the most objectionable persons."[12] Major General Quincy Adams Gillmore, the overall commander of the Department of South Carolina, voiced similar concerns.[13]

President Johnson continued to allow state leaders to undercut federal control and redirect power back into conservative hands. When Army commanders complained that state magistrates were administering the loyalty oath (only provost marshals were authorized to do so), Johnson overruled his officers, just as he did when Perry moved to reopen civil courts. Perry did allow one concession: the provost courts retained jurisdiction in cases involving freedmen. But in other matters, Johnson told his commanders "not to interfere with Governor Perry's reconstruction policy."[14]

Conservatives' independent course and defiant attitude were even more pronounced at the state convention. Among other tasks, the convention was charged with formalizing emancipation and drawing up a new state constitution. At the same time, delegates believed the convention was a step toward readmission and the end of Northern and federal supervision. Since voting for delegates was restricted to those who held political rights before the war, there seemed little chance for real change. Frederick Jackson's father had no illusions; writing from Boston to his son in Beaufort, he warned that "the ruling class at the South will resort to every means to embarras [sic] the Govt and retain the Negro's [sic] in a condition as near as possible to slavery."[15] Major General (Brevet) John Hatch had the same misgivings, believing that the old leaders "hope to obtain control of the State, and then pass laws with reference to the colored people which shall virtually re-establish slavery; and although they look upon secession as at present hopeless, a future war may enable them to again raise the standard."[16]

This seemed to be the case when the convention assembled on September 13. In his opening address, moderate judge James L. Orr—a leading Unionist before the war—spoke about the duties of "a white man's government." Delegates followed his lead and acted with the self-interest and defiance characteristic of South Carolina. For instance, instead of declaring secession "null and void" as Johnson required, delegates merely repealed it, thus recognizing its legitimacy. For some, even this conceded too much; A. P. Aldrich and three others voted against the measure outright (Aldrich was later unanimously elected Speaker of the House in the new legislature).[17]

Delegates had an even harder time recognizing Johnson's requirement for "unqualified abolition." There were many proposed amendments, such as one for compensation to ex-owners and another calling for a clause prohibiting freedmen from "engaging in any species of traffic and in any department of labor other than manual service." The outspoken A. P. Aldrich offered an amendment which stated that South Carolina would accept all conditions and "calmly await the time and opportunity to effect our deliverance from unconstitutional rule." No such amendments passed; those who opposed abolition merely voted against it, and the clause passed ninety-eight to eight. Still, the measure smacked of defiance, since the final version read: "the slave in South Carolina having been emancipated by the action of the United States Authorities, neither slavery nor involuntary servitude . . . shall ever be re-established in this State." The convention placed emancipation on the shoulders of the U.S. government; South Carolinians had not directly freed their slaves. The convention never even discussed the repudiation of the Confederate debt, thus rejecting outright one of Johnson's few stipulations.[18]

Carolinians were showing little in the way of submission or remorse. The convention's defiance met with general accord, as did its nomination of former General Wade Hampton for governor, to replace Provisional Governor Perry. A cavalry hero who had been perhaps the wealthiest planter in the antebellum South, Wade Hampton had opposed the convention altogether and was, according to one army officer, "the most objectionable man to the [federal] Govt in the State."[19] Hampton refused the nomination, so the choice fell to James L. Orr, a former Unionist-turned-Confederate senator. Orr was victorious in the election of October 18, but his margin was surprisingly slim considering Hampton was not running; in some cases entire districts went for Hampton. Such a showing, said one federal officer, revealed "how powerless the most liberal and enlightened men in the State are against the traditions of South Carolina."[20] Indeed, James DeCaradeuc declared proudly that "our little State is still defiant. Our Convention . . . has said nothing about the repudiation of all debts. . . . The Convention has not declared the act of Secession null & void . . . and lastly, our people in the late election for Governor have shown their spirit in the vote for Gen. Wade Hampton. . . ."[21] Nor was he alone in his satisfaction. The election for state and federal senators and representatives followed, and the *Edgefield Advertiser* was "proud" that "our State has not elected men whom *can take the test oath*. Away with men who can take the test oath!! South Carolina should want nothing to do with such."[22]

White Carolinians, again in legitimate control of the state, could now begin their reconstruction in earnest. Secession and war had failed to preserve slavery, but whites were determined to use every means at their disposal to limit the damage and recreate as near as possible their old order. The most critical issue was obvious, as N. L. Springs pointed out to his cousin A. B. Springs: "I trust you will be able to adopt some plan by which the negro can be made useful to you."[23] During the convention Governor Perry had commissioned prominent lawyers Armistead Burt and David Wardlaw to draft a code for the "regulation of labor and the protection and government of the Colored Population of the State."[24] Their mission was simple yet daunting: salvage as much of antebellum South Carolina as possible. Burt in turn solicited advice from Edmund Rhett, who suggested that since emancipation was so "sudden and abrupt," it should be "limited, controlled and surrounded with such safeguards as will make the change as slight as possible. . . . The general interest of both the white man and the negro requires that he should be kept as near to his former condition as Law can keep him. That he should be kept as near to the condition of slavery as possible, as far from the condition of the white man as is practicable."[25]

Rhett believed that South Carolina could reestablish systematic guidelines for the subjugation of blacks. Rhett's extensive proposal prohibited freedpeople and their posterity from ever owning real estate, restricted black mobility, and implemented a strict system of contracts and penalties regulated by the state. But Rhett also understood his state's tenuous position vis-à-vis the Union and warned Burt that "this is no time to do it. The question should not be broached until we are back in the Union [or] it will only strengthen the Black Republican Party and render the admission of the State difficult."[26]

Although Carolina's lawyers and legislators used many of Rhett's ideas, they rejected his advice on the proposal's timing. Introduced in October and passed in December, South Carolina's black codes clearly indicated the future of Carolina society should whites remain in control. The code itself was composed of three laws. The first recognized that slavery no longer existed and blacks can sue in court, own property, and make contracts. But the codes placed stringent economic and social restrictions upon the former slaves. The second law prohibited blacks "employed in husbandry" from selling anything without "written permission of the employer or District judge." Article 13 prohibited the ownership of weapons, and Article 30 put legal distinctions in order: in the case of any misdemeanor by a "person of color," any white can *arrest* the accused. If the misdemeanor is committed by a white, any person may *complain* to the magistrate. The third law imposed a "sunrise to sunset" workday, complete with restrictions on movement and liberal justifications for employee dismissal, following the trend set—and enforced—by planters privately since emancipation. In addition, the law effectively closed the door on black economic opportunity, for blacks could be only farm laborers or hired servants, unless they purchased a license from the judge of the district court.[27] Yet the license was too expensive for most, and white judges held the final say.[28]

For the North, South Carolina's black codes showed an obstinacy incompatible with defeat. The state had refused to repudiate the Confederate debt and had elected a full regimen of old leaders to its new legislature and to Congress. In the wake of all this, Congress faced the dilemma of admitting South Carolina—and the other Southern states—on a basis of representation that counted blacks as a full citizen (rather than three-fifths of one, as during slavery), while affording them few of the rights. With these new demographics, disloyal Southern states might well control Congress.[29] But it was the codes that forced congressional action, for they revealed, in the words of Eric Foner, "the likely shape of Southern economic relations if left to the undisputed control of the planters." The codes served up a "chilling object lesson" about the "prospect for self-generated change in the region," according to Dan Carter. The codes, then, were South Carolina's plan of reconstruction.[30]

III

Across the state, local private activity was supplementing the formal framework being erected in Columbia. Community-based action was a tradition in South Carolina, and by late 1865 former planters and other whites had come a long way towards regaining control over their state and its black population.

Some observers recognized that Carolinians would not accept anything but white domination in all aspects of society. In the summer of 1865, General Quincy A. Gillmore, commanding the Department of South Carolina, told Carl Schurz that "I do not think they [planters] will organize free labor upon any plan that would be of advantage to both whites and blacks. . . ."[31] Sidney Andrews agreed and, while visiting Aiken in October, warned that "if the nation allows that whites to work out the problem of the future in their own way, the negro's condition in three years will be as bad as it was before the war." "The viciousness that could not overturn the nation," Andrews continued, "is now mainly engaged in the effort to retain the substance of slavery. What are names if the thing itself remains?"[32]

One of the few obstacles to this effort was the War Department's Bureau of Refugees, Freedmen, and Abandoned Lands. As an agency of the government operating on Carolina soil with the responsibility of caring for freed slaves, the bureau represented a direct threat to white control.[33] Carolina's greatest son, cavalry hero Wade Hampton, complained that all labor problems after the war could be traced to "that incubus, that hydra-headed monster, the freedmen's bureau."[34] Eliza Fludd also complained of such interference, calling the bureau a *"National Pest* and a Sower of Discord between the whites and blacks."[35]

Suspicious whites had little to fear from the Freedmen's Bureau. The understaffed bureau faced local white hostility and had to manage with an indifferent—and even antagonistic—chief executive, Andrew Johnson. To make matters worse, the only realistic chance of the South's creating a new economic system all but vanished by late 1865 when the administration rejected the confiscation of Southern property. Without land, blacks were forced to work for white landowners, reestablishing a system of white control and black dependence.[36]

The best the bureau could do was keep *landlessness* from becoming *helplessness*. In the summer of 1865, the bureau began trying to regulate the relationship between the white employer and the black laborer through contracts. But bureau personnel were too few to examine every contract, and many army officials disregarded the duty altogether.[37] This resulted in confusion and the loss of productivity, for freed slaves often refused to deal with local whites alone. In addition, many ex-slaves, still holding out hopes for land, refused to sign contracts in order to avoid being under obligation if land redistribution began.[38]

Generally speaking, white employers in South Carolina created at the local level a system of restrictions parallel to the ones legislators were hammering out in Columbia. Former slaves were supervised carefully, and employers' notebooks tallied transgressions which translated into fines, forfeitures, and dismissals. Planters docked laborers for leaving the plantation without permission, damaging the planter's property, showing laziness, and laying off from work due to sickness. Hands were required to labor six days a week, from sunup to sundown, with breaks totalling one hour a day (one and a half in the summer). Contracts barred visitors without permission, and in some cases conversation was prohibited during working hours. H. A. Johnson, a Freedmen's Bureau agent in Cheraw, spoke from experience when he said, "they cannot trust to have a contract made by their late Masters."[39]

The Freedmen's Bureau did not have the resources to oversee all planters, so many continued to run their plantations as they had done before the war. Testifying on labor practices before the Joint Committee on Reconstruction, Assistant Bureau Commissioner Rufus Saxton chronicled shootings, beatings, tying-up-by-the-thumbs, whippings, patrol-and-pass systems, and instances of blacks' being driven off plantations without compensation.[40] James Beecher's Memorandum Book contains hundreds of complaints by blacks for unfair compensation, workers' children being removed to other plantations, and beatings.[41] After one harvest James Hopkinson drove eighty-one laborers off his land. Bureau Captain O. S. B. Wall remarked that some planters treated their ex-slaves *"the same as in former years."*[42]

The tools for meting out such treatment seemed the same as in former years as well. During the antebellum period, slave patrols were ever-present in South Carolina, riding through streets at night, roaming the countryside, and even visiting plantations to search slave quarters for weapons. By late summer 1865 the slave patrol had reappeared.[43] News came in from the up-country of bands called "regulators" enforcing a "pass-system." James Beecher reported from Barnwell District that "an armed patrol of civilians is organized for the summary punishment of negroes" and "a system of passes, similar to those under the Slave Code, is in effect and a negro found off the plantation is liable to severe flogging."[44] Even reporter Sidney Andrews knew of the "patrol-and-pass" systems.[45]

Central to this or any system of control was a readiness to use violence. Whites were ready, willing, and able to use physical force to demonstrate their authority and defy the federal government's attempts to revamp Southern society. John Picksley, a freedman, told Bureau agent G. W. Pease that in Edgefield "it is almost a daily occurrence for black men to be hunted down with dogs and shot like wild beasts." In November, Pease received an "appeal" by Edgefield freedmen, for "there is no safety in our lives, we hear of men being found dead in different places we apply to you to help us. . . ." Troubles were not confined to Edgefield; John Williams, Assistant Adjutant General at Bureau headquarters, stated that there "is no end to the complaints of brutal treatment to the freedpersons in the Upper Country."[46] In Saxton's November report to Bureau Commissioner O. O. Howard, nearly every county's entry ended the same: "it is thought that troops cannot be withdrawn with safety from this section."[47] In January, Saxton drew special attention to three blacks who had refused a "lifetime" contract by their employer. The planter, after driving them from the estate, had a band of whites hunt them, kill the two men, and carry the woman back to the plantation.[48]

Needless to say, the struggle for control of South Carolina and its black population was not limited to the planter class. In the words of one bureau agent, common whites openly *"announce their determination to take the law into their own hands, in defiance of our authority."*[49] At a speech intended to conciliate locals, bureau officer F. M. Montell, explaining that the war *was* over, had a man tell him "the war is not over . . . this thing will never die out!"[50] The up-country had men like "July" and "Largent," two ex-CSA soldiers who led bands that terrorized Unionists, federal soldiers, and Negroes. "Texas Brown" made his home in Abbeville along the Savannah River, where he amassed a fortune killing blacks who had fled their owners' plantations.[51] Even in the low-country, where troop concentration was the heaviest, whites defied the U.S. Army on behalf of white rule and Carolina honor. On Edisto Island in May 1865, Mary Ames noted in her diary that two companies were "stationed here to protect the island from guerrillas." Even with the troops "sleep was impossible. . . . I got out the hammer . . . and kept it in my hand all night, ready to beat out the brains of any one attacking us."[52] Sidney Andrews, now in Charleston, lamented the "indifference to the negro's fate and life." He reported the killing of a black soldier who had questioned a local white about wearing his CSA buttons; the man promptly produced a knife and slit the soldier's throat.[53] In the opinion of Carl Schurz, "since the negro has ceased to be property," they had no "pecuniary value," so "maiming and killing" went largely unnoticed.[54]

Carolinians reserved special enmity for black soldiers stationed in the state. Black troops violated Carolina tenets concerning racial dependence and white honor, and they feared the disruptive potential of such men in the midst of a collapsed slave society. Wade Hampton, writing to Andrew Johnson, was livid over the "pouring into our country [of] a horde of barbarians, your negro troops," which he saw as "a direct and premeditated insult to the whole Southern people."[55] Using "black savages," according to Henry W. Ravenel, was "vindictive."[56] Robert A. Pringle told his friend W. R. Johnson that submitting to a "guard of black troops" is the "severest trial" of all, but Carolinians "have exhibited a degree of self-control which our bitterest enemies would not (if he possessed the magnanimity) but admire."[57]

This self-control was not as universal as Pringle claimed. The whites of Anderson demonstrated little self-control toward the blacks stationed at the courthouse; a lieutenant and an enlisted man, both black, were murdered there. The unit was removed to ease tensions, but on the march back to Newberry, another soldier was waylaid and had his throat slit. Just to the north, in Chester District, a small assembly turned into a riot when black troops marched by. Although uniformed and armed, three blacks were killed and several wounded; no white casualties were reported.[58] On St. Helena, Laura M. Towne wrote in her diary that "it is so dangerous for a negro to go about, especially with the United States Uniform on, that orders are out that no more will be allowed to go to recover their families and bring them here. . . ."[59]

Despite this, whites argued that black troops were the real danger, and their presence would incite newly freed blacks to murder and riot. As usual, white Carolinians believed themselves to be the only force capable of controlling blacks, and so—as at other times—they took matters into their own hands. In an ominous letter, Henry Ravenel commented on the "better & more orderly spirit" among Cooper River blacks since the "presence of our Scouts & the summary executions of a few of the ring leaders." Ravenel offered chilling advice, that "the conduct of our Scouts should be no child's play, no taking up and whipping. . . . [Leaders] should be quietly disposed of. The mystery of disappearance has more awe in it, than any amount of punishment which is seen or known."[60] In Kingstree a "citizen's committee" whipped freedpeople and expelled Northern teachers as protection against an "imminent uprising."[61]

Fear of race war intensified as the 1865 Christmas season approached. Tensions had been building since the surrender, and in October an uprising in Jamaica (in which thirteen whites were killed) added fuel to white fears.[62] To this add the coming of Christmas, which had been the one holiday on which masters allowed their slaves some liberty to celebrate. Now whites feared the undisciplined spirit could overtake their former slaves, and blood would flow.

Again, private and state action complemented each other. While Cadawaller Jones of Rock Hill urged neighbors to create "an armed police organization before Christmas," Provisional Governor Benjamin F. Perry instructed the General Assembly to reorganize the state militia to guard against "insurrection and domestic violence."[63] On November 4 the "Committee on the Military" suggested creating "an organized, armed military force" to control the freed slaves, as they had "become so thoroughly contaminated with false notions as to their rights. . . ." The committee also advised the assembly to "keep on duty . . . a number of white mounted troops . . . sufficient to protect the country . . . until the Militia shall be perfected."[64] Reports filtered in as districts organized paramilitary units. In November, for instance, Edgefield reported that three companies had formed, all composed of veterans and led by "gentlemen." On January 10, 1866, the legislature named former Major General Martin W. Gary of Edgefield commander of the state militia—a man who would play a similar, less legal role just a decade later.[65]

IV

In October of 1865, an alarmed Wendell Phillips spoke on "The South Victorious," warning that the South was reemerging with "the same theories, with the same men to work them, and the same element to work them with. . . ."[66] Indeed, by December, as most white Carolinians saw it, their task was nearly complete. The state had (more or less) complied with Johnson's federal requirements, a new government had been established, and new regulations and structures had been developed to insure white dominance and security. Carolina whites were well on their way to regaining total control of their society.

Similar developments across the South presented Congress with a dilemma. Should it go along with President Johnson, reunion, and reconstruction Southern-style, or should it scrap nine months of work, and quite possibly its relations with the South and President Johnson, and start from scratch?[67] Congress convened in the fall of 1865 and assessed the extent of the South's defeat—its submissiveness, its willingness to change, its repentant behavior—and the decision came easily. Along with those from other Southern states, South Carolina's representatives to the august body in Washington found a cool welcome waiting, as Congress exercised its prerogative and refused to seat the Southern congressmen. The event caused traveler-journalist Whitelaw Reid to reflect back on secession. The fatal error of the North in 1860, he believed, was a failure to take South Carolina seriously. Following Congress's rejection, Reid warned the North to use caution, for a "majority" of Southerners saw the rebuff "as a studied, brutal insult to a beaten and helpless enemy."[68] Another phase began in this struggle for Southern rights, and Carolinians would soon show that they were neither beaten nor helpless.

Notes

1. Richard Henry Dana, quoted in Michael Les Benedict, *The Fruits of Victory: Alternatives in Restoring the Union, 1865–1877* (Philadelphia: J. B. Lippincott, 1975), 98.

2. See Eric L. McKitrick, *Andrew Johnson and Reconstruction* (Chicago: University of Chicago Press, 1960), 91–92; Eric Foner, *Reconstruction, 1863–1877: America's Unfinished Revolution* (New York: Harper and Row, 1988), 183; Dan T. Carter, *When the War Was Over: The Failure of Self-Reconstruction in the South, 1865–1867* (Baton Rouge: Louisiana State University Press, 1985), 25.

3. *The Private Journal of Henry William Ravenel, 1859–1887*, ed. Arney Robinson Childs (Columbia: University of South Carolina Press, 1947), 254; John

Hope Franklin, *Reconstruction: After the Civil War* (Chicago: University of Chicago Press, 1961), 33–34.

4. Emma LeConte, diary entry for May 17, 1865, Emma LeConte Diary, Southern Historical Collection, University of North Carolina, Chapel Hill, N.C. (hereafter SHC/UNC).

5. Carl Schurz, in *Report on the Condition of the South [Accompanied by a Report of] Carl Schurz*. (New York: Arno Press, 1969), 13; emphasis in original. The report was first published in *Message of the President of the United States. . . . Accompanied by a Report of Carl Schurz on the States of South Carolina, Georgia, Alabama, Mississippi, and Louisiana,* 39th Cong., 1st sess., 1865, S. Doc. 2 (Serial 1237), 2–46.

6. Sidney Andrews, *The South since the War* (Boston: Ticknor and Fields, 1866; Boston: Houghton Mifflin, 1971), 391.

7. John T. Trowbridge, *The South: A Tour of Its Battlefields and Ruined Cities* (Hartford, Conn.: L. Stebbins, 1866; New York: Arno Press, 1969), 568.

8. William Whiting, *War Powers under the Constitution of the United States* (Boston: Lee and Shepard, 1871), 232–33.

9. Perry succeeded Andrew McGrath, the last wartime governor, who was arrested by military authorities in May for illegally exercising his powers of office. See John Robert Kirkland, "Federal Troops in the South Atlantic States during Reconstruction: 1865–1877" (Ph.D. diss., University of North Carolina at Chapel Hill, 1968), 34; "Address to Young Men's Democratic Union Club of New York City," summer 1868, Ellison Summerfield Keitt Papers, South Caroliniana Library, University of South Carolina, Columbia, S.C. (hereafter SCL); Carter, *When the War Was Over,* 25–27, 31–55; E. Merton Coulter, *The South During Reconstruction, 1865–1877* (Baton Rouge: Louisiana State University Press, 1947), 33.

10. Stephen Meats and Edwin Arnold, eds., *The Writings of Benjamin F. Perry: Volume I: Essays, Public Letters, and Speeches* (Spartanburg, S.C.: Reprint Company, 1980), 204. See also Carter, *When the War Was Over,* 31.

11. Meats and Arnold, eds., *The Writings of Benjamin F. Perry* 1:204. See also James E. Sefton, *The United States Army and Reconstruction, 1865–1877* (Baton Rouge: Louisiana State University Press, 1967), 29; Francis Butler Simkins and Robert Hilliard Woody, *South Carolina during Reconstruction* (Chapel Hill: University of North Carolina Press, 1932), 34–37.

12. Brevet Major General Adelbert A. Ames to Lieutenant Clous, acting assistant adjutant general, April 4, 1866, in Record Group 94, Microcopy 619, Reel 512, National Archives, Washington, D.C. (hereafter RG, MC, Reel, NA). Ames's district was under the larger administrative unit of the Dept. of South Carolina, under Quincy A. Gillmore. This, in turn, was a subdivision of the Division of the Atlantic, commanded by George Gordon Meade.

13. Quincy A. Gillmore to Brigadier General Lorenzo Thomas, adjutant general, August 1, 1865, RG94, MC619, Reel 415, NA; Michael Perman, *Reunion without Compromise: The South and Reconstruction 1865–1868* (New York: Cambridge University Press, 1973), 132.

14. Meats and Arnold, eds., *The Writings of Benjamin F. Perry* 1:225–27.

15. "Father" to Frederick Jackson, June 24, 1865, Frederick Jackson Papers, SCL.
16. Brevet Major General John Hatch, quoted by Schurz in *The Condition of the South*, 50.
17. Roger P. Leemhuis, *James L. Orr and the Sectional Conflict* (Washington, D.C.: University Press of America, 1979), 99.
18. Andrews, *The South since the War*, 43, 54, 56–57; John William DeForest, *A Union Officer in the Reconstruction*, ed. James Croushore and David M. Potter (New Haven: Yale University Press, 1948), ix; Simkins and Woody, *South Carolina during Reconstruction*, 39; Carter, *When the War Was Over*, 69–73; Brevet Major General A. A. Ames to Lieutenant Clous, April 4, 1866, RG94, MC619, Reel 512, NA; Constitutional Convention of the State of South Carolina, *Journal of the Convention of the People of South Carolina Held at Columbia, S.C., September 1865* (Columbia: Julian A. Shelby, 1865), in South Caroliniana Library, Book Division, University of South Carolina, Columbia, S.C. (hereafter SCL).
19. Ames to Clous, April 4, 1866, RG94, MC619, Reel 512, NA.
20. *Edgefield Advertiser*, October 25, 1865; John Hammond Moore, ed., *The Juhl Letters to the Charleston Courier, 1865–1871* (Athens: University of Georgia Press, 1974), 51–52. Orr was the first governor ever chosen directly by popular vote in South Carolina; previous to Reconstruction and the new constitution, the General Assembly selected the state's chief executive.
21. James DeCaradeuc, James A. DeCaradeuc Diary, in Box 2, Folder 13, DeCaradeuc Family Papers, Southern Historical Collection, University of North Carolina at Chapel Hill (hereafter SHC/UNC).
22. *Edgefield Advertiser*, December 6, 1865; emphasis in original.
23. N. L. Springs to A. B. Springs, November 2, 1865, in Box 9, Folder 149, Springs Family Papers, SHC/UNC.
24. Benjamin F. Perry to Armistead Burt, October 15, 1865, Benjamin Franklin Perry Papers, Special Collections Library Research Room, Perkins Library, Duke University, Durham, N.C. (hereafter SCLRR, Duke); Joel Williamson, *After Slavery: The Negro in South Carolina during Reconstruction, 1861–1877* (Chapel Hill: University of North Carolina Press, 1965), 72.
25. Edmund Rhett to Armistead Burt, October 14, 1865, in Box 3, Armistead Burt Papers, SCLRR, Duke.
26. Rhett to Burt, October 14, 1865, in Box 3, Armistead Burt Papers, SCLRR, Duke; Foner, *Reconstruction: America's Unfinished Revolution*, 210.
27. South Carolina General Assembly, *Reports and Resolutions of the General Assembly of the State of South Carolina Passed at the Annual Session of 1865* (Columbia, S.C.: Julian A. Shelby, 1865), bound in *Acts and Resolutions, 1864–1865*. Copies of the code also appeared in the *Edgefield Advertiser*, December 20, 1865, and January 3, 1866, and are reprinted in Simkins and Woody, *South Carolina during Reconstruction*, 48–50.
28. For more "approving" reviews of the codes see Theodore Brantner Wilson, *The Black Codes of the South* (Tuscaloosa: University of Alabama Press,

1965), 71–80, 117, 119; and David Duncan Wallace, *South Carolina: A Short History, 1520–1948* (Columbia, S.C.: University of South Carolina Press, 1951), 566–67. It is difficult to argue the benevolent characteristics of the codes, since, as Thomas Holt pointed out, the laws actually *revoked* rights held by free blacks before the war. See Holt, *Black over White: Negro Political Leadership in South Carolina during Reconstruction* (Urbana: University of Illinois Press, 1977), 19–22.

29. David M. Potter, *Division and the Stresses of Reunion: 1845–1876* (Glenview, Ill.: Scott, Foresman, 1973), 171–75. For the significance of the codes, also see Alrutheus Ambush Taylor, *The Negro in South Carolina during the Reconstruction* (Washington, D.C.: n.p., 1924; New York: AMS Press, 1971), 50.

30. Eric Foner, *Nothing but Freedom: Emancipation and Its Legacy* (Baton Rouge: Louisiana State University Press, 1983), 52; Carter, *When the War Was Over*, 17.

31. General Quincy A. Gillmore, quoted by Schurz in *The Condition of the South*, 47.

32. Andrews, *The South since the War*, 225.

33. A negative view of the Freedmen's Bureau can be found in William S. McFeely's *Yankee Stepfather: General O. O. Howard and the Freedmen* (New York: W. W. Norton, 1968), while John Carpenter, in *Sword and Olive Branch: Oliver Otis Howard* (Pittsburgh: University of Pittsburgh Press, 1964), presents a more favorable view of Howard and the bureau's successes, although the discussion focuses more specifically on Howard and is somewhat weak on the local operations of the bureau. A sympathetic view of Southerners and their goals is in Martin Abbott, *The Freedmen's Bureau in South Carolina, 1865–1872* (Chapel Hill: University of North Carolina Press, 1967).

34. Wade Hampton, Broadside, on "A True Policy for the Restoration of the South," to President Andrew Johnson, August 25, 1866, Hampton Family Papers, SCL.

35. Eliza Fludd to "Friend," October 24, 1865, Eliza (Borden) Fludd Papers, SCLRR, Duke.

36. The dream of "forty acres and a mule" had a sad ending in South Carolina, leaving freedpeople bitter and, in the face of white ownership, nearly helpless. For a discussion of the events surrounding the retraction of federal promises and the returning of white lands, see McFeely, *Yankee Stepfather*, 97–106, 112–14, 127, 130–43; Abbott, *The Freedmen's Bureau*, 54–58; Mary Ames, *From a New England Women's Diary in Dixie in 1865* (n.p.: 1906; New York: Negro Universities Press, 1969), 96–101, 122; Andrews, *The South Since theWar*, 212–13; and Williamson, *After Slavery*, 79–84. Years later (on August 1, 1880) in a speech at Elimira, N.Y., Frederick Douglass said that "some of the evils which we now suffer would have been averted" had Congress provided real opportunity for blacks to own land; quoted in James McPherson, *The Struggle for Equality: Abolitionists and the Negro in the Civil War and Reconstruction* (Princeton: Princeton University Press, 1964), 416. One of the best short analyses of why Northerners opted against confiscation is the essay by Eric Foner titled "Thaddeus Stevens, Confiscation, and Reconstruction," in *The Hofstader Aegis: A Memorial,* ed.

Stanley Elkins and Eric McKitrick (New York: Alfred A. Knopf, 1974), esp. 159–83. Willie Lee Rose delivers an excellent discussion of the transition from slavery to freedom on the Sea Islands in *Rehearsal for Reconstruction: The Port Royal Experiment* (Indianapolis: Bobbs-Merrill, 1964). But as James Roark points out, Rose's study is not really a rehearsal for Reconstruction. The Port Royal area was unique: the transition took place without presence of the former masters, and blacks had an extended period to become accustomed to independent farming. I agree, and suggest that, in particular, the newly developing system of labor and the relationships between the former masters and the freedpeople played critical roles in the course of Reconstruction and cannot be examined through the Port Royal experiment. See James L. Roark, *Masters without Slaves: Southern Planters in the Civil War and Reconstruction* (New York: W. W. Norton, 1977), 112.

37. Donald Nieman, *To Set the Law in Motion: The Freedmen's Bureau and the Legal Rights of Blacks, 1865–1868* (Millwood, N.Y.: KTO Press, 1979), 41–42; 171–190.

38. Foner, *Reconstruction: America's Unfinished Revolution*, 157–70.

39. H. A. Johnson to "Samuel," July 14, 1865, Hannibal A. Johnson Papers, SHC/UNC. For examples of contracts see Box 2, Folders 26 and 27, Boykin Family Papers, SHC/UNC; Folders 2 and 3, Elias Horry Deas Papers, SCL; Box 9, Folder 152, Springs Family Papers, SHC/UNC; Allan Macfarlan Papers, SCLRR, Duke; Folder 4, Edward Stoeber Papers, SCL; Folder "1866," George Wise Papers, SCL.

40. U.S. Congress, *Report of the Joint Committee on Reconstruction at the First Session of the Thirty-ninth Congress* (Washington, D.C.: Government Printing Office, 1866), 222–29.

41. James Chaplin Beecher Diary and Memorandum Book, SCLRR, Duke.

42. Captain O. S. B. Wall, sub-assistant commissioner, Bureau of Refugees, Freedmen and Abandoned Lands, to Major O. D. Kinsman, assistant adjutant general, October 14, 1865, RG94, MC619, Reel 505, NA; emphasis in original.

43. H. M. Henry, *Police Control of the Slave in South Carolina* (n.p.: 1914; New York: Negro Universities Press, 1968), 28–52. Ira Berlin claimed that after emancipation, "whites almost instinctively applied the lessons of the past"; see Berlin, *Slaves without Masters: The Free Negro in the Antebellum South* (New York: Pantheon Books, 1947), 382–84. The point, although accurate, is not completely precise. White reactions after emancipation were not instinctive but based on experience and calculation. Joel Williamson agrees that there was a continuity of reaction: "Physical force . . . was, traditionally, the ultimate means of controlling the Negro. Such was the case in slavery, and it did not cease to be so afterward" (*After Slavery*, 256). In many ways this applies to later organizations as well, such as the Ku Klux Klan and the Democratic rifle clubs.

44. James C. Beecher to Major Stuart Taylor, assistant adjutant general, September 29, 1865, RG94, MC619, Reel 505, NA; Beecher, diary entry for September 27, 1865, James Chaplin Beecher Diary and Memorandum Book, SCLRR, Duke.

45. Andrews, *The South since the War*, 206, 220.

46. These reports are included in John Williams, assistant adjutant general,

Bureau of Refugees, Freedmen and Abandoned Lands, to Brigadier General C. H. Howard, chief of staff, December 4, 1865, RG94, MC619, Reel 505, NA.

47. Brevet Major General Rufus Saxton to Commissioner O. O. Howard, December 19, 1865, RG105, MC752, Reel 24, NA.

48. Saxton to O. O. Howard, January 15, 1866, RG105, MC752, Reel 24, NA.

49. Quoted by Schurz in *The Condition of the South,* 18; Kirkland, "Federal Troops in the South Atlantic States," 34.

50. F. M. Montell to O. D. Kinsman, January [?], 1866, RG94, MC619, Reel 505, NA.

51. Brown's band was so notorious that Governor James Orr, who succeeded Provisional Governor B. F. Perry, offered a reward of three hundred dollars for every member of Brown's gang captured. See DeForest, *A Union Officer in the Reconstruction,* 14–21.

52. Ames, *From a New England Woman's Diary,* 7, 13.

53. Andrews, *The South since the War,* 28.

54. Schurz, in *The Condition of the South,* 20.

55. Wade Hampton broadside on "A True Policy for the Restoration of the South," to President Andrew Johnson, August 25, 1866, Hampton Family Papers, SCL.

56. Childs, ed., *The Private Journal of Henry W. Ravenel,* 246.

57. Robert A. Pringle to W. R. Johnson, August 19, 1865, Robert A. Pringle Papers, SCLRR, Duke.

58. H. A. Johnson to "Samuel," September 9, 1865, Hannibal A. Johnson Papers, SHC/UNC; *Charleston Daily News,* August 29, 1865.

59. Rupert Sargent Holland, ed., *Letters and Diary of Laura M. Towne, Written from the Sea Islands of South Carolina, 1862–1884* (Cambridge: Riverside Press, 1912; New York: Negro Universities Press, 1969), 167–68.

60. Childs, ed., *The Private Journal of Henry W. Ravenel,* 223.

61. *Nation,* November 23, 1865; quoted in Carter, *When the War Was Over,* 193–94.

62. The uprising in Jamaica was not related to the stresses of emancipation, as slavery had ended there in the 1830s. However, this fact mattered little to the Southern press, which capitalized on the story and exaggerated greatly the destruction done and the scope of the insurrection. For example, see the *Edgefield Advertiser,* November 29, 1865; and Carter, *When the War Was Over,* 200–1. For the "scare" itself see Dan T. Carter, "The Anatomy of Fear: The Christmas Day Insurrection Scare of 1865," in *Journal of Southern History* 42 (August 1976): 345–64.

63. Cadawaller Jones to A. B. Springs, December 6, 1865, in Box 9, Folder 150, Springs Family Papers, SHC/UNC; Williamson, *After Slavery,* 251.

64. South Carolina General Assembly, *Reports and Resolutions of the General Assembly of the State of South Carolina, Session of 1864–1865* (Columbia, S.C.: Julian A. Shelby, 1866), SCL.

65. *Edgefield Advertiser,* November 15 and December 6, 1865, January 10,

1866. For the constitution of one such militia unit, and a list of its forty-five members, see Folder 29, Iredell Jones Papers, SCL.

66. Wendell Phillips, quoted in James M. McPherson, *The Struggle for Equality: Abolitionists and the Negro in the Civil War and Reconstruction* (Princeton: Princeton University Press, 1964), 335.

67. Benedict, *Fruits of Victory,* 16–18. As Eric McKitrick has argued, one cannot speak of "Radicals" yet, for Congress had not been in session, and no real ideology, plan, or policy existed to compete with Johnson's. See *Andrew Johnson and Reconstruction,* 55–64. Another view is expressed in Henry Thompson's pro–South Carolina argument that the refusal to seat the representatives was all part of plot to overthrow Johnson; the reaction to the codes was merely an excuse to act against the president's program. See Henry T. Thompson, *Ousting the Carpetbagger from South Carolina* (Columbia, S.C.: R. L. Bryan, 1926; New York: Negro Universities Press, 1969), 20–21.

68. Whitelaw Reid, *After the War: A Tour of the Southern States, 1865–1866* (Cincinnati: Moore, Wilstach and Baldwin, 1866; New York: Harper and Row, 1965), 445.

CHAPTER TWO

THE BATTLE IS JOINED—AGAIN

> Our people have not yet learned the lessons taught by adversity, & cannot see the hopelessness of maintaining a struggle in which a faded gentility has to do battle.... They can only impose ideas and sentiments resting on the *past*.
> Louise Porcher to Armistead Burt, December 11, 1866, Octavius Theodore Porcher Papers, Duke University

I

The refusal of the Thirty-ninth Congress to seat the Southern representatives—and the subsequent creation of the Joint Committee on Reconstruction—opened a new phase in the struggle over the future of the South. Many Northerners saw President Johnson's support for rapid restoration as precluding any real change in the region. Reports of violence against blacks and Unionists, the passage of black codes, and the preponderance of former Confederates among the Southern congressmen caused many to ponder what four years of bloodshed had achieved. But the president favored speedy readmission and minimal federal interference and, by accepting Southern self-rule, seemed determined to let slip the opportunity to reshape Southern society. Radical Republicans in Congress, aided by the growing concern of moderate Republicans, military officers, and

Northern citizens, embarked on a program in 1866 designed to supplant Johnson's policy and wrest control of the South from recalcitrant rebels. Only by taking control back from conservatives could the North protect the newly freed slaves and its own hold on national power.

This was not an easy task for the Radical Republicans to achieve. The chief guarantor of black rights in the South, the Freedmen's Bureau, was too understaffed to counter white efforts to dominate the freedpeople. For instance, although bureau officer John William DeForest received numerous complaints from freedmen, complaints usually concerning the retention of wages or concerning an unfair division of crops, he frequently advised plaintiffs to drop the matter. His reasoning was simple; without troops at his disposal, he had no real power to address the issue, and was required to let the civil courts (they were open in his district) handle most cases anyway.[1] General Robert K. Scott replaced Rufus Saxton as assistant commissioner on January 20, 1866, and soon learned the bitter truth about labor relations and the bureau's authority. Assistant Commissioner Scott even discovered one case of federal officers acting in cahoots with planters, who paid them a fee to cajole blacks into signing unfair contracts.[2] Whites were manipulating the freedpeople with impunity, and Scott lamented that "the Bureau, in its emasculated present condition, has no power" to secure justice.[3]

This was an understatement. The Freedmen's Bureau tried to guarantee blacks' economic rights through the contract system—whether for shares or wages—but it never functioned as intended. By 1866, planters had become proficient at writing contracts that "give the land owners as absolute control over the freedmen as though he was his slave." So many contracts were made by planters "with the sole view to *their* interests" that Assistant Commissioner Scott issued a standard contract that employers were expected to follow.[4] But the understaffed bureau could not provide constant supervision, and planters continued to issue their own. Julius Fleming commented on the drawbacks of the "shares" system, as blacks, contracting for a "share" of the crop after harvest, were forced to borrow to survive until then. After harvest, the planters added up all the advances, and often "the employee finds that he has actually worked himself into debt."[5] After the harvest many planters also drove off laborers without compensation, knowing that in order to survive—or at least to avoid vagrancy charges—blacks would be forced to contract again at planting time. As Scott informed Commissioner Howard, "now that the crops are made, some of the planters are driving their laborers off the plantations, without regard to the obligations of the contract . . . these instances are becoming more numerous daily. . . ."[6] Also becoming more numerous were incidents of violence, and by the summer of 1866, Scott was bombarding Howard with reports of whippings, shootings, stabbings, and outright murders.[7]

Whereas federal authority was hamstrung and tentative, white Carolinians willingly resorted to force to prove their power. Organized armed bands—often mounted, to the dismay of bureau officials and Army officers who had no cavalry support—continued to terrorize blacks across large portions of the state. The post commander at Greenville Court House reported that "Beat companies (so-called) are organized to go about whipping and driving back freedmen found employed away from their former owners."[8] In February the bureau agent for Newberry and Laurens Districts told of "bands of armed men whose avowed purpose is to prevent the Freedmen from hiring themselves to any one but their former owners . . . and through fear to keep him in a condition worse than slavery." The officer had infantry at his disposal, but the mounted "desperadoes . . . bid defiance to the garrisons who have to pursue them on foot."[9] Lieutenant Colonel John Devereux, the acting assistant commissioner for Edgefield and Abbeville Districts, sampled white defiance firsthand. Returning from Augusta, Georgia, one afternoon, he was set upon by a band of armed men and robbed of his pocketbook, his watch, his horse, and even his boots. Luckily he had been wearing his U.S. Army uniform, and no Southerner would have wanted to appropriate that.[10]

The War Department sent a formal "Board of Investigation" into the western part of South Carolina, hoping to learn more about the organizations that interfered with free labor. Consisting of Captain Henry Shorey for the army and Second Lieutenant G. H. Zeigler for the Freedmen's Bureau, the board began its inquiry in March 1866. Its findings described the situation in Newberry as "truly alarming." Violence went unpunished, and many blacks were living with the garrison and refusing to go to their plantations because of armed bands. The "Bushwhackers," as blacks called them, prohibited freedmen from working for anyone other than their former owners. One band had raided the Newberry jail and freed two men being held for murdering a black worker. The armed group rode up in broad daylight, demanded the keys from the U.S. soldier guarding the jail, and when he refused, shot him dead. The investigating body found that "public opinion at the time endorsed the assault." The officers concluded the bands met with general support, and "there can be little doubt that they have been harbored, aided, and assisted in some instances by the property holders in the District."[11]

The board of investigation found Laurens District more peaceful, although until recently "armed bands of lawless men most certainly did exist." As with other districts, these groups were tied to "men of property [who] actually paid for outrages." One individual, the notorious Texas Brown, who offered to kill anyone for five dollars, was given a prize stallion by "Colonel Williams" to "enable him to carry out his career of crime." But investigating officers deduced that when the probe was begun, local inhabitants had decided that "operations cannot now be considered as beneficial to the interests of the District." As a result, "the masses . . . have become, within the past few weeks, decidedly opposed to any further acts of lawlessness."[12]

Just as whites opposed Northern and federal involvement in labor matters, they also resisted outside ideas on education. The Freedmen's Bureau had been operating schools in South Carolina since late 1862—on the Sea Islands—and the number of schools and students increased rapidly after the surrender. By June of 1866, Commissioner Howard counted 75 Bureau schools in South Carolina, with 148 teachers and 9,017 students. However, bureau officials had no illusions about the state of black education in South Carolina. In his report to the secretary of war, Commissioner Howard cautioned that if "the federal power is withdrawn" then "public opinion and the government of the state [will] prove ineffectual to protect schools from the violence of evil-minded persons."[13] Captain William Leighton would have agreed; after establishing a school, he had been "repeatedly advised by prominent men of the place *to break it up*."[14]

An anonymous Carolinian expressed the same sentiment in a poem. Do not be "distressed," the author stated, for public schools and Yankee books were now for the "oppressed, and that the time would shortly come, when tyranny like this, would cease, & the clime would be a land of bliss."[15] A Carolinian's bliss could only come, according to Assistant Commissioner Robert K. Scott, if blacks were "as ignorant as when they were slaves."[16]

As with free labor, conservative Carolinians opposed this type of black advancement and federal interference. By Scott's November report to Commissioner Howard, the number of schools in the state had declined from 75 to 38, with only 91 teachers and 5,465 students.[17] Difficulties with finances and the availability of teachers hindered the program, but Southern hostility played a major role in its decline. Some schools went the way of the one at Lexington Court House, where gangs of whites harassed the students and teacher so badly that it "caused them to abandon the school."[18] In Edgefield, only a single school remained by October, and the teacher there finally fled under threats of death. That same month, in Barnwell, an armed mob appeared at another teacher's house and promised him "instant death" if he stayed in the district; he did not.[19]

II

Violence towards blacks and white Unionists, and the refusal of new state governments to intervene, forced the hand of Congress in December of 1865. But Congress's rejection of Southern representatives and the creation of the Joint Committee on Reconstruction failed to send a warning to the former Confederates. Republicans in Congress realized that if they wanted to build a new South, *they* would have to be the instruments of change.

President Johnson appeared unconcerned with the anti-black violence and the return to power of former Confederates, so by early 1866, congressional Republicans began taking a more active role in shaping Southern affairs. Congress embarked on a legislative package designed to do what Southern states would not: protect and provide for the freedpeople. Congress had opened the second phase of the Civil War with the passage of the Thirteenth Amendment. Now, Southern recalcitrance forced Congress to raise the stakes in the struggle over the nature of the citizen. On February 6, Congress passed the Freedmen's Bureau Act, intended to modify the bureau and extend its life. President Johnson vetoed the measure less than two weeks later. In March, Johnson vetoed a more significant piece of legislation, the Civil Rights Act. Moderate in nature, the act was designed to nullify the South's black codes and improve the chances for justice by transferring jurisdiction to federal courts if state courts discriminated by race. But Johnson had cast his lot with white self-rule in the South and could not accept what he saw as unwarranted and unconstitutional exercises of federal power. The president's vetoes of two necessary, moderate pieces of legislation, and his antagonistic messages to Congress, drove many moderate Republicans into the "radical" camp.

The future of Reconstruction—and possibly the South—hung in the balance as Congress and the president locked horns over Southern rights and black rights in the spring and summer. Hoping to hobble military authority in the South, Johnson declared on April 2, 1866, that "the insurrection which heretofore existed . . . is at an end, and is henceforth to be so regarded." The president honestly believed the nation had to move on, but he also sought to undercut the legitimacy Congress would need to pursue a course opposed to his own.[20] That course continued to take shape, as Congress overrode the Civil Rights Act veto only days later, and then proceeded to override another veto, for a revised Freedmen's Bill, in July. Congress also produced a weapon believed to be beyond presidential interference—the amendment. By June the so-called Howard Amendment had passed Congress, and awaited ratification from the states. If ratified, the Fourteenth Amendment would alter the course of Reconstruction, and perhaps the nature of the federal system itself.[21]

State conservatives were horrified at the turn of events in the North. To avoid the transfer of cases to federal courts under the Civil Rights Act, states had to insure that their laws did not discriminate on the basis of race—meaning an official end to the black codes. Julius Fleming, writing as "Juhl" to the *Charleston Courier*, called the act "most fatal to liberty and certainly most damaging to our great unrepresented southern domain."[22] Planter A. C. Garlington blamed Governor Perry and President Johnson for the sudden turn in South Carolina's fortunes, as they did "not properly estimate the strength of the opposition."[23] Having just returned from a service for Confederate dead in March, M. L. Brinkley mourned that the state "now [lies] powerless in the hands of a set of unprincipled bad men whose sole aim is how much they can oppress and degrade us. . . ."[24] To David Milling, South Carolina's "political horizon seems cloudy, and not much appearance of a clear atmosphere while the Radicals have the control," for they were undoubtedly bent on "hellish and evil designs."[25]

To the relief of many white Carolinians, congressional activity did not have as great an impact on the South as radical Republicans desired. Despite the Civil Rights Act, for instance, conservatives retained control over the legal affairs of the state by complying with its provisions. The act provided blacks equal access to the judicial system but was more carrot than stick, for if states removed discriminatory measures from their books, legal proceedings would not be transferred from state to federal courts. Once South Carolina altered its judicial codes and removed all racial references, by nullifying the black codes, the act was of limited value. State courts, with their white judges and whites juries, retained jurisdiction.

Even the last resort—the military's provost courts—were of limited value. The provost courts of the War Department maintained jurisdiction over cases involving blacks if the department commander decided civil courts were acting unfairly (the Freedmen's Bureau courts were small in number and smaller in authority, and after the president's proclamation, they ceased to be of import). The courts were intended to foil Southern prejudice by always including an army officer on the three-man panel. But the courts convened irregularly and infrequently, and, according to one army captain, "when it comes time to testify, through fear, he [the freedman] is very liable to contradict former statements." Even if victims testified—which was rare—whites always had an alibi or a solid character witness. As the officer observed, "it is almost impossible to find a white man here who will testify to the good character of any negro, or to the bad character of any white man."[26]

Former Confederates further consolidated their power after President Johnson's second peace proclamation was issued in August of 1866.

Johnson removed the military from civil affairs by declaring that the insurrection had ended in all states of the former Confederacy (his April proclamation had excluded Texas). In South Carolina, General Orders No. 15—which took effect on October 1, 1866—officially discontinued the provost courts in the state and handed all responsibility for justice over to the civil authorities.[27] Across the state, many local boys were behind bars for one reason or another, often held under the previous War Department orders. The return to the civil power brought rapid "justice" for whites, a confounded Assistant Commissioner Scott wrote to Commissioner Howard. In some districts, he stated, nearly all detainees escaped punishment, "either by failure of the Grand Jury to find a bill against them, of if tried they were acquitted. . . ."[28] Justice was swift indeed for the men held by Major Eugene Carter of the Eighteenth U.S. Infantry. On October 12, Carter handed the jail at Chester over to the civil constable; by October 16, six of the seven had escaped. In Carter's opinion, "the Sheriff and his deputies are responsible for this outbreak . . . [as] no effort was made to keep the prisoners safely."[29]

With their violent combinations unchecked and their legal control unquestioned, Carolina whites redoubled their efforts to relegate the freedpeople to their former status. In the wake of Johnson's proclamation, federal officers warned superiors that civil authorities either could not or would not control lawlessness. George W. Gile, the bureau agent for the Districts of Sumter, Darlington, and Chesterfield, was "not convinced that the interest of the freedmen would be safe in the hands of the civil authorities" if the army was removed.[30] He was right, for Brevet Brigadier General Benjamin Runkle informed Assistant Commissioner Scott that "armed men roam through the country shooting and assaulting blacks, and no effort is made by the civil authorities to check them." The exasperated Runkle pointed out that "the less a constable or sheriff does, the more popular he is, so *few do anything*."[31] It was difficult to even secure information necessary for an arrest. One officer said freedmen "dare not tell, even if they knew of these men, for if they did, the moment the troops were withdrawn they would be beaten or probably killed."[32] One judge simply refused to organize the court for his district, citing qualms about jurisdiction. The army officer on the scene, Lieutenant Colonel John Devereux, felt helpless, because "there is actually no means of obtaining justice and redress of wrongs in this part of South Carolina."[33] The same situation occurred in Darlington: since "there is no court to which the freedmen in this county can apply for redress or grievances," the magistrate admitted, ". . . wrongs can be inflicted upon them with absolute impunity."[34]

Even functioning courts did not guarantee justice, as whites used them as another tool of racial control. Julius Fleming, now a magistrate, wrote directly to General Scott to complain about the Honorable A. P. Aldrich and his district court. In cases involving whites killing blacks, even when "the *fact* of the killing in each case was admitted," Aldrich's charges to the juries were "plain *instructions to acquit.*" But Fleming admitted this probably did not alter the verdict, for juries were "composed chiefly of *planters*—the very class with whom the freedmen have their principal difficulties. Can such juries be expected to act without bias . . . ?" Fleming told Scott that "if the negroes are left in their present condition, then emancipation is a mockery and freedom a farce"—"Of course," Fleming added, "there are exceptions, but *as a race* their condition is worse than Slavery itself."[35]

III

Where some observers saw cruelty and reactionary vengeance, President Andrew Johnson saw Southern troubles as the result of unwarranted and unconstitutional interference with natural patterns and relationships. Incapable of compromise and determined to protect the Constitution and restore the alienated states, Johnson sought other safeguards against the upstart Congress. He envisioned a new political party, one designed to secure control of Congress in the 1866 elections. President Johnson hoped the "National Union" movement would unite moderates in the North and the South behind his programs.

From its outset the president's plan suffered from crippling problems, including poor management, the presence of too many extremists (who scared off many moderates), and the ever-antagonistic Johnson himself. Timing also played havoc; the National Union convention in Philadelphia opened on the heels of the New Orleans riot of July 30, in which white policemen had attacked a constitutional convention and killed thirty-four blacks, three white Republicans, and injured more than a hundred. The blatant aggression by official state forces on the eve of a convention proclaiming reconciliation made many question the accuracy, and the sincerity, of the movement.[36]

Southerners—South Carolinians included—saw the movement as another step to achieving control of their states. For hopeful conservatives, the opening procession on August 14—marked by the sickeningly dramatic gesture of James L. Orr of South Carolina and Darius Couch of Massachusetts entering the hall arm-in-arm—symbolized restoration and a return to state's rights and federalism.³⁷ Some, like Henry W. Ravenel, were convinced the convention would be "a great success."³⁸ Martin Wilkins agreed, but was less than satisfied with the whole project; he was tired of Southern concessions and looked for leaders who would come out and "assert the dignity and great argument of a lost cause."³⁹ But the only lost cause was Johnson's, who capped off his pre-election canvass with his "Swing Around the Circle," an embarrassing display of how out-of-touch the president had become.

Not unlike President Johnson, Republicans in Congress also looked toward the elections to vindicate their policy. The congressional alternative to Johnson had emerged as the proposed Fourteenth Amendment. Framers and supporters saw the amendment as a solution to violence and a guarantee of Northern dominance in Congress; change would come in the South, either through a black electorate or by a Northern, Republican-controlled Congress.

While the historical debates over the amendment continue to this day, one fact is clear: as written, it was unacceptable to the South. Southerners who seceded had fought for the right to regulate their own society, and they would not accept an amendment framed by a hostile Congress in which they lacked representation. The amendment presented the South with a no-win situation. Either blacks gained the franchise, or the South lost seats in Congress.⁴⁰

"We are on the eve of critical events in the elections which come on this autumn," wrote Henry W. Ravenel of the coming congressional elections. As Ravenel saw it, "the fate of the South (humanely speaking) depends on the result."⁴¹ The historian Eric Foner believed that the 1866 elections were a "referendum" on the Fourteenth Amendment and that voters would say yea or nay with their ballots.⁴² What they said was that the Fourteenth Amendment must become law, the South must adopt it, and Southerners must begin to show more compassion and humility if they expected to be allowed back into the Union. The sweeping Republican victories vindicated Congress, repudiated Johnson, and sent shock waves through the former Confederacy.

Regardless, Carolinians had no intention of ratifying the amendment. Months earlier, when it first became public, South Carolina Governor Benjamin Perry had written to the *New York Tribune* outlining the limits of Southern concessions. He declared the South desired only to govern itself, free from Northern interference. Perry wrote that "there is another punishment to be inflicted on the Southern people . . . a war of races . . . [for if] the negro will be invested with all political power, then the antagonism of interests between capital and labor is to work out the final result!" Perry reminded the paper's readers that "this Government has been the white man's government, both Federal and State. It was formed by white men and for white men exclusively." After all, he concluded, "the history of the world shows . . . that the negro is inferior to the white man."[43]

Others feared the social ramifications of the franchise. In a letter to Perry, J. M. Anderson explained that black suffrage was "the *ne plus ultra* of all evils . . . alone and of itself utterly intolerable and certainly ruinous . . . [since] it will certainly bring every other evil in its train. Give the negro political equality and he will legislate social equality."[44] In November 1866, Charles Woodward proposed altering the amendment to include "impartial suffrage," based on literacy qualifications designed to disfranchise very few whites and enfranchise only a few blacks. When he asked Perry if the South would accept it, Perry answered, "I do not think so."[45]

While Southern honor and Southern fears narrowed the chances for the Fourteenth Amendment's acceptance in the South, other factors seemed to seal its fate completely. For instance, try as they might, Southerners could get no guarantee of admission if they ratified the amendment. Topping it all off was President Johnson, who openly advised Southern states to reject the amendment. T. C. Weatherly, a member of South Carolina's General Assembly, was warned by President Johnson not to trust Republican promises. He included this news, and more of the president's advice to reject the amendment, in a frantic letter back to his state.[46]

Governor James L. Orr opened his address to the General Assembly by saying that "history furnishes few examples of a people who have been required to concede more to the will of their conquerors than the people of the South." Preposterous as they were, his words nonetheless prepared the way for his recommendation against ratification. Orr called on legislators to stand firm and declared that if the amendment does pass, "let it be done by the irresponsible power of numbers, and let us preserve our self-respect, and the respect of our posterity by refusing to be the mean instrument of our shame." Both the Senate and the House rejected it overwhelmingly, the House voting ninety-five to one.[47] Pleased with the result, James Wright of Laurensville wrote with news to his cousin Nickels Holmes, studying at the University of Edinburgh: "But there is life in the old land yet. The last one of the late confederate states has rejected, I believe, the odious, disgraceful amendment to the Constitution, preferring to be held as conquered provinces always to accepting such terms."[48] South Carolina and its Southern brethren had made their choice, as they had done the previous December and the December of 1860. Now the choices lay before the Thirty-ninth Congress of the United States, which had just begun its second session on December 4, 1866.

IV

The rejection of the Fourteenth Amendment, President Johnson's continued coddling of former Confederates, and the elections of 1866 ushered in a dramatic shift in the Reconstruction program. Taking the cue from Republican victories in the 1866 elections, Republicans in Congress embarked on a plan designed to reverse the damage done by Johnson. Congress would hold the states in a "political limbo" while a new power base—a new black electorate—was being prepared. Congress rendered impotent one obstacle, Andrew Johnson, but found that the other, the South, could not be subdued as easily.

Congressional leaders—from the old "radicals" Charles Sumner and Thaddeus Stevens, to the more recent recruits like Roscoe Conkling and John Logan, and moderates such as John Sherman and Lyman Trumbull—focused on the single element capable of transforming the South: black suffrage. With the black male population enfranchised, states could again become self-regulating, while their huge black constituencies formed a solid foundation for the extension of the Republican party.[49]

The congressional program began with the Military Reconstruction Act (or simply, the "Reconstruction Act"), which established a procedure for states to follow for both modifying their internal governance and reapplying for admission. The bill, passed March 2 over the President's veto, divided the Southern states into five military districts, each under a commanding general. South Carolina and North Carolina comprised the Second Military District, under the command of Major General Daniel E. Sickles. While under military control, the state proceeded toward civil restoration and readmission through the election of a new constitutional convention on the basis of *full male suffrage*. The convention then drafted a new constitution, to include equal male suffrage, which had to be ratified at a second election. Lastly, the state legislature had to be elected anew, based on the voting provisions of the new constitution, and it had to ratify the Fourteenth Amendment. If Congress approved the constitution, the state would regain its place in Congress and the Union.[50]

Congress quickly passed measures designed to minimalize Southern and presidential interference with the program. The Army Appropriations Act required the general-in-chief to reside in Washington, and stipulated that all official correspondence must flow through him. With General Ulysses S. Grant leaning toward the Radicals, such a law allowed Congress and the War Department to circumvent and undercut the president. A rider attached to the bill disbanded all military organizations in the late rebel states—*including* all state militias. The same day, March 2, Congress planted the seed of Johnson's demise by passing the Tenure of Office Act.[51]

The Supplementary Reconstruction Act, passed on March 23, provided specific instructions for implementing the Reconstruction Act. District commanders were to register all eligible males by September 1 for the purpose of electing delegates to the state constitutional convention. Commanders could establish registration boards, select registrars, and supervise the actual counts. Once registration was complete, a vote would be held for or against a convention. It was possible, depending on the vote, for states to avoid congressional Reconstruction and remain under military control. If a voter opposed the convention, he merely voted "no." If a voter was in favor of the convention to modify the constitution, he voted "yes" and wrote in his choice for a delegate. If a *majority* of those registered voted *for* a convention, then a convention had to convene within sixty days of the vote.[52]

Disagreeable as it was, Carolinians understood that these military operations paved the way for a far more devastating blow. Within a year, the operating theory behind Reconstruction had shifted dramatically. Under President Johnson, and even with Congress's measures of 1866, the focus had been on influencing, conciliating, and cajoling the white population. The Reconstruction Acts, however, placed the focus on the voting population at large, including the black portion of it. For South Carolina, with a black majority, this meant whites faced the possibility of becoming less powerful at best, *ruled* at worst.

A consensus soon emerged in opposition to the new convention. If no convention were held—if the vote were somehow defeated—the state would remain under military supervision. This situation would be temporary, lasting only until Congress developed a new plan or Northern opinion shifted; besides, conservatives had already demonstrated their ability to undermine federal authority. On the other hand, once a new constitution granted blacks political power, they might control the legislature, the judiciary, and the governorship, and whites would face a grueling uphill struggle to reclaim power.

So, contrary to logic and the course pursued by other Southern states, Carolina whites attempted to derail the convention. It would appear, in a state with a black majority, that there was little doubt as to the outcome of the convention vote. As Michael Perman pointed out, whites in states with large black populations accepted the inevitable, and instead of opposing the convention, tried to elect conservatives to it.[53] South Carolina whites opted for the opposite strategy. In order for a convention to be held, a majority of those registered had to vote for it. Whites, therefore, registered in record numbers to swell the figure, then voted "no" or boycotted the election.

As early as May, months before registration began, leading conservatives took the stump arguing that temporary submission was better than permanent subjugation. Writing to former governor Benjamin Perry, W. E. Martin of Charleston was optimistic: "let us not despair. I urge everybody who can to register, and vote *no convention*."[54] Perry was in fact leading the drive to block the convention: "If we are to wear manacles," he proclaimed in May, "let them be put on by our tyrants, not ourselves."[55] Carolinians must avoid "disgracing themselves for ever and ever by adopting a negro government and giving up the rights of their State...."[56] When the *Columbia Phoenix* warned that rejecting a convention might lead to worse consequences, Perry fired back. "In my opinion," he exclaimed, "nothing worse than negro suffrage and a negro government can be forced upon us. It would be a thousand times preferable to remain under military rule...."[57] He also chastised those who spoke of directing the negro vote. Once granted, he argued, it would prove uncontrollable, the "*ne plus ultra* of all political and social evils." The only solution, according to Perry, was total registration and total rejection.[58] The aging but influential Alfred Huger agreed that Carolinians should not "hastily escape a 'Military Government,' administered by intelligence and policy, to embrace such a one as Negro suffrage ... *must* provide."[59]

By April, war hero Wade Hampton, who at first had argued that whites should try to direct the black vote, agreed that unified opposition offered an escape from black rule. All energies, the cavalier-planter argued, must be directed to preserving white rule in the state: "I will not give up," the defiant planter said, "I will fight on every battlefield shown by the enemy till I fall or till we are free...." As he told John Mullaly, "the very existence of our country" was a stake, for "we are fighting for bread and for life, & a desperate battle we are waging."[60] Gone were his speeches to black assemblies and the messages sweet with conciliation. "Our State Conventions were mistakes," Hampton informed the *Charleston Mercury*, "so were the changes of our constitutions; greater that all others was the legislation ratifying the amendment ... known as Article 13."[61] Hampton told the lawyer Armistead Burt "it would be better for the State to be remanded to Military Government rather than that which places the negro permanently in power."[62]

On November 6, two weeks before the election, conservative whites gathered in Columbia for a "Conservative State Convention" in a final effort to spread the message of "register-and-reject." Participants included James Chesnut, Benjamin Perry, Wade Hampton, A. P. Aldrich, and William DeSaussure. Resolutions proclaimed the Reconstruction Acts "illegal" since they would "place the best interests of society in the hands of an ignorant mob." The convention also issued an open letter to the people of the United States, assuring them that white Carolinians "would never acquiesce in Negro equality or supremacy."[63] White Carolinians had declared war on their state government even before it existed.

On the election days (voting was on November 19 and 20), whites stuck by their plan. Observers might have suspected that something was amiss, for although the black vote was heavy, the white turnout was light, especially considering the number of eligible whites registered. Abstinence was deliberate; the convention required support of a majority of those registered, so not voting produced the same effect as voting "no." As Henry W. Ravenel noted in his journal, "there is a general indisposition among the whites to take any part in the election. . . . The whites will absent themselves from the polls. . . ."[64] Thomas Pinckney Lowndes observed that whites "took no part in the election, many of them from fear of social ostracism and others from pride of race, that pride which alone could save us from the fearful consequences of miscegenation."[65]

The results were surprisingly close. Preliminary reports indicated that whites had been successful. Hoping against hope to avoid a black government, Andrew Cornish wrote to his brother: "How wonderful the result! No Convention in South Carolina! How contrary to all predictions! What next? Well, we can be thankful for Military Rule!"[66] He was not thankful for long, as the final figures showed that the white strategy had failed. The vote was as follows:

Total Registered:	127,550
black:	80,379
white:	47,171
Voting for convention:	68,768
Voting against:	2,278
Not voting:	55,798

The numbers support two general conclusions. First, state conservatives did not accept the convention as a certainty. They organized and applied a coherent strategy in an attempt to thwart the plans of Congress and the Republican party. Looking at the final figures, one sees that the conservatives came very close to victory. Black voters had an overwhelming advantage in numbers, yet cleared their goal—they needed 63,776 "yes" votes—by only a slim margin. Secondly, while there is no single explanation for why many *blacks* did not vote, the experience of the past few years suggests that more aggressive white tactics were also at work.[67]

Prior to the election, Julius Fleming, a voice of moderation in a wilderness of extremism, had pleaded with his fellow Carolinians to accept the terms of the Reconstruction Acts. "The man who has his hand in the lion's mouth," Fleming counseled, "if a sensible man, will do nothing to irritate the animal."[68] But whites had ignored Fleming, and in the end the freedmen had beaten them. With Republican help, an inexperienced mass of former slaves had mobilized, unified, and seized the future.

The victory that blacks achieved in 1867 did not bring peace, stability, or prosperity either to the state or to their own lives. South Carolina whites viewed Reconstruction as the continuation of the Northern attack on their rights and their way of life. They had sought security in independence, and failing that, they had attempted to rebuild their shattered world under the guidelines established by President Johnson. Now a new force had emerged to interfere with conservatives' rights, a force that until recently had been property. South Carolina's traditional values of white supremacy, self-government, and local control tottered near the brink. But the state remained determined and defiant. As one editorial from the *Charleston Mercury* claimed, whites "are not *ruled* by any governments they do not recognize as legitimate over them. . . . The white race of the South have only to will the rule of the South, and there is no power on this continent which can prevent it."[69]

Notes

1. John William DeForest, *A Union Officer in the Reconstruction*, ed. James Croushore and David M. Potter (New Haven: Yale University Press, 1948), 29–30.

2. Robert K. Scott to Commissioner O. O. Howard, "Annual Report," November 1, 1866, in Box 1, Folder 3, Robert K. Scott Papers, Ohio Historical Society, Columbus, Ohio (hereafter OHS).

3. Scott to Howard, June 20, 1866, in Record Group 105, Microcopy 752, Reel 35, National Archives, Washington, D.C. (hereafter RG, MC, Reel, NA).

4. Scott to Howard, "Annual Report," November 1, 1866, in Box 1, Folder 3, Robert K. Scott Papers, OHS; emphasis in original.

5. John Hammond Moore, ed., *The Juhl Letters to the Charleston Courier: A View of the South, 1865–1871* (Athens: University of Georgia Press, 1974), 110–11.

6. Scott to Howard, "Annual Report," November 1, 1866, in Box 1, Folder 3, Robert K. Scott Papers, OHS.

7. Scott to Howard, June 20, 1866, RG105, MC752, Reel 35, NA.

8. The report by Greenville's commander is contained in Scott to Howard, "Freedmen's Bureau Report for February 1866," RG105, MC752, Reel 29, NA.

9. Captain A. Coan to Captain J. A. Blank, acting assistant adjutant general, February 10, 1866, RG94, MC619, Reel 512, NA.

10. See Lieutenant Colonel John Devereux to Robert K. Scott, March 7, 1866, RG105, MC752, Reel 29, NA; Dan T. Carter, *When the War Was Over: The Failure of Self-Reconstruction in the South, 1865–1867* (Baton Rouge: Louisiana

State University Press, 1985) 20–21; and Orville Vernon Burton, *In My Father's House Are Many Mansions: Family and Community in Edgefield, South Carolina* (Chapel Hill: University of North Carolina Press, 1985), 289.

11. Captain Henry Shorey, "Report of the Board of Investigation," March 19, 1866, RG94, MC619, Reel 512, NA.

12. Shorey, "Report of the Board of Investigation," March 19, 1866; DeForest, *A Union Officer in the Reconstruction*, 15–21; Joel Williamson, *After Slavery: The Negro in South Carolina during Reconstruction, 1861–1877* (Chapel Hill: University of North Carolina Press, 1965), 97.

13. Commissioner O. O. Howard, "Report of the Freedmen's Bureau for South Carolina," 737, in *Annual Report of the Secretary of War for 1866*.

14. Captain William Leighton to Robert K. Scott, March 5, 1866, RG105, MC752, Reel 29, NA; emphasis in original.

15. No author, n.d., in Folder 20, Conway, Black, and Davis Family Papers, South Caroliniana Library, University of South Carolina, Columbia, S.C. (hereafter SCL).

16. Scott to Howard, "Annual Report," November 1, 1866, in Box 1, Folder 3, Robert K. Scott Papers, OHS.

17. Scott to Howard, "Annual Report," November 1, 1866.

18. Report of F. Simmons of Lexington Court House, in a letter from Brevet Brigadier General R. Ely, acting assistant commissioner, to Scott, April 25, 1866, RG105, MC752, Reel 29, NA.

19. Burton, *In My Father's House Are Many Mansions*, 251; Brevet Major L. Walker to H. W. Smith, assistant adjutant general, October 12, 1866, RG105, MC752, Reel 39, NA.

20. James D. Richardson, *A Compilation of the Messages and Papers of the Presidents, 1789–1902* (Washington, D.C.: Bureau of National Literature and Art, 1904), 6:429–32; John Robert Kirkland, "Federal Troops in the South Atlantic States during Reconstruction: 1865–1877" (Ph.D. diss., University of North Carolina at Chapel Hill, 1968), 123.

21. For an overview of the estranged relationship between the executive and the legislative branches of the federal government, see Eric L. McKitrick, *Andrew Johnson and Reconstruction* (Chicago: University of Chicago Press, 1960); 274–325; Eric Foner, *Reconstruction 1863–1877: America's Unfinished Revolution* (New York: Harper and Row, 1988), 247–51. The debate continues over the intent and extent of the Fourteenth Amendment. But, as happens more often than not, the truth lies somewhere in the middle: the amendment was not wholly "revolutionary," but it did set new precedents and modify the relationship between the states and the federal government. For a "conservative" view of the measure, see Michael Les Benedict, "Preserving the Constitution: The Conservative Basis for Radical Reconstruction," *Journal of American History* 61 (June 1974): 76. A more radical perception of the amendment's potential powers can be found in Robert J. Kaczorowski, "To Begin the Nation Anew: Congress, Citizenship, and Civil Rights after the Civil War," *American Historical Review* 92 (February 1987): 45–68.

22. Moore, ed., *The Juhl Letters*, 88–89.

23. A. C. Garlington to A. B. Springs, February 17, 1866, in Box 9, Folder 152, Springs Family Papers, Southern Historical Collection, University of North Carolina, Chapel Hill, N.C. (hereafter SHC/UNC).

24. M. L. Brinkly to "Sister," March 19, 1866, in Box 7, Daniel W. Jordan Papers, Special Collections Library Research Room, Perkins Library, Duke University, Durham, N.C. (hereafter SCLRR, Duke).

25. David Milling to James S. Milling, August 30, 1866, in Folder 10, James S. Milling Papers, SHC/UNC.

26. Captain A. Evans to Captain J. A. Clark, acting assistant adjutant general, January 27, 1866, in Folder 5, George Coffin Taylor Papers, SHC/UNC.

27. See General Orders No. 15, Dept. of the South, October 15, 1866, RG105, MC752, Reel 39, NA.

28. Scott to Howard, "Annual Report," November 1, 1866, in Box 1, Folder 3, Robert K. Scott Papers, OHS; Scott to Howard, report for December 1866, dated January 23, 1867, RG105, MC752, Reel 44, NA.

29. Brevet Major Eugene Carter to Lieutenant Colonel H. W. Smith, assistant adjutant general, October 16, 1866, RG105, MC752, Reel 39, NA.

30. Brevet Brigadier General George W. Gile to Scott, n.d.; quoted in Scott to Howard, "Annual Report," November 1, 1866, in Box 1, Folder 3, Robert K. Scott Papers, OHS.

31. Brevet Brigadier General Benjamin Runkle to Scott, n.d.; quoted in Scott to Howard, "Annual Report," November 1, 1866; emphasis in original.

32. Major Stowe to Scott, quoted in Scott to Howard, "Annual Report," November 1, 1866.

33. Lieutenant Colonel John Devereux to H. W. Smith, assistant adjutant general, June 6, 1866, RG105, MC752, Reel 35, NA.

34. Quoted in Scott to Howard, "Annual Report," November 1, 1866.

35. Julius Fleming to Scott, February 8, 1867, RG105, MC752, Reel 44, NA; emphasis in original.

36. Foner, *Reconstruction: America's Unfinished Revolution*, 262–64; McKitrick, *Andrew Johnson and Reconstruction*, 394, 410–19, 422–27, 428–38.

37. Carter, *When the War Was Over*, 242–48; Michael Perman, *Reunion without Compromise: The South and Reconstruction 1865–1868* (New York: Cambridge University Press, 1973), 198–228.

38. Arney Robinson Childs, ed., *The Private Journal of Henry William Ravenel, 1859–1887* (Columbia: University of South Carolina Press, 1947), 293.

39. Martin Wilkins to "Uncle" (J. B. Grimball), August 29, 1866, in Folder 18, Grimball Family Papers, SHC/UNC.

40. The staunchest advocate for the conservative nature of Fourteenth Amendment is Michael Les Benedict in "Preserving the Constitution," *Journal of American History* 61 (June 1974): 76. On the opposite side, arguing for radical intent, is Kaczorowski in "To Begin the Nation Anew," *American Historical Review* 92 (February 1987): 45–68.

41. Childs, ed., *The Private Journal of Henry W. Ravenel*, 293, 295.

42. Foner, *Reconstruction: America's Unfinished Revolution*, 267.

43. Governor Benjamin Perry to the *New York Tribune,* April 15, 1866, in Scrapbook, Benjamin F. Perry Papers, SHC/UNC.

44. J. M. Anderson to Perry, [n.d.], 1865; quoted in Lou Faulkner Williams, "The Great South Carolina Ku Klux Klan Trials, 1871–1872" (Ph.D. diss., University of Florida, 1991), 21; emphasis in original.

45. Perry to Charles W. Woodward, November 30, 1866, in Scrapbook, Benjamin F. Perry Papers, SHC/UNC.

46. See McKitrick, *Andrew Johnson and Reconstruction*, 471.

47. Quoted in Francis Butler Simkins and Robert Hilliard Woody, *South Carolina during Reconstruction* (Chapel Hill: University of North Carolina Press, 1932), 62–63. Some historians have implied that without Johnson's intercession, Southern states would have ratified the proposed amendment. See, for example, Roger P. Leemhuis, *James L. Orr and the Sectional Conflict* (Washington, D.C.: University Press of America, 1979), 121; and David M. Potter, *Division and the Stresses of Reunion, 1845–1876* (Glenview, Ill.: Scott, Foresman, 1973), 179. This was unlikely, for the provisions of the Fourteenth Amendment address ancient issues, including fundamental questions of state's rights, a limited federal government, and a state's control over its races, society, and politics. These issues had driven Southern secession and had cost millions of dollars and thousands of lives. Michael Perman has reasoned that even without Johnson's prompting, rejection was probable, for the amendment was too high a price to pay for readmission. See Perman, *Reunion without Compromise*, 235–47. See also Michael Les Benedict, *The Fruits of Victory: Alternatives in Restoring the Union, 1865–1877* (Philadelphia: J. B. Lippincott, 1975), 28–30.

48. James Wright to Nickels J. Holmes, January [n.d.], 1867, Nickels J. Holmes Papers, SCLRR, Duke.

49. I agree with Michael Les Benedict on the inherent "conservative" nature of the Reconstruction Acts. James Blaine and John Bingham had modified Stevens's original bill from the Joint Committee, and helped insure its moderate intentions. The bill proposed only limited and temporary territorialization—all following existing state lines, so no redrawing occurred. In addition, there was no provision for confiscation or redistribution. As Benedict has pointed out, the stipulation for inclusion of black males in the political sphere provided an escape for the federal government, which could turn affairs back over to the states and hope that blacks—having the power of the ballot—could protect themselves and their party. See Benedict, *The Fruits of Victory*, 31–33; and "Preserving the Constitution," *Journal of American History* 61 (June 1974): 65–90 passim.

50. Benedict, "Preserving the Constitution," *Journal of American History*, 82–84.

51. James E. Sefton, *The United States Army and Reconstruction, 1865–1877* (Baton Rouge: Louisiana State University Press, 1967), 111–13; Otis Singletary, "The Negro Militia during Radical Reconstruction," *Military Affairs* 19 (Winter 1955): 177. On the Tenure of Office act, see William S. McFeely, *Grant: A Biography* (New York: W. W. Norton, 1981), 262–73.

52. In South Carolina, General Sickles had the assistance of Governor Orr, who, unlike many of his fellow Carolinians, accepted the act and sought to follow its provisions. Orr himself dragooned many people into assisting with the registration and created an almost comical network of men dragging other men into the same distasteful duty. See James L. Orr to A. B. Springs, A. B. Springs to

Cadawaller Jones, Cadawaller Jones to A. B. Springs, and J. Wallace to A. B. Springs, in Box 10, Folder 163, Springs Family Papers, SHC\UNC; Kirkland, "Federal Troops in the South Atlantic States," 194–96; Williamson, *After Slavery,* 337; and Reconstruction Scrapbook, 21–22, SCL.

53. Perman, *Reunion without Compromise,* 278–79, 299.

54. W. E. Martin to Benjamin F. Perry, May 7, 1867, in Box 4, Armistead Burt Papers, SCLRR, Duke.

55. Benjamin F. Perry, in *Charleston News,* May 18, 1867; quoted in Simkins and Woody, *South Carolina during Reconstruction,* 85.

56. Perry to Dr. F. Marion Dye, May 25, 1867, in Box 1, Folder 11, Benjamin Franklin Perry Papers, SHC/UNC.

57. Perry to editors, *Columbia Phoenix,* n.d., in Scrapbook, Benjamin Franklin Perry Papers, SHC/UNC.

58. Perry, in *Charleston Courier,* April 19, 1867; emphasis in original.

59. Alfred Huger to Perry, quoted in Perman, *Reunion without Compromise,* 312; emphasis in original. For other support see Lizzie [Elizabeth] Perry to Armistead Burt, May 11, 1867, Benjamin Franklin Perry Papers, SCLRR, Duke.

60. Wade Hampton to James Conner, April 9, 1867, and Hampton to John Mullaly, April 11, 1867, in Box 5, Hampton Family Papers, SCL.

61. Hampton to D. W. Ray, W. H. Talley, and J. P. Thomas, editors of the *Charleston Mercury,* August 29, 1867, in Box 5, Hampton Family Papers, SCL.

62. Hampton to Armistead Burt, n.d., in Box 3, Armistead Burt Papers, SCLRR, Duke.

63. Simkins and Woody, *South Carolina during Reconstruction,* 87; Perman, *Reunion without Compromise,* 334; *Charleston Courier,* November 9, 1867; *Charleston News,* November 9, 1867.

64. Childs, ed., *The Private Journal of Henry William Ravenel,* 314.

65. Thomas Pinckney Lowndes, "Reminiscences," 110–11, in Box 2, Folder 21, William Lowndes Papers, SHC/UNC. For a similar report see the Robert Wallace Shand Journal, SCL.

66. Andrew Cornish to John Hamilton Cornish, December 2, 1867, in Box 2, Folder 28, John Hamilton Cornish Papers, SHC/UNC.

67. My numbers are from a clipping in the Reconstruction Scrapbook, SCL. The piece appears to be a printed notice and is signed by Louis Caziarc, the acting assistant adjutant general of the Second Military District. Carol Bleser, however, has given different figures. She listed 80,550 as the total registered—with 66,418 blacks voting for the convention; 2,350 whites voting for the convention; and 2,278 whites voting against the convention. See Carol K. Bleser, *The Promised Land: The History of the South Carolina Land Commission, 1869–1890* (Columbia: University of South Carolina Press, 1969), xii.

68. Moore, ed., *The Juhl Letters,* 160.

69. *Charleston Mercury,* December 12, 1867; quoted in Perman, *Reunion without Compromise,* 339; emphasis in original.

CHAPTER THREE

"WE MUST FIGHT THE DEVIL WITH FIRE"

> For us the war was not ended. We had met the enemy in the field and lost our fight, but now we were threatened with a servile war, a war in which the negro savage backed by the U.S. and the intelligent white scoundrel as his leader was our enemy.
>
> Thomas Pinckney Lowndes, "Reminiscences," William Lowndes Papers, Southern Historical Collection, University of North Carolina

I

Since Appomattox, conservatives in South Carolina had worked to regain control over their affairs, relying on a sympathetic executive, legal loopholes, a divided Congress, and brute force. The events of 1867 swept away what they had constructed and threatened them with permanent removal from power. Indeed, that year marked the opening of a new age in America, for black males now had the ballot, and the election demonstrated that they could dominate politics. The state convention of 1868 and the elections for the new government further confirmed this fact, as an alliance of blacks and Republican whites—many of them "carpetbaggers" from outside the South—pushed aside the conservatives and took control of the government.

This shift in power forced conservative whites to operate *outside* the normal channels. Their response was a necessary one if they were to restore white rule. Intimidation, economic extortion, and outright terrorism became integral components of state politics as whites began an eight-year effort to regain political power. What Herbert Shapiro has called the "counterrevolution of white supremacy" began as black suffrage forced these "counterrevolutionaries" to adopt new means to secure their ends.[1]

The state's constitutional convention both authorized and symbolized the dramatic shift in power. The convention assembled on January 14, 1868, and of the 124 delegates meeting in Charleston, 73 were black, 36 were Southern whites (nearly all Republicans), and the remaining 15 were carpetbaggers—that is, whites from outside the South. The chief task facing the convention was the drafting of a new constitution, which, by order of Congress, must include impartial male suffrage. The final document used explicit language in regard to "race" and "color," delegates wisely avoiding loopholes that might spell trouble in the future. As delegate Francis L. Cardozo, a free-born mulatto, argued, "if we do not" make the document explicit, "we deserve to be, and will be, cheated again. Nearly all the white inhabitants of the state are ready at any moment to deprive us of our rights, and not a loop-hole should be left that would permit them to do it constitutionally." By the middle of March, in preparation for the April elections for a new state government, the revised constitution was ready.[2]

Conservatives made no effort to hide their anxiety and distress. When the convention opened in January, Dr. John Davis reported gloomily that "everything looks to the speedy Africanization of the South & there seems to be no way of escape."[3] The editor of the *Edgefield Advertiser* agreed, claiming that "South Carolina is Polandized—aye worse than that, *Africanized* . . . the South Carolina of the great men, great services and great distinction *is no more!*"[4] Reviewing the new constitution, the *Fairfield Herald* called it "the maddest, most unscrupulous, and most infamous revolution in history."[5] Dr. Henry D. Green lectured a Democratic club in a similar way, urging whites to oppose the constitution simply because "it is a *negro constitution, of a negro government, establishing negro equality.*" "I am opposed to negro suffrage," Dr. Green declared, "*because he is a negro,* independent of anything else."[6] The Democratic state central executive committee even went so far as to send a formal protest to Congress. The "Respectful Remonstrance on Behalf of the White People of South Carolina" listed the committee's objections to the new constitution. Article 1, section 19 allowed, in the committee's words, "ignorant, vicious negroes" to be justices of the peace. The first of many charges of "taxation without representation" appeared in this petition. The committee also opposed the provision for free public schooling, for it might integrate schools. The greatest outrage was black suffrage, by which "intelligence, virtue and patriotism are to give way . . . to ignorance, stupidity and vice. The superior race is to be made subservient to the inferior." Whites warned Congress that "the white people of our State will never quietly submit to negro rule. We may have to pass under the yoke you have authorized, but . . . we will keep up this contest until we have regained the heritage of political control handed down to us by our honored ancestry."[7]

State whites had rejected out-of-hand the constitution and the government it would establish. For Carolinians, although the new constitution "may have the authority of law . . . it has not and never can have the moral sanction of right, truth, or justice. . . ."[8] This attitude is significant, for as Eqbal Ahmad—who has spent most of his life studying revolutionary war and guerrilla movements—concludes, the greatest factor involved in an insurgency's success is "the absence or loss of governmental legitimacy."[9] There is no greater liability to a government than the population's refusal to accept it as legitimate. For South Carolina whites, a Republican state government would never have legitimacy; it might have power, but not authority. The problem, as seen by Francis Simkins and Robert Woody, was that the federal government "succumbed to the temptation of trying to legislate into the political complex of the state innovations which were repellent to its traditions. They created a situation which made revolution against their decrees inevitable." It was "unthinkable," they surmised, that white Carolinians "would consent to be ruled by alien whites and native blacks."[10]

That rule came closer as the constitutional convention evolved into the Republican state convention. Although contemporaries and even some historians criticize the "Black and Tan" convention as "Negro rule," whites, not blacks or mulattoes, constituted the majority of the nominees for state positions. The overwhelming choice for governor was Ohioan Robert K. Scott, currently the assistant commissioner for the Freedmen's Bureau in South Carolina. The candidate for lieutenant governor was a native white and former slaveholder, Lemuel Boozer. The only black among those holding top-level positions was Francis Cardozo, the choice for secretary of state.[11]

The Democratic state convention met at the opening of April, and at first appeared willing to compromise. Some moderates, hoping that by meeting Republicans halfway they could stave off black rule, offered to accept *qualified* Negro suffrage in a new, amended constitution. However, William Dunlop Porter, whom the convention nominated for governor, refused to accept the nomination unless the convention shunned such groveling and repudiated the constitutional convention. The outspoken A. P. Aldrich agreed, arguing "we must go into this fight with the party banner that this is 'A White Man's Government.'" Moderates capitulated, and the convention issued a statement formally protesting the validity of the "Black and Tan" convention and the constitution it produced.[12]

Former Confederates stood aghast as the elections of April 13, 14, and 15 ushered in a government controlled by native blacks, alien whites, and traitorous scalawags. The new governor was Republican Robert K. Scott, a native of Ohio who was inaugurated on July 9, three days after James L. Orr left office. Scott would govern beside a legislature unprecedented in Carolina history—and unforeseen in the worst conservative nightmare. Nearly the entire Republican ticket was elected, and black and white Republicans filled local and state offices, as well as the state legislature. Republicans controlled both houses of the South Carolina legislature, but a majority of senators were white. The majority in the House of Representatives was black, giving blacks a majority in the General Assembly overall.[13] The election also resulted in a victory for the new constitution, which Congress quickly accepted. Governor Scott called the new General Assembly into special session in July, it quickly ratified the Thirteenth Amendment, and South Carolina reentered the federal Union.[14]

Upon South Carolina's readmission, the War Department turned over to the new rulers all of the state's administrative and judicial functions. In June, Congress eliminated the Second and Third Military Districts, established under the Reconstruction Acts, and created the "Department of the South" as an umbrella unit under General George Gordon Meade. The army, no longer involved in civil affairs, retained only three posts in the state: Columbia, Charleston, and Aiken. Intervention, even if necessary, might not be forthcoming, since General Meade and the new secretary of war, John Schofield, both opposed military involvement in civil affairs.[15]

The presence of the Freedmen's Bureau diminished accordingly. On July 25, Congress declared that with the exception of the educational and pension departments, the bureau would cease to exist on December 31, 1868.[16] By autumn of that year, a total of only ten officers—including the assistant commissioner—were present in South Carolina.[17] With the army withdrawing from civil affairs, one officer predicted that "the South, as a whole, will not soon see more quiet and more satisfactory control . . . for some time to come, than in the twelve-month just past."[18]

II

There was an irony to the Republican victory. While it displaced the former ruling elite and filled blacks with hope, it also cleared away an obstacle to native white control: the U.S. Army. For the first time since

Appomattox, civil authorities stood clear of military interference. In other words, the state Republican party had to face conservative opposition alone.

Carolina whites understood this, and they made no effort to disguise their opposition to the new government. D. T. Wells, a lieutenant in the Eighth U.S. Infantry, claimed that the general attitude in Laurens County was that whites need not submit to any laws passed by the "negro government."[19] Confederate cavalry hero Martin Witherspoon Gary stated that the "attempt to place the negro over the white man, was not only a violation of the supreme law of the land, but at war with the noblest instincts of our races. . . ." He proclaimed that "usurpations and the abuses of power" had driven secession, and that the same fight still raged, as the Reconstruction Acts, the Freedmen's Bureau, and the enfranchisement of blacks were all unconstitutional.[20] The editor of the *Edgefield Advertiser* agreed, asserting that "the continued denial of our God-given privileges and rights justify the resort to extraordinary means for their recovery and perpetuation! To our apprehension, that moment is approaching in the history of our down-trodden people. . . ."[21]

For conservatives, that moment was the upcoming presidential election of 1868. The state was in the hands of blacks and Radical whites, with Congress as the instigator of this atrocity. But a Democratic president might rein in the national legislature, bolster the judiciary, and keep the military out of Southern affairs. The Democratic ticket of Horatio Seymour and Francis P. Blair, Jr., had already sent signals that encouraged conservative hopes. Vice presidential nominee Blair remarked in June that "there is but one way to restore the Government and the Constitution, and that is for the President-elect to declare these acts null and void . . . disperse the carpet-bag State governments, and allow the white people to reorganize their own governments and elect Senators and Representatives."[22] When Governor Robert Scott learned of the pronouncement, he wrote to General Meade that Blair had "declared war; he has plainly told us that the Reconstruction of Congress is revolutionary and must be set aside. The leading men in the Rebellion understood him to mean it must be done by force if need be and they are prepared to act."[23]

Many historians have seen this election—and 1868 in general—as a watershed in Reconstruction, when violence and political designs formally dovetailed. Both Joel Williamson and George Rable have noted that violence was present before 1868, but was random and without political content. This analysis is only partly accurate. Although not aimed directly at regaining political control, pre-1868 violence had the same larger goal in view: white domination of the political, economic, and social life of the state. After 1868, violence was directed at regaining political control so as to allow the rebuilding of South Carolina as white Carolinians saw fit. As with the war itself, scholars have drawn distinctions between periods of the Reconstruction that were in fact linked by aims; only the means differed.[24]

For whites the campaign was part of the continuing struggle over the future of their state and their race. Trying to mobilize disheartened voters, Martin W. Gary called on whites to support the belief that "this shall remain purely a White Man's Government and that the negro shall not become a part of the body politic, or from any qualification either as to education or property, be allowed to vote in this country."[25] Armistead Burt sounded the same note of racist defiance at the state Democratic convention held in Columbia in August. Carolinians, he announced, were ready to fight for control of their state and their country, "which was discovered by the white man, settled by the white man, made illustrious by the white man, and must continue to be the white man's Country."[26] Ellison S. Keitt asked "will they impose, at the point of a bayonet, negro governments upon the Southern States ... will they Africanize the South?" "These are the questions you will answer," he stated, "in November next when you cast your ballots in the Presidential election."[27] Joseph Abney, speaking before a Democratic club in Edgefield, called on fellow whites to "gather in all the votes we can from the ranks of the adversary, and by all the legitimate means in our power. And in such a strife, we need not be dainty as to the means employed; we must fight the Devil with fire." Abney reminded his listeners of "our duty to God and our country ... to wage incessant, restless, and eternal war."[28]

Economic coercion was one weapon to which whites turned readily. The failure to revolutionize the Southern economy after Appomattox left whites in control of the land, and kept the economy rooted in the plantation system. White employers and black laborers soon learned that economic inequality translated into political pressure. In his last report as assistant commissioner for the Freedmen's Bureau, Robert K. Scott warned his superior O. O. Howard that blacks would vote the Democratic ticket because of their need to work and have a place to live. According to his report, black laborers are "freely and publicly told that unless they voted the Democratic Ticket, they should never get any more work."[29]

If anything, Scott underestimated conservative determination and organization. Immediately after the Democratic failure in the April elections, a Democratic club in Edgefield County passed a resolution requiring members to keep a list of their employees and their political affiliations. Members voted "not employ any negro or white man, or any member of their families, who fails to bring with him a written certificate from his former employer that he is a Democrat and has voted with the Democrats at some election."[30] Benjamin F. Perry advised his friends to tell their laborers to "go to their friends, the carpet-baggers and scalawags, for their favors and employment." In another letter, Perry simply wrote that "if they will not vote with us we should not employ them."[31] The press echoed these sentiments. One newspaper urged planters to remind each worker that he cannot "make war upon the capital from which he derives his support . . . he is quarreling with his meat and his bread."[32] When planter George Ghislen discovered that his hands had attended Radical meetings, he called them together and told them that if they voted "in favor of radicalism . . . they can no longer work for me." Other locals would refuse them work as well, and plans had been made to go to Augusta, Georgia, to get new workers.[33] Clubs existed in Edgefield, Charleston, and Orangeburg Counties, all conspiring to pressure whites into conformity, and pressure blacks into obedience.[34]

Whites also turned to their most traditional instrument of control, physical force. The new governor, Robert K. Scott, informed General Edward R. S. Canby in September that the so-called "innocent lambs of the Democratic Plank are shooting Negroes almost daily" because "the old leaders are determined to control this country again."[35] Scott's replacement in the Freedmen's Bureau, John R. Edie, learned that assassination attempts had been made upon congressional candidates, and that some men had been killed just for admitting they were Republicans. Edie told Commissioner Howard that the "destruction of human life is appalling."[36]

The few remaining bureau officers, Edie stressed in his report to the commissioner, agreed. Lieutenant M. DeKnight in Abbeville believed that "unless the colored man either votes the Democratic Ticket or stays away from the Polls altogether, he will be shot down." Lieutenant William Stone in Edgefield had confessed that it was impossible "to protect the lives and property of those who do not agree politically with the large majority of white citizens." Officers reported that armed groups of whites had visited workers in the fields and forced them to sign papers pledging support for the Democratic party, "with the direct threat that unless they do so, or if they attempt to vote the Republican ticket, they shall assuredly be killed."[37] A petition from blacks claimed the "Rebel element" was "in a state bordering on insurrection."[38] A similar account for the counties of Clarendon, Kershaw, and Lancaster came from B. F. Whittemore, sent by the governor to investigate the region. Whittemore found Republicans "intimidated by threats of the most violent and dangerous character," and confirmed that "armed bands of men" patrolled the public roads.[39]

As Whittemore noted in his report, opposition forces were very well supplied. An organized effort was under way by summer to supply guns to conservatives who needed them. For instance, James Pagan sent a letter to A. B. Springs alerting him that a shipment of guns was on its way. Pagan had tested one of the rifles and proclaimed that "in a bush fight or in the open field—no American citizens of African decent [sic] could stand up against such arms."[40] Democratic clubs raised funds locally—each district was assessed a certain sum—and then sent buyers north to procure weapons. For example, a few days before Pagan shipped the guns to Springs, Iredell Jones of Rock Hill had informed Springs that he was coming by with fifty dollars that the State Central Club had allotted for his district.[41]

The degree of organization in the procurement of arms was surpassed only by the degree of ruthlessness in the use of them. Testifying before a congressional investigating committee months later, William Tolbert bluntly stated the aims of his Democratic club: "To find out where the negroes were holding Union Leagues . . . kill the leaders; fire into them and kill the leaders if [we] could." He was also ordered to find the Republicans who kept the ballots before the election and to take the ballots from them; if they resisted, "shoot them and take them by force." Orders regarding Republican speakers were similarly straightforward: "Shoot them, kill them, stop it."[42]

This they did frequently and effectively. General Canby recorded the first "assassination," as he called it, on June 4, when state senator Solomon Washington Dill was shot dead in his own home.[43] A few weeks later James Martin, a legislator from Abbeville, was killed outside of the town of Abbeville. In early October, Johnson Stuart, a prominent Republican from Newberry, was shot to death riding home from a political meeting. A few weeks later his friend Lee Nance, president of the local Union League, was found murdered in his front yard.[44] About the same time, B. F. Randolph, a black carpetbagger and member of the General Assembly, was assassinated as he stepped off a train at Hodges Depot.[45] There were rumors of plots to kill the governor, Attorney General Daniel Chamberlain, and prominent Republicans Thomas Jefferson Mackey and Christopher C. Bowen.[46] It is not surprising that many Republicans feared the worst when the Freedmen's Bureau's superintendent of education, Pennsylvania Quaker Reuben Tomlinson, disappeared during the campaign; he was, in fact, deliberately keeping a low profile because of threats against his life.[47] In the midst of this wave of terrorism, Governor Scott received a chilling telegram signed by William Lawton, "A Republican Democrat." The message contained the usual banter about saving the state from tyranny and battling for rights. Its closing, however, was brief and direct: "By the 'Law of Success' the murder of your enemy is the righteous vindication of your 'Right to Rule.'"[48]

III

The most feared band of assassins was the Ku Klux Klan, an organization which utilized all weapons at the whites' disposal with such cold-blooded determination that the organization became the nemesis of Republicans, a creature of mythical proportions for conservatives. The Ku Klux Klan had originated in Tennessee in 1866, but it was not until 1868 that cells of the association first appeared in the Palmetto State.[49] The creation of a South Carolina Klan was only a matter of time, for it incorporated two longstanding Carolina traditions. The first was the localized, community-oriented, extralegal response to fears and crimes which were seen as a threat to Carolina society. The second was the establishment of organizations that were designed to carry out the tasks desired by the fearful citizens—the slave patrols of the antebellum period being the most obvious example. In 1868 these elements combined to create an organization that could operate in a systematic way to confront Republican party in the state.

The Ku Klux Klan has long been viewed in the context of Southern traditions of extralegal activity. Edward Ayers admits that the Klan "reflected a tradition of extralegal retribution," and Bertram Wyatt-Brown has neatly linked classic patterns of community-based punishment to the activities of the hooded order. "The community," Wyatt-Brown argues, "was the final arbiter of morals and justice" and outbreaks of vigilante action were "the ultimate expressions of community will."[50] In her dissertation on the Klan, Lou Falkner Williams points out that antebellum South Carolina had no prison and few jails, so often "social control was largely a community matter among whites." In addition, since regular police forces were rare outside major cities, law enforcement rested in the hands of volunteers and individual citizens.[51]

Not all violence in antebellum South Carolina was spontaneous, in other words, and the creation of the slave patrols was a measured step toward an organized vigilante arrangement. This situation too carried directly into Reconstruction, first with the roving bands that followed the surrender, and later with the Ku Klux Klan. Like the patrols, the Klan was a mounted, armed symbol of white authority that held the unquestioned power of life or death in racial matters. Like its predecessor, the Klan lacked statewide organization, being based instead on local and regional membership and jurisdiction. As South Carolinian Belton O'Neal Townsend put it, "the Ku Klux Klan with its night visits and whippings and murders was the legitimate offspring of the patrol." To Townsend, neither the deeds nor the system itself was "unnatural." As a matter of fact, he had rather come to expect them.[52]

There is less of a consensus on the aims of the organization. Historians Bertram Wyatt-Brown, Edward Ayers, Lou Williams, and Charles Flynn see many purposes to Klan activity, centering in the enforcement of public morals, ethics, and "acceptable" behaviors. Charles Flynn's study of the Georgia Klan ably dismantles J. C. A. Stagg's "labor-control thesis," but Flynn also criticizes what he calls the "liberal school" for its focus on racism. Flynn sees Klanism as the result of class conflict and "caste" expectations, and places it firmly within the school of ethical and moral control. The latest proponent of this explanation of the Klan's aims is Lou Faulkner Williams, who agrees that the organization sought to reassert community values and enforce a specific code of ethics and honor. Only Edward Ayers admits that "racial control" was central to the function of the Klan, but he also refuses to accept a solidly political focus.[53]

These historians, however, appear to be working backward toward the answer. To be sure, the Klan did harass thieves, adulterers, drunks, rapists, arsonists, and other individuals who posed a threat to public order. However, research beginning with the Klan and moving outward produces a different conclusion. A massive amount of documentary material exists on the Klan from 1868 to 1871, including letters, military reports, newspaper accounts, journals, and the voluminous findings of a congressional investigation. Cases do exist of hooded horsemen abusing suspected thieves and chastising adulterers, but instances of "moral enforcement" are negligible when compared to the number of political attacks. Historians do see the bigger picture: the aim of the Klan was the restoration of a society founded on traditional Southern values. But Carolinians knew the only way to that goal was through political power, and the Klan was a weapon designed to strike directly at the Republican political machine.[54]

The timing of the organization's appearance in the state illustrates its political nature. Some historians have erred in dating the Klan's appearance, and so have misinterpreted its purpose. David Duncan Wallace claimed the creation of the state's black militia brought on the Klan as a defensive force.[55] The pro-Southern Henry Thompson agreed, claiming that "the arrogance of the negro militia . . . became so great that the people . . . banded themselves together for self-protection in the famous organization known as the Ku Klux Klan."[56] More recently, Ida Waller Pope has stated that the Klan followed the formation of the militia.[57] This is erroneous, for the Klan was operating in South Carolina by the late spring of 1868. No militia of any kind existed in the state until the spring of 1870; all such forces had been disbanded by the Reconstruction Acts of March 1867. Another favorite explanation, one used at the time by Democrats in Congress, was that the Klan arose to counter Republican corruption and fraud.⁵⁸ As many Republican congressmen undoubtedly pointed out, it is difficult to find the connection between corruption in Columbia and the whipping of a black family one hundred miles away in Spartanburg. Certainly South Carolina had more than its share of mismanagement during Reconstruction, but these problems had not yet arisen. In 1868 the government had barely begun operation, and fiscal (and moral) problems were no more pervasive than would be expected in a government struggling to get on its feet.⁵⁹

The Klan appeared in the spring of 1868 immediately after the failure of the whites to defeat the new state constitution. The success of the state Republican party—based on an efficient network of Union Leagues and an enthusiastic black population—forced whites to seek an organized, coherent response. Historians studying the Union Leagues have found them a particular object of Klan attention. Michael Fitzgerald believes that the Klan deliberately targeted the roots of black political activity, the Leagues.⁶⁰ Even Lester and Wilson's contemporary work on the Klan mentioned the importance of counteracting League influence.⁶¹ Iredell Jones, one of founders of the Chester Conservative Clan, avowed that he and his fellows would "do all in our power to counteract the evil influences exerted by a secret radical organization known as the *Union* League," proposing that they keep track of "all meetings or proposed meetings of negroes and Radicals" in the area so that they could conduct visits to such gatherings if need be.⁶²

Historians who do recognize the political nature of the Klan hint at, but do not fully enunciate, the existence of a conflict that had been under way between Carolina conservatives and Republican ideology for years. Allen Trelease, for instance, calls the organization the "terrorist arm of the Democratic party," while Eric Foner considers it "a military force serving the interests of the Democratic Party, the planter class, and all those who desired the restoration of white supremacy."⁶³ Even George Rable, who argues that much of the violence at the time was random, admits that the Klan had a singular purpose: the destruction of the Southern republican party.⁶⁴ Otto Olsen believes the Klan to be "a unique guerrilla movement dedicated to the destruction of an alien regime, and the restoration of white supremacy and home rule." Klan hostility represented a "continuation of the war against the North" through the use of "guerrilla-like tactics."⁶⁵ Historians, however, must not perceive Klanism in a vacuum; it evolved out of the white resistance and desires of the previous three years, a new means to an old end.

That the Klan was a political organization with political goals was clear to citizens of South Carolina at the time. William Tolbert, who took part in the assassination of Randolph, told investigators that the Klan "was a political organization of the Democratic Party." Its goals, he stated, were "to regulate the republican party, break it up if they could, and strengthen the democratic party." In other words "kill out the leaders of the republican party and drive them out of the state."[66] David T. Corbin, a Dartmouth attorney who served as the U.S. district attorney for South Carolina, had in his possession a Klan notice which spelled out its aims. "We are on the side of justice, and constitutional liberty, as bequeathed to us in its purity by our forefathers," the memorandum read, "and we oppose and reject the principles of the Radical party." Corbin emphasized that the organization "is on the side of the Constitution *as it was,* not as it *now is.*"[67]

The Klan's drive to destroy the Republican party and return South Carolina to the way "it was" began immediately after the April elections. Just days after the election, Richard Clark Springs wrote to his nephew that "the colored and white Radicals are very much excited by the Secret Society called *Ku Klux Klan* which has recently formed here at Spartanburg Village."[68] By late April, reports of the Ku Klux Klan appeared in the *Yorkville Enquirer,* the *Charleston Daily News,* and the *Edgefield Advertiser.*[69] Governor-elect Robert Scott informed Commissioner Howard of the organization and noted uneasily that most newspapers spoke "approvingly" of the combination.[70]

By the summer of 1868, state Republicans and military officials had became convinced that the Klan was a serious threat to law, order, and the Republican party. Scott's monthly report for June carried numerous accounts of Klan visitations, warnings, and whippings. Freedmen's Bureau agent DeKnight reported from Abbeville that the Klan had taken to placing coffins in the yards and on the porches of Republicans (according to DeKnight, the impact of this was "considerable").[71] As the state's chief executive, Scott became the focus for hundreds of complaints, calls for help, and petitions for redress. Many sounded like that of Mrs. John Cochran, who was writing because her husband was "engaged in guarding our house, as we expect an attack to night from the Ku Klux Klan." "I never lie to sleep with that sense of safety which I could feel," Mrs. Cochran stated, "if my husband's principles were *democratic!*"[72]

As the November election drew closer, both Klan activity and Republican fears intensified. By the end of October, A. S. Wallace, a candidate for Congress, predicted that in Abbeville the "reign of terror" would prevent "a fair election," because Klan riders announced they "would patrol that whole Co the night before the election."[73] One native white Republican wrote that the "Rebel KKK's" were out in full force in Walhalla, and "our lives are in danger among them they are all armed." The author had rejected advice given him by a neighbor—to become a Democrat—and announced he would "rather die and fill a Republican grave than go with the Enemies of my Mother Government."[74]

As Klan operations increased in scope and intensity, so too did reports of black militancy. The cause-and-effect relationship was actually the reverse of that posited by some historians: the Ku Klux Klan was the catalyst for black militancy in the state. In June hundreds of blacks in Darlington, fearing a Klan attack, had gathered guns and transformed their Union League into a paramilitary unit. They seized control of an entire town and threatened to burn it if whites attacked (it appears they did not).[75] Henry Ravenel jotted down up-country rumors that armed black units were meeting and drilling regularly. "As the term [sic] of the Presidential election draws nearer," Ravenel fretted, "apprehensions are felt of a collision between parties."[76] William Porcher DuBose also recorded that blacks had grown "very dangerous." The women of his house were so frightened that they demanded pistols to defend themselves. (Riding home one day, DuBose saw one young lady, Miss Peronneau, on the back porch screaming at the children to "get away!" Dubose, rushing to rescue her from some unseen threat, arrived to find that she had cocked her pistol and did not know how to release the hammer safely. He gave her a dinner bell instead.)[77]

Although some Republicans argued that arming blacks would deter white violence, Governor Scott initially opposed the idea, believing such a move would only provoke conservatives. In July, Scott received the conservative view of the situation in Union County. A letter stated that "we are looking for it to commence . . . all that wonst to see the Negroes and Rebels fight can com up here they say that war has to start."[78] In a similar way, conservative M. L. Bonham warned Governor Scott of "sowing for the negro the 'wind,' of which he will reap the whirlwind." Beware, Bonham told Scott, for "when a war of races shall be inaugurated, it requires no prophet to predict the result."[79] Scott knew this, and had no illusions about the ability of blacks to challenge seasoned whites. "It would have been folly," he said, "to have placed inexperienced and unarmed men against organized and disciplined ex-Confederate soldiers. . . ."[80]

Nonetheless, advisors insisted that some action was necessary to demonstrate that the state government would protect its citizens. Cabinet members suggested recruiting and equipping more men for the state constabulary (since a state militia was still prohibited), but not until September did the governor approve the purchase of Springfield and Enfield rifles from Meigs Patent Arms of Lowell, Massachusetts. Even so, Scott had waited so long that the company had no guns on hand, and it would take time to produce more.[81] Republican T. J. Mackey advocated the creation of special police units under the supervision of the state's chief constable,

New Yorker John B. Hubbard. Hubbard wanted to recruit toughs from up North, and organize two-hundred-man companies to sweep without warning across lawless counties.[82] S. L. Hoge, a candidate for Congress, pleaded with Scott to declare martial law. Having spoken with Secretary of War John Schofield, Hoge felt confident that General Meade of the Department of the South would use his troops if state forces were opposed.[83] Thomas Tullock believed "the only remedy now left for the lawlessness and violence" was a declaration of martial law. "This measure," Tullock believed, "cannot fail to have a beneficial effect upon rebel assassins."[84]

Instead Governor Scott sought to stem the tide of violence by gambling on his political skill with a clever bluff. A month before the presidential election, just after the assassination of B. F. Randolph, Scott met with Colonel L. D. Childs, a close friend of Wade Hampton and a member of the Democratic state central committee. Scott related details of Republican forces, plans, and arms, and informed Colonel Childs that he was doing everything possible to keep blacks from starting a race war. Unless Hampton spoke openly against violence, Scott assured Childs that he would allow retaliation against "those who inaugurated a system of political campaigning which could be compared to nothing but the bloody Revolution of Robespierre in France." At another meeting Scott repeated his warning to Hampton directly. Violence would beget violence, he assured them, but the bloodshed would not gain Democrats control of the state. Recent Democratic defeats in Northern elections already indicated that Ulysses S. Grant would probably win the presidency, and South Carolina could not influence the outcome.[85]

Governor Scott's ruse may have soothed tensions. Hampton, possibly fearing that a substantial outbreak would bring federal intervention—regardless of the instigators—complied with Scott's request. On October 23, Hampton's address appeared in newspapers across South Carolina. Hampton invoked the readers' "earnest efforts in the cause of peace and the preservation of order. . . ." The former general declared that violence and lawlessness were counterproductive, for they brought criticism down upon the Democratic party and the state.[86] Almost immediately the governor heard from J. M. Morris, who said, "I do not deem all danger past. But I do feel that the popular mind is in a better state than it has been for months."[87] Violence did decline sharply in late October, possibly due to the proclamation, or to the acceptance of a coming Republican victory. Even the Klan began curtailing its activity, one of its orders warning members to be "moderate" and not to "redress grievances of a general character or act in any manner calculated to produce a breach of the peace without orders. . . ."[88] The impetus for the decline in violence may be difficult to determine, but the operative force is not: white Carolinians controlled the tempo, and it was their decision to ease up. They were not suppressed, cowed, or intimidated, but merely took a step back, in order to take two steps forward in the future. This terrorist tactic—going underground when the risk becomes too great—was to come into play several more times before Reconstruction was over.

IV

The truce that existed in South Carolina was a fragile one, and it grew more brittle as the election approached. Speakers like former Confederate colonel Alexander C. Haskell seemed intent on shattering the relative calm, reminding voters that "this is the Plataea . . . it is the same great cause of life and liberty," a chance to "prove that . . . we *will not* permit the white race to be degraded and trampled underfoot by the negro. . . ." A "combination" had taken control of the federal government and the state governments, and "it has to be *made* to die." The weapon was the ballot, which would bring "the purification of the Government, and the overthrow of the Reconstruction Acts of Congress as unconstitutional, null and void, and the restitution of the Constitution as it was."[89]

Republicans prepared as best they could, but their options were few. Governor Scott finally found some members of his party who were daring enough to serve as special deputies, and General Meade spread federal troops among the counties as a sign of support. But by law the soldiers could not be present at an election poll, and had to be posted some distance away. In addition, they could not interfere in cases of fraud, intimidation or mismanagement; they could act only if formally called on by a federal marshal who had met resistance in his duties.

Not surprisingly, measures intended to insure a fair vote in South Carolina were far from adequate. Testimony taken by a congressional committee confirmed that Klan visits began again just prior to the election on November 3. John Watson, an election commissioner for York County, said that a great many blacks refused to leave their homes on election day because of threats from Klansmen the night before. Harry McDaniel stayed home after receiving a visit and a pistol ball in the shoulder from Klansmen. The Klan had also threatened to enforce the discharge of any workers who voted Republican, McDaniel claimed. In his opinion, the election in his county was "carried by violence and fraud." The manager of the election at Laurens Court House, G. E. Tuxbury, made similar charges, stating that Democratic clubs had agreed not to hire anyone who voted Republican. In Union County, conservatives took another approach.

Just prior to the election a band of whites waylaid Judd Porter, keeper of the Republican tickets, and stole all the Republican ballots. In the words of James Henderson, this was part of a "systematic plan on the part of the democratic party to keep the colored voters from the polls."[90]

Democrats were equally well prepared to deal with those Republicans who managed to vote. At one poll in York County, for instance, a group of whites who held no official capacity sat at a desk writing down the names of everyone who voted Republican! In Union County, Richard Kinyon testified that Democratic managers claimed they "could not find names on the list" of registered voters, and therefore refused to allow many to vote. Samuel Nuckles, a Baptist minister in the same county, said that at one poll Democrats deposited their tickets into containers on a window ledge, while Republicans handed their ballots to a man inside the window. At Rock Hill, whites turned blacks away for "not being registered," while blind and lame Democrats were carried to the polls; in one instance Democrats carried the ballot box to the house of an old man so he could vote. One witness in Oconee County claimed that the entire student body of Newberry College, a Lutheran institution then located in Walhalla, voted—even though many were underage, and some were residents of other states![91]

The meager Republican forces were powerless to stop the onslaught. Constable W. P. Harris of Newberry, for example, had appointed thirteen deputies for the election, but not one appeared. "They were afraid to serve," he testified, "afraid of violence from the Democrats." Following the election, the Board of State Canvassers accused the Democratic party of "a wholesale system of proscription, terrorism, and assassination" designed to influence the election. The entire campaign had been "accompanied by such grave and widespread disorder and outrages" that it "prevented anything like a free expression of political opinion. . . ."[92]

In spite of all this, election results again demonstrated that solid organization, raw courage, and sheer numbers could overcome intimidation and fraud. The Republican majority in the state overcame conservative opposition, and South Carolina went for Grant by a margin of 62,916 to 45,237. A closer look, however, indicates that the Democratic strategy was not a complete failure. In the up-country counties, where violence and Klan activity were more intense, the vote was 14,186 for Seymour, and only 10,379 for Grant, despite a slight black voting majority in the region. In Abbeville, although 2,400 blacks were registered, only 800 voted. Laurens County—with a black enrollment of almost 2,500—had only 1,174 blacks turn out. And in Anderson, between 700 and 800 of a potential 1,400 blacks voted. The previous April, Republicans had swept the congressional elections. In November the Democrats won two seats, as J. P. Reed defeated S. L. Hoge in the Third District and William Simpson beat A. S. Wallace in the Fourth.[93]

Nevertheless, the South Carolina Republican party had reason to be confident. It had weathered its first major storm, and now a Republican prepared to assume the presidency. Regardless of white hostility, the future looked bright, for in the words of William Gillette, "if Reconstruction ever had a chance, it was during Grant's administration, when the Republicans controlled—in fact, not just in form—both the presidency and Congress for the first time during the postwar period."[94] This sent shudders through conservatives like W. L. Trenholm, who sensed "a peril upon us that few realise [sic] & yet it is imminent, the danger of passing forever under the local domination of strangers . . . [and] a foreign & barbarous race. . . ."[95]

The campaign of 1868 was only one battle, and although South Carolina's conservatives had lost, the struggle went on. R. C. Poole of Spartanburg knew this, and warned Governor Scott that a Grant victory would not bring peace to the state. Poole feared that "if Grant was elected . . . Revolution would be inevitable, for I am confident that negro Supremacy never will be submitted to by the former Slave States. . . ."[96] Poole, Scott, and Grant would soon discover that his prediction was disturbingly accurate.

Notes

1. Herbert Shapiro, *White Violence and Black Response: From Reconstruction to Montgomery* (Amherst: University of Massachusetts Press, 1988), 8.

2. Lawanda Cox and John H. Cox, eds., *Reconstruction, the Negro, and the New South* (Columbia: University of South Carolina Press, 1973), 217; Francis Butler Simkins and Robert Hilliard Woody, *South Carolina during Reconstruction* (Chapel Hill: University of North Carolina Press, 1932), 104; Richard Current, *Those Terrible Carpetbaggers* (New York: Oxford University Press, 1988), 91. Among other changes, the new constitution abolished the use of "district" as an administrative unit. Beginning with the convening of the General Assembly in November, the term "county" was used. This book changes usage accordingly.

3. Dr. John H. Davis to John C. Davison, in Folder 14, Conway, Black, and Davis Family Papers, South Caroliniana Library, University of South Carolina, Columbia, S.C. (hereafter SCL).

4. *Edgefield Advertiser,* May 30, 1868; emphasis in original.

5. *Fairfield Herald,* April 29, 1868.

6. Henry D. Green, in *Edgefield Advertiser,* June 24, 1868; emphasis in original.

7. Cox and Cox, eds., *Reconstruction,* 229–35. The grand old historian of South Carolina, David Duncan Wallace, shared the views of the committee. The

constitution of 1868 provided that "one of the most ignorant and undeveloped of races was to be placed by mere legislative fiat in absolute power over a large portion of a race notable for centuries for the highest success in self-government. . . ." See Wallace, *South Carolina: A Short History, 1520–1948* (Columbia: University of South Carolina Press, 1951), 569.

8. *Sumter News,* June 27, 1868.

9. Eqbal Ahmad, "Revolutionary Warfare and Counterinsurgency," in *Guerrilla Strategies: An Historical Anthology from the Long March to Afghanistan,* ed. Gerard Chaliand (Berkeley: University of California Press, 1982), 262.

10. Simkins and Woody, *South Carolina during Reconstruction,* 94, 112.

11. Henry T. Thompson, *Ousting the Carpetbagger from South Carolina* (Columbia, S.C.: R. L. Bryan, 1926; New York: Negro Universities Press, 1969), 28; *Speech of the Honorable J. J. Wright at Liberty Hall, Charleston S.C., May 31, 1872,* in *Pamphlets: Reconstruction in South Carolina, Democratic and Republican, 1869–1880* (n.p., n.d.), 11, South Caroliniana Library, Book Division, University of South Carolina, Columbia, S.C. (hereafter SCL). Scott has been much maligned for using his office in the Freedmen's Bureau to promote himself in politics. Martin Abbott leans toward the view that he did use his military post to gain valuable contacts and advance his political ambitions. A large amount of correspondence, however, exists showing that it took several weeks—and scores of appeals—for him to decide to leave his post as army general and assistant commissioner and accept the nomination for governor. See Abbott, *The Freedmen's Bureau in South Carolina, 1865–1872* (Chapel Hill: University of North Carolina Press, 1967), 32–35; and Box 1, Folder 5, Robert K. Scott Papers, Ohio Historical Society, Columbus, Ohio (hereafter OHS).

12. Simkins and Woody, *South Carolina during Reconstruction,* 109–11; *Charleston Mercury,* May 25, 1868.

13. Edward King, *The Great South* (Hartford, Conn.: American Publishing, 1875; Arno Press, 1969), 454. Richard Current has in the Senate twenty whites and ten blacks, and in the House forty-six whites and seventy-eight blacks. His overall figures favor blacks sixty-six to eighty-eight (see Current, *Those Terrible Carpetbaggers,* 143). Others' numbers differ, but the percentages remain basically the same. Thomas Holt counted twenty-one whites and ten blacks in the Senate, and forty-seven whites and seventy-four blacks in the House. See Holt, *Black over White: Negro Political Leadership in South Carolina during Reconstruction* (Urbana: University of Illinois Press, 1977), 97. Michael Thompson's dissertation offers still other figures, with the Senate having twenty-two whites and thirteen blacks, and the House at forty-eight whites and eighty-five blacks. See Michael Edwin Thompson, "Blacks, Carpetbaggers, and Scalawags: A Study of the Membership of the South Carolina Legislature, 1868–1870" (Ph.D. diss., Washington State University, 1975), iv–vi. As David M. Potter has stated, "negro domination" was only a myth, for the closest state to such a situation was South Carolina, and the numbers were not all that dominating. All state positions were in the hands of whites (except that of secretary of state), and the vast voting power of the black constituency gave only a bare majority in the legislature. See Potter, *Division and the Stresses of Reunion: 1845–1876* (Glenview, Ill.: Scott, Foresman, 1973), 220.

James McPherson has made the same point: between 1868 and 1876, blacks held sixty-one percent of the House and forty-two percent of the Senate, and a total of only fifty-two percent of all state and federal elective offices, a number far below the numerical majority. See McPherson, *Ordeal by Fire: The Civil War and Reconstruction* (New York: Alfred A. Knopf, 1982), 557.

14. Simkins and Woody, *South Carolina during Reconstruction*, 109. Thompson has the ratification occur in late May and early June, with readmission on June 25 (*Ousting the Carpetbagger*, 31).

15. *Annual Report of the Secretary of War for 1868*, 40th Cong., 3d sess., 1868, H. Doc. 1 (Serial 1367), xv; James E. Sefton, *The United States Army and Reconstruction, 1865–1877* (Baton Rouge: Louisiana State University Press, 1967), 186–87. Troops in South Carolina were the Eighth Infantry at Columbia, six companies of the Sixth Infantry at Charleston, and two cavalry companies at Aiken. See *Army and Navy Journal*, August 29, 1868, 18; and John Robert Kirkland, "Federal Troops in the South Atlantic States during Reconstruction: 1865–1877" (Ph.D. diss., University of North Carolina at Chapel Hill, 1968), 233–39.

16. "Report of the Freedmen's Bureau," 1039, in Commissioner O. O. Howard, *Annual Report of the Secretary of War for 1868*.

17. *Army and Navy Journal*, December 5, 1868, 242–43.

18. *Army and Navy Journal*, July 11, 1868, 741.

19. Testimony of Lieutenant D. T. Wells, in *Additional Papers in the Case of Wallace vs. Simpson*, 41st Cong., 1st sess., H. Doc. 17 (Serial 1402), 32, 48, 52.

20. Martin W. Gary, in *Edgefield Advertiser*, September 9, 1868. For a view similar to Gary's, see the address of the Honorable Ellison S. Keitt to the Young Men's Democratic Union Club of New York City, summer 1868, Ellison Summerfield Keitt Papers, South Caroliniana Library, University of South Carolina, Columbia, S.C. (hereafter SCL).

21. *Edgefield Advertiser*, August 26, 1868.

22. Francis P. Blair, Jr., quoted by John Shellabarger, in the latter's speech on enforcing the Fourteenth Amendment, delivered April 6, 1871; cited in *J. W. Keifer Collection of Speeches and Pamphlets* (n.p., n.d.), 6:5.

23. Robert K. Scott to General George Meade, September 18, 1868, in Box 2, Folder 1, Robert K. Scott Papers, Ohio Historical Society, Columbus, Ohio (hereafter OHS).

24. In his excellent work on Reconstruction in South Carolina, Joel Williamson states that Ku Klux Klan activity began in 1870. As the present chapter shows, however, the Klan was active from the spring of 1868. George Rable, one of the few historians to recognize the "revolutionary" nature of Southern violence, has nevertheless intimated that the pre-1868 violence was random. This supposition ignores the connections between such violence and the basic assumptions, traditions, and desires of conservatives. See Joel Williamson, *After Slavery: The Negro in South Carolina during Reconstruction, 1861–1877* (Chapel Hill: University of North Carolina Press, 1965), 257–58; and George C. Rable, *But There Was No Peace: The Role of Violence in the Politics of Reconstruction* (Athens: University of Georgia Press, 1984), 69.

25. Martin W. Gary, quoted in *Edgefield Advertiser*, September 9, 1868.

26. Armistead Burt, quoted in Williamson, *After Slavery,* 73.
27. Speech of Hon. Ellison Keitt to Young Men's Democratic Union Club of New York City, 1868 (no day), Ellison Summerfield Keitt Papers, SCL.
28. Joseph Abney, quoted in *Edgefield Advertiser,* June 10, 1868.
29. Robert K. Scott to Commissioner O. O. Howard, monthly report for June, dated July 20, 1868, in Record Group 105, Microcopy 752, Reel 60, National Archives, Washington, D.C. (hereafter RG, MC, Reel, NA).
30. Minutes for May 16 and June 6, 1868, Records of the Democratic Club of Liberty Hill, SCL. The club secretary, William Yeldell, asked for advice on using economic pressure from Francis W. Pickens, the chair of Democratic central committee of Edgefield County. See William Yeldell to Francis W. Pickens, June 13, 1868, Francis Warrington Pickens Papers, Special Collections Library Research Room, Perkins Library, Duke University, Durham, N.C. (hereafter SCLRR, Duke).
31. Benjamin F. Perry to E. L. Parker, August 10, 1868, and to S. D. Keith, August 22, 1868, in Scrapbook, Benjamin Franklin Perry Papers, Southern Historical Collection, University of North Carolina, Chapel Hill, N.C. (hereafter SHC/UNC).
32. *Edgefield Advertiser,* August 28, 1868.
33. George Ghilsen to T. J. McKie, October 27, 1868, in Thomas Jefferson McKie Papers, SCLRR, Duke.
34. See for instance the minutes for July 22, 1868, Records of the Democratic Club of Ward No. 4, Charleston, and the minutes for October 10, 1868, Records of the Democratic Club of Liberty Hill, SCL.
35. Governor Robert K. Scott to General Canby, September 8, 1868, in Box 2, Folder 1, Robert K. Scott Papers, OHS.
36. Assistant Commissioner and Brevet Colonel John Edie to Commissioner O. O. Howard, October 19, 1868, RG105, MC752, Reel 60, NA.
37. Edie to Howard, monthly report for September, dated October 20, 1868, and monthly report for October, dated November 21, 1868, RG105, MC752, Reel 60, NA.
38. John Woolly and John Devill to Robert Scott, October 27, 1868, in Box 3, Folder 14, Governor Robert K. Scott Papers, South Carolina Department of Archives and History, Columbia, S.C. (hereafter SCDAH).
39. B. F. Whittemore to Scott, October 28, 1868, in Box 3, Folder 17, Governor Robert K. Scott Papers, SCDAH.
40. James Pagan to A. B. Springs, October 21, 1868, in Box 11, Folder 181, Springs Family Papers, SHC/UNC. See also James Baxter to "Wife," September 25, 1868, James Baxter Papers, SCL.
41. Iredell Jones to A. B. Springs, October 11, 1868, in Box 11, Folder 181, Springs Family Papers, SHC/UNC.
42. William Tolbert, quoted in *Additional Papers in the Case of Hoge vs. Reed,* 41st Cong., 1st sess., H. Doc. 18 (Serial 1403), 31–33, 45–46.
43. General Canby, "Report of the Second Military District" in *Annual Report of the Secretary of War for 1868,* 339.
44. *Anderson Intelligencer,* October 21 and 28, 1868, and *Newberry Herald,* October 21, 1868; quoted in Williamson, *After Slavery,* 260, and Peggy Lamson,

The Glorious Failure: Black Congressman Robert Brown Elliott and the Reconstruction in South Carolina (New York: W. W. Norton, 1973), 82–84.

45. See U.S. Congress, Joint Select Committee to Inquire into the Conditions of Affairs in the Late Insurrectionary States, *Testimony Taken by the Joint Select Committee to Inquire into the Conditions of Affairs in the Late Insurrectionary States (The Ku-Klux Conspiracy)* (Washington, D.C.: Government Printing Office, 1872; New York: AMS Press, 1968), 4:1258–60 (cited hereafter as *KKK Report*); and Allen W. Trelease, *White Terror: The Ku Klux Klan Conspiracy and Southern Reconstruction* (New York: Harper and Row, 1971), 116. For fascinating details on the murder of Randolph—including an account given by the principal gunman—see *Additional Papers in the Case of Hoge vs. Reed,* 41st Cong., 1st sess., H. Doc. 18 (Serial 1403), 32–33; *Additional Papers in the Case of Wallace vs. Simpson,* 41st Cong., 2d sess., H. Doc. 17 (Serial 1402), 40, 47; and John Edie to O. O. Howard, monthly report for October, dated November 21, 1868, RG105, MC752, Reel 60, NA.

46. Richard Cain to Robert K. Scott, October 24, 1868, in Box 3, Folder 12, Governor Robert K. Scott, SCDAH.

47. Rupert Sargent Holland, ed., *Letters and Diary of Laura M. Towne, Written from the Sea Islands of South Carolina, 1862–1884* (Cambridge: Riverside Press, 1912; New York: Negro Universities Press, 1969), 199.

48. Telegram from William Lawton to Robert Scott, October 10, 1868, in Box 2, Folder 2, Robert K. Scott Papers, OHS.

49. Neither this chapter nor this book is meant to be a complete explanation or study of the Ku Klux Klan. I will discuss such elements and background as they are necessary for an understanding of the Klan's place in this project. The Klan itself is only one factor, one manifestation, in a long and complicated struggle. The best work on the Reconstruction Klan remains Trelease, *White Terror,* while the most interesting—from a historian's viewpoint—may be J. C. Lester and D. L. Wilson, *The Ku Klux Klan: Its Origin, Growth, and Disbandment* (n.p.: 1884; New York: Da Capo Press, 1973). This is the only known work on the original Klan that is written by a founding member.

50. Edward Ayers, *Vengeance and Justice: Crime and Punishment in the 19th-Century American South* (New York: Oxford University Press, 1984), 161–64; Bertram Wyatt-Brown, *Southern Honor: Ethics and Behavior in the Old South* (New York: Oxford University Press, 1982), 369, 370, 384, 401.

51. Lou Faulkner Williams, "The Great South Carolina Ku Klux Klan Trials, 1871–1872" (Ph.D. diss., University of Florida, 1991), 67. Also interesting are the findings of Jack Kenny Williams, who shows that while normal crimes were handled by regular authorities, the most threatening and dangerous affairs fell within the bounds of extralegal punishment. After 1840, ninety percent of all lynch-law cases were related to slavery or abolitionism. The reasons for this fact are many, including the public's hysteria, a pressing need for haste, the desire to create examples of the offenders, and, sometimes, a need for preemptory action not possible under ordinary civil law. See Williams, *Vogues in Villainy: Crime and Retribution in Ante-Bellum South Carolina* (Columbia: University of South Carolina Press, 1959), 120–21.

52. Belton O'Neal Townsend ("A South Carolinian"), "South Carolina Morals," *Atlantic Monthly* 39 (1877): 470–71. Lou Faulkner Williams also regards the Klan as an outgrowth of the slave patrol system; see "The Great South Carolina Ku Klux Klan Trials," 58.

53. Wyatt-Brown, *Southern Honor,* 435–61; J. C. A. Stagg, "The Problem of Klan Violence: The South Carolina Up-Country, 1868–1871," in *Journal of American Studies* 8 (December 1974): 303–18; Charles L. Flynn, Jr., "The Ancient Pedigree of Violent Repression: Georgia's Klan as a Folk Movement," in *The Southern Enigma: Essays on Race, Class and Folk Culture,* ed. Walter J. Fraser and Winfred B. Moore, Jr. (Westport, Conn.: Greenwood Press, 1983), 189–98; Lou Faulkner Williams, "The Great South Carolina Ku Klux Klan Trials," 69–78; Ayers, *Vengeance and Justice,* 161–64, 183.

54. One of the clearest indicators of the political nature of the Klan is the large number of assaults made upon *white* Republicans in the state.

55. Wallace, *South Carolina: A Short History,* 580, 582.

56. Thompson, *Ousting the Carpetbagger,* 53, 54.

57. Ida Waller Pope, "Violence as a Political Force in the Reconstruction South" (Ph.D. diss., University of Southwestern Louisiana, 1982), 136.

58. For the corruption argument, see Coulter, *The South during Reconstruction,* 165.

59. On the unlikely notion that government corruption brought about the Klan, see Everette Swinney, *Suppressing the Ku Klux Klan: The Enforcement of the Reconstruction Amendments 1870–1877* (New York: Garland, 1987), 51–52. See also William Porcher DuBose, "Reminiscences," SHC/UNC.

60. Michael W. Fitzgerald, *The Union League Movement in the Deep South: Politics and Agricultural Change during Reconstruction* (Baton Rouge: Louisiana State University Press, 1989), 200.

61. Lester and Wilson, *The Ku Klux Klan: Its Origins, Growth, and Disbandment,* 24.

62. Iredell Jones, "General Orders, Chester Conservative Clan," dated June 28, 1868, and October [n.d.] 1868, Iredell Jones Papers, SCL.

63. Trelease, *White Terror,* xlvi–xlvii; Eric Foner, *Reconstruction 1863–1877: America's Unfinished Revolution* (New York: Harper and Row, 1988), 425.

64. Rable, *But There Was No Peace,* 95.

65. Otto Olsen, ed., *Reconstruction and Redemption in the South* (Baton Rouge: Louisiana State University Press, 1980), 179–80.

66. William Tolbert, quoted in *Additional Papers in the Case of Hoge vs. Reed,* 41st Cong., 1st sess., H. Doc. 18 (Serial 1403), 34.

67. *Speech of the Honorable D. T. Corbin, U.S. District Attorney for So. Ca.,* in *Collected Pamphlets Including Preston, John Smith Address Delivered before the Survivor's Association of South Carolina* (L. F. Youmans, n.d.), 6, SCL; emphasis in original.

68. Richard Clark Springs to "Nephew" (A. B. Springs), May 5, 1868, in Box 11, Folder 177, Springs Family Papers, SHC/UNC; emphasis in original.

69. Lacy K. Ford, "One Southern Profile: Modernization and the Development of White Terror in York County, 1856–1876" (Master's thesis, University of

South Carolina, 1976), 94; *Speech of the Honorable David Thomas Corbin, U.S. District Attorney for So. Ca.,* in *Collected Pamphlets,* 6, SCL.

70. Robert K. Scott to O. O. Howard, April 22, 1868, RG105, MC752, Reel 55, NA.

71. DeKnight's report is contained in Scott's report to Howard for the month of June, dated July 20, 1868, RG105, MC752, Reel 60, NA.

72. Mrs. John Cochran to Robert K. Scott, October 27, 1868, in Box 3, Folder 15, Governor Robert K. Scott Papers, SCDAH; emphasis in original. A few days later John Cochran wrote to Governor Scott, assuring him of the truth of his wife's remarks and asking him, for safety's sake, to keep the letters secret. John Cochran to Scott, October 28, 1868, in Box 3, Folder 15, Governor Robert K. Scott Papers, SCDAH.

73. A. S. Wallace to Scott, October 29, 1868, in Box 3, Folder 18, Governor Robert K. Scott Papers, SCDAH.

74. W. O. B. Hiott to Scott, November 7, 1868, in Box 3, Folder 25, Governor Robert K. Scott Papers, SCDAH.

75. Scott to Howard, July 20, 1868, RG105, MC752, Reel 60, NA.

76. Arney Robinson Childs, ed., *The Private Journal of Henry William Ravenel, 1859–1887* (Columbia: University of South Carolina Press, 1947), 326, 328.

77. William Porcher DuBose, "Reminiscences," 144–45, SHC/UNC.

78. Robert Martin and B. W. Duncan to Robert Scott, July 25, 1868, in Box 1, Folder 17, Governor Robert K. Scott Papers, SCDAH.

79. M. L. Bonham to Scott, August 15, 1868; quoted in *Edgefield Advertiser,* September 9, 1868.

80. Robert K. Scott, quoted in *Additional Papers in the Case of Wallace vs. Simpson,* 41st Cong., 2d sess., H. Doc. 17 (Serial 1431), 46.

81. T. J. Mackey to Scott, September 16, 1868, in Box 2, Folder 22, and J. V. Meigs to Scott, October 20, 1868, in Box 2, Folder 3, Robert K. Scott Papers, OHS.

82. T. J. Mackey to Scott, September 16, 1868, in Box 2, Folder 22, Governor Robert K. Scott Papers, SCDAH.

83. S. L. Hoge to Scott, October 22, October 23, 1868, in Box 2, Folder 3, Robert K. Scott Papers, OHS.

84. Thomas Tullock to Scott, October [n.d.], 1868, in Box 2, Folder 3, Robert K. Scott Papers, OHS.

85. Scott to the Republican party executive committee, October 12, 1868, in Box 6, Folder 1, Robert K. Scott Papers, OHS.

86. *Columbia Phoenix,* quoted in Current, *Those Terrible Carpetbaggers,* 148.

87. J. M. Morris to Scott, October 24, 1868, in Box 2, Folder 3, Robert K. Scott Papers, OHS.

88. "Orders from Rock Hill," October 1868, Iredell Jones Papers, SCL.

89. Colonel Alexander C. Haskell, speech delivered at Edgefield Court House, September 2, 1868; quoted in *Edgefield Advertiser,* September 9, 1868; emphasis in original.

90. James Henderson, testimony in *Papers in the Case of S. L. Hoge vs. J. P. Reed,* 41st Cong., 1st sess., H. Rept. 6 (Serial 1403), 4–5; see also *Additional Papers in the Case of Wallace vs. Simpson,* 41st Cong., 1st sess., H. Doc. 17 (Serial 1402), 18–20, 47.

91. *Additional Papers in the Case of Wallace vs. Simpson,* 41st Cong., 1st sess. H. Doc, 17 (Serial 1402), 5, 16–21, 56–57; Lamson, *The Glorious Failure,* 83.

92. W. P. Harris, quoted in *Papers in the Case of S. L. Hoge vs. J. P. Reed,* H. Rept. 6 (Serial 1403), 4. The State Board of Canvassers consisted of Francis L. Cardozo, Niles Parker, Daniel H. Chamberlain, and J. L. Neagle.

93. For election statistics see Herbert Shapiro, "The Ku Klux Klan during Reconstruction: The South Carolina Episode," *Journal of Negro History* 49 (January 1964): 38–39. Congressional investigations overturned the Democratic congressional victories several months later, giving the seats to the Republican candidates (Trelease, *White Terror,* 117).

94. William Gillette, *Retreat from Reconstruction, 1869–1879* (Baton Rouge: Louisiana State University Press, 1979), xii.

95. W. L. Trenholm, "The South since 1865," in Box 1, Folder 1, Trenholm Family Papers, SHC/UNC.

96. R. C. Poole to Robert Scott, October 16, 1868, in Box 3, Folder 6, Governor Robert K. Scott Papers, SCDAH.

CHAPTER FOUR

DIVIDE AND CONQUER
THE ELECTION OF 1870

> All fear the woolf [sic] is in the sheep's skin they are the same kind of creatures but they have have [sic] changed their coat but once and again they wear out the old coat and then the good old Democrat pokes out his head and we can get a look at his deformed principals [sic].
>
> W. W. Tucker on the Union Reform party,
> Robert K. Scott Papers, Ohio Historical Society

I

Democratic defeat in the presidential election of 1868 forced South Carolina conservatives to turn their attention back to state politics. So as the new state legislature convened and began to reshape South Carolina society, white opposition intensified and gained focus. But now both the executive and legislative branches were in Republican hands, so conservative whites knew the federal government would support, rather than restrain, state Republicans. But as the future grew more bleak, conservatives discovered unlikely allies, for by 1870, corruption would lead to a division in Republican ranks, giving conservatives an opportunity to weaken seriously the state Republican party.

"It is the most degrading sight I have seen," wrote Edward Crosland after visiting the General Assembly in February 1869.[1] His was the reaction of most conservatives in South Carolina, who looked upon the body dominated by blacks, carpetbaggers, and scalawags as an affront to God, nature, and the state itself. Martha Schofield had a different opinion of the legislature, "where those whose race had been oppressed for two centuries, were now making laws for the oppressors." The mingling of black and white, Democrat and Republican fascinated her, and she wryly commented that the situation "would disturb the dead bones of many of Carolina's proud sons."[2]

More important, the legislature and its accomplishments disturbed the live bones of many Carolinians. The South Carolina General Assembly opened its first regular session on November 24, 1868, and proceeded to redefine state society. Among its first actions was the ratification of the Fifteenth Amendment in March 1869, which directly restricted the state's control over its suffrage policy. In vain, William Trescot had tried to warn his fellow Carolinians that "the sooner we recognize the right of qualified suffrage—the *qualification being under our own control,* the better for us,—a little later and the qualifications *will not* be under *our* control."[3] The Fifteenth Amendment removed the most important qualification—race—from the hands of the states.

A truly significant achievement, the Fifteenth Amendment was tainted nonetheless by congressional conservatism and public ambivalence. As Michael Les Benedict has shown, the amendment "was the culmination of state-protecting Republican Reconstruction policy." It did not grant the right to vote, but only banned voting restrictions based on race, leaving open other methods of discrimination and private (as opposed to state) action.[4] Both Benedict and Robert Sawrey, in his recent work on Ohio and Reconstruction, see the Fifteenth Amendment as an attempt to settle the issues of Reconstruction without disturbing the traditional balances involved in federalism. Once the amendment was ratified and blacks were "protected" in their right to vote, the convulsive issues of race and Reconstruction could be forgotten.[5]

But former Confederates would neither forget nor forgive what this "outrage" meant to the South, to quote Thomas Pinckney Lowndes.[6] As a result, the violence and hostility that characterized the 1868 election continued through the winter and spring. Miss Amie Young claimed that "those assassins" had begun "a Second Rebellion upon us." In the summer of 1869, she told Governor Scott that "the Secepionist [sic] party had become . . . a deadly weapon to the Republican Party."[7] In fact, the Ku Klux Klan actually expanded its operations in 1869. A native white sheriff in Edgefield County reported that "every day colored men would come in and report the death, also whipping and abusing of persons. . . . [I] have seen the wounds on the parties."[8] Counties that had been relatively quiet in 1868 were ravaged by political violence. As was the case during the campaign, victims had little or no recourse. Abbeville Constable Lew Guffin, for instance, told Governor Scott that in his county, Democratic club presidents had warned him that if he issued warrants, "they would not responsible for the consequences." Guffin believed local whites "would not let those old matters to be investigated if I attempted it it would inaugurate *civil war* here at once."[9] In Sumter, whites who "sympathized" with blacks fell prey to a new form of economic pressure. Disguised men rode through the night, burning the stores and businesses of anyone who traded with the freedmen. Merchant John Fereter informed the governor that "the parties committing these outrages were comprised at least in part by some of our first families."[10]

If they intended to enforce their authority, state Republicans had to build a law enforcement system practically from scratch. A small state constabulary did function in the major cities, but early attempts at gaining control of the legal system foundered badly. The administration of justice, for instance, was both inefficient and corrupt. During the first term of the legislature, "trial justices" replaced the state magistrates, a move which smacked of politics from the beginning: the governor had the sole power to appoint trial justices, and the system soon became a leading source of "spoils." In a more honest effort at injecting justice into the justice system, Republicans hoped that black jurors and black judges would eliminate some of the bias that plagued state courts. (Appalled by this, Edward Lipscomb gave thanks for a law which exempted those over age sixty-five from sitting on a jury: "it makes me glad that I am so near the end of my race—to sit on a jury with them I don't intend to do, but we have a law that exempts a man at 65 & I take the advantage of it.")[11] Still, whites often managed to pack juries and circumvent the law. In March of 1869, a self-appointed committee from Edgefield notified Governor Scott that not a single black had sat as a juror in the town of Edgefield Court House, even though blacks had a voter majority of over 1,800 in the county.[12]

Although not without impact, none of these would-be remedies could change the fact that whites constituted the real power in the state. State and federal courts remained largely ineffective, for it was nearly impossible to procure witnesses and testimony for trials. Conservative whites were as a whole uncooperative or dishonest, and blacks often refused to testify from fear of retribution. The Klan had succeeded in showing that state authorities were unable to protect citizens, so blacks and Republican whites rarely pressed a case. It was also unlikely that the U.S. Army would intervene, for Major General Henry Wager Halleck, commanding the newly created Division of the South, was a stalwart opponent of military interference in civil affairs. Halleck even posited that "no such general organization [as the Klan] now exists in the southern states." Therefore, Halleck ordered, "no such military interference should be permitted, except on requisition of the governor of a State, and by order of the President."[13]

Instead, Governor Scott and the legislature turned to a plan many believed dangerous and impractical. The movement for a new state militia to bolster the tiny constabulary began during the campaign of 1868, but the Reconstruction Acts of March 1867 had made standing militias illegal in the Southern states. Once states were readmitted to the Union, however, Congress repealed the restriction. Although Scott had previously refused to consider arming blacks, he now saw its potential as another source of patronage; the offices and pay would go far to win allies, and—thinking optimistically—the force might even serve to curb violence. So on March 16, 1869, despite his earlier misgivings, Governor Scott signed a militia bill into law, organizing the National Guard Service of South Carolina. All males—*white and black*—between the ages of eighteen and forty-five were eligible. Whites, however, refused to serve with—and possibly under—blacks, so the force very quickly became a "black militia" (although most officers were white). Former Confederates offered their own all-white militia companies, but Scott refused to accept them for state service. Some followed the lead of Charleston's Carolina Rifles, which changed its identity to a "social club" in July 1869; its members, however, continued to drill regularly.[14]

For the most part, black Carolinians greeted the formation of the militia with unbridled enthusiasm. Freedmen flocked to the rolls in overwhelming numbers, for reasons ranging from self-defense to a sense of duty to the Republican party, from financial compensation to the appeal of the uniform and militia pageantry. Black women promoted enrollment; some refused to do laundry or have sexual relations if their husbands did not join. Other pressures were at work as well, for an avowed Republican who spurned service might find his principles under suspicion. Some historians have estimated the total force to number close to 100,000 men by the fall of 1870.[15]

Of course many Republicans appreciated the risk inherent in arming former slaves. Southern white concepts of honor and tradition would never allow it, untrained blacks were no match for former Confederates, and there were no guarantees of federal support should bloodshed occur. Deputy Constable Benjamin Yocum asked, "does he [Scott] think a lot of ignorant colored men with clumsy muskets in their hands can catch a squad of experienced soldiers on blooded horses?"[16] When John Haymond learned that Scott intended to ship a hundred rifles to a militia unit near him, he warned the governor that local whites will "misconstrue any action having a tendency to place the negro, armed and equipped for war, in an antagonistic position to them." If the whites sensed a threat, Haymond stated, the blacks will "be crushed by an uprising of these miserable misquieted people here, which with the arming of this number of freedmen would almost a certainty follow."[17] State Adjutant and Inspector General Franklin J. Moses moved in March to arm blacks in Charleston, but Mayor Gilbert Pillsbury advised against it. Pillsbury told Moses not to send arms "unless it could be done in perfect secret (which is hardly possible), the excitement, and danger, would be rather enhanced, than allayed, just at this crisis."[18]

Despite such reservations, the state government quickly began to arm its militia. In the summer of 1869, Franklin J. Moses, the scion of an old Jewish Carolina family and currently state adjutant and inspector general, went to Washington and managed to convince the War Department's Militia Bureau to issue the state's quota of arms *for the next ten years* to the state immediately. (In 1878, the state's adjutant general, John Scoffin, would lament that "we cannot obtain any [guns] from U.S. Gov't as they have a claim for 88,000 for those issued to Scott and Co. in 1869 and illegal as that issue was the War Dept can not erase it from their books. . . .")[19] Scott and Moses also concluded contracts with the Roberts Breech-Loading Company (totaling $44,250), C. H. Pond (for $45,000), and the American Metallic Ammunition Manufacturing Company (for $37,000). The militia was to have the finest in rifles—all converted Springfields or new Winchesters—bayonets, accoutrements, and uniforms.[20] With "conservatives" and "radicals" each preparing their separate armies, South Carolina, looking like an armed camp, entered its next political contest for control of the state.

II

The 1870 campaign eclipsed the 1868 election in complexity, intensity, and hostility. As before, conservative whites resorted to intimidation, economic pressure, and violence, but in 1870 they had some unlikely allies. Fraud and corruption split Republican ranks, and many Republicans bolted the organization. Seeking to restore honest government, "reform" Republicans sought alliance with "moderate" conservatives. But what reformers saw as political realignment many "moderate" conservatives saw as political expediency; the "moderates" were only using the Republican division to gain a foothold in the government, wielding dissenters as another weapon in the struggle for control.

Rumors of dissension in the Republican camp had been circulating for months. The problem was corruption, which by 1870 had become so widespread that one scholar claims there was a general "absence of a sense of responsibility to the society, white as well as black."[21] Certain figures stood out in Carolina's new elite, including Pennsylvanian John J. Patterson, a former railroad financier who "enjoyed legislative bribery as a game."[22] There was also T. J. Mackey, a close friend of Governor Scott's, who used his proximity to collect all sorts of offices and positions, despite a loud outcry even within his own party.[23] Richard B. Carpenter, a white Republican judge who would bolt the party in 1870 because of its corruption, called Mackey a "reckless revolutionary," and "the worst and most unprincipled man" in Columbia.[24] Robert Brown Elliott, the black assistant adjutant and inspector general, was so disgusted that he resigned in December 1870. Richard Realf felt similarly, telling Scott *we are ashamed of them*" and unless corruption was controlled "our present power will at the next election slide from our grasp into the hands of our Enemies. . . ."[25]

His prediction was not far wrong, and in the spring of 1870 a new political movement began to take shape. The "Citizen's Party" was composed of disaffected Republicans who planned on uniting with members of the Democratic Party "in order to put the present leaders out of power."[26] In April the Citizen's Party found a leader, Judge Richard B. Carpenter, a Vermont Republican and one of the most respected men in the party. This worried Republicans, who feared his message of reform might lure away other important figures and their followers.[27] For example, Richard Cain, an influential black leader and editor of the *Missionary Herald,* bolted the party soon after.[28]

Some state conservatives quickly latched on to the Citizen's Party as a means of weakening the Scott government. A victory for the bolters promised two important changes. First, it might establish a more honest government, and second, if conservatives joined the new party, it might bring Democratic influence to bear on the new government. Near the end of April, Governor Scott received the news he was dreading: some leading conservatives were pledging their support to Carpenter and had unofficially offered him the nomination for governor.

Just prior to the bolter's convention, the designation "Union Reform" replaced "Citizen's Party," and conservative Democrats began enlisting in the movement. The Union Reform convention, which met in June, gathered together leading reformers seeking honest government, leading conservatives seeking their own government, and a large number of blacks seeking the two dollars a day that Democrats promised them. But the proceedings, like the convention and the party itself, were a charade, manipulated by conservatives intent on winning black votes and allaying Northern suspicions. By prearranged agreement, the nomination for governor went to Richard Carpenter. The nomination for lieutenant governor took longer, also by prior arrangement. Conservatives enthusiastically offered the position to various blacks, until finally blacks themselves responded with the name of Matthew Calbraith Butler. His nomination—especially because it was done by blacks—was a farce, serving no purpose other than to reassure conservatives that whites had not "sold out." Prior to the war Butler had been a successful planter and slaveholder, and had served gallantly in the Confederate Army, finishing with the rank of general and one less leg. He had opposed the state government and had never even bothered ridding himself of his political disqualifications because of his rank and wealth. Legally entitled to vote and hold office because of President Johnson's final general amnesty, Butler never desired or applied for such for himself.[29]

Conservatives' grand gestures of compromise and conciliation were only a performance, for they sought no permanent allegiance with Republicans of any sort. As Eric Foner has shown, these alliances—the Southern New Departure—were wholly politically motivated, for conservatives had not really accepted the spirit of the new constitution.[30] To be sure, issues of honesty concerned Democrats, but they had opposed Reconstruction and the Republicans long before such matters existed. In 1870 the corruption dispute had created an opening, a chance to secure a foothold in the government as a stepping stone to full control. Whites accepted the Machiavellian logic of this strategy. Discussing the reform movement with his close friend James Conner, arch-conservative Wade Hampton declared that "we must by steady, patient, and persevering work, get possession of the State Government. This we can do if we determine to accomplish it, and after that all the way is plain and easy." As for the alliance with Republicans, Hampton explained that "we must work out our own political salvation and work it out with such instruments as we find at hand."[31] Wilmot DeSaussure told William Porcher Miles that an "effort is being made to overturn that party & Hampton, Butler, Kershaw & gentlemen of that character are earnestly at work, I hope for success." Accepting the alliance but nonetheless embarrassed by it, DeSaussure explained that the conservatives "have been obliged to work with the best tools at their command, & one of the adventurers, & probably one of the best of them, Judge Carpenter, is the candidate for Governor." "You will readily perceive," DeSaussure posited, how disgusted Carolina's great sons "must be with the tools they are obliged to use."[32]

Despite the elaborate song-and-dance, whites were unable to fool many "regular" Republicans, who saw through the conservative charade. For instance, although Robert Brown Elliott had resigned as assistant adjutant and inspector general because of corruption in the government, he refused to join the reform movement. Elliott warned fellow blacks to be wary, for "today we are welcomed by those who have always declared that we were not fit to occupy a position entrusted to us." "It behooves us to be careful of these men," Elliott advised, "whether they come in the name of the Democrats, Conservatives, or Citizen's Party."[33] Speaking two years later, black state Supreme Court Justice Jonathan J. Wright explained that the Union Reform party found meager support among freedmen "because we so highly prize our liberty." Wright admitted that there was "corruption in the Republican Party," but believed that the Union Reform party would bring about "the destruction of our liberties, which we value higher than life." Justice Wright quoted the Union Reform platform, which embraced "local self-government, with impartial suffrage, [to] guard the rights of all citizens more securely than any centralized power," and "a return to the ... constitutional limitation of power." In other words, according to Wright, the platform was "let us alone and permit us to do as we choose," the classic battle cry of South Carolina.[34]

The "regular" Republican party faced other threats as well, for conservative whites never seemed at a loss for schemes. Soon after the Union Reform convention, state constables informed Governor Scott that several hard-line conservatives had suddenly taken an interest in joining the "regular" Republican party. Scott's agents were suspicious and warned the governor to avoid letting them into the party. According to one officer in Columbia, such men were planted by the conservatives "to bring Democratic influence to bear on our nomination." One aspirant was described as being a "Ku-Klux," a "violent, outrageous and insulting" individual who had drawn a knife on a constable during the 1868 campaign.[35] Government agents also learned that state Democrats had hired Northern blacks of questionable character to win over the freedmen. B. F. Whittemore alerted Scott from Washington that one George Natter "is a dangerous man so watch out for him." Natter was headed to South Carolina "to work in the interest of the Union Reform Party" and was bringing thirteen hundred dollars to aid his efforts.[36]

It was also clear that terrorism would again play a role in Carolina politics. As whites began to implement their strategy of intimidating Republicans, government officials were buried under a deluge complaints and requests for help. The constable in Newberry, James Leahy, reported to Chief Constable John B. Hubbard that bands of well-armed whites were indeed threatening blacks but had declared that "they would begin by killing all the damned *white* Republicans first."[37] S. A. Swails in Kingstree claimed, "you cannot speak without a guard if you are a Republican, I see plainly that the Reformers wish to raise a row...."[38] Some Republicans, such as James Bonsall, decided that caution was the better part of valor; after suffering numerous visits and one attack, Bonsall withdrew from the local race in Union County. Tension there continued, and Bonsall feared that "we will have trouble here, I am confident," for conservatives were well armed—one arsenal at a depot was even under guard—but Republicans were not.[39]

Indeed, despite the official proclamations about creating a formidable militia, whites continued to win the arms race. Where Republicans were beset with divisions, corruption, and delay, conservatives were organized and unified. Deputy Constable J. W. Anderson warned Chief Constable Hubbard that "the Democrats . . . say they intend to organize all over the State against Scott's militia. I have it from good authority that whites are receiving guns through the merchants and are secretly organizing."[40] J. A. Jackson also reported that the "Democrats are organizing companies, I hear, in several counties against the militia." Jackson warned Hubbard that former Confederates "are working on the quiet to fool us all, and are getting guns all the time. . . ."[41] Deputy Constable Benjamin Yocum also notified Hubbard that "the opposite party make no secret of thier [sic] intention of arming against our militia."[42] In September, Chief Constable Hubbard received news from Union that a "regular company" of men had left for Laurens after hearing rumors of black rowdiness. One officer reported that whites had been receiving guns for some time; just recently a local business had "received a very large invoice of pistols and guns—so large that it does not look all right."[43] A month later J. P. Wharton informed Hubbard that a shipment of guns was making its way across Newberry.[44] From Chester came a report that "there are Winchester rifles being received here almost every day, but in such a way as they cannot be easily detected." Buyers went North, and then shipped guns into the state "in packages of dry goods." "The people are very well supplied with them now," a constable in Chester said; "they are playing a pretty smart game. . . ."[45]

As had occurred with the franchise, the effort to protect blacks and Republicans through the militia fostered, rather than deterred, white aggression. An escalation of sorts resulted, for as white aggression intensified, so too did interest in the state militia. New companies appeared in the up-country, where violence was most prevalent and state constables less numerous (they were concentrated around larger towns). Militia proliferation in 1870 was astounding; three new units appeared in York County, three each in Fairfield, Chester, Union, and Spartanburg, and several other piedmont counties added one or two each. E. L. Mann reported nine companies in Abbeville alone, and Laurens had eight.[46] In response the conservative *Unionville Times* in Union County declared "In Peace Prepare for War!" The governor, the paper suggested, would not be "happy until he has brought about a collision of the races." Therefore, "it would be our surest policy to hold ourselves prepared to accommodate him to the utmost of his desire."[47] Republican Isaac Witherspoon believed that Carolinians saw arming the blacks "as a declaration of war between the races."[48] Conservative W. R. Robertson of Winnsboro told A. B. Springs that the "stupid leading darkies are determined to provoke a conflict with the white race." His advice was to "meet it promptly and *terribly* and make the issue short and quick." "We should," explained Robertson, "by all means let *them* inaugurate the movement, and when they do we should strike fast and quick, and can soon settle it."[49]

A case in point took place in Laurens County in September, when whites moved against local militia companies. In the town of Clinton, a minor disturbance—probably instigated deliberately by whites—provided the excuse for town whites to call for help from surrounding paramilitary companies. When news spread that conservative "clubs" were coming to suppress the riot, black militia companies responded, and within hours three hundred blacks and over one thousand whites converged on the town. The whites were better organized and equipped, and they quickly cut off the towns of Clinton and nearby Laurensville, the county seat. Wagons loaded with guns and ammunition arrived shortly after the men, and reports circulated that more men and munitions were on the way.[50]

News of the riot quickly reached Columbia, and Chief Constable Hubbard sent Deputy Constable Henry Wilson to investigate. What he found shocked and frightened him. On his way to Clinton, Wilson discovered "all roads leading to and from the Railroad, and all the stations on the line of the road . . . a distance of about twenty-five miles, guarded by armed bodies of white men." Stealing his way into Clinton, he realized the town was in the possession of between eight hundred and one thousand armed whites, many of whom were mounted. Moving on to Laurensville, Wilson noted armed white patrols in the streets, and saw a wagonload of guns roll in. Sneaking around behind a store (no doubt thankful he was white), Wilson saw men opening crates of new Winchester rifles and handing them out to eager whites.[51]

The extent and sophistication of white organization convinced Wilson that state authorities faced more that just a crime wave. The constable claimed that the men in Clinton "came in organized companies from the Counties of Abbeville, Union, Spartanburg, and Newberry." He noted a structure of command and the smooth operation that came only with experience and discipline; a guard posted on one road said he was positioned there "by the man in command at Clinton." Women whom Wilson questioned told him their husbands and sons "had all been *ordered* off to Clinton to the war." Their purpose was similarly well thought-out; at both Clinton and Laurensville, whites ordered blacks to hand over their militia guns and disband their companies. As Wilson concluded, "this in no mere disturbance of the peace . . . it is a complete military organization, armed and equipped for the purpose of defying the Laws and menacing the authorities of the State."[52]

Wilson's report capped a series of investigations carried out under Hubbard and prompted the Chief Constable to warn the governor about imminent war. "I am satisfied," Hubbard informed Governor Scott, "that a complete organization exists from the Savannah river to Chester, a distance of nearly two-hundred miles in length, and embracing and including all the counties above Edgefield, and that its object is to intimidate Republican voters on Election day and if necessary murder leading Republicans." Hubbard even reported that "large numbers of the citizens of Georgia and North Carolina are employed . . . with the object of voting and aiding in this organization."[53]

Hubbard hoped Governor Scott would convince the federal government to take a more active role in the state. Indeed in 1870 the federal government had seemed to take a renewed interest in protecting suffrage. On May 31, Congress had passed the Enforcement Act, designed to discourage fraud at the upcoming fall elections. Under the act, it became a federal offense to bribe a voter or to punish any voter because of his voting behavior. The law made it a felony to conspire or to go in disguise for the purpose of infringing upon a citizen's voting rights, and authorized the president to use the military to enforce its provisions. Overseeing these measures was the new Department of Justice, which formally came into being in June of 1870, under the direction of the U.S. attorney general.[54]

Unfortunately these developments had little impact on the terrorism in South Carolina. Less than a month after its inception, the Justice Department got a new director, Amos Tappan Akerman, an advocate of stronger civil rights enforcement in the South. The enthusiastic enforcer from Georgia found himself hamstrung by strict budgets, cabinet infighting, a conservative administration, and even more conservative laws. Nor was the military ready to assist in law enforcement. General Henry Halleck, commanding the sprawling Division of the South, told his officers to avoid intervention in civil affairs. Any marshal asking for assistance must present a court order declaring he was unable to call on civilians to execute his *posse comitatus*. Halleck believed such "embarrassing" duties "can hardly be said to legitimately belong to the military service."[55] Even the Enforcement Act passed in May left much to be desired; a bulk of the expenditures and most of the marshals went to the North during the campaign and election. As Allen Trelease has observed, the law's effect on Southern violence was "wholly negligible."[56]

Left to confront what amounted to armed insurrection, state Republicans frantically sought means to protect their constituents. Governor Scott and Chief Constable Hubbard were forced to rely on temporary deputies, much as they had done in the 1868 election. William Taft, commissioner of elections for Charleston County, demanded at least two deputies at each of his forty-eight polls "to preserve the peace."[57] O. C. Folger in Pickens alerted Hubbard to the "considerable excitement" in his region and also wanted men to protect Republicans on election day.[58] Frantic activity filled the days prior to the election, as requests came to escort voters to the polls to guard the ballot boxes after the election had finished and to watch out for counterfeit tickets. But while the threat of violence created a need for protection, it also made that protection difficult to find. Not enough men volunteered as deputies and managers, a situation forcing the administration to offer compensation and opening Republicans to further charges of graft. Such meager efforts to stave off the onslaught made Republican Alonzo J. Ransier's comment all the more appropriate: "Our Thermopalae [sic] is to be here."[59]

October 19 had none of the noble splendor of that ancient battle, with abuses occurring on both sides. Republicans and those under the Union Reform umbrella resorted to fraud—and worse—in an attempt to carry the day. Officers' accounts claimed that in several townships "Republicans were driven from the polls and some were compelled to vote the Demo [Union Reform] ticket" while others refused to leave their homes for fear of attack or economic retribution. But regular Republicans also resorted to fraud as a means of countering deceitful conservative tactics. Isaac McKissick contested the victory of Republican A. S. Wallace in the Fourth Congressional District, claiming black militia units threatened freedmen who voted for McKissick. He also alleged—and the evidence supports the charge—that Republicans moved the polls at the last minute without a public announcement. Bolter Christopher Columbus Bowen also contested his defeat, alleging that Republican managers erased his name from ballots and wrote his opponent's in its place. Some witnesses even claimed they saw women voting the Republican ticket![60]

Once the dust settled, Republican numbers had held firm, defeating the Union Reformers and the conservatives partially allied with them.[61] Robert K. Scott garnered 85,071 votes, while his opponent, the Union Reform candidate Richard Carpenter, received 51,537 votes.[62] Party-racial loyalties still held, so while the black population remained the backbone of the Republican party, Governor Scott recognized that most of the native white population still opposed him. In his second inaugural address Scott publicly apologized for the corruption that had plagued his first administration. The bulk of his message, however, was a call for peace.

"There cannot be prosperity in the State unless there is peace," Scott stated, and "there cannot be peace unless there is respect for law and for the rights of all.... A little forbearance will save us from the dangers which threaten the peace and prosperity of the State."[63]

Forbearance in the face of continued alien-and-black rule was too much to demand from conservative South Carolinians. Frustration with their failed alliance in 1870, combined with their realization that state and federal Republicans had not taken action to suppress political violence, launched conservatives into the most devastating campaign of terror yet seen in the state. The twelve months following the election of 1870 would test the determination of conservatives, the mettle of state Republicans, and the will of the federal government to enforce its Reconstruction program.

Notes

1. Edward Crosland to "Mother," February 27, 1869, Edward Crosland Papers, South Caroliniana Library, University of South Carolina, Columbia, S.C. (hereafter SCL).

2. Martha Schofield, diary entry for January 22, 1869, Martha Schofield Diaries, in Folder 3, Southern Historical Collection, University of North Carolina, Chapel Hill, N.C. (hereafter SHC/UNC).

3. William H. Trescot to Henry Simpson, December 22, 1868, William Henry Trescot Papers, SHC/UNC; emphasis in original.

4. Benedict regards the Fifteenth Amendment as the conclusion of a policy of conservativism and believes that the so-called retreat in 1870s was a natural consequence of this limited, restricted program. See Michael Les Benedict, "Preserving the Constitution: The Conservative Basis for Radical Reconstruction," *Journal of American History* 61 (June 1974): 87.

5. Robert Sawrey, *Dubious Victory: The Reconstruction Debate in Ohio* (Lexington: University Press of Kentucky, 1992), 142–44. See also Everette Swinney, *Suppressing the Ku Klux Klan: The Enforcement of the Reconstruction Amendments 1870–1877* (New York: Garland, 1987), 22–23; and William Gillette, *Retreat from Reconstruction, 1869–1879* (Baton Rouge: Louisiana State University Press, 1979), 17–19.

6. Thomas Pinckney Lowndes, "Reminiscences," 109, in Box 2, Folder 21, William Lowndes Papers, SHC/UNC.

7. Amie L. Young to Robert Scott, July 8, 1869, in Box 8, Folder 8, Governor Robert K. Scott Papers, South Carolina Department of Archives and History, Columbia, S.C. (hereafter SCDAH).

8. Quoted in Orville Vernon Burton, *In My Father's House Are Many Mansions: Family and Community in Edgefield, South Carolina* (Chapel Hill: University of North Carolina Press, 1985), 289.

9. Lew Guffin to Robert Scott, July 22, 1869, in Box 8, Folder 17, Governor Robert K. Scott Papers, SCDAH; emphasis in original.

10. T. B. Johnson and W. H. Gardner to Scott, October 26, 1869, in Box 9, Folder 29, and John Fereter to Scott, November 9, 1869, in Box 9, Folder 35, Governor Robert K. Scott Papers, SCDAH.

11. Edward Lipscomb to "Brother," June 30, 1869, in Folder 6, Lipscomb Family Papers, SHC/UNC.

12. Ned Simkins to Robert Scott, March 13, 1869, in Box 6, Folder 11, Governor Robert K. Scott Papers, SCDAH.

13. Major General Henry W. Halleck, "Report on the Division of the South," in *Annual Report of the Secretary of War for 1869,* 41st Cong., 2d sess., 1869, H. Doc. 1 (Serial 1412), 75, 77–78; James E. Sefton, *The United States Army and Reconstruction, 1865–1877* (Baton Rouge: Louisiana State University Press, 1967), 190.

14. Peggy Lamson, *The Glorious Failure: Black Congressman Robert Brown Elliott and the Reconstruction in South Carolina* (New York: W. W. Norton, 1973) 80–82, 85–87, 96; Allen W. Trelease, *White Terror: The Ku Klux Klan Conspiracy and Southern Reconstruction* (New York: Harper and Row, 1971), 349; Alrutheus Ambush Taylor, *The Negro in South Carolina during the Reconstruction* (Washington, D.C.: n.p., 1924; New York: AMS Press, 1971), 190; Joel Williamson, *After Slavery: The Negro in South Carolina during Reconstruction, 1861–1877* (Chapel Hill: University of North Carolina Press, 1965), 260–61.

15. In her dissertation Lou Faulkner Williams puts the number enrolled at between 90,000 and 100,000; Joel Williamson has estimated that 90,000 names were on the rolls by the election of 1870. See Williams, "The Great South Carolina Ku Klux Klan Trials, 1871–1872" (Ph.D. diss., University of Florida, 1991), 54; and Williamson, *After Slavery,* 261. The most thorough works on the militia are Otis Singletary, *Negro Militia and Reconstruction* (Austin: University of Texas Press, 1957), see esp. 24, 101, 103; and Singletary, "The Negro Militia during Radical Reconstruction," *Military Affairs* 19 (Winter 1955): 179.

16. Deputy Constable Benjamin Yocum to Chief Constable John B. Hubbard, September 2, 1870, in the South Carolina General Assembly's *Report of the Joint Investigating Committee on Public Frauds and the Election of Hon. John J. Patterson to the U.S. Senate* (Columbia, S.C.: Calvo and Patton, State Printers, 1878), 9:26; hereafter cited as *Report on Public Frauds.*

17. John W. Haymond to Robert Scott, June 20, 1869, in Box 7, Folder 41, Governor Robert K. Scott Papers, SCDAH.

18. Gilbert Pillsbury to Adjutant and Inspector General Franklin J. Moses, March 16, 1869, in Box 3, Folder 1, Robert K. Scott Papers, Ohio Historical Society, Columbus, Ohio (hereafter OHS). On the need for "discretion," also see P. A. Eichelberger to Scott, June 19, 1869, in Box 7, Folder 10, Governor Robert K. Scott Papers, SCDAH.

19. John Scoffin to Benjamin S. Williams, August 7, 1878, Benjamin Stuart Williams Papers, SCL.

20. *Report on Public Frauds* 9:23–24, 29–32, 49–51; O. F. Winchester to Robert Scott, June 22, 1869, in Box 7, Folder 43, Governor Robert K. Scott Papers, SCDAH; Benjamin Ryan Tillman, "Autobiography," SCL.

21. Williamson, *After Slavery,* 387.

22. *After Slavery,* 387–88. For details on particular frauds, see Henry T. Thompson, *Ousting the Carpetbagger from South Carolina* (Columbia, S.C.: R. L. Bryan, 1926; New York: Negro Universities Press, 1969), 32–45.

23. For a look into the interesting career of T. J. (Thomas Jefferson) Mackey, see T. J. Mackey to Robert Scott, July 11, 1869, in Box 8, Folder 10, Governor Robert K. Scott Papers, SCDAH; Secretary (to the Governor) Hart to the Honorable W. J. Whipper, August 3, 1869, in Box 3, Folder 6, Robert K. Scott Papers, OHS; Scott to T. J. Mackey, August 7, 1870, and [unknown] to Scott, August 16, 1870, in Box 5, Folder 5, Robert K. Scott Papers, OHS.

24. Richard B. Carpenter to Scott, February 22, 1870, in Box 4, Folder 4, Robert K. Scott Papers, OHS.

25. Richard Realf to Scott, October 26, 1869, in Box 3, Folder 6, Robert K. Scott Papers, OHS; emphasis in original.

26. J. Donaldson to Scott, April 22, 1870, in Box 4, Folder 7, Robert K. Scott Papers, OHS.

27. For example, see T. J. Mackey to Scott, April 24, 1870, in Box 4, Folder 7, Robert K. Scott Papers, OHS.

28. Taylor, *The Negro in South Carolina,* 193–94.

29. J. M. Morris to Scott, March 27, 1870, in Box 4, Folder 7, Robert K. Scott Papers, OHS; *Charleston Daily Courier* June 18, 1870; Lamson, *The Glorious Failure,* 101–104; Richard Current, *Those Terrible Carpetbaggers* (New York: Oxford University Press, 1988), 225. Eric Foner cites one instance that sums up Butler's take on Reconstruction: testifying before the congressional committee investigating the Ku Klux Klan, Butler described the body politic by saying "I mean the white people." See U.S. Congress, Joint Select Committee to Inquire into the Conditions of Affairs in the Late Insurrectionary States, *Testimony Taken by the Joint Select Committee to Inquire into the Conditions of Affairs in the Late Insurrectionary States (The Ku-Klux Conspiracy)* (Washington, D.C.: Government Printing Office, 1872; New York: AMS Press, 1968), 4:1190 (cited hereafter as *KKK Report*); and Foner, *Reconstruction: America's Unfinished Revolution 1863–1877* (New York: Harper and Row, 1988), 412, 417. For information on the convention, including a complete list of participants, see John S. Reynolds, *Reconstruction in South Carolina, 1865–1877* (Columbia, S.C.: State Company, 1905), 139–43; and Francis Butler Simkins and Robert Hilliard Woody, *South Carolina during Reconstruction* (Chapel Hill: University of North Carolina Press, 1932), 448–50.

30. Foner, *Reconstruction: America's Unfinished Revolution,* 417.

31. Wade Hampton to James Conner, April 11, 1869, in Box 5, Hampton Family Papers, SCL.

32. Wilmot DeSaussure to William Porcher Miles, September 21, 1870, in Box 4, Folder 55, William Porcher Miles Papers, SHC/UNC.

33. Robert Brown Elliott, in *Charleston Daily Republican,* April 29, 1870; quoted in Lamson, *The Glorious Failure,* 101.

34. *Speech of the Honorable J. J. Wright at Liberty Hall, Charleston, S.C., May 31, 1872,* in *Pamphlets: Reconstruction in South Carolina, Democratic and Republican, 1869–1880* (n.p., n.d.), 13–14.

35. P. Connell to Scott, June [n.d.], 1870, in Box 5, Folder 3, Robert K. Scott Papers, OHS.

36. B. F. Whittemore to Scott, June 17, 1870, in Box 5, Folder 5, Robert K. Scott Papers, OHS.

37. James Leahy to John B. Hubbard, August 16, 1870, in Box 1, Folder 10, Chief Constables' Letterbooks, SCDAH; emphasis in original.

38. S. A. Swails to Hubbard, August 23, 1870, and August 27, 1870, in Box 1, Folder 11, Chief Constables' Letterbooks, SCDAH.

39. J. Bonsall to Hubbard, August 28, 1870, in Box 1, Folder 11, Chief Constables' Letterbooks, SCDAH.

40. J. W. Anderson to Hubbard, June 25, 1870, in *Report on Public Frauds*, 9:26.

41. J. A. Jackson to Hubbard, July 3, 1870, in *Report on Public Frauds*, 9:27.

42. Benjamin Yocum to Hubbard, September 2, 1870, in *Report on Public Frauds*, 9:26.

43. J. C. Bonsall to Hubbard, September 19, 1870, in *Report on Public Frauds*, 9:28.

44. J. P. Wharton to Hubbard, October 7, 1870, in *Report on Public Frauds*, 9:28.

45. John Burke to Hubbard, October 10, 1870, in *Report on Public Frauds*, 9:27–28.

46. Reynolds, *Reconstruction in South Carolina*, 137; Thompson, *Ousting the Carpetbagger*, 47; E. L. Mann to Scott, June 13, 1870, in Box 5, Folder 3, Robert K. Scott Papers, OHS.

47. *Unionville Times*, n.d.; quoted in the *Edgefield Advertiser*, September 15, 1870.

48. Isaac Witherspoon, quoted in *KKK Report* 5:1515.

49. W. R. Robertson to A. B. Springs, August 23, 1870, in Box 12, Folder 201, Springs Family Papers, SHC/UNC; emphasis in original.

50. *KKK Report* 5:1304–05, 1329–30; Trelease, *White Terror*, 350–51.

51. Henry Wilson to John B. Hubbard, September 21, 1870, in Box 1, Folder 12, Chief Constables' Letterbooks, SCDAH.

52. Wilson to Hubbard, September 21, 1870; emphasis in original. Even a month later, armed bands continued to patrol Laurens County. In October, James Leahy in Newberry even reported refugees coming in from the stricken county; they told of an attack on a black church that left fifteen blacks dead or wounded. See James Leahy to Hubbard, October 24, 1870, in Box 1, Folder 14, Chief Constables' Letterbooks, SCDAH.

53. Hubbard to Robert K. Scott, September 21, 1870, in Box 1, Folder 12, Chief Constables' Letterbooks, SCDAH.

54. "An Act to Enforce the Right of the Citizens of the United States to Vote in the Several States of the Union, and for Other Purposes," in *Statutes at Large of the United States of America, 1789–1873*, vol. 16 (Washington, D.C.: Government Printing Office, 1870), chap. 114.

55. General Henry Halleck, "Report on Division of the South," in *Annual Report of the Secretary of War for 1870*, 41st Cong., 3d sess., H. Doc. 1 (Serial 1446), 37–38.

56. Trelease, *White Terror*, 385–86. See also William S. McFeely, *Grant: A Biography* (New York: W. W. Norton, 1981), 362–65; and Gillette, *Retreat from Reconstruction*, 45–51.

57. William N. Taft to John B. Hubbard, October 10, 1870, printed in *Report on Public Frauds*, 9:61.

58. O. C. Folger to Hubbard, October 13, 1870, in Box 1, Folder 13, Chief Constables' Letterbooks, SCDAH.

59. Robert K. Scott to E. W. Seibals, September 30, 1870, in Box 6, Folder 1, Robert K. Scott Papers, OHS; Edward King, *The Great South* (Hartford, Conn.: American Publishing, 1875; Arno Press, 1969), 457; Alonzo Ransier to Scott, October 15, 1870, in Box 6, Folder 2, Robert K. Scott Papers, OHS.

60. Lamson, *The Glorious Failure*, 109–15; *Papers in the Case of Issac G. McKissick vs. A. S. Wallace*, 42d Cong., 2d sess., H. Doc. 48 (Serial 1525), passim; *Papers in the Case of Christopher C. Bowen vs. Robert C. DeLarge*, 42d Cong., 2d sess., H. Doc. 37 (Serial 1525), 10–25, 30, 36–38; "George" to Robert Scott, October 20, 1870, in Box 6, Folder 2, Robert K. Scott Papers, OHS.

61. Swinney, *Suppressing the Ku Klux Klan*, 207–8.

62. Lamson, *The Glorious Failure*, 109–15; *Edgefield Advertiser*, December 1, 1870.

63. Robert Scott, in Box 6, Folder 5, Robert K. Scott Papers, OHS.

CHAPTER FIVE

"A PERFECT REIGN OF TERROR"

> Defeated on the battle-field, defrauded at the ballot box, we have but one remedy—The dagger that was made illustrious in the hands of Brutus. . . .
>
> from a Ku Klux Klan posting, late 1870

I

The election of 1870 brought no peace to South Carolina. The passage of time and the victories of the Republican party only increased conservative hostility. Moreover, a lack of forceful action from state and federal authorities encouraged further lawlessness. As a result, the first half of 1871 was the most violent period in South Carolina since General William T. Sherman had burned a path across the state. In an attempt to bring order after years of lawlessness, legislation, and investigation, the federal government finally stepped in to suppress the rebellion against state and federal authority. In 1871 the Grant administration attempted to make an "example" of South Carolina by destroying the Carolina Klan. The federal "crackdown," however, demonstrated the enforcement program's weaknesses rather than its strengths and ultimately damaged the Reconstruction effort more than it did the Klan.

The need for federal assistance became clear in the days immediately following the election of 1870. In Laurensville, on the day after the election, a scuffle broke out between a local white and a state constable. Pushing and shoving escalated, several shots were fired, and blacks who had come to help the constable ran into their armory. A crowd of whites followed and began firing into the building. Fearing an assault, the militiamen dove out the back windows and bolted for the nearby woods. Fifteen minutes after the riot began, three blacks lay dead; two were killed inside the armory, and another was shot while fleeing.[1]

The bloodletting in Laurensville continued through the evening and into the night. One witness recorded that whites flooded into the town and "formed themselves into squads and took different roads to hunt for the leaders of the radical party."[2] Dawn the next day revealed the grisly fruits of their search: the bodies of at least nine Republicans. Included among the dead were a white probate judge, a black member of the legislature, and a state constable. The town itself was in the hands of armed whites—between 2,000 and 2,500 of them—who had already confiscated the militia guns from both the armory and a nearby barn.[3]

Governor Scott again vacillated on taking severe action, perhaps coming to recognize that his militia program only exacerbated problems. The bloody display of white power seemed to further convince the governor to tread softly. He ordered all militia guns in the county handed over for transfer to Columbia. Only then did he declare martial law in the counties of Laurens, Newberry, Union, and Spartanburg.[4] Of course the proclamation had only a symbolic effect, for the state government had no real enforcement mechanism. Conservative forces had shown time and again that they could best the state militia and constables, and the governor had made no request for federal assistance.

Not surprisingly, whites ignored the governor's declaration, and postelection violence spread throughout the up-country. Across Laurens and Union appeared new organizations called "councils of safety," which served as an information network between townships and counties, reporting on the movements and activities of black militia units.[5] In November, Captain Felix Torbell of the Eighteenth U.S. Infantry confirmed at least two Klan murders—one victim was a trial justice—and a score of beatings and whippings. Torbell believed "the ulterior objects of the Ku Klux party to be against the U.S. Government . . . in the mean time they mean to break the spirit of local loyalty, so that control of the state may be first secured. . . ."[6]

Trouble was not restricted to Laurens and Union, and up-country terrorism showed that despite the Republican victories at the polls, whites still held a monopoly on violence. In Chester, just east of Union, constable Benjamin Yocum, having learned of a planned attack on Chester Court House by armed bands, mobilized a group of men to defend the town.[7] Similar reports came from Spartanburg, where constables called for more men and guns, since "difficulty may occur momentarily and we will be the first persons subjected to violence."[8] In York County, along the North Carolina border, the Klan attacked the home of County Treasurer Edward M. Rose, who, luckily, was not at home when they riddled his house with bullets.[9] Among the murder victims in Rock Hill was Tim Black, who was shot eighteen times and had his throat slit. In every case, a constable reported, there was "no offence given except that the murdered men were leading Republicans."[10] James Leahy, to the south in Newberry, feared for the recently elected officials, for "bets are offered that *some of the elected* officers will not get their places." Like others before him, Leahy told Chief Constable John B. Hubbard that only the U.S. Army could suppress the lawlessness.[11]

With political violence on the rise and his militia clearly useless, Governor Scott pleaded with Washington for assistance. He informed President Grant that "an organized force" was "creating a general reign of terror and lawlessness" throughout the piedmont region. Black and white Republicans were being beaten and murdered because "they dared to exercize their own opinions upon political subjects." Scott explained the weaknesses of the civil courts and the militia, and reasoned that "if the State is powerless the duty clearly devolves upon the National Government" to quell the disorder. State forces could not oppose bands "largely composed of those who were engaged in the Confederate Armies, accustomed to the use of fire arms, thoroughly drilled, and armed with the most improved weapons...." "Humanity," the imperiled governor stated, "as well as every sound principle of policy would dictate, that regular troops should be employed in this service."[12]

Governor Scott also contacted General Alfred H. Terry, commander of the Department of the South under Henry Halleck's Division of the South. Holding a law degree from Yale, Terry was more sympathetic to military intervention than his superior. To use the militia, Scott informed Terry, would be a "signal for a general uprising and slaughter of those not in sympathy with the marauders." Scott had the same request for the commander as he did for the commander-in-chief: South Carolina needed federal soldiers.[13]

As if to vindicate the governor's claims, the Ku Klux Klan put on a murderous display of its power in the winter of 1871. In Union County, a dozen black militiamen had been arrested for the murder of a handicapped Confederate veteran, Mat Stevens.[14] On the night of January 4, two days after the arrests, a band of forty or fifty mounted, disguised men rode into Unionville, chopped down the jail door with axes, and removed five of the prisoners. Klansmen led them away from the town and shot all five; two died, and the three others were soon recaptured and returned to the jail. When news of this episode reached Columbia, the judge of the district court ordered the prisoners transferred to the capital for holding and trial. The sheriff of Unionville received the order on Thursday night, February 9, but was unable to make arrangements for the Friday train; the next available train was on Monday. Some of the prisoners would never make that trip, for at midnight on Sunday the Klan struck again. A vast mounted force—estimates place it between eight hundred and fifteen hundred men—seized the town, blocked all exits, and posted guards along the streets. Operating in complete silence, using only gestures and whistles, the Klan surrounded the jail and demanded the keys. When the deputy sheriff refused, masked men promptly exhibited his wife to him—held in captive by a Klansman, a gun to her head. The Klan tied up the deputy and the jailer, and removed ten black prisoners. Searchers discovered eight dead men the following morning; the two others were never found. In the opinion of Robert Wallace Shand, the night "had a most quieting effect on the negroes."[15]

State authorities redoubled their efforts to attract federal intervention. On February 14, Governor Scott again wrote to President Grant to "demand the interposition of the Federal Government for the protection of the lives and persons of our people." Without federal troops, said Scott, he would be forced to rely on the militia and "inaugurate a war in which the loyal people would be sacrificed."[16] The General Assembly sent a delegation to Washington with facts and figures designed to sway the administration. Despite their fears that a "bloody war of extermination" was imminent, the delegation received no guarantees of assistance.[17]

While politicians debated in Washington, conservatives continued their assault on the forces of the state government. In Chester County in March, trouble began when armed whites set out after a group of militiamen who were harboring a fugitive. The militia captain, Jim Wilkes, called for help from other units, and within a day, over one hundred armed blacks had pitched camp in Chester Village. Hundreds of armed and mounted whites arrived, some bands coming from as far as Rock Hill and Winnsboro. When the militia moved into the woods during the night, the main force of whites, under command of Joseph Gist of Union, set up a skirmish line around their position. In the morning the whites advanced but were repelled by heavy fire. Changing his tactics, Gist ordered a flanking attack, which drove the blacks out of the woods. Pursuit continued for a short while, but the militia scattered and escaped. At least five blacks were killed and several wounded; Gist reported one dead from his forces. A few days later Scott disbanded several of the county's militia units and suggested to John Reister, colonel of the county militia, that he leave the county.[18]

By March it was apparent that—at least in much of the up-country—

state Republicans were losing what little authority they had. Again in mid-March the governor pleaded with Grant, informing the chief executive of the latest round of outrages, raids, and murders. The "organized combinations," according to the besieged governor, were so well trained and equipped that they "render the power of the State and its officers unequal to the task of protecting life and property."[19] In the middle of March another delegation arrived in Washington—a group composed of twenty prominent white and black Republicans, including Lieutenant Governor Alonzo Ransier. They brought boxes of evidence and many horror stories, all in the hope of convincing the administration to take decisive action.[20]

While federal officials pondered and state officials waited, many local officials found themselves seeking another line of work. Klan terrorism was quite effective at forcing Republican resignations. As it had done with the recall of militia guns, the Scott administration chose to concede defeat rather than to push the issue. In several instances, in order to avoid further violence, the governor appointed a conservative white to a vacant position—but considering the threats made against the previous officials, these men may have been the only ones available. H. R. White, the commissioner of Union County, told Scott to hold a new election there because the other two commissioners had resigned under pressure. At one point Scott had tried to stand up to the opposition by refusing to accept any resignation given "under the influence of intimidation or fear," hoping this would dissuade the Klan. This policy was short-lived as well, for violence continued, and Republican officeholders opposed the plan; some believed resignations might restore peace, while others wanted to leave office to protect themselves.[21]

Perhaps more surprising than Scott's sudden—albeit minor—stand against the opposition was the announcement that U.S. troops were headed for South Carolina. In March, General William T. Sherman ordered a major reshuffling of the regiments in the West to free up companies of cavalry for service in the South. In mid-March, Scott received word that four companies of the Seventh U.S. Cavalry would arrive shortly, and that more could follow. These forces would serve alongside the five companies of the Eighteenth Infantry already in the state and provide much-needed mobility.[22]

The promise of federal aid emboldened Governor Scott to seek a truce with his enemies. On March 13, the governor met with seventeen of Carolina's "best citizens" in hopes of finding a solution to the disorder. The resulting informal arrangement called on Governor Scott to refrain from declaring martial law, disband many of the up-country militia companies, and replace selected local officials. In return, the conservatives present pledged to use their "utmost influence" to end the violence and preserve peace. At first glance, Scott appeared to have ceded a great deal. But in reality the governor did not relinquish anything that the Klan would not have taken by force. Resignations were already a problem, and officials continued to leave office. After the meeting, both Edward Lipscomb and Robert H. Hemphill recorded that the governor removed many blacks and corrupt whites and replaced them with "respectable white men."[23] As for the militia, Scott had already disbanded several units following the tumultuous events of the past few months. In January he had disbanded the Union militia, followed by York companies in February and Chester units in March. Eliminating a few other units disrupted the governor's patronage system, but there was no chance of using them against the Klan. Disbanding them merely prevented the bloodshed that would have resulted had the Klan done it instead.[24]

II

The federal government supplied the stick to Governor Scott's carrot. Or, more accurately, the government provided the *threat* of the stick, since it increased the number of troops in the state without really altering their mission. Companies B, E, and K of the Seventh Cavalry were in South Carolina by the end of March—stationed at Unionville, Spartanburg, and Yorkville respectively—and companies C and D arrived in April. With the transfer into the state of companies G, L, and M in May and June, cavalry forces numbered nearly four hundred officers and men. Nearly five hundred other troops from the Eighteenth Infantry and Third Artillery already garrisoned the state.[25]

But the stick remained small in comparison to the task at hand. As long as Congress and the administration restricted the army from an active role—and such limitations were appropriate under civil law—the size of the force meant little. The army could only react to crimes in progress, and it was highly unlikely that the Klan, with its information network and knowledge of the region, would be caught unawares. Nor were the numbers themselves impressive; nine hundred soldiers garrisoned South Carolina, but the Klan had mobilized that many in one town in a matter of hours. In late March the *Nation* made these observations in an article that mourned the "failure" of the "social revolution" in the South. The forces of conservativism "have taken the field against the new regime," the author wrote, and the government's reaction was lackluster at best. A European power, the article continued, would have sent a hundred thousand men to crush the insurrection and "strike terror" in the hearts of the rebels. In the United States, "we vote a regiment of cavalry and two companies of infantry . . . about enough men to make one county tolerable safe." "We cannot interfere effectively," the author believed, "and had better not interfere at all."[26]

No one understood the dilemma facing the army better than Major Lewis Merrill of the Seventh Cavalry. Merrill, who arrived in Yorkville on March 26 to assume command of the cavalry in the state, had a background that prepared him for the duty he faced. A graduate of West Point, Merrill had earned four brevets for service during the Civil War, finishing as a Brevet Brigadier General. He had also commanded pacification operations in Missouri and Arkansas, and had served as a Judge Advocate (he came from a family of lawyers) and headed military commissions.[27]

Personally capable of severe action, but understanding the limitations under which he operated, Merrill pursued a "carrot-and-stick" policy of his own. Like the *Nation*, the cavalry officer knew his meager force was incapable of restoring peace to the beleaguered state. More importantly, and not unlike Governor Scott, he realized that any significant change would have to come from the population itself. First, Merrill constructed an apparatus that could, if the decision were made, do direct damage to the Klan. He conducted an exhaustive investigation into the York County Klan. Merrill and a battery of secretaries, some paid directly by him, conducted interviews and took testimony from anyone who had a story to tell. He created a vast file which cross-referenced outrages, victims, and suspects, so as to verify names and events. To encourage and protect victims, he opened his camp at Yorkville as a refuge where anyone fearing danger could stay. He also used sympathetic native whites and at least one disillusioned former Klansman as spies to infiltrate Klan dens. In a speech given a year later, U.S. District Attorney David T. Corbin applauded Merrill as the man who broke the organization's "veil of secrecy" and made federal intervention in the fall of 1871 possible.[28]

The other half of Merrill's policy took advantage of a movement against violence that had begun before he had even arrived. When the major assumed command in Yorkville on March 26, he found a local movement against lawlessness already under way, probably in response to the recent meeting between Scott and the state's conservative leaders. Local merchants and planters had hosted town meetings on March 13 and 16, and their resolutions had been printed in the *Yorkville Enquirer*.[29] Drawing on this sentiment, Merrill hosted his own meeting with prominent locals. The major hinted at the incriminating evidence he was gathering, commented on the growing restlessness in Washington and among his troops, and made allusions to federal action.[30]

Merrill's involvement spurred on the reaction against political violence. Informers reported that local leaders held meetings of their own, and many bands and "committees" decided to curtail activity. As more cavalry units entered the state through the spring, Klan meetings became more frequent, and "resolutions" and "warnings" urging calm were published in local papers. "We earnestly raise a warning voice," one resolution read, "that force, if persisted in, will be suppressed by the power of the Federal Government." The *Carolina Spartan* and the *Yorkville Enquirer* published "cards" with signatures of those urging peace, some of which carried over five hundred names. The movement soon spread beyond York County; by June, meetings were occurring in Spartanburg, Clarendon, and Sumter.[31]

Oddly enough, while hostilities in the Palmetto State seemed to be on the decline, activity in Washington was on the rise. In the first week of March, President Grant indicated Southern violence was a top priority. At the close of the regular session of Congress, he called a new one immediately rather than allow Southern hostility to fester until fall. A week later the Senate issued a call for tougher legislation to combat the "organized bands of desperate and lawless men . . . [who have] subverted all civil authority" in parts of the South.[32] After the defeat of one bill, Grant made a personal appeal to the House of Representatives, declaring that "a condition of affairs now exists . . . rendering life and property insecure . . . [and] the power to correct these evils is beyond the control of State authorities. . . ."[33]

But the situation in the South called for action, not more legislation. Between the Enforcement Act of May 1870 and the Civil Rights Act, enough legislation already existed to authorize federal intervention in the South. The problem was not necessarily one of legitimacy or legality, but one of nerve and will. Even without further legislation, decisive action was possible. Laws already provided that soldiers could be used as *posse comitatus,* and Grant need only order General Halleck to cooperate. The Enforcement Act of May 31, 1870, provided for federal action in lieu of state performance, and even authorized the president to use the military to enforce the law. In February 1871, Congress had added a Second Enforcement Act, which placed congressional elections under federal supervision but otherwise added little of substance to the first.[34]

Clearly, the federal government was not ready to take the radical steps necessary to curb violence in the South. For instance, one option was for the president to declare martial law, or unswervingly support a governor who did. Although the legal and constitutional basis of such a move was questionable, it was not without precedent. Grant might reach back to

Dana's "Grasp of War" idea to show that even with readmission and the return to civil law, the late rebel states continued their defiance of the Union and its principles. Congress and the Supreme Court could temporarily suspend civil law, and military officers and courts would take matters into their hands. If the president and Congress truly felt that a "rebellion" was in progress, Grant could invoke General Orders No. 100, "Instructions for the Government of Armies of the United States in the Field." Written by Francis Lieber during the Civil War for the War Department, "Lieber's Code" offered only one justification for martial law: necessity. If war existed, the one-time professor at South Carolina College argued, everything was fair game. When caught, "rebels" and "partisans" should be executed. Speedy, severe action was the only way to respond to an insurrection, which Lieber defined as "the rising of a people in arms against their government, or a portion of it, or against one or more of its laws, or against an officer or officers of the government."[35] While such steps appear extreme, the use of federal power to preserve the peace was not unprecedented; the Whiskey Rebellion and Fries Rebellion of 1789 are two examples, as was Lincoln's call for volunteers in 1861.[36]

But in this case the federal government opted for what Michael Les Benedict has called "the bare minimum." On April 20, 1871, Congress passed the Third Enforcement Act, also called the Ku Klux Act, which demonstrated how conservative and tentative Congress was being.[37] The new law did not provide for martial law, military commissions, or any other of the harsh responses that rebellion seemed to demand. It was crafted with the South in mind, however, and it specifically targeted the "unlawful bands" that denied persons the "equal protection of the laws." By creating a new federal crime, the framers solved the puzzle of how to allow the federal government to punish state crimes, such as murder: "the deprivation of any rights, privileges, and immunities secured by the Constitution."[38]

Perhaps the biggest difference between this law and its predecessors was the fourth section, which allowed the president to suspend *upon his own discretion* the privilege of the writ of habeas corpus in a finite area. Habeas corpus is the constitutional guarantee against arbitrary arrest, for it prohibits holding a suspect who has not been charged or against whom no indictment is pending. Not the equivalent of martial law, a suspension would affect only holding procedures, not arrest procedures. Law enforcement remained in the hands of civil authorities and warrants were still required for arrests. The same day that it passed the Ku Klux Act, Congress created the Joint Select Committee to Inquire into Conditions of Affairs in the Late Insurrectionary States. Congress was not ready to plunge into extremes, and sought to justify the new law by making a political case for its existence. Members began hearing testimony in Washington in May and, in June, started their tour of the South in South Carolina.[39]

Another sign that the federal monolith was rising from its slumber occurred on May 3. President Grant issued a proclamation declaring that if the Southern people did not see fit to end the lawlessness, the federal government would step in. President Grant ordered federal marshals to arrest all transgressors of the new law, and reiterated the use of soldiers as posses.[40] As stirring as it may have sounded, the proclamation did nothing. Federal authorities were already authorized to do all of this under the 1870 Enforcement Act; a lack of marshals, court terms, and witnesses willing to testify had usually stopped investigations in their tracks. Major Merrill informed Edward Townsend, adjutant general of the army, that he was both confused and disappointed, since the order gave the military no additional authority. Merrill complained that the army should not be blamed for any lack of activity, for officers had to follow the civil authorities; and marshals, attorneys, and judges were irresponsible and apathetic.[41]

Merrill's commanding officer, General Alfred Terry, was also concerned with the federal government's refusal to assume responsibility for insuring peace and security. By summer Terry, a lawyer in civilian life, was convinced that the federal government's policy—if it could be called that—was a failure. Writing to his superior in the Division of the South, Terry declared that the only way to crush the "insurrectionary movement" was through the use of military force. Terry knew the entire South could not be reconquered, but "if in a single state it [the Klan] could be suppressed, and in that State *exemplary* punishment meted out to some of the most prominent criminals, I think that a fatal blow would be given to it everywhere...." The commander suggested South Carolina as the target, for there the organization seemed most dangerous and active, and a considerable military force was already present.[42]

The congressional subcommittee investigating illegal organizations in the South reached the same conclusions. Republicans John Scott and Job Stevenson and Democrat Philadelph Van Trump arrived in South Carolina in late June. For three weeks they heard testimony from conservatives and Republicans, whites and blacks, during interviews conducted in Columbia, Unionville, Spartanburg, and Yorkville. At Yorkville, Major Merrill supplied them with the data he had gathered on the organization and its activities. Senator Scott, the chairman of the subcommittee, was so struck by the findings that he suggested Grant declare martial law and use the army to break up the Klan.[43]

Slowly the administration came to accept the necessity of intervention. In late August, President Grant received the congressional subcommittee's report, which included Major Merrill's files. After meeting with his cabinet individually and as a group, Grant sent U.S. Attorney General Amos Akerman into the state for an expert opinion. Akerman would confer with leading state and federal officials to get their input on possible intervention.[44] Akerman's stand on the government's responsibilities was clear, as he told a friend from Mississippi: "the Government is there by right, and not by the tolerance of the population. This disaffection is a thing not to be won by wooing. Enough of that has already been done in vain."[45]

Akerman first met with U.S. District Attorney David T. Corbin and Governor Robert Scott, informing them of the president's intention to invoke the power of the Ku Klux Act. The governor approved of the "intended operation," pledged his full support, and even suggested the counties where the writ of habeas corpus should be suspended. In Yorkville, Akerman met with Major Merrill and discussed how the Departments of War and Justice would cooperate. Akerman acquired such respect for Merrill that he authorized the major to make arrests as the district attorney directed. In the beginning of October, Akerman reported to the president in Dayton, Ohio, and advised him to invoke the Ku Klux Act. Grant immediately sent his attorney general back to South Carolina to oversee preparations.[46]

On October 12, Grant called for all bands to disperse within five days, and demanded they turn in all weapons, disguises, and paraphernalia of the organization.[47] On October 16, Akerman contacted the president, urging him to proceed with the operation.[48] The next day, October 17, President Grant suspended the privilege of the writ of habeas corpus in nine counties of the South Carolina up-country, to last "during the continuance of such rebellion." The counties were York, Chester, Spartanburg, Chesterfield, Laurens, Newberry, Fairfield, Lancaster, and Marion. Marion was included by clerical error; the proper county was Union, but the correction was not made until November 3.[49]

If arrests are indicative of success, the federal operation appeared to be an enforcement victory. The months spent accumulating evidence and the smooth cooperation between marshals and their cavalry escorts resulted in scores of arrests within just a few days. Numbers of prisoners grew rapidly, outstripping the capacity of many of the small county jails. A report in early November listed dozens of suspects who had been apprehended, and within a month the number had passed one hundred.[50] On January 8, District Attorney Corbin informed Akerman that 472 persons had been arrested thus far.[51] In April 1872, the time of the attorney general's annual report, the figures had grown to the following:

Spartanburg	230 arrests
York	183 arrests
Chester	43 arrests
Laurens	40 arrests
Union	36 arrests
Newberry	1 arrest
TOTAL:	533 arrests[52]

A large number of Klansmen surrendered to federal authorities, further swelling the number of men in jail. Merrill claimed that "unbelievable numbers" turned themselves at Yorkville. Louis Post, a "carpetbagger" who served as Merrill's chief secretary, believed that the fear of punishment—hanging seemed to be on the tips of many tongues—convinced Klansmen to give up and seek clemency.[53] A *New York Evening Post* correspondent estimated that three hundred men had surrendered at Yorkville in the two weeks after the suspension.[54] Crowding was so bad that Merrill allowed many of the "lesser" criminals to go home on bail.[55] The rush to surrender—and avoid punishment—was "like the sudden breaking of a flood," according to Mary Davis Brown. Across the piedmont, jails filled to capacity and beyond, and *confessed* murderers were allowed to return home to make room for "bigger fish."[56]

III

The federal operation was off to an impressive start, but poor preparation and lack of foresight would eventually bring the enforcement effort to a whimpering close. For instance, although the arrest numbers were impressive, they created a judicial and logistical nightmare. Lacking men, money, and time, Attorney General Amos Akerman realized almost immediately that it was impossible to try all the offenders. In November he instituted a policy of "selective prosecutions." The attorney general ordered District Attorney David T. Corbin to prepare cases only for those suspected of being leaders of the Klan, and those involved in crimes of "deep criminality." Others were to be released on light bail, while those whom the district attorney believed had played "a reluctant part" because of "compulsion" should be released altogether.[57] A week later Corbin replied that prisoners were being classified, and most "will be set at liberty."[58]

Prosecutions commenced in the federal circuit court in Columbia in late November. From the outset, however, it was evident that the trials would not be the decisive blow the government had intended. Days before the trials opened, the chief prosecuting attorney, District Attorney Corbin, laid his doubts before Attorney General Akerman. The fact that most of the alleged crimes "were committed prior to the Act of April 20, 1871," worried the district attorney, who feared an *ex post facto* ruling (in fact most cases had to be prosecuted under the 1870 Enforcement Act). In addition, Corbin believed that a "conspiracy" would be difficult to prove and that pressing violations against the right to bear arms or the right to be secure in one's own house would indicate weakness in the government's case. It was weak, as Corbin knew, and he openly solicited advice from his superior Akerman.[59]

The head of the Justice Department shared Corbin's doubts. Writing to an old friend, Attorney General Akerman admitted that "indeed it seems to me that it is too much for even the United States to undertake to inflict adequate penalties through the courts." Akerman confessed that he had too few men, too little money, and too little time to punish all the perpetrators. "Really these combinations amount to war," Akerman declared, "and cannot be effectively crushed on any other theory."[60]

Instead it was the opposition who went all-out during the trials. A week after the habeas corpus suspension, conservative leaders began an organized effort to secure the best defense money could buy. On October 22, Wade Hampton suggested to Armistead Burt that they should hire Northern lawyers "to defend our Ku Klux cases . . . they would have more weight than our own advocates & could speak more freely." Hampton, Burt, Matthew C. Butler (the Union Reform nominee for lieutenant governor), and others estimated that fifteen thousand dollars would be needed to procure the finest men. Each county was assessed a specific sum.[61]

The campaign raised nearly ten thousand dollars and secured two of the most capable lawyers in the country, Reverdy Johnson and Henry Stanbery.[62] Reverdy Johnson of Maryland had argued for the defense in *Dred Scott v. Sanford,* served as attorney general of the United States, and had been a member of the Joint Committee on Reconstruction. (Ironically his son was a U.S. marshal in South Carolina, so Johnson knew more than most about the horrors of the Klan.) Henry Stanbery of Ohio had also been attorney general and had defended President Johnson at his impeachment trial.[63] Corbin's confidence slipped further when he learned the identities of his counterparts, but Akerman reassured him that "the very fact of sending far off for celebrated counsel often strik[es] the jury as evidence of a cause inherently weak."[64]

Just which cause was the weaker was still in dispute at the close of the Columbia trials. Nearly 500 men awaited trial in November, but when the term closed in early 1872, only 54 men had been convicted and sentenced. Of these, only 5 had actually been found guilty by trial, while 49 had pleaded guilty; 38 men were acquitted, and 30 cases thrown out.[65] The Circuit Court's April 1872 term at Charleston faced a carryover of 278 cases involving over 400 persons, in addition to new cases from ongoing arrests. In terms of convictions the government fared better in April: 18 men were found guilty, while 18 pled guilty. Hundreds of cases remained on the docket, with hundreds of men indicted and awaiting trial.[66]

Swift justice was not forthcoming, much to the dismay of federal authorities. "It is obvious," Attorney General Akerman complained in early January, "that the attempt to bring justice, through the forms of law, to even a small portion of the guilty in that State must fail, or the judicial machinery of the United State must be increased." "If it takes a court over a month to try five offenders," Akerman asked, "how long will it take to try four hundred, already indicted, and many hundreds more who deserve to be indicted?"[67]

Corbin agreed, believing that "Congress ought to afford some more speedy and effective means. It must do so or permit most of the prosecutions to fail."[68] Despite requests for additional funding and extra court terms, Congress did nothing. A year after the initial crackdown, Major Merrill observed the same problems: "The machinery for the execution of the these [laws] . . . is wholly inadequate to the task. . . the United States courts are choked with a quantity of business which amounts practically to a denial of a hearing of four-fifths of the cases."[69]

Nor was justice severe, especially considering that prosecutions focused on Klansmen of highest standing and crimes of the most serious nature. Punishments were light, due to the need to prosecute in federal courts under the Enforcement Acts. For instance, since murder is a state crime, the charge brought against Robert Hayes Mitchell, suspected of involvement in the premeditated murder of militia captain Jim Williams, was "a conspiracy to deprive a citizen of his right to vote on account of race and color."[70] Five years in prison was the most severe sentence handed down during the Columbia trials. Most sentences ranged from six to eighteen months, with fines running from ten to one hundred dollars.[71]

Another explanation for the light punishment is that despite the federal authorities' claims, most of the Klan's leadership escaped the federal operation. Arrests and prosecutions dealt only with the lesser members. Historians generally agree that although the Klan drew its membership from all strata of white society, those prominent in the community were often leaders in the organization.[72] According to District Attorney Corbin, the "saddest aspect" of "the whole affair" was that "many of the most intelligent and wealthy men, even ministers of the Gospel of Christ, have been active, energetic members of these Klans."[73] Ann Eliza Marshall concurred, and noted in her journal that "the original Ku Klux was composed of the gentry—they were particular with who they admitted." It was not long, however, before "the common people took it up."[74] Yet Secret Service investigations at the Albany Penitentiary revealed men from the lowest social classes, many of whom were completely illiterate. Amos Akerman's successor in the Justice Department, George Williams, believed these men took the blame for outrages "that were planned and executed by men of intelligence . . . [who] are responsible for the sentiment and action of the communities."[75]

In fact, evidence indicates that the most notorious Klansmen may have escaped the federal crackdown completely. Robert W. Shand believed that with few notable exceptions, only "low elements" surrendered and were arrested, because most of the important figures had fled the state.[76] For several years, through better information and organization and sheer cunning, conservatives had outwitted state authorities; now they outmaneuvered federal ones. Mary Brown Davis recorded that by October 16—*before* the suspension—"a good many of the men left York" County to avoid arrest.[77] Once the crackdown began, a shortage of marshals provided the opportunity for many suspects to flee; one officer complained that "many of the members are now leaving the State" before he could arrest them.[78] One judge estimated that over fifteen hundred of his "neighbors" had "absconded." The problem became so acute that Merrill asked Akerman to explain extradition guidelines to him, since the major knew of fugitives in Mississippi, Georgia, Arkansas, Virginia, Maryland, and even Pennsylvania.[79] Among those singled out by Major Merrill as Klan leaders were J. Banks Lyle, believed to be the chief in Spartanburg County; James Avery, alleged chief in York County; and Dr. J. Rufus Bratton. Avery had fled to Ontario, and Bratton followed him there; their haven was the home of expatriate Edward Manigault.[80] None of these men, as was the case with most leaders, were ever brought to trial. Instead of permanently decapitating the movement—an accomplishment that generally acts to crush an insurrection—the federal operation only temporarily dispersed its leadership.

The enforcement operation in South Carolina was already slipping towards failure when Attorney General Amos Akerman resigned on December 12. Akerman had been a constant advocate for the federal protection of civil and political rights in the South. He departed under mysterious circumstances, and could not even explain his reasons to Corbin "without saying what perhaps, ought not to be said."[81] His replacement, George

Williams, had been a "radical" for some time; he had sponsored the Tenure of Office Act, helped to frame the Reconstruction Act, and voted against Andrew Johnson at his trial. His record, and the political benefits of having a Westerner in the cabinet (Williams was from Oregon), made him acceptable to many in Washington. The only complaints might come from advocates of a strict enforcement policy, since Williams had no history of or experience in civil rights enforcement.[82]

Amos Akerman's resignation was in a way symbolic of the government's waning commitment to civil rights enforcement. Before leaving office on January 10, Akerman commented on the North's fading interest in protecting political and civil rights in the South. To an old friend in Cartersville, Georgia, Akerman wrote from Washington that "the feeling here is very strong that the Southern republicans must cease to look for special support to action."[83] To a member of Georgia's Republican party Akerman said that "our friends" in the South must learn "to stand on their own feet. They must not depend always on propping from Washington, and might as well learn the lesson now."[84] To Benjamin Conley in Atlanta, Akerman confessed that "the real difficulty is that very many of the Northern Republicans shrink from any further special legislation in regard to the South. Even such atrocities as Ku Kluxery do not hold their attention. . . . The Northern mind, being full of what is called progress runs away from the past."[85]

Nonetheless, some historians contend that federal intervention in South Carolina restored peace, destroyed the Klan, and bolstered the administration's enforcement program. Herbert Shapiro has argued that the federal government's "limited" steps (true enough) were enough to "destroy the organization," while Joel Williamson believes "a crushing imposition of federal power" stopped the violence.[86] James Sefton stresses the army's role, arguing that "the application of military force broke the Klan in South Carolina," and Allen Trelease maintains that the violence "finally ended as a result of federal intervention."[87] Even Robert Kaczorowski, who sees Klan violence as the rebellion it was, argues that "federal prosecutions in South Carolina so demoralized members of the Ku Klux Klan that its leaders issued orders to stop all Klan activity."[88] The strength of this myth is evident by its inclusion in the most important Reconstruction synthesis of our time, Eric Foner's *Reconstruction: America's Unfinished Revolution*. Foner accurately depicts the "crackdown" as a tactical failure; the immediate results were negligible, and the problems of the trials and speed of the retreat outweighed any short-term gains. But Foner sees a strategic victory. In his opinion, with regard to the "larger purposes—restoring order, reinvigorating the morale of Southern

Republicans, enabling blacks to exercise their rights as citizens—the policy proved a success."[89]

But what did the federal government really accomplish? After a wave of political terrorism unprecedented in the history of the United States, a handful of low-ranking Ku Klux Klan members had been sentenced to a few years in jail. To be sure, hundreds had been arrested, indicted, and now awaited trial. But many more had avoided arrest, while a large proportion of those arrested were walking around free—and would never see the inside of a courtroom.

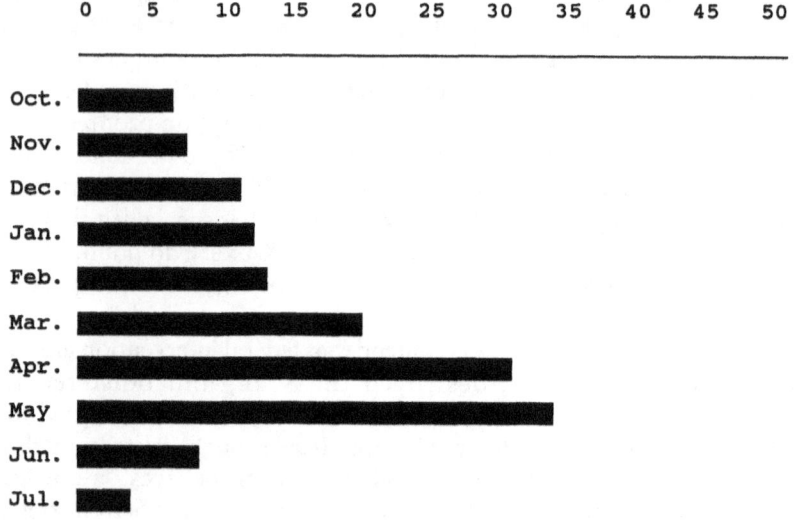

Frequency of Klan outrages, October 1870–July 1871. Taken from the *Ku Klux Klan Report,* passim.

Nor was federal intervention responsible for ending the Klan's wave of terror or breaking the back of the organization. The timing of the outrages catalogued in the *Ku Klux Klan Report* indicate that the Klan's "reign of terror" had subsided before the president suspended the writ of habeas corpus. Figure 2, above, presents a bar graph representing outrages that can be verified by cross referencing witnesses in the *KKK Report*. The same information—the number of outrages and their dates of occurrence—appears in the table that follows. Here, however, the author has used the appropriate page numbers from the *KKK Report* to illustrate the pattern of violence:

"A Perfect Reign of Terror"

1870			1871						
Oct.	Nov.	Dec.	Jan.	Feb.	Mar.	Apr.	May	Jun.	Jul.
365	289	353	40	309	29	316	386	327	400
380	296	552	580	440	37	320	400	327	407
427	901	585	681	690	392	349	403	436	603
632	974	595	723	1472	393	376	411	440	
895	1071	595	875	1475	531	560	416	568	
901	1081	685	1000	1475	538	571	520	616	
	1511	974	1159	1475	602	576	524	687	
		1069	1159	1475	620	576	564	1182	
		1070	1475	1475	1096	576	574		
		1173	1478	1479	1472	600	585		
		1472	1480	1479	1472	668	591		
			1481	1479	1472	695	597		
				1479	1475	696	676		
				1578	1475	698	678		
					1478	700	680		
					1478	1082	790		
					1479	1474	1406		
					1479	1478	1474		
					1593	1479	1474		
					1593	1479	1475		
						1480	1475		
						1480	1475		
						1480	1475		
						1480	1476		
						1480	1476		
						1481	1476		
						1481	1477		
						1481	1477		
						1574	1478		
						1577	1478		
							1478		
							1479		
							1479		
6	7	11	12	13	20	31	34	8	3

Klan outrages as indicated in the *Ku Klux Klan Report*. These figures represent pages with descriptions of incidents. Cross-checked for accuracy and to avoid repetition, identical numbers mean different attacks were recounted on the same page.

A similar pattern emerges from Major Merrill's report on York County, which is also included in the *KKK Report*:

Dec.	Jan.	Feb.	Mar.	Apr.	May	June	July
1	1	8	4	9	14	0	0

In fact Corbin knew that Klan activity had declined. He informed Akerman before the Columbia trials that charges needed to come under the Enforcement Act of 1870, since most crimes were committed *before* the Ku Klux Act had passed.[90] The indictment charts for the Columbia trials listed the dates of the crimes, and confirmed Corbin's information:[91]

Oct.	Nov.	Dec.	Jan.	Feb.	Mar.	Apr.	May	June	July	Aug.	Sept.
1	2	5	6	19	30	20	7	1	0	2	0

Men on the scene also reported a decline in Klan activity well before the federal "crackdown." Sergeant Winfield S. Harvey, a Seventh Cavalry

105

farrier, arrived in Yorkville on March 26 and recorded in his diary that "plenty of Ku Klux" were in the area. By late spring, his entries were more like "no further news of the KKs, all have settled down and gone home to stay." By the end of July the comments were the same, that "the K.K.K. have all gone home and no more heard of them [sic]."[92] The Seventh Cavalry's Major Marcus A. Reno established the post of Spartanburg on July 19, and reported in September that not a single outrage had occurred since he had arrived. Reno attributed the calm to "the active part taken by some of the men of property, to show the folly of such deeds & the harm it might bring the county...."[93]

What accounted for the decline in violence *before* the federal government intervened? As Major Reno observed, local whites took the initiative in curtailing Klan activity. The Ku Klux Klan was a product of the community, designed to enforce community values and fight for community goals. If the community believed the organization had outlived its usefulness, the local population—including Klan leaders, members, and sympathizers—would simply shut the system down; the same had occurred earlier in Reconstruction, on a smaller scale, with "bushwhackers" and the "night patrols." In the spring and summer of 1871, the Klan had already achieved a great deal. Klan activity had resulted in the disbanding of many militia companies, the removal of Republican officials, and the general intimidation of the black population. At the same time, the federal government was focusing new attention on South Carolina. The influx of troops into the state, the passage of the Ku Klux Act, and the May proclamation of President Grant indicated that federal intervention might not be far off. Rather than risk losing what it had gained, the Klan—i.e., many conservative whites across South Carolina—opted for peace.

In fact, evidence that the federal operation did not destroy the Klan came from those credited with its destruction. On December 3, less than two months after the habeas corpus suspension, District Attorney Corbin informed Attorney General Akerman that new Klan dens were forming in Laurens County. Corbin learned this from local whites who had been driven from their homes after refusing to join.[94] In January, both Major Merrill and the General Assembly advised Washington against removing soldiers from the state. Merrill did not believe peace was permanent, for the cause of turmoil still existed in "the dissatisfaction of the white leaders with the results of the war and their determination to nullify these as far as possible...."[95] District Attorney Corbin shared the major's doubts. Although he believed that the prosecutions had a "demoralizing effect" on the Klan, he did not think they were responsible for peace. Corbin told the new attorney general, George Williams, that he had information showing that "orders were given last summer" to stop the violence *"for the present.*" The Klan would wait *"until the storms blew over"* and then "resume operations."[96]

Evidently some Carolinians did not take the federal storm very seriously, for in the winter of 1872, while the federal enforcement operation was still under way, violence began anew. In February, reports filtered into Columbia about disguised white riders in Abbeville calling themselves "regulators."[97] In Union County, despite the presence of federal troops and U.S. marshals, the *Columbia Phoenix* claimed that there was "a perfect reign of terror throughout the County."[98] In a plea for permanent military posts in Laurens County, a state senator and several representatives claimed that a "state of terror still exists" and that "Republican citizens are not safe in life or property."[99] Major Merrill confirmed this fact and offered suggestions for transferring men to free up enough soldiers.[100] The South Carolina General Assembly became concerned over rumors about plans to begin moving troops out of the state. Fearing that "any withdrawal would jeopardize peace," the legislature passed on March 11 a resolution urging its congressmen to lobby to keep soldiers in the state.[101]

As Merrill and others had anticipated, a hostile spring blossomed into a violent summer, and it appeared that the Ku Klux Klan was again on the rampage in the up-country. Reports from marshals, army officers, constables, and private citizens depicted a rapidly deteriorating situation. As before, some Republicans received notices to leave, signed by the "KKK." As before, some men ignored them, and suffered the consequences. W. W. Davis, for example, stayed after receiving a Klan warning and awoke one night in June to find his house aflame.[102] Republicans were in such danger in the counties of Newberry and Laurens—again despite the fact that arrests had just begun there in late winter—that District Attorney Corbin himself applied to Major Merrill for military aid. Corbin had information that "a number of leading K.K." were reorganizing their dens in the region and that only the presence of cavalry could preserve the peace.[103] In a letter to Attorney General Williams, Corbin reported that "the K.K's [sic] are becoming very much emboldened and their organizations are coming together again." "I see no peace or safety," the District Attorney said, "and no end to this business, unless the Govt proceeds with a steady hand to meet [sic] out justice to these people."[104] In September, Major Merrill confessed that "in my experience . . . [South Carolina] has no parallel, either in wanton and brutal cruelties inflicted . . . or in the utter deadening of the moral sense in large parts of white communities reputed and believed to be far removed from the barbarism of savages."[105]

In light of this situation, it is difficult to argue that the federal enforcement effort in South Carolina achieved any of its goals. Continued violence—while the federal operation was still under way—demonstrated that intervention had not destroyed the Klan, restored law and order, or bolstered federal authority. Tardy government action had come only after scores of murders, hundreds of assaults, and months of investigations, reports, and petitions. The operation itself was conducted under the restraints of civil law and did nothing more than harass hundreds of people whom the government ended up sending back to their homes anyway. The prosecutions, according to W. McKee Evans, "were largely a matter of sweeping the dirt under the rug." The government failed "to understand that conditions of war still prevailed in the South" and relied on "gestures" instead of acting quickly and forcefully "to convey convincingly the message that it would not tolerate a renewal of terrorism."[106] William Gillette also criticized the "pitiable" effort that did little to combat the violence which was "so persistent, so widespread, and so formidable as to constitute civil disobedience and guerrilla warfare."[107]

The failure of the government to meet such a threat swiftly and adequately did irreparable damage to the Republican cause in the South. To be sure, the *threat* of federal intervention had had considerable impact at first, helping to prod locals into taking an active stand against violence. But the government's bite was not up to its bark, and the police action that followed months of preparation brought only short-term benefits. Conservatives' worst fears went unrealized; Republicans—at the state and federal levels—dealt in bluff, while conservatives dealt in blood. The fiasco that resulted from Grant's attempts to make an example of South Carolina encouraged Carolina whites. The problems that beset the operation and the doubts about its success convinced conservatives that the federal government would not again interfere in such a way. In the end, it was the Klan and hostile whites who scored the strategic victory. By forcing federal action, they exposed the inadequacies of the enforcement program for all to see—and for some to use.

Notes

1. See below Box 3, Folder 25, William Dunlap Simpson Papers, South Caroliniana Library, University of South Carolina, Columbia, S.C. (hereafter SCL); John A. Leland, *A Voice from South Carolina: Journal of a Reputed Ku-Klux* (Charleston, S.C.: Walker, Evans, and Cogswell, 1879), 58–59; John S. Reynolds, *Reconstruction in South Carolina, 1865–1877* (Columbia, S.C.: State Company, 1905), 150.

2. "Mother" Pelot to "Robert," October 22, 1870, in Lalla Pelot Papers, Special Collections Library Research Room, Perkins Library, Duke University, Durham, N.C. (hereafter SCLRR, Duke).

3. In the words of John Leland, "the severe lesson taught our colored fellow-citizens on the 20th of October, 1870, had proved most salutary. They then found out, that however forbearing and long-suffering the white man had shown himself to be, there was a limit beyond which they could only go at the peril of their lives; pass that limit, and he would not only resist, but he would *kill*" (*A Voice from South Carolina*, 91). See also *Edgefield Advertiser,* October 27, 1870; Allen W. Trelease, *White Terror: The Ku Klux Klan Conspiracy and Southern Reconstruction* (New York: Harper and Row, 1971), 352; U.S. Congress, Joint Select Committee to Inquire into the Conditions of Affairs in the Late Insurrectionary States, *Testimony Taken by the Joint Select Committee to Inquire into the Conditions of Affairs in the Late Insurrectionary States (The Ku-Klux Conspiracy)* (Washington, D.C.: Government Printing Office, 1872; New York: AMS Press, 1968), 1:558, 3:336 (cited hereafter as *KKK Report*); Records of the Office of the Adjutant and Inspector General, Letterbook, South Carolina Department of Archives and History, Columbia, S.C. (hereafter SCDAH).

4. Robert Scott, "Proclamation," in Box 6, Folder 2, Robert K. Scott Papers, Ohio Historical Society, Columbus, Ohio (hereafter OHS). John Leland reacted to the declaration of martial law by saying "old Laurens could boast of *one* day, at least, under a white man's government" (*A Voice from South Carolina,* 60).

5. Trelease, *White Terror,* 352.

6. Captain Felix Torbell to U.S. District Attorney David T. Corbin, December 3, 1870, in Box 13, Folder 18, Governor Robert K. Scott Papers, SCDAH.

7. Benjamin Yocum to Chief Constable John B. Hubbard, October 29, 1870, in Box 1, Folder 14, Chief Constables' Letterbooks, SCDAH.

8. C. H. Bankan to Hubbard, October 30, 1870, in Box 1, Folder 14, Chief Constables' Letterbooks, SCDAH.

9. Bankan to Hubbard, October 30, 1870.

10. Report compiled by Colonel Robert Brown Elliott, acting adjutant and inspector general, South Carolina National Guard, "Reports of 1870 and 1871," Military Affairs File, SCDAH; J. S. Watson to Robert Scott, December 9, 1870, in Box 13, Folder 23, Governor Robert K. Scott Papers, SCDAH.

11. James Leahy to John B. Hubbard, November 12, in Box 1, Folder 15, Chief Constables' Letterbooks, SCDAH; emphasis in original.

12. Robert Scott to Ulysses S. Grant, n.d. (but, by context, either November or December 1870), in Box 6, Folder 5, Robert K. Scott Papers, OHS.

13. Scott to Brigadier General Alfred Terry, January 17, 1871, in *Letter of the Secretary of War Communicating a Copy of a Letter of the Governor of South Carolina Relative to Outrages Committed upon Citizens of the United States Resident in that State,* 41st Cong., 3d sess., S. Doc. 28 (Serial 1440), 1–2.

14. *KKK Report* 1:549–50, 3:98, 4:969.

15. *KKK Report* 1:36–37, 550–51; 3:64, 74, 98; 4:971–72, 975–77, 979–80, 984; Robert Wallace Shand Journal, 144, SCL; *Edgefield Advertiser,* February 23, 1871; Reynolds, *Reconstruction in South Carolina,* 185; Henry T. Thompson, *Ousting the Carpetbagger from South Carolina* (Columbia, S.C.: R. L. Bryan, 1926; New York: Negro Universities Press, 1969), 55; J. C. Lester and D. L. Wil-

son, *The Ku Klux Klan: Its Origin, Growth, and Disbandment* (n.p.: 1884; New York: Da Capo Press, 1973), 193.

16. Robert Scott to Ulysses S. Grant, February 14, 1871, in Record Group 94, Microcopy 666, Reel 4, National Archives, Washington, D.C. (hereafter RG, MC, Reel, NA).

17. Warren Wilkes and Samuel Nickles to Grant, March 2, 1871, RG94, MC666, Reel 43, NA.

18. *KKK Report* 1:1563–73; 3:38–41; 4:1028–29, 1035; 5:1428–43, 1580–90; *Yorkville Enquirer,* March 9, 16, and 30, 1871. Trelease provides an account that does not match the *KKK Report.* Among his claims are that "Woods" was the militia captain at the center of the fray and that Colonel Reister provided the militia with ammunition in Chester (*White Terror,* 355–56).

19. Robert Scott to Ulysses S. Grant, March 16, 1871, in Box 6, Folder 7, Robert K. Scott Papers, OHS.

20. March 28, 1871, in Ellison Summerfield Keitt Papers, SCL.

21. An example of a Klan resignation warning is "General Order No. 97, KKK," in Box 15, Folder 36, Governor Robert K. Scott Papers, SCDAH. See also John W. Martin to Scott, April 28, 1871, Governor Scott Papers, SCDAH; W. B. Peake to Scott, May 3, 1871, in Box 6, Folder 8, Robert K. Scott Papers, OHS; H. R. White to Scott, May 31, 1871, in Box 16, Folder 14; John Tinsley to Scott, March 18, 1871, in Box 15, Folder 20; and R. M. Stokes to Scott, April 24, 1871, in Box 15, Folder 34, Governor Robert K. Scott Papers, SCDAH.

22. General Alfred Terry to Adjutant General Edward D. Townsend, March 25, 1871, RG94, MC666, Reel 6, NA.

23. Edward Lipscomb to "Brother," April 11, 1871, in Folder 6, Lipscomb Family Papers, Southern Historical Collection, University of North Carolina, Chapel Hill, N.C. (hereafter SHC/UNC). Robert H. Hemphill to William Hemphill, May 9, 1871, in Box 4, Hemphill Family Papers, SCLRR, Duke.

24. In his excellent work on the Southern politics during Reconstruction Michael Perman characterizes Scott as a "centrist." But this idea only partly explains the situation in South Carolina. Scott's refusal to declare martial law, for instance, was not completely due to a desire to win white approval. As we have seen, Scott had already declared martial law once before, and its effects were negligible to the point of embarrassment. He chose the course he did—avoiding martial law, disbanding the militia—because it was the most direct course to achieving his object, the restoration of peace. Had Scott wanted to conciliate conservatives, he would have disbanded the militia much earlier, removed local officials more readily, and not applied over and over to President Grant for aid. See Michael Perman, *The Road to Redemption: Southern Politics, 1869–1879* (Chapel Hill: University of North Carolina Press, 1984), 34–35. For the disbanding of the militia, see *KKK Report* 3:215; 4:705–11; 5:1366–70, 1395, 1556; Trelease, *White Terror,* 365, 367, 378–80; Herbert Shapiro, "The Ku Klux Klan during Reconstruction: The South Carolina Episode," *Journal of Negro History* 49 (January 1964): 47; Thompson, *Ousting the Carpetbagger,* 55; March 30, 1871, "Letter from Ellison S. Keitt to Editors [paper unknown], March 30, 1871," Ellison Summerfield Keitt Papers, SCL; Joel Williamson, *After Slavery: The Negro in South*

Carolina during Reconstruction, 1861–1877 (Chapel Hill: University of North Carolina Press, 1965), 265; *Yorkville Enquirer,* February 16, 1871; Robert K. Scott to "The Ku Klux in South Carolina," n. d., in Box 10, Folder 3, Robert K. Scott Papers, OHS.

25. "Report of General Alfred Terry for the Department of the South," in *Message of the President of the United States and Accompanying Documents. . . . Including the Annual Report of the Secretary of War,* 42d Cong., 2d sess., H. Doc. 1 (Serial 1503), 61–63.

26. *Nation,* March 27, 1871, 192–93.

27. Reynolds, *Reconstruction in South Carolina,* 197.

28. Lewis Merrill's files attracted many interested readers: the congressional subcommittee that visited the state in July used them during their interviews, Attorney General Amos Akerman found them vital in convincing Grant to suspend the writ of habeas corpus, and Corbin himself utilized them during the famous Ku-Klux trials in November 1871. For Merrill's reports on the inner workings of the Klan, see his letters to Edward D. Townsend, adjutant general, June 9, June 10, June 11, July 17, and September 14, 1871, RG94, MC666, Reel 26, NA; Everette Swinney, *Suppressing the Ku Klux Klan: The Enforcement of the Reconstruction Amendments 1870–1877* (New York: Garland, 1987), 228; Trelease, *White Terror,* 370; *Speech of the Honorable David Thomas Corbin, U.S. District Attorney for South Carolina,* in *Collected Pamphlets Including Preston, John Smith Address Delivered before the Survivors' Association of South Carolina* (L. F. Youmans, n.d.), 10.

29. Sheriff R. H. Glenn to Robert Scott, March 13, 1871, in Box 15, Folder 17, Governor Robert K. Scott Papers, SCDAH; *Yorkville Enquirer,* March 16 and 30, 1871.

30. *Yorkville Enquirer,* April 6, May 25, 1871; *KKK Report* 5:1500–2, 1516, 1520, 1540–41.

31. Major Lewis Merrill to the adjutant general, Department of the South, June 9 and July 17, 1871, RG94, MC666, Reel 26, NA; Trelease, *White Terror,* 354, 361, 368–73.

32. "Resolution Submitted by Senator John Sherman," in *Resolution of the Senate of the United States,* 42d Cong., 1st sess., S. Doc. 16 (Serial 1467).

33. *Message of the President of the United States Relative to the Condition of Affairs in the South,* 42d Cong., 1st sess., H. Doc. 14 (Serial 1471).

34. *Statutes at Large of the United States of America, 1789–1873,* vol. 16 (Washington, D.C.: Government Printing Office, 1871), chap. 433; Trelease, *White Terror,* 387.

35. Lieber's code can be found in U.S. War Department, *War of the Rebellion: A Compilation of the Official Records of the Union and Confederate Armies,* ser. 3 (Washington, D.C.: Government Printing Office, 1880–1901), 3:148–64.

36. To be sure, the argument over who has the power to declare martial law, Congress or the president, complicates matters. But there is precedent for executive jurisdiction. It can be argued that the authority to declare martial law is part of the War Powers, or that it falls under the Constitution's direction that the chief executive "take care that the laws be faithfully executed" (ARTICLE II, SECTION 3).

Both *Martin vs. Mott* and *ex parte Field* support the presidential declaration of martial law, and even *Luther vs. Borden,* which grew out of Dorr's Rebellion in 1842, provided that the president had the obligation to protect states from domestic violence. In *Luther vs. Borden,* Roger B. Taney indicated that domestic violence could comprise a "state of war," and require the federal government to take extraordinary steps. See Bennet Milton Rich, *The Presidents and Civil Disorder* (Washington, D.C.: Brookings Institution, 1941), 19–20, 21–27; 63; and Robert S. Rankin, *When Civil Law Fails: Martial Law and Its Legal Basis in the United States* (Durham: Duke University Press, 1939), 26–32, 181–83, 195–97.

37. The act as passed was called the "Ku Klux Act," *not* the Ku Klux Klan Act. Although I use the word "Klan" throughout this work, contemporaries did not. The organization was the "Ku Klux," and a member was a "Ku Klux." "Klan" was not a common part of the name and did not appear as such in the act.

38. *Statutes at Large of the United States of America, 1789–1873,* vol. 17 (Washington, D.C.: Government Printing Office, 1781), chap. 22; Robert J. Kaczorowski, *The Nationalization of Civil Rights: Constitutional Theory and Practice in a Racist Society 1866–1883* (New York: Garland, 1987), 167–200; Trelease, *White Terror,* 388; Michael Les Benedict, *The Fruits of Victory: Alternatives in Restoring the Union, 1865–1877* (Philadelphia: J. B. Lippincott, 1975), 55; Swinney, *Suppressing the Ku Klux Klan,* 162.

39. *Statutes at Large of the United States of America, 1789–1873,* vol. 17 (Washington, D.C.: Government Printing Office, 1781), chap. 13; Swinney, *Suppressing the Ku Klux Klan,* 156–75; Benedict, *The Fruits of Victory,* 53–54.

40. Ulysses S. Grant to Secretary of War William W. Belknap, May 13, 1871, RG94, MC666, Reel 13, NA; Adjutant General Edward D. Townsend to Brigadier General Alfred Terry, May 13, 1871, RG94, MC666, Reel 17, NA.

41. Alfred Terry to Robert Scott, May 15, 1871, in Box 6, Folder 8, Robert K. Scott Papers, OHS; Lewis Merrill to Edward D. Townsend, May 26, 1871, RG94, MC666, Reel 17, NA.

42. Alfred Terry to the assistant adjutant general, Division of the South, June 11, 1871, RG94, MC666, Reel 17, NA; emphasis in original.

43. *Charleston Courier,* September 9, 1871, in Ellison Summerfield Keitt Papers, SCL.

44. Trelease, *White Terror,* 401–3; Swinney, *Suppressing the Ku Klux Klan,* 212–13; *New York Tribune,* September 2, 1871.

45. Attorney General Amos Akerman to R. A. Hill, September 12, 1871, in Book 1, Amos Tappan Akerman Letterbooks, Alderman Library, University of Virginia, Charlottesville, Va. (hereafter UVA).

46. Akerman to General Alfred Terry, November 18, 1871, in Book 1, Amos Tappan Akerman Letterbooks, UVA; Trelease, *White Terror,* 403; Swinney, *Suppressing the Ku Klux Klan,* 213.

47. Ulysses S. Grant, "Proclamation of October 12, 1871," RG94, MC666, Reel 35, NA; *Edgefield Advertiser,* October 19, 1871. According to Lou Faulkner Williams, "as expected, the proclamation was ignored by Klansmen in South Carolina." This conclusion is not supported by the facts, however, for the Klan had

already ceased activity in the state. See Williams, "The Great South Carolina Ku Klux Klan Trials, 1871–1872" (Ph.D. diss., University of Florida, 1991), 96.

48. *Message of the President of the United States in Answer to a Resolution of 25 January Last Relative to the Lawlessness in Insurrectionary States,* 42d Cong., 2d sess., H. Doc. 268 (Serial 1515). For more on Attorney General Akerman's opinions on the Klan, see Akerman to Terry, November 18, 1871, in Book 1, Amos Tappan Akerman Letterbooks, UVA.

49. Ulysses S. Grant, "Proclamations of October 17 and November 3," both in RG94, MC666, Reel 35, NA; Swinney, *Suppressing the Ku Klux Klan,* 213–14. For the confusion over the Marion mistake, see U.S. Marshal E. Perry Butts to A. J. Falls, chief clerk, Department of Justice, October 17, 1871, RG60, MC947, Reel 1, NA.

50. L. E. Johnson to Akerman, November 4, 1871, and Lewis Merrill to Akerman, November 27, 1871, RG60, MC947, Reel 1, NA.

51. David T. Corbin to Akerman, January 8, 1872, RG60, MC947, Reel 1, NA.

52. The chart is compiled from the following sources: Lewis Merrill to Edward Townsend, January 17, 1872, RG94, MC666, Reel 26, NA; *Annual Report of the Attorney General for 1871,* 42d Cong., 2d sess., H. Doc. 55 (Serial 1510); and *Message from the President of the United States,* 42d Cong., 2d sess., H. Doc. 268 (Serial 1515).

53. Louis Post, "A Carpetbagger in South Carolina," *Journal of Negro History* 10 (January 1925): 44–45.

54. *New York Evening Post,* quoted in *Army and Navy Journal,* November 18, 1871, 224.

55. Lewis Merrill to Edward Townsend, January 17, 1872, RG94, MC666, Reel 26, NA; Swinney, *Suppressing the Ku Klux Klan,* 232.

56. Mary Davis Brown, diary entry for November 18, 1871, Book 3, Mary Davis Brown Dairies, SCL.

57. Amos Akerman to David T. Corbin, November 10, 1871, RG60, MC701, Reel 3, NA; Swinney, *Suppressing the Ku Klux Klan,* 185, 194–99, 233; Trelease, *White Terror,* 406–7.

58. Corbin to Akerman, November 17 and 20, 1871, RG60, MC947, Reel 1, NA.

59. Corbin to Akerman, November 13, 1871, RG60, MC947, Reel 1, NA.

60. Akerman to B. D. Silliman, November 9, 1871, in Book 1, Amos Tappan Akerman Letterbooks, UVA.

61. Wade Hampton to Armistead Burt, October 22, 1871, Wade Hampton Papers, SCLRR, Duke; Circular on the Ku-Klux assessments, in Folder 1, Wallace-Gage Papers, SHC/UNC.

62. Mary Davis Brown, diary entry for December 1, 1871, Book 3, Mary Davis Brown Diaries, SCL.

63. *Charleston Courier,* November 25, 1871; Williams, "The Great South Carolina Ku Klux Klan Trials," 111–14.

64. Amos Akerman to David T. Corbin, December 6, 1871, in Book 1, Amos Tappan Akerman Letterbooks, UVA.

65. *Speech of the Honorable D. T. Corbin, U.S. District Attorney for So. Ca.,* in *Collected Pamphlets,* 11, SCL. For the most complete account of the trials available, see *Proceedings in the Ku Klux Trials, at Columbia, S.C. in the United States Circuit Court, November Term, 1871* (Columbia, S.C.: Republican Printing, 1872; New York: Negro Universities Press, 1969).

66. *Speech of the Honorable D. T. Corbin,* in *Collected Pamphlets,* 11, SCL; *Message from the President of the United States,* 42d Cong., 2d sess., H. Doc. 268 (Serial 1515), 3.

67. Amos Akerman, *Annual Report of the Attorney General,* 42d Cong., 2d sess., 1871, H. Doc. 55 (Serial 1510), 5.

68. Below *Message from the President of the United States,* 42d Cong., 2d sess., H. Doc. 268 (Serial 1515), 19.

69. Lewis Merrill to Adjutant General, Department of the South, September 23, 1872, "Annual Report of the Secretary of War for 1872," 42d Cong., 3d sess., H. Doc. 1 (Serial 1558), 90.

70. Post, "A Carpetbagger in South Carolina," *Journal of Negro History* 10 (January 1925): 65.

71. For the sentences delivered at the Columbia trials, in particular for *United States v. J. W. Avery et al.* and *United States v. Robert Hayes Mitchell et al.,* see *Proceedings in the Ku Klux Trials,* 765–87.

72. Sympathetic Southerner Francis B. Simkins believed that it was impossible for noble Southern gentry to take part in such atrocities: "One must lose complete faith in Southern chivalry," Simkins argued, "to believe that South Carolinians of standing could have committed the horrible crimes of which the Klan was actually guilty." See Simkins, "The Ku Klux Klan in South Carolina," *Journal of Negro History* 12 (1922) 618. One needs only to look at South Carolina's history of dealing with blacks to find Simkins's argument difficult to accept. For opinions on Klan leadership see George C. Rable, *But There Was No Peace: The Role of Violence in the Politics of Reconstruction* (Athens: University of Georgia Press, 1984), 94–95; and Michael W. Fitzgerald, *The Union League Movement in the Deep South: Politics and Agricultural Change during Reconstruction* (Baton Rouge: Louisiana State University Press, 1989), 216.

73. *Speech of the Honorable D. T. Corbin,* in *Collected Pamphlets,* 7–8, SCL.

74. Ann Eliza Marshall, "Reminiscences," in Joseph Warren Waldo Marshall Papers, SCLRR, Duke.

75. Attorney General George Williams to Secret Service Agent H. C. Whitely, August 2, 1872, RG60, MC699, Reel 14, NA; Williams to Alexander Stephens, September 16, 1872, RG60, MC699, Reel 14, NA; *New York Tribune,* December 28, 1871.

76. Robert Wallace Shand Journal, 145–46, SCL.

77. Mary Davis Brown, diary entries for October 15 and 16, 1871, in Book 3, Mary Davis Brown Diaries, SCL.

78. Marshal L. E. Johnson to Attorney General Amos Akerman, November 4, 1871, RG60, MC947, Reel 1, NA.

79. Lewis Merrill to Amos Akerman, November 13, December 10, 1871, RG60, MC947, Reel 1, NA. District Attorney David T. Corbin also knew of sev-

eral Klan leaders who had escaped, and he too wanted the Justice Department to pursue them. See Corbin to Akerman, November 13, 1871, RG60, MC947, Reel 1, NA.

80. J. Newton Lewis to Dr. John Anderson, November 30, 1871, in Box 7, Folder 96, Bratton Family Papers, SCL; Akerman to B. D. Silliman, November 9, 1871, in Book 1, Amos Tappan Akerman Letterbooks, UVA.

81. Akerman to Corbin, December 15, 1871, in Book 1, Amos Tappan Akerman Letterbooks, UVA. Historians continue to debate the reasons for Akerman's resignation. Akerman may have been prompted to resign because the administration no longer shared his gusto for enforcement. This theory is difficult to prove, as his replacement, George Williams—although having no background in civil rights enforcement—was a "radical" Republican who had a hand in much of the party's legislation, including the Reconstruction Act. Yet Williams readily followed the administration when it began dismantling the enforcement program in 1872. Other theories focus on Akerman's personality conflicts with more important cabinet members, such as Secretary of State Hamilton Fish, on problems generated by unfavorable Justice Department rulings against prominent railroads, and on the administration's desire to balance the cabinet "geographically" with a Westerner. For discussion of Akerman's resignation see William S. McFeely, *Grant: A Biography* (New York: W. W. Norton, 1981), 373–74, and McFeely, "Amos T. Akerman: The Lawyer and Racial Justice," in *Region, Race, and Reconstruction: Essays in Honor of C. Vann Woodward*, ed. J. Morgan Kousser and James M. McPherson (New York: Oxford University Press, 1982), 395–415; Kaczorowski, *The Politics of Judicial Interpretation*, 91–93; and Trelease, *White Terror*, 411.

82. Kaczorowski, *The Politics of Judicial Interpretation*, 93; Swinney, *Suppressing the Ku Klux Klan*, 182.

83. Amos Akerman to the Honorable J. R. Parrott, December 6, 1871, in Book 1, Amos Tappan Akerman Letterbooks, UVA.

84. Akerman to "Mr. Atkins," December 12, 1871, in Book 1, Amos Tappan Akerman Letterbooks, UVA.

85. Akerman to Benjamin Conley, December 28, 1871, in Book 1, Amos Tappan Akerman Letterbooks, UVA.

86. Shapiro, "The Ku Klux Klan during Reconstruction," *Journal of Negro History* 49 (January 1964): 46; Williamson, *After Slavery*, 266.

87. James E. Sefton, *The United States Army and Reconstruction, 1865–1877* (Baton Rouge: Louisiana State University Press, 1967), 226; Trelease, *White Terror*, 361.

88. Kaczorowski, *The Politics of Judicial Interpretation*, 93.

89. Eric Foner, *Reconstruction: America's Unfinished Revolution 1863–1877* (New York: Harper and Row, 1988), 458.

90. David T. Corbin to Amos Akerman, November 13, 1871, RG60, MC947, Reel 1, NA.

91. See *Proceedings in the Ku Klux Trials*, passim.

92. Winfield S. Harvey, diary entries for March 26, June 15, and July 28, 1871, Winfield S. Harvey Diary, in Edward Settle Godfrey Papers, Library of Congress, Washington, D.C.

93. Major Marcus A. Reno to Senator John Scott, chairman of congressional subcommittee investigating the condition of the South, September 6, 1871, RG60, MC947, Reel 1, NA.

94. David T. Corbin to Amos Akerman, December 3, 1871, RG60, MC947, Reel 1, NA.

95. Lewis Merrill to Edward Townsend, January 17, 1871, RG94, MC666, Reel 26, NA. For the South Carolina petition see *Joint Resolution of the Legislature of South Carolina, Asking That the Federal Troops Be Not Removed from That State,* 42d Cong., 2d sess., H. Doc. 160 (Serial 1526).

96. David T. Corbin to George Williams, quoted in *Message from the President of the United States,* 42d Cong., 2d sess., H. Doc. 268 (Serial 1515), 19; emphasis in original.

97. Charles Wright to Robert Scott, February 13, 1872, in Box 19, Folder 28, Governor Robert K. Scott Papers, SCDAH.

98. *Columbia Phoenix,* March 10, 1872.

99. The petition, addressed to the adjutant general of the Department of the South, is in *Message of the President Transmitting Statements on the Use of the Army in Certain of the Southern States,* 44th Cong., 2d sess., H. Doc. 30 (Serial 1755), 69. The petition is also located in RG94, MC666, Reel 63, NA.

100. Lewis Merrill to the assistant adjutant general, Department of the South, May 28, 1871, RG94, MC666, Reel 16, NA. Merrill also rearranged units because he was concerned that some of soldiers suffered from a "lack of sympathy with the wish of the Executive to execute the law." Merrill later reported on other difficulties regarding his troops, including too much drinking, bad manners, and "unduly frequent" desertions. He was sure that everything from access to liquor to the opportunity to desert was "encouraged and facilitated by Ku-Klux and their sympathizers." "No effort has been spared by these persons," he insisted, "to breed disaffection and dissatisfaction among the men." See Merrill's report in *Annual Report of the Secretary of War for 1872,* 42d Cong., 2d sess., 1872, H. Doc. 1 (Serial 1558), 86–87.

101. The resolution, as presented to Congress, is the *Joint Resolution of the Legislature of South Carolina, Asking that the Federal Troops Be Not Removed from That State,* 42d Cong., 2d sess., H. Doc. 160 (Serial 1526).

102. W. W. Davis to Robert Scott, June 2, 1872, in Box 20, Folder 44, Governor Robert K. Scott Papers, SCDAH.

103. David Corbin to Lewis Merrill, June 30, 1872, RG94, MC666, Reel 16, NA.

104. Corbin to George Williams, July 22, 1872, RG60, MC947, Reel, NA; Kaczorowski, *The Politics of Judicial Interpretation,* 107–9.

105. Lewis Merrill to the adjutant general, Department of the South, September 23, 1872; quoted in *Annual Report of the Secretary of War,* 42d Cong., 3d sess., 1872, H. Doc. 1 (Serial 1558), 91.

106. W. McKee Evans, "The Ku Klux Klan and the Conservative Triumph" (Paper delivered at the Pacific Coast Branch Meeting of the American Historical

Association, 1971); quoted in Herbert Shapiro, *White Violence and Black Response: From Reconstruction to Montgomery* (Amherst: University of Massachusetts Press, 1988), 14–15.

107. William Gillette, *Retreat from Reconstruction, 1869–1879* (Baton Rouge: Louisiana State University Press, 1979), 42–45, 55.

CHAPTER SIX

TRUCE AND CONSEQUENCES
FEDERAL RETREAT AND THE CONSERVATIVE RESURGENCE

> It is my individual opinion than nothing is more idle than to attempt to conciliate by kindness that portion of the Southern people who are still malcontent. They take all kindness on the part of the Government as evidence of timidity, and hence are emboldened to lawlessness by it.
> Attorney General Amos T. Akerman, Amos Tappan Akerman Letterbooks, Alderman Library, University of Virginia

I

The joint civil-military operation in 1871 represented the climax of the federal enforcement program in South Carolina—and in the South—and, in a way, the climax of Reconstruction itself. But serious questions remain about the success of this enforcement effort. Already by early 1872 the Klan had reappeared across portions of the Palmetto State. There was even more trouble on the horizon: in 1872 both the national and state Republican parties were racked by schisms. Most important for Carolinians—white and black—was the flagging federal interest in the enforcement of civil rights. Both Republicans and conservatives recognized that the national party and national government were cutting loose from the Southern imbroglio.

In the opening months of 1872, the government gave no indication of abandoning its enforcement effort. Civil and military officers of the federal government continued their sweep through the South Carolina upcountry. In late winter Major Lewis Merrill and District Attorney David T. Corbin had shifted their theater of operations from York, Spartanburg, and Union to concentrate on the counties of Newberry and Laurens.[1] The results were not very different from those achieved elsewhere; U.S. marshals apprehended a large number of suspects, but perhaps a larger number escaped. The *Laurensville Herald* estimated that five hundred men had fled Laurens County alone, fearful of implications in the riot of 1870 and other outrages.[2]

Enforcement in the courtroom showed only marginal improvement over that of the previous November. Republicans hoped that the Charleston court term would reiterate the message of enforcement and nip renewed violence in the bud. To a small extent, the April term was an improvement: the government secured eighteen convictions, as opposed to only four in November. But the earlier problems persisted, and the overcrowding on the docket grew worse as the arrest rate far outpaced the rate of trials and convictions. Corbin wrote to Attorney General Williams and Senator George Edmunds, trying to force some change in the court system, but Washington turned a deaf ear. Corbin even had difficulty procuring a capable stenographer; the man Williams sent to do the job never attended a day's proceedings, preferring to spend his days lying around drunk.[3]

Facing rising violence, overcrowded courts, and the escape of the most serious offenders, the government opted for a new tactic to shore up its flawed operation. Major Merrill had insisted in late 1871 that the government needed to pursue fugitives, and in 1872 other officials began pushing for the extradition of refugees.[4] But knowing their whereabouts was only half the battle, for extradition was no easy task. In late May, District Attorney Corbin sent marshals, with federal warrants, all the way to Arkansas to nab two high-ranking Klansmen. When authorities in the state refused to honor the warrants, a dumbfounded Corbin sought the intercession of the Attorney General.[5] There is no evidence that he was successful in the attempt.

The most famous extradition effort turned into such a fiasco it virtually ended the practice. As it had happened with the October crackdown as a whole, the capture of Dr. J. Rufus Bratton began with noble intentions, but an inability to foresee consequences lead to embarrassment and failure. Suspected as being leaders in the up-country Klan, Bratton and James W. Avery had escaped in late October to Ontario.[6] S. B. Cornell, a spy in the employ of Governor Robert K. Scott, had tracked Bratton to Canada, and in 1872 the federal government launched an operation to capture the fugitives. Secret Service agents took up positions in the post office, and one day in May they plucked Bratton off the street and tossed him into a passing coach. Agents covered Bratton's face with a handkerchief soaked in chloroform and smuggled him into Detroit, where they presented him with a warrant for his arrest. On June 10, Merrill reported to Attorney General Williams that Bratton was safely tucked away in the Yorkville jail.[7]

But like some omen foreshadowing the enforcement effort's embarrassing disintegration, Dr. Bratton got the last laugh. Upon discovering the "kidnapping," the Canadian government and the British minister lodged formal protests with Washington for a breach of national sovereignty. The Canadian government also began proceedings against local constables who had assisted the U.S. agents.[8] Secretary of State Hamilton Fish quickly backpedaled, and Attorney General Williams put the brakes on Bratton's prosecution in South Carolina. By the beginning of November, President Grant, Secretary of State Fish, and Attorney General Williams had all formally apologized to Canadian and British authorities, and Dr. J. Rufus Bratton was making his merry way back to Ontario. He returned, as did most others, following a general pardon a few years later.[9] As it was with other fugitives, Bratton's flight was involuntary and disruptive, but only a temporary nuisance that afforded the government no permanent results.

Waning support from Congress further hobbled the enforcement effort. Already by the spring of 1872, Congress had taken steps indicative of a new interest in conciliation and a desire for sectional rapprochement. Arch-radical Charles Sumner's civil rights bill had been watered-down, and then defeated, in the spring, while an amnesty bill had passed easily.[10] At the same time, Congress refused to extend the president's suspension of the habeas corpus in South Carolina, despite clear evidence that political violence was again on the increase. In his last annual report as attorney general, Amos Akerman had urged Congress to extend the suspension, and even hoped it could be applied on an *individual* basis to suspects who escaped from the "insurrectionary districts."[11] His plea, and those of state and federal officials in the Palmetto State, went unheeded, and the suspension of the privilege of habeas corpus expired in June.[12]

Republicans in South Carolina feared Congress's decision would exacerbate an already desperate situation. In early July, Major Merrill warned that "affairs are getting into a very bad condition, by reason of hopes excited by refusal of Congress to extend suspension of *habeas corpus*." There is a "belief," the major reported, that "all proceedings are to be abandoned": "If this impression is confirmed" by such signs as "the present inaction in pushing proceedings, there will most certainly be renewal of serious trouble before the election. It is vital to the interests of peace that there shall be no relaxation or appearance of it as yet."[13] Merrill stepped up his criticism after learning that, in order to cut costs, Attorney General Williams refused to hold an extra court term (which Corbin had requested earlier). Responding to Williams's decision that lawlessness could be punished in state courts, Merrill warned War Department officials that "it is idle to expect for a long time to come that the State laws will be enforced in any Ku-Klux cases." Experience prior to the crackdown had proven that state courts were not a viable option; "I doubt the possibility," Merrill said, "of bringing any offender to justice before the state courts."[14] Merrill admitted to his commanding officer that his earlier optimism concerning peace was "premature" and that a spirit of rebellion still pervaded the state; "either through ignorance or prejudice or both combined," Merrill wrote, "the majority of whites here learn but little by experience."[15]

Despite the cavalry officer's admonitions, the government continued to coax rather than coerce. In September, Merrill learned that Attorney General Williams was considering a more selective prosecution system and planned on reducing prison sentences. Merrill sent a frantic plea to Williams, pointing out that a selective system was already under way, too few suspects had been tried, and of those only a smattering had been convicted. Hundreds of suspects were out on bail, living at home and going about their everyday business, unpunished for their crimes! "The causes from which Ku Kluxism sprung are still potent for evil," Merrill told the Attorney General. "The blind, unreasoning, bigoted hostility to the results of the war is only smothered, not appeased or destroyed," he continued, "and whenever there appears anything which can be construed into weakness or releasing of purpose in enforcing that protection the head of the snake may be instantly seen."[16]

District Attorney Corbin also warned his superior about a policy that might encourage lawlessness. Corbin informed Williams that the Klan was still alive, "clinging together" in the up-country counties. Corbin believed that "there still remains . . . much of the feeling and sentiment which has heretofore, and could hereafter, under favorable circumstances, become developed, into Ku Klux organizations." As he had done many times in the past, the district attorney urged the attorney general to call new court terms and pleaded with him to avoid discharging cases already on the docket. Like his military colleague, Corbin wanted to hold and try all offenders, believing that only severe punishment would bring peace to the state.[17]

Yet the federal government continued to disengage from both South Carolina and civil rights enforcement. The first cavalry companies had begun leaving the state in March 1872, even though violence was on the rise. In June, the House of Representatives had refused to extend the habeas corpus suspension, and it expired later that month. In September and October, Attorney General Williams reviewed the cases for prisoners convicted under the enforcement acts and notified Amos Pilsbury, the Superintendent of the Albany Penitentiary, of reductions to be made in prisoners' sentences.[18]

Williams went further, and actually ordered the curtailment of enforcement activities in South Carolina. The attorney general examined the files of persons awaiting trial, as well as the petitions and pleas for clemency that accompanied them. Beginning in October, Williams interceded directly for individual suspects, often ordering Corbin to close a case or release a suspect. For example, John A. Leland had been arrested in March for his involvement in the Laurens riot of 1870. After reviewing the case, in which a grand jury had indicted Leland for murder and conspiracy, Williams told Corbin to "let the case pass along the docket without trial."[19]

By the close of the circuit court's November 1872 term, the statistics appeared as follows:

Term	Convicted	Pleaded Guilty	Acquitted
Fall '71	4	54	1
Spring '72	18	18	1
Fall '72	3	4	1

Corbin tallied that of the 1,355 indictments, the government convicted 27 men, while 75 pled guilty, 5 were acquitted, and 54 cases fell *nolle prosequi*.[20] Two weeks later, at the year's end, Attorney General Williams counted 1,207 cases pending under the enforcement acts, while only 96 cases had been terminated since prosecution began in 1870.[21] Regardless of the tally, the message was the same. The government could not complete the prosecutions, and it had no intention of trying.

With prosecutions dwindling and new arrests at a standstill (ever since the habeas corpus suspension had expired), the War Department happily stepped up its withdrawal of troops from the state. Cavalry units were required out West as the Indian Wars grew in intensity. Two more companies of the Seventh Cavalry left in December 1872, leaving only six in January 1873. By March 1873, all of the Seventh Cavalry would be out West, serving in the Department of the Dakota.[22]

II

While the federal government's policy worried state Republicans, two other developments also indicated a breakdown of the war consensus, that "North versus South" and "Republican versus Democrat" polarity that had underwritten many achievements. These events were the Liberal Republican movement and a parallel Republican schism in South Carolina. But in the face of opportunity, state conservatives remained cautious and largely aloof. White Carolinians played only a minor role in the state and national elections of 1872, abstaining from the polls to avoid driving rival Republican wings together. Many conservatives believed their participation in 1870 had been wasted, so leaders decided on a policy of watchful waiting. Even violence abated as the election neared; aggression was more to probe federal sentiment than topple the state government, and whites avoided backing the Grant administration into a corner.

The split in the national Republican party grew in part out of the stresses of Reconstruction and the controversies it spawned. The "reformers" who broke away in the spring of 1872 to create the Liberal Republican party stood for honesty and liberty in the broadest sense. Although Southerners cheered the Liberal Republican's bitter denunciations of the corruption associated with the Grant administration, the new party's pro-conciliation stance was its most appealing feature. Reformers targeted Southern Republicans—noted for their corruption and their selective legislation—and criticized the continuance of anti-Southern policies which only hindered national healing and economic prosperity. Following the precepts of "new thinking" founded upon the nascent principles of "natural law" and "laissez-faire," these "best men" moved away from artificial, made-man devices which disrupted the natural order of things. To a Liberal Republican, this represented the most good for the best people. To a Southerner, this represented redemption and home rule.[23]

Liberal Republicans chose *New York Tribune* editor Horace Greeley to oppose Grant and the regular Republicans. Greeley was a national figure, a man whose eclectic past might make him the best candidate—or the worst. Although an early Radical, Greeley had openly opposed confiscation in the South and favored allowing former Confederates into local and state governments to ease the transition to civil rule. Yet at the same time, Greeley was an outspoken critic of the Ku Klux Klan and called for severe enforcement measures. Also important for Southerners—Republicans and Democrats—was the fact that Greeley had no patience for the corruption and fraud characteristic of Southern Republican regimes. Such practices alienated the local population and ruined the chance for the outside investment that was necessary for regional and national growth.[24]

Although Northern Democrats did not find Greeley's sudden about-face entirely convincing, their options were limited. The Democratic party could run an independent ticket, but by 1872, recent defeats and demographic realities had forced the party to think pragmatically. Since 1870, Northern Democrats had embarked on their own "New Departure," not unlike the policy followed by the ill-fated Union Reformers in South Carolina in 1870. Moving away from issues of race, New Departure Democrats focused on economics, sectional conciliation, and corruption in an effort to win votes and shed old baggage. The party had finally accepted the Fourteenth Amendment and, after failing to defeat the Fifteenth Amendment, turned its attention to less divisive issues. Similarly, although many Democrats agonized over supporting a man who spent most of his life assailing them, they had little choice if they wanted to defeat Grant. The July Democratic National Convention, with its banners pushing reform instead of racism, endorsed the Greeley ticket and the entire Liberal Republican platform.[25]

Partly as a result of the devastating defeat of the Union Reform ticket in 1870 and a wariness about conciliation and cooperation, few South Carolina whites supported Greeley. Following the maxim that "the enemy of my enemy is my friend," some conservatives saw Greeley as "an instrument in the hands of Providence to work out our destiny in the path of virtue and peace." As T. P. Bailey put it, the "South had almost better vote for Satan himself rather than allow Grant to be reelected."[26] Such prominent men as Benjamin F. Perry and Matthew C. Butler took the stump for Greeley and called on voters to take a stand on the "question of liberty, of local government, of civil as against military rule."[27] Although most county committees seemed indifferent, a few counties held campaign meetings in the summer, and some endorsed the Greeley ticket.[28]

State conservatives did send a delegation to the Democratic convention in Baltimore, but many leading conservatives disagreed with the decision to participate. At first Wade Hampton had written that "it would be folly for the Dem. Con. to place a ticket in the field, as our only hope to defeat Grant is in supporting the Liberal nominations." "Of course," Hampton continued, "we hope that Greeley's letter of acceptance will be satisfactory, and that he will above all avoid all reference to 'Civil Rights.'"[29] Upon further consideration, Hampton lobbied against a delegation, announcing that "our true policy is to abstain altogether from all participation in the next National Democratic Convention."[30] Thomas Magrath agreed, arguing that South Carolina should not even attend the convention. Since Southern delegates could not exert any real power, and the

Northern party would bear the brunt of the election, Northern delegates alone should decide on the platform and candidates.[31]

Oddly enough, the state elections of 1872 generated scarcely more enthusiasm. As it had done in 1870, the state Republican party split, with a bolt by "reformers" who challenged the regular Republicans. For state voters, the issues were the same as those in the national election, corruption and honesty in government; and, as in the national election, South Carolina's conservatives played a conspicuously small part.

In the two years since Governor Scott's reelection, the divisions in the state Republican party had only deepened. The reforms promised by Scott never materialized, and the fraud and swindling only grew worse. Party in-fighting reached a climax in December 1871, when, at the height of the Ku-Klux crackdown, members of Scott's own party tried to impeach him and his treasurer, Niles G. Parker. One legislator claimed that Scott survived the narrow vote by bribing members of the General Assembly![32]

The state Republican convention assembled on August and furnished the blow which formally divided the party. Incumbent Governor Scott had given a half-hearted nod to former Speaker Franklin J. Moses, Jr., a native white from an old Jewish Carolina family who was deeply involved with some of the administration's most notorious deals.[33] Late in the afternoon on August 22, Moses secured the nomination, with Richard H. Gleaves, a black lawyer from Pennsylvania and former state legislator, selected to run as lieutenant governor. Upon hearing the vote, former governor James L. Orr, now a delegate from Anderson, walked out of the convention. Moses's close relationship to Scott, and his well-known affinity for "perks," indicated that no reform would be forthcoming from his administration. Nearly a third of the delegates left the convention and followed Orr back to his hotel.[34]

The bolting delegates reconvened on August 23 at the Richland County Courthouse. Prominent faces included B. F. Whittemore, Christopher Columbus Bowen, William J. Whipper, and even District Attorney David T. Corbin. Their nominee for governor was Reuben Tomlinson, the Pennsylvania Quaker who had served as superintendent of education under the Freedmen's Bureau. James H. Hayne, a native black schoolteacher from Barnwell, was the nominee for lieutenant governor. The bolters, like their national counterparts, stressed "reform and retrenchment," but they *did not* endorse the Liberal Republican ticket and instead promoted Grant and the regular Republicans, just as the Moses ticket did.[35]

The similarity did not end there. Neither faction sought alliance with state conservatives, a stance which was just fine with Carolina whites. Reform nominee Tomlinson was heard to say that "we have not now, and will not make any alliance with the Democratic Party."[36] Nor did the regular Republicans seek to bolster their position by recruiting conservative numbers. Conservatives decided to settle back and watch Republicans do battle with themselves. On August 27, the Conservative Executive Committee met in Columbia and decided to abstain from the gubernatorial contest.[37] Conservatives declined to formally endorse either Republican ticket, and offered no third alternative. Corruption was not the overriding issue; home rule and racial control were priorities, and leading whites had discarded the 1870 notion that support for one side would further white goals (although failure here would force yet another shift later). "We shall support neither," declared the *Orangeburg Times*. "We have a preference for both party and color," the editorial stated, "[but] a cowardly policy of temporary self-degradation to prostitute their sacred rights of ballot, we never shall, nay, never can believe." "Self-respect is the virtue of life," the author contended, "and the man who once bows his neck to the yoke, will ever after carry the bend of the neck though the weight be taken off."[38] The *Charleston News* had the same advice, "if we cannot vote for those worthy of our suffrage, we will not vote at all."[39] As at the national level, an independent ticket was out of the question, for it might drive the warring Republican factions into one another's arms. In the words of the *Aiken Journal*, if the Democratic party were to organize, "all schisms in the ranks of the Radicals would at once be healed."[40]

In the first violence-free election of Reconstruction, the regular Republicans were victorious at both the state and national levels. Since conservatives had no candidate in the field, there was no reason for terrorism or intimidation—further evidence of the overwhelmingly political nature of the lawlessness. As in 1870, state Republicans withstood a reformer's challenge, and Franklin J. Moses, Jr., became governor with 69,838 votes to Reuben Tomlinson's 36,533. As in previous elections, the midlands and the heavily black low county allowed the regular Republicans to carry the day. The count showed that in 1872, over 30,000 fewer votes were cast than in 1870—a fact reflecting the policy of abstention followed by white conservatives.[41] Richard Carpenter, the Union Reform candidate in 1870, had garnered 51,537 votes, over 15,000 more than Tomlinson. The bolter's poor showing in 1872 allowed the regular Republicans to sweep the congressional positions and most of the county offices.[42] At the national level, Grant and the regular Republicans crushed Horace Greeley and the Liberal Republican movement, with South Carolina going overwhelmingly for Grant. As in the state elections, the South Carolina's total turnout was low; one historian has estimated that 40,000 registered voters abstained.[43]

Aside from ushering in yet another Republican government, the election also brought about a significant change in conservative sentiment. Although many whites eschewed participation out of a sense of honor or out of spite, many had nonetheless harbored hopes that at least the "lesser of two evils" might be elected. Another victory by the regular Republicans—who retained the loyalty of black voters—discredited any cooperation policy. In 1870 and 1872 the results had been the same, despite different conservative approaches—cooperation and abstention. Consequently, both strategies were thrown into disarray.[44]

A shift in sentiment was immediately apparent. After receiving word in Baltimore that Moses had been elected governor, Wade Hampton delivered a speech that all but called his fellow Southerners to unfurl their flags and pick up their guns. Hampton enjoined his brethren, "by the graves of your fathers, by your duty to your children, by the love of all these noble women who will share your fate, by all the hallowed memories of the past, by all the sacred duties of the present, by all your dearest hopes for the future, to dedicate yourselves to the redemption of the South." Dredging up an allusion from the classics, Hampton claimed that when barbarians had invaded Rome, one centurion had halted the panic by telling a soldier, "Plant your colors; we will remain here." "So be it with us!!" shouted Hampton; "The South now, the South forever!"[45] Similarly, the *Fairfield Herald* called on whites to stand against "the hell-born policy which has trampled the fairest and noblest States of our great sisterhood beneath the unholy hoofs of African savages and shoulder-strapped brigands—the policy which has given up millions of our free-born, high-souled brethern and sisters—to the rule of gibbering, louse-eating, devil-worshipping, barbarians, from the jungles of Dahomey, and peripetetic buccaneers from Cape Cod, Memphremagog, Hell, and Boston."[46]

III

Grant's victory may have meant that white intransigence and black safety in the South still stirred Northern interest. But the opposite may have also been the case. Republican voters may have been indicating their support for the administration's more recent—meaning more moderate—stance on enforcement activities. Perhaps convinced of the latter, the administration persisted in abandoning a progressive civil rights policy.

The removal of federal soldiers from South Carolina clearly indicated the waning of enforcement enthusiasm. Most cavalry units had already departed the state in 1872, and the remaining ones—three companies in all—followed in March 1873.[47] Learning beforehand of the withdrawal of the last cavalry companies, the General Assembly passed a resolution declaring that the transfer would be "detrimental to the permanent establishment and maintenance of law and order."[48] General-in-Chief William T. Sherman countered that the cavalry was required on the frontier "for defense of life and property"; Congress and the Grant administration concurred. Ten companies of the Eighteenth Infantry remained in the state, but with the exception of one company at Newberry and one at Yorkville, they were located in major cites, such as Greenville, Columbia, and Charleston, and were not deployed around the state to keep the peace.[49] Federal officials may have inwardly agreed with the *Charleston News and Courier,* which sarcastically commented on the lack of state power: "Is it not a cowardly act to admit that the whole State Government of South Carolina is incompetent to maintain the public security and preserve the public peace?"[50]

Cowardly as it was, state Republicans had to admit that their government lacked the wherewithal to control violence. Even though political assaults and illegal bands had resurfaced while troops were in the state, Republicans believed the military's presence was necessary to prevent the destruction of the party or even all-out war. In March, just after the last cavalry units had departed, S. E. Lane of Chesterfield told Governor Franklin J. Moses of a "state of things in our County as reported to me that is alarming." Instead of being destroyed, Lane argued, the Klan had "grown defiant." "The withdrawal of U.S. Troops, I fear, will prove disastrous," Lane continued, for "intimidation is daily practiced" with "leading K.K.s" stirring up the whites and recruiting new members.[51] Henry Wall, the sheriff of Edgefield, argued that without a "sufficient number of United States Soldiers," he would be "totally unable to execute" the law.[52]

Help was not forthcoming from the Justice Department either, since its policy really drove the troop withdrawal. After a year and a half of prosecutions, the government had dispensed with only a sliver of the cases on the docket. Like their War Department counterparts, Justice officials—caught between conflicting emotions on the uselessness of their mission and the idyllic hope that they had in fact succeeded—believed men and money could be better used elsewhere. In April of 1873, Attorney General George Williams effectively ended the government's short-lived and poorly fought war on the Klan by suspending all cases already carrying indictments.

In South Carolina, over 1,000 Enforcement Act cases never made it to the courtroom. The government convicted 4 men in 1873, but dismissed 540 cases. In 1874, there were no convictions, but 555 dismissals. By 1877, 162 men had been convicted, but approximately 1,233 cases had been dismissed.[53] In July of 1873, Williams had permitted all refugees from the state to return to their homes without fear of prosecution.[54] The attorney general also restricted arrests to "flagrant cases of murder" and even chastised District Attorney Corbin for arresting individuals suspected of lesser crimes.⁵⁵ By the end of 1874—only three years since the "crackdown" began—the last convicted Ku Klux left prison; all other men had been pardoned, had their sentences shortened, or had already served their terms.

Even before this "retreat" policy was complete, however, it was evident that the attempt to cajole recalcitrant rebels into good behavior was a wasted effort. The Klan, and the spirit supporting it, had not been crushed, and as an editorial in the *South Carolinian* put it, "it is but a question of time how long it will take the prostrate figure to rise in its former strength, and resume its broken sceptre."⁵⁶ "The South has Tried Cringing and Fawning Long Enough!" cried the *Chester Reporter*. Shunning conciliation, the paper claimed that "whatever the politicians seeking place may say, the heart of the people is as true now to that cause for which they gave and suffered so much as it was when the colors of the South were floating most bravely."⁵⁷ "THE PEOPLE," declared the *Edgefield Advertiser*, "the long-suffering patient but OMNIPOTENT PEOPLE—will ere long rally around the glorious banner of 'STATE SOVEREIGNTY, WHITE SUPREMACY, AND A UNIVERSAL OVERTHROW OF USURPERS AND THIEVES,'" and sweep the "nigger-exalting, state destroying . . . mob o'liars to a figurative hell . . . THE PEOPLE ARE MOVING!"⁵⁸ One contributor reminded readers of the utter failure of conciliation and cooperation. All attempts to win over blacks "have proved futile," he stated, and "there is no use in attempting to disguise the fact, the blacks *will not* cast in their lot with us." The alternative was clear: "We must make the political issue an *issue of races*. We must *vote* for A. B. *because* he is a white man, simply and nothing more, provided, always, he be honest and capable."⁵⁹

About this time, in the fall of 1873, Henry Hayne, the black secretary of state, enrolled in the medical school of South Carolina University. White reaction, petty in comparison to the terror of the Klan, nonetheless symbolized their desire to preserve a racist, supremacist society. Leading whites noted that "a wise regard for the welfare of the University had, until now, prevented that attempt at a mixing of the whites and blacks which must destroy any institution" by forcing out intelligent whites. Prominent conservatives pleaded with Republican state officials, arguing that since blacks had their own state-sponsored university, there was no reason to admit Hayne. Nevertheless, Hayne took his place at the school, prompting nearly the entire faculty and student body to depart (the second time this had happened; the university closed in 1861 when the entire student body and most of the faculty volunteered for military service).⁶⁰ Most students went so far as to erase their names from the "roll of honor" kept by the school, to avoid any connection with the establishment.[61] The *Edgefield Advertiser* summed up the event (and white views on Reconstruction in general): "The laws of God and of Nature cannot be changed or abrogated by the edict of a carpet-bag administration."[62]

The Hayne affair, and white's uncompromising approach to it, reiterated the central themes of South Carolina history. Whites demanded the right to control "their" society and "their" blacks, and reacted emotionally—and even violently—to any threat to this domination. In the mid-1870s, as the Republican party both inside and outside of the state struggled to remain intact and the issues of Reconstruction became less pressing, Carolina conservatives sensed that their day might be approaching. Cooperationalists, although discredited, saw new opportunities to divide and conquer, while those who favored a more violent strategy believed the time had come for a fight to the finish. By 1874, only one thing seemed clear—that Republicans in South Carolina were on their own.

Notes

1. Andrew Cornish to James Hamilton Cornish, April 10, 1872, in Box 3, Folder 37, John Hamilton Cornish Papers, Southern Historical Collection, University of North Carolina, Chapel Hill, N.C. (hereafter SHC/UNC); *Edgefield Advertiser*, April 18, 1872.

2. *Laurensville Herald*, April 12, 1872.

3. David T. Corbin to George Williams, January 27, February 10, 1872, in Record Group 60, Microcopy 947, Reel 1, National Archives, Washington, D.C. (hereafter RG, MC, Reel, NA); Corbin to Justice Department Chief Clerk A. J. Falls, April 18, 1872, RG60, MC947, Reel 1, NA. Corbin sent the chief clerk reports on the April trials nearly every other day. See Corbin to Falls, April 18, 20, 23, 25, 26, 29, and May 1, 5, 1872, RG60, M947, Reel 1, NA.

4. See for instance Major W. Harry Brown to U.S. Marshal R. M. Wallace, April 13, 1872, and Wallace to Attorney General George Williams, April 19, 1872, RG60, MC947, Reel 1, NA.

5. David T. Corbin to George Williams, June 1, 1872, RG60, MC947, Reel 1, NA.

6. Dr. J. Rufus Bratton—suspected of taking part in the murder of militia captain Jim Williams and of being a leader of the York County Klan—had escaped to Ontario. Friends in South Carolina kept him informed of court proceedings and military movements through the fall and spring. Included in the letters from "C. D. Melton" and "T. L. J." are warnings about the danger of replying, and advice to "keep out of the public eye." See C. D. Melton to Bratton, December 14, 1871, in Folder 96, and "T. L. J." to Bratton, January 23, 1872, in Folder 97, Bratton Family Papers, South Caroliniana Library, University of South Carolina, Columbia, S.C. (hereafter SCL).

7. *Edgefield Advertiser,* June 20, 1872; "Truth" [author], *Statement of Dr. Bratton's Case Being an Explanation of the Ku-Klux Prosecutions in the Southern States* (London, Ont.: "Free Press" Steam Book and Job Printing, 1872), 18, SCL-BD; Major Lewis Merrill to George Williams, June 10, 1872, RG6O, MC947, Reel 1, NA.

8. *Rock Hill Lantern,* July 20, 1872; quoted in *Edgefield Advertiser,* July 25, 1872.

9. George Williams to Hamilton Fish, November 2, 1872, RG60, MC702, Reel 2, NA; David T. Corbin to George Williams, November 5, 1872, RG60, MC947, Reel 2, NA.

10. Eric Foner, *Reconstruction, 1873–1877: America's Unfinished Revolution* (New York: Harper and Row, 1988), 504–5.

11. Amos Akerman, *Annual Report of the Attorney General for 1871,* 42d Cong., 2d sess., H. Doc. 55 (Serial 1510), 6.

12. The decision not to renew the suspension, and the reasons for that decision, are the subject of a seminar paper completed by the author for Michael Les Benedict in 1989. "Congress and the Habeas Corpus Suspension Bill: A Study of Influences on the Congressional Decision-Making Process" revealed that many Republicans acted out of a concern for their party and their seats when they voted against the bill. Success or failure against the Klan was secondary to protecting the party from charges of corruption, class legislation, and tyranny, especially in light of the Liberal Republican Bolt and the campaign of 1872.

13. Lewis Merrill to Edward Townsend, July 11, 1872, RG60, MC947, Reel 1, NA.

14. Merrill to the adjutant general, Department of the South, September 23, 1872; quoted in *Annual Report of the Secretary of War for 1872,* 42d Cong., 3d sess., H. Doc. 1 (Serial 1558), 89, 90.

15. Merrill to the adjutant general, Department of the South, September 23, 1872; quoted in *Annual Report of the Secretary of War for 1872,* 89.

16. Merrill to George Williams, September 30, 1872, RG60, MC947, Reel 1, NA.

17. Corbin to Williams, November 2, 1872, RG60, MC947, Reel 2, NA.

18. Williams to Amos Pilsbury, October 21, 1872, RG60, MC699, Reel 14, NA.

19. Corbin to Williams, November 21, 1872, RG60, MC947, Reel 2, NA; Williams to Corbin, November 26, 1872, RG60, MC701, Reel 3, NA.

20. These numbers do not add up to those in the chart, which are also taken from Corbin's report. Attorney General Williams's figures do not match the total listings either, but the slight difference is irrelevant; the fact remains that a vast majority of cases never came to trial. See Corbin to Williams, December 15, 1872, RG60, MC947, Reel 2, NA.

21. *Annual Report of the Attorney General for 1872,* 42d Cong., 3d sess., S. Doc. 32 (Serial 1545), 11, 36.

22. General Orders No. 2, U.S. War Department, February 8, 1873, RG391, MC744, Reel 71, NA.

23. Michael Les Benedict, "Reform Republicans and the Retreat from Re-

construction," in *The Facts of Reconstruction: Essays in Honor of John Hope Franklin,* ed. Eric Anderson and Alfred A. Moss (Baton Rouge: Louisiana State University Press, 1991), 54, 56–58. The best book-length examinations are John G. Sproat, *"The Best Men": Liberal Reformers in the Gilded Age* (New York: Oxford University Press, 1970); and Earle Dudley Ross, *The Liberal Republican Movement* (New York: n.p., 1919).

24. Foner, *Reconstruction: America's Unfinished Revolution,* 502–5.

25. William Gillette, *Retreat from Reconstruction, 1869–1879* (Baton Rouge: Louisiana State University Press, 1979), 62, 70; Michael Perman, *The Road to Redemption: Southern Politics, 1869–1879* (Chapel Hill: University of North Carolina Press, 1984), 10, 19–20; Foner, *Reconstruction: America's Unfinished Revolution,* 505–6.

26. T. P. Bailey to Thomas Jefferson McKie, May 29, 1872, Thomas Jefferson McKie Papers, Special Collections Library Research Room, Perkins Library, Duke University, Durham, N.C.

27. *Greenville Enterprise,* August 7, 1872; quoted in the *Edgefield Advertiser,* August 15, 1872.

28. Ellison Keitt to [unknown], June 5, 1872, in Ellison Summerfield Keitt Papers, SCL.

29. Wade Hampton to John Mullaly, May 19, 1872, in Box 5, Folder 87, Hampton Family Papers, SCL; see also Charles Cauthen, ed., *Family Letters of the Three Wade Hamptons, 1782–1901* (Columbia: University of South Carolina Press, 1953), 143–44.

30. Letter of Wade Hampton, dated September 9, 1872, printed in issue 19 of *Southern Home* [date not found]; in Ellison Summerfield Keitt Papers, SCL.

31. *Edgefield Advertiser,* May 30, 1872.

32. Francis Butler Simkins and Robert Hilliard Woody, *South Carolina during Reconstruction* (Chapel Hill: University of North Carolina Press, 1932), 465; *Charleston Courier,* December 28, 1871; Allegedly, Senator "Honest John" Patterson took $48,000 from the "Armed Force Fund" and used it to swing votes among members in the General Assembly. One account even claimed that Robert B. Elliott—who had once resigned from the cabinet due to corruption—alone received $10,500. See *Report of the Joint Investigating Committee on Public Frauds and the Election of John J. Patterson to the U.S. Senate* (Columbia, S.C.: Calvo and Patton, State Printers, 1878), 7:7–8; hereafter cited as *Report on Public Frauds.*

33. Simkins and Woody, *South Carolina during Reconstruction,* 465–66.

34. John S. Reynolds, *Reconstruction in South Carolina, 1865–1877* (Columbia, S.C.: State Company, 1905), 222–25.

35. *Reconstruction in South Carolina,* 224–25; Simkins and Woody, *South Carolina during Reconstruction,* 466; Roger P. Leemhuis, *James L. Orr and the Sectional Conflict* (Washington, D.C.: University Press of America, 1979), 159–61. For a full treatment of the bolt, see Robert H. Woody, "The South Carolina Reform Movements of 1870 and 1872" (Master's thesis, Duke University, 1928).

36. *Charleston Courier,* August 24, 1872; quoted in Simkins and Woody, *South Carolina during Reconstruction,* 466.

37. *Charleston News,* August 29, 1872.

38. *Orangeburg Times*, n.d.; quoted in the *Edgefield Advertiser,* October 3, 1872.
39. *Charleston News*, n.d.; quoted in the *Edgefield Advertiser,* October 10, 1872.
40. *Aiken Journal*, n.d.; quoted in the *Edgefield Advertiser,* August 8, 1872.
41. Simkins and Woody, *South Carolina during Reconstruction*, 468.
42. Perman, *The Road to Redemption*, 122, 298.
43. Reynolds, *Reconstruction in South Carolina*, 226.
44. Foner, *Reconstruction: America's Unfinished Revolution*, 510–11.
45. Wade Hampton, quoted in *Edgefield Advertiser,* November 7, 1872.
46. *Fairfield Herald*, November 20, 1872.
47. Many men of the Seventh Cavalry had looked forward to the transfer to the Department of the Dakota. Tired of law enforcement—which usually meant patrolling now and then, and little else—troopers wanted to fight Indians out West. Unfortunately they got their wish. Many of the men who had served in South Carolina died in 1876 at the Battle of the Little Bighorn with Colonel (Brevet General) George Armstrong Custer (see RG391, MC744, Reel 71, NA, and RG94, MC665, Reel 194, NA). Not all troopers left the state in 1873; Major Lewis Merrill stayed behind at the request of District Attorney Corbin. See David T. Corbin to George Williams, February 14, 1873, RG60, MC947, Reel 2, NA; and Williams to William W. Belknap, February 18, 1873, RG60, MC702, Reel 2, NA.
48. The resolution is in RG94, MC666, Reel 104, NA, and is printed as *Resolution of the Legislature of South Carolina, Remonstrating Against the Withdrawal of the United States Troops from That State,* 42d Cong., 3d sess., S. Doc. 81 (Serial 1546).
49. *The Annual Report of the Secretary of War for 1873,* 43d Cong., 1st sess., H. Doc. 1 (Serial 1597), 36, 48–49.
50. *Charleston News and Courier,* February 12, 1873.
51. S. E. Lane to Franklin J. Moses, Jr., March 15, 1873, in Box 3, Folder 11, Governor Moses Papers, South Carolina Department of Archives and History, Columbia, S.C. (hereafter SCDAH).
52. Henry Wall to Moses, October 16, 1873, in Box 5, Folder 30, Governor Moses Papers, SCDAH.
53. For these statistics see *Annual Report of the Attorney General for 1873,* 43d Cong., 1st sess., H. Doc. 6 (Serial 1606), 28; *Annual Report of the Attorney General for 1874,* 43d Cong., 2d sess., H. Doc. 7 (Serial 1638), 27.
54. Allen W. Trelease, *White Terror: The Ku Klux Klan Conspiracy and Southern Reconstruction* (New York: Harper and Row, 1971), 417.
55. In fact Attorney General Williams reacted angrily in the spring of 1874 when he learned that arrests had been made in York County. Williams questioned Corbin as to "how it is that my instructions not to make arrests of persons charged with offenses of this kind, except in flagrant cases of murder, have been disregarded." The district attorney assured the attorney general that no more arrests would occur and that he would officially "discontinue, at the coming [April 1874] term of the Circuit Court, most of the indictments against K.K.'s." See George

Williams to David T. Corbin, March 17, 1874, RG60, MC701, Reel 4, NA; and Corbin to Williams, March 28, 1874, RG60, MC947, Reel 2, NA.

56. *South Carolinian,* quoted in the *Edgefield Advertiser,* May 29, 1873.
57. *Chester Reporter,* quoted in the *Edgefield Advertiser,* September 4, 1873.
58. *Edgefield Advertiser,* October 16, 1873; emphasis in original.
59. *Edgefield Advertiser,* September 4, 1873; emphasis in original.
60. *Charleston News and Courier,* October 9, 1873.
61. Edward King, *The Great South* (Hartford, Conn.: American Publishing, 1875; Arno Press, 1969), 462.
62. *Edgefield Advertiser,* October 23, 1873. In response to the great exodus from South Carolina University, the state legislature hired Northern professors, abolished tuition, and created a preparatory program for incoming students. The white reaction brought about what they had feared, for the student body at the formerly all-white school became dominated by blacks. Foner, *Reconstruction: America's Unfinished Revolution,* 368.

Benjamin F. Perry. Portrait by W. G. Brown, owned by Mrs. Sam Baker, Montgomery, Alabama. Reproduced in Lillian Kibler, *Benjamin F. Perry, South Carolina Unionist* (Durham, N.C.: Duke University Press, 1946). Photograph courtesy of the South Caroliniana Library, University of South Carolina.

A. P. Aldrich. Courtesy of the South Caroliniana Library, University of South Carolina.

Wade Hampton III. Courtesy of the South Caroliniana Library, University of South Carolina.

James L. Orr. Courtesy of the South Caroliniana Library, University of South Carolina.

Matthew C. Butler. Courtesy of the South Caroliniana Library, University of South Carolina.

Robert K. Scott. Photograph from *South Carolina during Reconstruction,* by Francis B. Simkins and Robert H. Woody (1966). Courtesy of the South Caroliniana Library, University of South Carolina.

Alonzo Ransier. From the Collections of the Avery Research Center for African American History and Culture, College of Charleston, Charleston, South Carolina.

Francis L. Cardoza. From the Collections of the Avery Research Center for African American History and Culture, College of Charleston, Charleston, South Carolina.

Daniel H. Chamberlain. Reproduced in Walter Allen, *Governor Chamberlain's Administration in South Carolina: A Chapter of Reconstruction in the Southern States* (New York: B. P. Putnam's Sons, 1888). Photograph courtesy of the South Caroliniana Library, University of South Carolina.

Martin Witherspoon Gary. Courtesy of the South Caroliniana Library, University of South Carolina.

Johnson Hagood. Courtesy of the South Caroliniana Library, University of South Carolina.

The State House in Columbia, circa 1887. Courtesy of the South Caroliniana Library, University of South Carolina.

Wade Hampton calming the crowd outside the State House in 1876. *Leslie's Illustrated,* December 16, 1876. Reprint courtesy of the South Caroliniana Library, University of South Carolina.

CHAPTER SEVEN

THE TIDE TURNS
REPUBLICAN ISOLATION
AND DEMOCRATIC MOBILIZATION

> Good government indeed was now restored in our State, and by their assistance could be maintained. But it was not a government under their own auspices, or those of the democratic party; and while it continued they could hope neither to be heard at Washington nor to practice their cherished traditions at home.
>
> Belton O'Neal Townsend on South Carolina
> under Governor Daniel Chamberlain, *Atlantic Monthly*

I

In the mid-1870s, Republican and Democratic fortunes seemed to exchange trajectories on some "political effectiveness" chart. Northern—and federal—interest in the South was on the wane, and the Republican party at the state and national levels was having severe internal problems. South Carolina Republicans still held the reins of command, but their power—specifically their ability to enforce law and bring order—was as negligible as ever. Even worse were their ethics, for the period from 1872 through 1874 saw the worst corruption and abuse in any state during Reconstruction. By 1874, South Carolina conservatives agreed that the need for Redemption—the need to deliver the state from carpetbag and black rule—was never greater, and the time never riper; the emergence of new paramilitary forces and an increase in violence symbolized the return of conservative confidence and a growing restlessness in the conservative camp. Still, while whites were unified on goals, serious differences over strategy continued to hamper their efforts. In 1874, Republicans managed to secure one more opportunity to prove they were capable of governing.

Republican state officials did appear to be capable in one area—making themselves rich. Native whites did not oppose the Reconstruction government because of corruption—they opposed Republicans before such problems existed. Rather, it was the administration's mismanagement that served as their rallying point—and as the shrewd mechanism which allowed them to use racial assumptions to sway moderates and Northerners. To conservative whites, Republican abuses were further evidence of the immorality and impossibility of a government supported by, and staffed by, blacks. Added to this was the fact that whites were largely responsible, through their taxes, for paying the bills. The reform and retrenchment promised by Governor Franklin J. Moses never materialized, and the improprieties swelled until the stories and monetary figures made the corruption of the two Scott administrations pale in comparison. A. O. Jones, the Republican clerk of the House of Representatives, had receipts for government "supplies" that included "groceries, clocks, horses, carriages, dry goods, furniture of every description . . . [and] the finest wines, liquors, and cigars." Jones tallied up the liquor bill for one session; it amounted to $125,000 for sherry, brandy, and whiskey (all of which were purchased by the gallon).[1] One of the greatest outrages to conservatives was the state printing system, which allowed the party in control to use the printing facilities at state expense. The printing fund supported the *Charleston Daily Republican* and the *Columbia Daily Union*, which by this time had become the *Columbia Union-Herald*. From 1872 through 1873, the printers cost the state $450,000; by comparison, the state of Ohio spent $63,000 for printing during the same period.[2] This was, in the words of journalist Edward King, "mighty theft; colossal impudence like this was never surpassed . . . never was a revolution, originally intended as humane, turned to such base uses."[3] Although far from being an objective observer, Paul Hamilton Hayne was not far wrong when he mourned for "South Carolina, where *millions* have been stolen from the People . . . in order to support *rogues* & *negroes,* and *alien* blackguards in political power—where every trace or fragment of 'States Rights' was long ago obliterated under the heel of the most *vulgar, upstart tyranny* that ever defiled the honor of a gallant nation."[4]

In the winter of 1874, hoping that corruption would again split the Republican party, Carolina whites began to mobilize for the fall election. Lead by former provisional governor Benjamin Perry, leading conservatives decided to discard their 1872 strategy of noninvolvement, which Perry argued had given Franklin Moses the election.[5] State conservatives sifted through their legal and illegal options in hopes of finding a way to overcome the black majority and bring victory in the fall.

Formal political mobilization started at the second "Taxpayers' Convention," held in late February 1874. In 1871, conservatives had begun forming state "tax unions," a network of cells that replaced the onerous "Democratic" title but performed the same function. The Taxpayers' Convention of 1874 was really a pre-Democratic state convention, with state leaders discussing options for the upcoming campaign. For a time, discussion centered around a tactic proposed by the president of the convention, William Dunlap Porter, and Edgefield's cavalry hero, Martin Witherspoon Gary. After the failure of violence (the Klan), cooperation (1870) and abstention (1872), conservatives sought a new approach. Porter and Gary's plan was simple, legal, and fairly inexpensive: bring white immigrants to the state to shift the voting balance and secure a Democratic victory.[6] Gary, chair of the convention's committee on immigration, had no doubts that Germans would make good Democrats, for he believed the difference between Democrats and Republicans was "race, not party."[7] Those who favored drawing the "white line" in society and politics were already hard at work. Five thousand dollars had been raised thus far, and Gary had hired an agent in Germany. Immigration into the United States and the trip south was to be handled by an agent in New York, Tilman R. Gaines. Gary argued that since ten South Carolina counties had white majorities, and twelve were split rather closely, "the introduction of a few hundred immigrants" into each of the marginal ones would bring Democratic control of the legislature, and possibly even the executive.[8]

Gary's immigration plan had many supporters, but his open emphasis on race was the spark that electrified whites. The editor of the *Charleston News and Courier* agreed with Gary, that "it was entirely a question of race." The paper quoted Gary's convention speech at length and voiced its approval with the belief that "God had destined the caucasian race to rule the other, and if the white men of this state would be true to themselves, they could speedily release themselves from their troubles. The great trouble was that the white men did not unite among themselves." The *News and Courier* applauded the war hero for vowing to restore "the dominance of the white race" and attempting to "protect his self-respect and restore his race to their natural rights."[9]

Other papers concurred with the philosophy and the plan. Commenting on Gary's speech, the *Constitutionalist* claimed that "a more sensible speech in the main, had never been uttered in the Palmetto State." Only a focus on race could unify whites and prevent defection, for "the *race question* is the mighty problem in this State, and that any compromising with or any evasion of it is the secret of every disappointment in politics." "White immigration and white consolidation," the column proposed, "are the two forces advocated by Gen. Gary. We believe he has hit upon the absolute and only perfect methods of deliverance. . . ."[10]

The scramble for a novel strategy even had some whites looking to a very unlikely place for support—the Grant administration. Lawyers drafted a petition detailing the outrageous behavior of state officials, trying to sway Grant into endorsing moderate conservatives, or at least hoping that a reprimand from the president might further divide state Republicans. In March, William D. Porter, Matthew C. Butler, and James Kershaw presented the information to Grant in person. In Grant's words, he "sympathized" with the citizens of the "ill-governed" state, but the president took refuge behind growing constitutional conservatism and state's rights. Grant reminded his visitors that since South Carolina was a "sovereign state," it was wholly unacceptable for the federal government to interfere in such internal state matters.[11] Perhaps a tactical victory for Republicans, Grant's statement nonetheless encouraged conservatives. For many conservatives—in particular, those who were growing restless and advocated a more confrontational approach to securing power—this was a direct acknowledgment by the executive of the policy of nonintervention. To be sure, situations might arise that the federal government could not ignore, but how far could conservatives go before bringing intervention?

Considering the brevity of the enforcement effort and the rapidity of the military withdrawal, whites gambled on federal indifference and began rebuilding the paramilitary forces that had been variously known as bushwhackers, patrols, and the Ku Klux Klan. Conservative bands now became known as rifle clubs, gun clubs, and sabre clubs. Some of these had made their appearance alongside the Klan in 1871 and 1872 in the larger cities of South Carolina (the Klan was concentrated in the piedmont and rural areas of the state), allegedly for "recreational" purposes. One of the first, the Carolina Rifle Club, was founded in Charleston on July 30, 1869. In the words of Irvine C. Walker, long-time member and one-time leader, the club existed "ostensibly for social intercourse and amusement." However he admitted, in a rather confusing fashion, that "as the weapon which was adopted was not a sporting or target rifle, but a sixteen shooter Winchester, it is not hard to appreciate that its hidden defensive object was not so peaceable as its constitution professed." Even the club members' attire had significance; they wore a "hideously ugly gray hunting shirt, as worn by our Revolutionary ancestors, during their struggle, in the swamps of South Carolina."[12]

The victory of Franklin Moses in 1872, and the federal government's laxity in punishing civil rights violations, sparked the formation of more clubs. In addition, since the government's attention had been focused on gowned Klansmen, Carolinians again found means of getting around the law and capitalizing on loopholes. Unlike the dozen or so gun-and-sabre clubs of the first wave, new ones were located in smaller towns, with many appearing across the up-country region to replace the Ku Klux Klan network. Organization in Edgefield County, for example, began in late 1872 and carried enthusiastically into 1873. Several rifle clubs, such as the Palmetto Sabre Club and the Sweetwater Sabre Club, grew out of the "agricultural clubs" that conservatives had relied upon to control black labor (along with performing more legitimate agricultural functions).[13] The Sweetwater Sabre Club of Edgefield, under the leadership of Andrew Pickens Butler, offered no pretenses about its purpose. The club aimed to cow, and if necessary destroy, the nearby militia units under local blacks Richard Bullock and Ned Tennant.[14]

As whites mobilized politically, the rifle clubs became their local operational units. Like the Klan, leadership was drawn from the elite, the finest of gentry culture, a "Who's Who" of the politically and socially powerful. Unlike the Klan, rifle clubs appeared in public and were involved in a host of social functions. Clubs held parades and picnics, orchestrated festivals and balls, and wined and dined with politicos from both parties.[15] D. E. Huger-Smith of Charleston believed that "every respectable white man in the city must have belonged to the 'organization for mutual protection.'"[16]

But parades and balls could not conceal the clubs' raison d'être. When the Sally Rifles formed in Columbia in 1870, its drill routines were specified in its constitution, and its members—ranked as captains, lieutenants, and sergeants—were divided into squads. A quartermaster was in charge of the arms and ammunition, and there were even specified punishments for an untidy uniform, a dirty rifle, or an unshined bayonet (nearly all clubs were equipped with bayonets, an odd accoutrement for a recreational organization).[17] As with the Sally Rifles, many clubs, such as the Georgetown Rifles and the Richland Rifles, regularly included in their meeting agenda a report on arms and ammunition—a topic that would have been out of place in a social club. In August 1874, the committee on arms of the Richland Rifles reported, for instance, that a shipment of guns "had been secured and distributed, ammunition purchased and ready for distribution."[18] A month later, the Georgetown Rifle Guards Club held a meeting to decide whether to buy Winchesters or Remingtons, and announced that poorer members need not contribute towards a rifle as long as they owned a shotgun.[19]

The proliferation of armed, all-white clubs in a campaign year had state Republicans clamoring for protection. On September 3, Republican congressman Robert M. Wallace wrote to Attorney General George Williams about attempts to "excite the people" and incite a "war of races" in South Carolina. Wallace claimed that clubs held themselves "ready for any emergency, and such language among a people who are easily excited to rashness has a comprehensive meaning." The congressman predicted that "outrages will be committed which will intimidate men from going to the polls, [but] it will be made to appear . . . that the poor victims were breathing death and destruction to the white race and that politics had no connection with it."[20] The next day Lewis Cass Carpenter, the editor of the *Columbia Daily Union,* corroborated Wallace's story: rifle clubs were drilling "day and night . . . with the thermometer in the nineties," and an outbreak was imminent.[21]

Conservative whites were either better informed than Republicans knew, or they excelled at anticipating Republican moves. The day *before* Wallace's letter arrived, the attorney general received word from the Columbia Board of Trade that "agitators" were stirring up trouble among blacks. The letter mentioned once such troublemaker by name—"R. M. Wallace." The board assured Williams that all was calm in the city and that rifle clubs were "not military organizations in any sense," but were "merely social, for the purpose of training our young men in the use of arms which, by the Constitution of the United States, they are entitled to bear."[22]

With whites mobilizing for war and federal soldiers few and far between, Republican authorities decided they had no choice but to reorganize the defunct state militia. The new militia system was not a revitalized version of the one under Governor Robert K. Scott; in some ways it was far worse. In 1873 the General Assembly began reviewing its programs, and by the spring of 1874, new companies appeared across the state. Again the whole system was noxious to whites, who supported with their tax dollars a political machine composed of Republican cronies and gun-toting former slaves. Exacerbating the problem was the act of February 20, 1874, "Providing for the Granting of Certain Charters," which created a parallel militia by allowing "groups of men" to apply to the clerk of the court in any county for a charter for a military organization.[23]

In the spring of 1874, blacks flocked to both "militias," eager to prove their loyalty, protect their homes, and in the case of the regular militia, pick up a paycheck. Only five days after the act's passage, Adjutant and Inspector General Henry Purvis told Governor Moses of the "alarming" number of companies applying for charters and requesting state arms. The legislature insisted that state arms be furnished even to the unofficial companies. Purvis notified Moses that it was impossible to arm them all, since the militia department had barely enough guns for the regular militia (yet by his annual report in October, Purvis counted 627 Winchesters and over 22,000 cartridges "in the hands of sundry persons," his term for the "independent" militia units).[24] Purvis also questioned the sudden growth of the regular militia, especially the need for a whole new regiment in Beaufort and cavalry units in Edgefield.[25] He reported to the governor that the militia expansion, which increased the size of the force to nearly eighteen regiments by the summer of 1874, would soon bankrupt his department.[26]

As in 1870 and 1871, the struggle for control of the Palmetto State turned bloody as white forces moved against black militia units. An outbreak in August seemed to indicate that the federal government would continue to remain aloof. A white club seized control of Georgetown, set several buildings afire, shot into homes, and even attacked the stagecoach of the U.S. Mail. When the town's intendant applied to the commanding officer at Charleston for assistance, the officer refused, stating it was a matter "for the state authorities."[27] Perhaps emboldened by this, whites on the opposite side of the state confronted their local militia. In Ridge Spring, not far from the Georgia border, a group of black militiamen refused a white company's order to stop drilling, and soon "three of four hundred men armed and equipped" rode into town, "carrying terror wherever they went." Arson and bloodshed followed, but, according to Lewis Cass Carpenter, whites pointed toward a threatened "negro insurrection" to excuse the "deeds of blood committed" by the whites.[28]

Fortunately for some blacks and white Republicans, there were a few military officers in the state who acted without waiting for orders. Such was the case in the end of August, when federal troops intervened in Edgefield to prevent a bloodbath. By late August, 1874, whites had had enough of the drilling of Ned Tennant's militia company, and showed their displeasure by shooting into his house one evening. The "First Ned Tennant Riot" erupted when Tennant sent his emergency signal, the loud beating of his drum. Militiamen rushed to Tennant's house on Glover's Plantation, while fearful locals—white and black—rushed to Edgefield Court House to alert the federal officer there.

Without orders—in fact technically in violation of them—Lieutenant Matthew Leahy set out for the plantation with a small detachment. On the way Leahy met a large armed band of whites who informed him that "everything was settled" with Tennant. Luckily, Leahy insisted on his own inspection, which revealed that nothing was yet settled. Upon arrival the officer discovered between seventy and eighty blacks facing over three hundred whites. Acting quickly, Leahy interposed his detachment between the enemy groups and set up negotiations for the following day, hoping tempers would ease overnight. Leahy, a few leading whites, and Tennant spoke the following morning, and all parties agreed to disperse—a decision accepted "rather reluctantly on the part of the whites." Leahy let go a sigh of relief, and noted in his report that the whites were more than a match for any state forces. "In fact," the lieutenant admitted, "the whole [white] county is perfectly organized, and ready to take the field at any time."[29]

All through the period of Reconstruction, whites understood—and took advantage of—one simple fact: their desire to control the black population was greater than the North's desire to prevent it. Such was the case in Edgefield, where, despite the U.S. Army's best intentions, local whites refused to let the matter drop. A few days later, prominent whites met and decided that militiamen would either have to hand their guns over to authorities, or leave the county. Blacks got wind of the meeting, and by evening Tennant's company had gathered around his dwelling to make a stand. Whites acted quickly, and by midnight their units had surrounded the entire camp. Tennant decided to gamble; he stole a march on the whites by driving his men through the woods all night, and arrived at Edgefield Court House the next morning. The militiamen surrendered their arms to Colonel Lawrence Cain, the commander of the county's state militia. Lieutenant Leahy provided escorts for the militiamen as they returned home, but feared that "this is a prelude to like disturbances," as "whites evidently intend to disarm the negroes in order to carry the ensuing election by intimidation."[30]

II

Once again, the state Republican party was besieged by enemies from within and without. In 1874, with corruption reaching epic proportions and the governor a leading culprit, the party jettisoned Franklin Moses. But as late as September, with the Republican convention fast approaching, there was no clear gubernatorial candidate. Josephus Woodruff, an employee of the Republican printing company and the clerk of the Senate, commented on the confusion in the Republican ranks. In the thick of the corruption and the factional infighting, Woodruff could only remark, "wish I was with the democrats." The clerk did not trust any of the Republican factions and, in writing, showed equal contempt for all office-seekers, including Francis Cardozo, T. J. Mackey, C. C. Bowen, and Daniel Chamberlain. As secretary during the Republican convention in September, Woodruff observed that "the Republican party are in a perilous condition [sic]."[31]

With corruption rampant and the Republican party in disarray, leading conservatives hatched yet another plot which they hoped would deliver the coup de grace. Learning that the state's entire Republican party had received a stern reproof from President Grant in August (possibly due to the earlier meeting with state conservatives), another delegation left from South Carolina to pry from Grant his endorsement of conservatives in the state elections. Conservatives hoped Grant's backing would bring scalawag whites and some blacks into their camp. Former governor Andrew Magrath, Francis W. Dawson (the English-born editor-in-chief of the *Charleston News and Courier*), James Conner, and George Trenholm met with the president and tried to get a few public words of support for possible candidate General James B. Kershaw. Armed with findings damaging to Republican front-runner Daniel Chamberlain, conservatives wanted Grant to endorse Kershaw as a "reform" candidate, or at least to rebuke Chamberlain for his earlier misdeeds (he had been involved in several notorious schemes during the Scott administration). Although Grant appeared interested at first, the conservative plan failed. The combination of Republican counter-arguments provided by South Carolina's senators and white violence convinced Grant to withhold any endorsement.[32]

The failure of one conservative gambit did nothing to solve Republican problems. The party was still in disorder when the nominating convention opened on September 8 in Columbia. For five days delegates argued, threw chairs, punched one another, and cut back-room deals in efforts to promote one name over another. Amidst the fortune seekers and careless adventurers were men genuinely concerned about the future of the Republican party in the state. They understood, as did lawyer William Heath, that if the party did not elect better people, then "the State of South Carolina in 1876 will go back in the hands of the Democrats as sure as fate."[33] After hours of wrangling, Daniel H. Chamberlain, a Massachusetts-born, Harvard-educated lawyer, won the nomination for governor (Francis W. Dawson, who had met earlier with Grant, again tried to spoil the nomination, but "they beat me out by using more money than I had").[34]

A founding member of the state's Republican party, Chamberlain was not the man who had come to the state in 1866. A former abolitionist who had commanded black troops in the Civil War, he now backed away from "radical" policies and was thought moderate enough to lure white voters to the party. As attorney general during the Scott administrations, Chamberlain had played a significant part in many dubious state scams, yet lately he had made Republican enemies as a proponent of honest government and fiscal reform. For the second time, incumbent Richard Gleaves edged Martin Delany for the lieutenant governor's position.[35]

As many Republicans expected, the nomination of Chamberlain led to yet another party bolt. On October 2, two weeks after the Republican convention closed, the "Independent" Republicans held their nominating convention in Charleston. Delegates chose as governor and lieutenant governor two men who came close to carrying the regular convention: John T. Green, a native white Republican, and the well-educated free black Martin Delany. The platform of the Independents was similar to the regular one—both stressing fiscal reform—with one major difference. Remembering the defeat suffered by a similar group of bolters in 1872, Independents openly appealed to conservatives for support. Promising "good government" under a native white governor, the Independents hoped to woo enough conservatives to tip the balance against Chamberlain and the regulars.[36]

Perhaps encouraged by the choice of native John Green, conservative cooperationalists experienced a brief rebirth in popularity. In a campaign reminiscent of 1870, state conservatives again turned to the bolters, hoping to weaken Republicans and move closer to gaining control of the government. Again as in 1870, conservatives applied a dual strategy, operating within the system as well as beyond its legal constraints: some of the most feared gun club commanders—such as James B. Kershaw and James Conner—openly allied with the Independent Republicans while the members of their clubs waged a campaign of terror against black and white "regular" Republicans. Independents eagerly welcomed the additional voters, but most conservative whites saw the Independents merely as an inroads to power. On October 8, conservative delegates gathered in Columbia and endorsed the Independent platform and candidates.[37]

The Independents' conservative allies were not prepared to rely simply on the power of numbers and messages promising political reform. Even before the Republican split, Carolina whites were gearing up for a new assault. While Republicans were thrashing each other at the convention in September, Senator John Patterson was in Washington, telling tired ears that—in the words of one newspaper reporter—"has never seen such a condition of affairs in the State before; that murders and outrages are of almost daily occurrence," and that "the ones who led in the Kuklux outrages are organizing and drilling rifle clubs all over the State. . . ."[38] Attorney General Williams received so many pleas for help in September that he tried—unsuccessfully—to convince Secretary of War William W. Belknap to return cavalry units to South Carolina.[39] B. L. Brisbane of Port Royal had another solution, since "these rebels, without fault on my part, are persecuting me and my family to death," he asked that the Attorney General "send Ben Butler."⁴⁰ Congressman Robert M. Wallace held the federal government responsible for the disturbed condition of affairs in the state, because "justice, in my opinion, has been too long delayed."⁴¹

Republican J. G. Winsmith of Spartanburg was not so concise in his letter to President Grant. "South Carolina is now passing through a bloody ordeal" the "scalawag" informed the president. During the Klan's reign of terror in 1871, Winsmith had written to Grant and asked that General Philip Sheridan be sent into the state to wipe out "the hideous monster—Ku Kluxism." Instead, Winsmith pointed out, the government sent "a committee from Congress on Southern outrages, at an enormous cost to the Federal Government," followed by "a few trials and convictions in the U.S. Courts; and then the pardoning of the criminals." Because of federal hesitation and conservatism, Winsmith argued, Republicans in the South now suffered under a "third rebellion" waged by "white leagues, rifle clubs, and a secret police," composed of men who vow "never to acknowledge the results of the war." Do not look for a fair election, the Carolinian informed the chief executive, for "the Ku Klux are organized to murder, and the Republicans are not."⁴²

Violence may have been the most persuasive weapon, but whites had other, less blatant tactics as well. William Heath, a Northern lawyer now living in Edgefield, informed Attorney General Williams that conservative leaders planned to use economic blackmail to intimidate black voters. Heath learned that employers planned to discharge workers who favored Republican Daniel Chamberlain, but to argue that they had discharged their hands "because it pays better to keep fewer hands. And you see there would be no colliding with the General Government, for there is no law either in State or National, to compel a man to employ hands to his own disadvantage."⁴³

On October 28, just days after Heath's letter, whites held a "tax union meeting" at Edgefield Court House, allegedly to resolve the financial and agricultural difficulties facing planters. Those present, including chairman Martin W. Gary, concluded that the best solution to troubled times was to cut labor. Each township would create a committee to decide which laborers would leave, and once selected, they could not rent or occupy land in that township. The notice in the paper carried 137 names of men who were, according to Gary, "ready to strike for white supremacy."⁴⁴ Such proscriptions were not to be taken lightly. Following the "Ned Tennant Riots," Meriwether township whites had circulated a pledge that no white should rent land to militiamen. Planter Joshua McKie ignored the notice and rented a dwelling to none other than Tennant himself. McKie found himself totally isolated, ostracized by his friends and even his own family; he soon committed suicide.[45]

Nor were conservatives above fraud in their struggle to destroy the Republican party. In his private journal, Robert Wallace Shand admitted that some whites sought a short-cut by simply buying the pre-printed Republican tickets! "We did try to purchase all the printed Republican tickets from their county chairman by offering him 500 [dollars] for them," Shand confessed, "but he demanded 1000, and we did not purchase." The episode reveals as much about Republican integrity as it does conservative probity. Shand also helped concoct another plan to lower the Republican vote. For a fee (of course), Republican election managers at one poll had agreed to leave a few ballot boxes overnight, the ballots to be counted the following day. "A party had been chosen to raid the room and carry off the boxes," but that part of the plan collapsed because "the hearts of the chosen raiders failed them and the boxes were counted the next day," after all.[46]

Not all "raiders" were so timid or so conscientious and, as a result, November 4 was as bloody an election as South Carolina had seen. In Laurensville, Lieutenant John Anderson reported an election day "difficulty" in which two blacks were shot. Anderson stepped in and stopped the fighting, but believed that without his intervention "a very serious riot" would have resulted, for "a plan had been arranged to murder the leading Republican Politicians, and negroes."[47] A lieutenant from the Eighteenth Infantry described a riot that took place in Winnsboro and left at least three blacks wounded.[48] So many offenses took place in Edgefield that officers of the Eighteenth Infantry spent much of November accompanying U.S. marshals serving warrants under the Enforcement Acts (as one might suspect, these were never prosecuted).[49] Reflecting on the campaign years later, Benjamin Ryan Tillman recalled that at Shaw's Mill, a precinct with five times the number of black voters as white ones, "democrats" carried it in 1874 "by some manipulation which nobody ever clearly understood except those who performed it. . . ." "It was an object lesson," wrote Pitchfork Ben, "in the possibilities of what white nerves and brains can accomplish when desperation and necessity prompt."[50]

The election of 1874 again demonstrated black loyalty, courage, and endurance. Despite attempts to force the election through fraud and violence, Daniel Chamberlain and the regular Republicans emerged victorious. Chamberlain received 80,403 votes to Green's 68,818, a wide margin but one not so vast as the winners' in previous elections; opponents, either bolters or conservatives, had made substantial headway. Ironically, had the Independents won, South Carolina may well have had the nation's first black governor; John T. Green died in January 1875, an event which would have elevated Lieutenant Governor Martin Delany to the post of the state's chief executive.[51]

Election day news was not all bad for conservatives. Elections across the North signified that the national tide was indeed turning. The year 1874 saw voters more interested in reform, the West, and the depression than Southern issues. In state elections, Democrats took control of the governorship or the legislature in several states, including New Hampshire, Connecticut, Ohio, and Indiana. Out of twenty-five gubernatorial races, Democrats won nineteen.[53] The trend continued through the congressional elections in November, and for the first time since before the Civil War, the Republican party lost control of Congress. Republicans, going into the election with a majority of 110 in the House of Representatives, received a stunning public rebuke. A Republican majority was wiped clean, replaced by a *Democratic majority* of sixty.

Scholars still debate the meaning of such a stunning turnaround. Eric Foner has argued that economic depression combined with agricultural distress in the South was responsible for the Republican defeat.[53] Other historians disagree, and firmly place Reconstruction at the center of the election disaster. William Gillette has called the election a "referendum on Reconstruction." Gillette sees the results as a direct repudiation of Grant, his administration, and his Reconstruction policies.[54] Regardless of the motivation *behind* the vote, the *effect* of the vote was clear: the Republican party no longer controlled the federal government, and the likelihood of major federal action in the South dwindled further. As George Rable puts it, the 1874 elections were the "turning point" in Reconstruction, or, to be more accurate, *another* turning point: for the first time, Democrats had leverage, and a fresh path was about to be hewn.[55]

For conservatives in South Carolina the election marked the dawning of a new era. Carolinians lived with the reality of Reconstruction every day, and issues of local control, self-determination, and black subjugation—issues that shaped their lives, their society, and the destiny of their state—far outweighed the temporary trauma of depression or the romance of westward expansion. For South Carolinians, there was only one way to interpret the election results: voters rejected the Republican party, federal interference in the South, and the entire program of Reconstruction. Belton O'Neal Townsend, writing as "A South Carolinian" to the *Atlantic Monthly*, spoke for countless conservatives when he said that the Democratic victory was "hailed with Thanksgiving in South Carolina, as an indication that the North had determined to protest against the oppression of the Southern whites by their old slaves and the carpet-baggers."[56]

III

As 1874 drew to a close, many Republicans sensed that the winds of change were decidedly unfavorable. The federal government—for years the omnipresent, although often reluctant and usually tardy, defender of the state government—had been castigated by the electorate. The Supreme Court had begun frittering away at the laws that enabled state authorities to hold would-be redeemers in check. Violence, fraud, and intimidation were rampant, and it seemed doubtful that the cavalry would literally ride up to protect Republicans. Plus, the state Republican party had just suffered its worst schism. Daniel H. Chamberlain, sworn in on December 1, presided over a party and a state that were tearing themselves apart at the seams.

Almost immediately, the new governor learned the illusory nature of his power. In an object lesson on who monopolized violence in South Carolina, Edgefield gun clubs lashed out at local blacks. On the evening of January 12, a dwelling caught fire on the plantation of Matthew C. Butler, former Union Reformer and current captain in a local rifle club. Whites captured a black man, who claimed that Ned Tennant, the black captain of the local militia, had paid him to commit arson. A warrant was issued for Tennant's arrest, but the militia leader, guarded by his men (whose guns had been returned to them), defied the constable sent to bring him in. Before long, M. C. Butler and his gun club caught up with the militia company, only to come under fire from other blacks hiding in ambush. Within hours white reinforcements appeared—Benjamin R. Tillman placed the number at over one thousand—and "they began to scour the whole region. . . ." Sporadic firefights continued for days, several blacks were captured, and both sides had its share of wounded. Again Tennant eluded pursuit, and by January 20, he and the bulk of his men had reached Edgefield Court House and deposited their guns in the jail. But Tennant would not reclaim them again; a few nights later, whites raided the jail, "and all of the arms disappeared."[57]

As powerless as his predecessors, Daniel H. Chamberlain followed in their footsteps by issuing proclamations and calling for federal help. On January 28, the governor called for all Edgefield militia companies to turn in their arms and for all companies "not being part of the regular State militia" to disband (there is no evidence that either white or black groups complied).[58] Chamberlain also contacted Attorney General George Williams, alerting him to the "disturbed condition of affairs" in Edgefield and to his fear that "further collisions may occur" if a permanent garrison of troops is not assigned there. As it turned out, the secretary of war complied, and a company of infantry made its way from Columbia to the turbulent county.[59]

Despite this, conservatives still gambled that an active federal role was only a remote possibility, and events elsewhere bolstered their confidence. The Louisiana legislature provided a critical "test case" for President Grant when five Democrats seized their disputed seats in January 1875. Under orders from Grant, General Philip Sheridan, commanding the department, had his troops enter the legislative hall and forcibly remove the five Democrats. The South Carolina General Assembly sent Grant a formal letter of appreciation, thanking the President "for his prompt and efficient action" in preventing disorder and protecting the legal government.[60] Such a response was in the minority, for the rest of the nation did not share these views. Both Grant and Sheridan came under fire for their actions, seen by many—Democrats as well as Republicans—as a serious breech of civil-military relations. The controversy over the disputed seats was eventually solved by a bit of political manipulation called the Wheeler Compromise, but it did not erase the memory of Grant's decision—or of the public and political response. The embarrassment and clamor that followed the military's intervention cast further doubts over the future of federal activity in the South.[61] Of course Northern opposition to interference in the South—another manifestation of the "laissez-faire" attitude that was taking hold in economic and social circles—did not begin with Louisiana.[62] Nevertheless the public outcry may have finally convinced the president, in the words of the *Spartanburg Herald,* that the Southern Republican party "must stand upon its own merit."[63]

Events in the fall of 1875 confirmed what Republicans suspected and conservatives anticipated. Grant remained neutral during the political disorders in Georgia in August, reflecting a more circumscribed federal role in the South. Georgia whites from gun clubs and other volunteer military companies, using the standard excuse that blacks were preparing "to open a war of races," struck against Republican militia units, arresting and injuring scores. Whites in South Carolina fully supported mob action to control the black population, and it appeared that the Northern public, and President Grant, did as well.[64]

The Mississippi campaign was the most telling display of the administration's—and Southern whites'—new policy. The struggle for control of Mississippi reached its climax in 1875, when the "White Man's" (or "People's") party waged a campaign characterized by violence, fraud, and open intimidation. Numerous riots occurred in August and September, and the death toll among black and white Republicans grew as the election approached. Governor Adelbert Ames pleaded with Washington for federal assistance, but to no avail.⁶⁵ According to one Carolina paper, Grant informed Attorney General Edwards Pierrepont, who replaced George Williams in May of 1875, that "the annual autumnal outbreaks and calls for troops are getting to be nauseating to the American people."⁶⁶ In turn, Pierrepont instructed Governor Ames that state resources must be used to quell any disturbances. Unfortunately, as with South Carolina, state forces were no match for white experience, training, and determination. Democrats took control of the legislature, which then impeached the lieutenant governor and forced Ames to resign and return to his native Massachusetts. Writing to his wife in the North, Ames said, "a revolution has taken place—and a race are disenfranchised—they are to be returned to a country of serfdom—an era of second slavery."⁶⁷ Across the North and now across the South, the tide had indeed turned.

Conservatives in South Carolina, chaffing under their own Massachusetts-born governor, had paid close attention to events in Mississippi. South Carolina correspondents covering the campaign in that state reported on the open intimidation blended with a careful use of force, and the conspicuous lack of federal interposition. The *Spartanburg Herald*'s correspondent, explaining "How It Was Done In Mississippi," reported that the election itself was "as quiet an election as ever I attended. When every man knew that every White man was armed . . . there was great circumspection of conduct." "I would not have believed," the correspondent wrote, "that so many colored people could have been got to vote the Democratic ticket as I have seen do it here today." Mississippi whites drew the line in 1875, and blacks—recognizing that the state party was defunct and the federal government indifferent—had to "accept the inevitable."⁶⁸

IV

With Republicanism collapsing across the South—even before the Mississippi debacle—many Republicans in South Carolina hoped that Daniel H. Chamberlain might be the miracle worker they needed. To be sure, the Republican party still labored under the divisions that had accompanied the 1874 campaign. At the same time, however, some conservatives were embracing Chamberlain as a harbinger of change—a moderate, honest carpetbagger fighting for reform. For a small group of conservatives and many (though not all) Republicans, Chamberlain offered the potential of party realignment, an escape from the pitfall of Republican debauchery on the one hand and violent revolution on the other.

Daniel H. Chamberlain, a veteran of South Carolina Reconstruction politics, believed—perhaps naively—that the only way to win over conservative voters was to eliminate corruption. The new governor oversaw spending cuts and militia reform, heavily curtailing the activist tendencies of previous administrations. The governor also removed dozens of state and local officials whom he believed to be incompetent or corrupt, and replaced them with native whites.[69] Chamberlain wrestled with the state legislature and used his veto power generously against unwarranted and irresponsible legislation.[70] Chamberlain won over several leading conservatives with his reforms, including Francis Warrington Dawson, the editor of the *Charleston News and Courier*. Carolinian John C. Davis applauded Chamberlain's efforts in March, telling the governor that "I see and approve much your endeavours to reform the vile practices of Public officers. In this you have any thinking man's sympathy."[71]

If Chamberlain indeed had the support of the thinking man, there was a serious lack of such individuals among the state's Republicans, for some of Chamberlain's most vociferous critics came from within his own party. Many of his loudest detractors were dishonest men who found themselves quickly displaced. Chamberlain was well aware that his programs were creating enemies of men he had once considered to be his friends, but as he explained to newfound ally Francis W. Dawson, "my evils have heretofore come from the *friendship* of bad men. Perhaps I shall fare better if I have their *hatred*."[72] There were some, however, who objected to Chamberlain's course not because of their own selfish greed but because of the new governor's threat to vital Republican programs. The governor's downsizing of the militia and the subsequent reduction in pay dealt many black families a severe economic blow. Chamberlain also sought to cut school expenditures, which would affect mostly black children who studied under the state-sponsored system. As Michael Perman has observed, Chamberlain's efforts to redefine South Carolina politics resulted in his abandoning of the old Republican constituency. Chamberlain began to drift away from the Republican core, but at the same time was unable—because of the growing attractiveness of white-line politics—to fully win over white conservatives. Yet in the end, it was Republicans' defiant opposition to his policies that brought about the final rupture of the state party.[73]

The rupture came on December 15, 1875, a day Carolinians came to call "Black Thursday." Six months earlier, arch-conservative A. P. Aldrich, watching Chamberlain's progress with growing interest, had warned a friend that "Chamberlain will have a harder fight next winter that he has yet had, with the Radical Ring—and his hardest fight will be in the election of the Judges."[74] Aldrich was right, for the General Assembly elected the circuit court judges, positions traditionally regarded as plum rewards for cronies and insiders. Corrupt or unqualified judges could do irrevocable damage to Chamberlain's programs, while the right men might insure justice and honesty on the bench. The General Assembly and the governor were locked on a collision course over policy and power.

On December 15, while Chamberlain was visiting Greenville, the General Assembly held its elections for the state's eight circuit court judgeships—even though legislators had assured Chamberlain they would wait for his return. Two men who were considered among the most debased in the state—former governor Franklin J. Moses, Jr., and Northerner William J. Whipper—managed to get themselves elected to judgeships. Whipper was chosen for the First Circuit (Charleston), and Moses for the Third (Sumter).[75]

Chamberlain returned to Columbia to counter the attack on his reform policy and his administration. The governor signed the commissions for six of the eight judges, but refused to approve those for Moses or Whipper, calling their election "a horrible disaster" and "a calamity."[76] Chamberlain feared that this "terrible crevasse of misgovernment and public debauchery" would convince conservatives that he did not have the mettle to run his party.[77] Writing to President Grant, Chamberlain expressed the belief that "no act of mine, if I were the greatest living traitor to my party, could be so fatal to that party as the election of Whipper and Moses has been and will be."[78]

The governor's concerns were well-founded, for white conservatives made clear that this last outrage eliminated any chance of cooperation between the parties. On December 27, conservative Carolinians held a mass rally in Hibernian Hall in Charleston to protest the election. Former Confederate General James Conner opened with the rousing declaration that "the question is not, how can you live here, but *whether you can live here at all.* You have to either redeem the State or quit it." "There are two courses open," explained Conner, "abject submission to this and the worse yet to come, or a firm, determined resistance." He called for "organization, thorough, complete over the whole State, to sweep from power those who have betrayed the trust which was confided to them." Knowing that his audience wanted more than just honest government, Conner reminded them that "secure the election, and the rest will follow!"[79]

Even those leading conservatives who praised Chamberlain's defiant stance understand that any hope of union was lost. Former Confederate Colonel B. C. Pressley applauded the governor's refusal to sign the commissions, and added that if the General Assembly tried to impeach him, "well—I wouldn't like to be the insurance agent that held policies on their lives." But Chamberlain was isolated, Pressley knew, so for Carolinians "the time has come for action."[80] Even Chamberlain's ally, Francis W. Dawson, admitted that the election spelled doom for cooperation. Republicans would soon learn that "no man, no party, no State can resist the awful power of public opinion."[81] An editorial in Dawson's *News and Courier* described "The Conspiracy to Africanize South Carolina," arguing that the election of Moses and Whipper was "evidence of a determination to Africanize, by and through the Black Thursday Judges, the low country of South Carolina, and, by and through the majority voting of the whole voting population in the low-country, to rule the State."[82]

From across South Carolina came peals of protest and calls for action. In early January, a public meeting at Marion announced that the election "has brought the people to the point beyond which forbearance ceases to be a virtue." Whites present produced a resolution which declared that "Moses shall never take his seat as Judge in our Courthouse unless placed there by Federal bayonets."[83] Various Charleston rifle clubs—cooperating under the command of James Conner—stood ready to oppose any attempt by Republicans or the black militia to seat William Whipper.[84] Horry County whites resolved that "we will take such actions as shall result in the overthrow and banishment of the faction which has so long ruled, robbed, and degraded us."[85] From Spartanburg came the declaration that the election was "the last feather to break the camel's back." The *Herald* called for whites to stop talking and start acting: "something more than out-bursts" was needed to redeem the state.[86]

So as early as January, Carolina whites were serving notice that the election of 1876 was to be the climactic battle. One letter to the *News and Courier* asked "what of the God-given, the American right of Revolution? What of *manhood* and *honor*?" The author stated that the "American people had better understand now" that if whites were called on "to give up South Carolina to the negro, scalawag, and the carpetbagger . . . we will bridge every old field in the State with dead first."[87] Never one to hold his tongue, former judge A. P. Aldrich called for Carolinians to "drive these brigands, these banditti, out at the next election" or, better yet, to "form a committee of vigilance and safety from our best citizens . . . who will give them a fair trial and swift justice." Aldrich appealed to Southern tradition and honor when he told his fellow Carolinians that failure in 1876 meant "you are a disgrace to your ancestry; you commit a crime against your posterity; your mothers will weep that you were born; your sisters blush that you live."[88] As the nation approached its centennial celebration, South Carolina whites eagerly and diligently set out on a revolution of their own.

Notes

1. *Report of the Joint Investigating Committee on Public Frauds and the Election of John J. Patterson to the U.S. Senate.* (Columbia, S.C.: Calvo and Patton, State Printers, 1878) 2:7–8, 13, 25–28; hereafter cited as *Report on Public Frauds*.
2. *Report on Public Frauds* 3:6–7.
3. Edward King, *The Great South* (Hartford, Conn.: American Publishing, 1875; Arno Press, 1969), 457.
4. Paul Hamilton Hayne to "Mrs. Preston," January 13, 1873, in Box 3, Folder 1, Paul Hamilton Hayne Papers, Special Collections Library Research Room, Perkins Library, Duke University, Durham, N.C. (hereafter SCLRR, Duke); emphasis in original.
5. See Stephen Meats and Edwin Arnold, eds., *The Writings of Benjamin F. Perry: Volume I: Essays, Public Letters, and Speeches* (Spartanburg, S.C.: Reprint Company, 1980), 1:419–23.
6. *Charleston News and Courier*, February 21, 1874; clipping in Folder 65, Martin Witherspoon Gary Papers, South Caroliniana Library, University of South Carolina, Columbia, S.C. (hereafter SCL).
7. Martin W. Gary, quoted in William Arthur Sheppard, *Red Shirts Remembered: Southern Brigadiers of the Reconstruction Period* (Atlanta: Ruralist Press, 1940), 15–16.
8. *Charleston News and Courier*, February 21, 1874.
9. *Charleston News and Courier*, February 21, 1874.
10. *Constitutionalist*, April 7, 1874; clipping in Folder 65, Martin Witherspoon Gary Papers, SCL; emphasis in original.
11. Ulysses S. Grant, quoted in *Columbia Daily Union-Herald*, March 31, 1874.
12. Irvine C. Walker, *Carolina Rifle Club*, July 30, 1869, in *Pamphlets: Reconstruction in South Carolina, Democratic and Republican, 1869–1880* (n.d., n.p.), 3, 16, 19, 21, 27.
13. *Edgefield Advertiser*, November 21, 1872; Orville Vernon Burton, "Race and Reconstruction: Edgefield County, South Carolina," *Journal of Social History* 12 (Fall 1978): 40.
14. See Francis Butler Simkins, *The Tillman Movement in South Carolina* (Durham: Duke University Press, 1926), 58.
15. For instance, on March 7, 1873, the *News and Courier* contained news about the activities of the Sumter Rifle Club, the German Rifle Club, the Irish Rifle Club, and the Palmetto Guards. Not at all unique, this was typical of the large number of clubs and the attention constantly paid them.
16. D. E. Huger-Smith, *A Charlestonian's Recollections, 1846–1913* (Charleston, S.C.: Walker, Evans, and Cogswell, 1950), 140.
17. "Constitution and Bye-Laws [sic]," Records of the Sally Rifles Club, SCL.
18. "Minutes and Pictures," August 24, 1874, Records of the Governor's Guards/Richland Rifle Club, SCL. The Governor's Guards had existed in the antebellum period, but died out during Reconstruction. The company was reestab-

lished in 1878, and then the Richland Rifles assumed its title. This collection includes material through 1879, and so bears the dual heading. See also *Constitution and Rules of the Richland Rifle Club, Columbia, S.C.*(Columbia, S.C.: Williams Sloane, 1874), SCL-BD; and "Minute Book," September 18, 1874, Records of the Georgetown Rifle Guards Club, SCL.

19. "Minute Book," August 20 and September 18, 1874, Records of the Georgetown Rifle Guards Club, SCL.

20. Robert M. Wallace to George Williams, September 3, 1874, in Record Group 60, Microcopy 947, Reel 2, National Archives, Washington, D.C. (hereafter RG, MC, Reel, NA).

21. Lewis Cass Carpenter to Williams, September 4, 1874, RG60, MC947, Reel 2, NA.

22. Board of Trade of Columbia, S.C. to Williams, September 2, 1874, RG60, MC947, Reel 2, NA.

23. Henry W. Purvis, the state adjutant and inspector general, warned that having armed bodies "entirely separate and not under the control of the laws that govern the militia" was "injurious to the perfection and good government of military bodies, and also one of the most dangerous elements of good and safe society." His protests fell on deaf ears, however, and the party approached the campaign with a two-tier militia defense. See "Annual Report of the Adjutant and Inspector General," in "Reports for 1870/1874," Military Affairs File, South Carolina Department of Archives and History, Columbia, S.C. (hereafter SCDAH).

24. Henry Purvis to Franklin Moses, February 24, 1874, in Box 6, Folder 35, Governor Moses Papers, SCDAH; "Annual Report of the Adjutant and Inspector General," Military Affairs File, SCDAH.

25. Purvis, entries for May 28, October 17, and December 3, 1874, in Letterbook, Records of the Office of the Adjutant and Inspector General, SCDAH.

26. Purvis to Franklin Moses, March 23, 1874, in Box 7, Folder 4, Governor Moses Papers, SCDAH.

27. *Annual Report of the Secretary of War for 1874,* 43d Cong., 2d sess., H. Doc. 1 (Serial 1635), 47.

28. Lewis Cass Carpenter to Ulysses S. Grant, August 26, 1874, RG60, MC947, Reel 2, NA.

29. Lieutenant Matthew Leahy to the assistant adjutant general, Department of the South, September 1, 1874, RG94, MC666, Reel 170, NA. Leahy's report is reproduced in the *Annual Report of the Secretary of War for 1874,* 49–50. Future governor Benjamin Ryan "Pitchfork Ben" Tillman was a member of the Sweetwater Sabre Club, which participated in the "riot." His account is useful for its social and ethnic commentaries, but contains many factual inaccuracies. For instance, Tillman places the riot in July 1874, but it actually occurred at the end of August and into September. See Benjamin Ryan Tillman, "Autobiography," 3–7, SCL.

30. Matthew Leahy to the assistant adjutant general, Department of the South, September 16, 1874, RG94, MC666, Reel 170, NA.

31. Josephus Woodruff, diary entries for August 2 and 17, and September 10, 1874, Josephus Woodruff Diary, SCLRR, Duke.

32. Thomas Holt, *Black over White: Negro Political Leadership in South Carolina during Reconstruction* (Urbana: University of Illinois Press, 1977), 177–78; Francis W. Dawson to "Wife," August 2 and 29, September 3, 8, and 13, 1874, Francis Warrington Dawson Papers, SCLRR, Duke.

33. William M. Heath to George Williams, October 24, 1874, RG60, MC947, Reel 2, NA.

34. Francis W. Dawson, quoted in Joel Williamson, *After Slavery: The Negro in South Carolina during Reconstruction, 1861–1877* (Chapel Hill: University of North Carolina Press, 1965), 400.

35. Eric Foner, *Reconstruction, 1863–1877: America's Unfinished Revolution* (New York: Harper and Row, 1988), 543; Francis Butler Simkins and Robert Hilliard Woody, *South Carolina during Reconstruction* (Chapel Hill: University of North Carolina Press, 1932), 471. For a complete list of the nominations, including those for national and local offices, see John S. Reynolds, *Reconstruction in South Carolina, 1865–1877* (Columbia, S.C.: State Company, 1905), 276–85.

36. Foner, *Reconstruction: America's Unfinished Revolution,* 543; Simkins and Woody, *South Carolina during Reconstruction,* 471–73.

37. *Charleston News and Courier,* September 17, October 9 and 10, 1874; Simkins and Woody, *South Carolina during Reconstruction,* 471–73.

38. Reynolds, *Reconstruction in South Carolina,* 270.

39. George Williams to William W. Belknap, September 30, 1874, RG94, MC666, Reel 170, NA.

40. B. L. Brisbane to Williams, September 22, 1874, RG60, MC947, Reel 2, NA.

41. Robert M. Wallace to Williams, September 18, 1874, RG60, MC947, Reel 2, NA.

42. J. G. Winnsmith to Ulysses S. Grant, October 5, 1874, RG60, MC947, Reel 2, NA.

43. William M. Heath to George Williams, October 24, 1874, RG60, MC947, Reel 2, NA.

44. Originally in the *Edgefield Advertiser,* reprinted in the *Columbia Daily Union-Herald,* October 29, 1874; clipping in Martin Witherspoon Gary Papers, Folder 65, SCL.

45. Tillman, "Autobiography," 7, SCL; Burton, "Race and Reconstruction," *Journal of Social History* 12 (Fall 1978): 42.

46. Robert Wallace Shand, Robert Wallace Shand Journal, 148, SCL.

47. Lieutenant John Anderson to the assistant adjutant general, Department of the South, November 4, 1874, RG94, MC666, Reel 172, NA. County officers wrote to Anderson's superiors in support of his action and warned against removing any troops from the area, for "serious disturbances would follow." See "County Officers of Laurens County" to [unknown, but eventually endorsed by the adjutant general of the Department of the South and Major General Irwin McDowell], November 5, 1874, RG94, MC666, Reel 171, NA.

48. *Message of the President Transmitting Statements on the Use of the Army in Certain of the Southern States,* 44th Cong., 2d sess., H. Doc. 30 (Serial 1755), 71.

49. Captain R. Morris to the assistant adjutant general, Department of the South, November 22, 23, and 25, 1874, RG94, MC666, Reel 172, NA.

50. Tillman, "Autobiography," 7, SCL.

51. Simkins and Woody, *South Carolina during Reconstruction*, 473; Alrutheus Ambush Taylor, *The Negro in South Carolina during the Reconstruction* (Washington, D.C.: n.p., 1924; New York: AMS Press, 1971), 211–12.

52. William Gillette, *Retreat from Reconstruction, 1869–1879* (Baton Rouge: Louisiana State University Press, 1979), 189, 247.

53. Foner, *Reconstruction: America's Unfinished Revolution*, 524, 528.

54. Gillette, *Retreat from Reconstruction*, 246, 250, 252–54.

55. George C. Rable, *But There Was No Peace: The Role of Violence in the Politics of Reconstruction* (Athens: University of Georgia Press, 1984), 121.

56. Belton O'Neal Townsend ("A South Carolinian"), "The Political Condition of South Carolina," *Atlantic Monthly* 39 (1877): 182.

57. Tillman, "Autobiography," 8–10, SCL; Burton, "Race and Reconstruction," *Journal of Social History* 12 (Fall 1978): 42.

58. Reynolds, *Reconstruction in South Carolina*, 301–2. No evidence exists that the rifle clubs disbanded; fourteen months later, Orville Vernon Burton estimated, no less than thirty such clubs existed in Edgefield County alone. See Reynolds, "Race and Reconstruction," *Journal of Social History* 12 (Fall 1978): 42. See also Walter Allen, *Governor Chamberlain's Administration in South Carolina: A Chapter of Reconstruction in the Southern States* (New York: G. P. Putnam's Sons, 1888), 68–69. Allen's work, while suffering from some of the flaws typical of its period, is nonetheless a gold mine for primary evidence on Chamberlain's administration; scores of letters, messages, declarations, and military orders are reprinted there.

59. Daniel H. Chamberlain to George Williams, January 27, 1875, RG60, MC947, Reel 2, NA; William Belknap to Major General McDowell, February 3, 1875, RG94, MC666, Reel 173, NA; Williams to Chamberlain, February 2, 1875, RG60, MC699, Reel 15, NA.

60. General Assembly of South Carolina to Ulysses S. Grant, February 20, 1875, RG60, MC947, Reel 2, NA.

61. Foner, *Reconstruction: America's Unfinished Revolution*, 554–55.

62. For an interesting discussion of "laissez-faire" and its impact on Reconstruction, see Michael Les Benedict, "Reform Republicans and the Retreat from Reconstruction," in *The Facts of Reconstruction: Essays in Honor of John Hope Franklin*, ed. Eric Anderson and Alfred A. Moss (Baton Rouge: Louisiana State University Press, 1991), 53–77.

63. *Spartanburg Herald*, September 29, 1875.

64. *Spartanburg Herald*, September 1, 1875.

65. *Spartanburg Herald*, September 15, 1875; Foner, *Reconstruction: America's Unfinished Revolution*, 558–63.

66. *Spartanburg Herald*, September 22, 1875.

67. Foner, *Reconstruction: America's Unfinished Revolution*, 558–62; William S. McFeely, *Grant: A Biography* (New York: W. W. Norton, 1981), 421–22.

68. *Spartanburg Herald*, December 11, 1875.

69. Foner, *Reconstruction: America's Unfinished Revolution*, 543–46.

70. The best study of Chamberlain remains Walter Allen's *Governor Chamberlain's Administration in South Carolina: A Chapter of Reconstruction in the Southern States* (New York: G. P. Putnam's Sons, 1888). For Chamberlain's struggles with the general assembly, and details on some of his nineteen vetoes, see Allen, 80–114.

71. John C. Davis to Daniel Chamberlain, March 5, 1875, in Folder 15, Conway, Black, and Davis Family Papers, SCL.

72. Chamberlain to Francis W. Dawson, May 11, 1875, in Francis Warrington Dawson Papers, SCLRR, Duke.

73. See Michael Perman, *The Road to Redemption: Southern Politics, 1869–1879* (Chapel Hill: University of North Carolina Press, 1984), 142–46. See also Foner, *Reconstruction: America's Unfinished Revolution*, 543–46; Williamson, *After Slavery*, 402–5; and Holt, *Black over White*, 175–76.

74. A. P. Aldrich to William Dunlap Simpson, June 30, 1875, in Box 4, William Dunlap Simpson Papers, SCLRR, Duke.

75. Although Walter Allen states (see *Governor Chamberlain's Administration*, 193) that Moses was chosen for the Charleston circuit and Whipper for Sumter, primary evidence, largely from the mass meetings held by whites after the election, shows that Allen has the seats reversed.

76. Daniel H. Chamberlain, quoted in Allen, *Governor Chamberlain's Administration*, 195, 197. See also Henry T. Thompson, *Ousting the Carpetbagger from South Carolina* (Columbia, S.C.: R. L. Bryan, 1926; New York: Negro Universities Press, 1969), 86; Sheppard, *Red Shirts Remembered*, 39–43.

77. Chamberlain, quoted in *Charleston News and Courier*, December 20, 1875.

78. Chamberlain to Grant, n.d.; quoted in the *Spartanburg Herald*, April 12, 1876.

79. James Conner, quoted in Allen, *Governor Chamberlain's Administration*, 203; emphasis in original.

80. *Governor Chamberlain's Administration*, 205–7.

81. Francis W. Dawson, quoted in *Charleston News and Courier*, December 20, 1875.

82. *Charleston News and Courier*, January 21, 1876.

83. *Charleston News and Courier*, January 5, 1876.

84. Walker, *Carolina Rifle Club*, in *Pamphlets: Reconstruction in South Carolina*, 52–53, SCL-BD.

85. *Charleston News and Courier*, January 7, 1876.

86. *Spartanburg Herald*, January 6, 1876.

87. *Charleston News and Courier*, January 7, 1876; emphasis in original.

88. Speech of A. P. Aldrich at Barnwell Court House on January 4, 1876; printed in the *Charleston News and Courier*, January 6, 1876.

CHAPTER EIGHT

"IT IS IN EVERY SENSE A MILITARY CAMPAIGN"

> Was all this justifiable? Yes—for unlike elections at other times our very civilization was at stake. We could not live in South Carolina if negro rule continued. . . . We had to fight as we could. Our plan of campaign was an evil, but its success overcame a greater evil.
>
> Robert Wallace Shand, on the campaign of 1876,
> Robert Wallace Shand Journal, South Caroliniana Library

I

The Circuit Court elections signaled the opening of the 1876 political campaign. For nearly a decade Carolina conservatives had lived under what they deemed an illegitimate alien-and-black government, and all their efforts to overturn it—by way of violence, fraud, or conciliation and alliance—had failed. But 1876 would be different, for rifts in Republican ranks, changes in Northern sentiment, and a new unity among conservatives created an environment ripe for revolution. Whites unfurled their banner of white supremacy and unsheathed their sword of the paramilitary citizen force. Both had appeared before in Reconstruction, but their use had been sporadic and local. In comparison, the 1876 campaign marked the culmination of white organization and mobilization; action moved from the county level to the state level, with thousands of conservative soldiers under the direction of would-be redeemers. Formally returning to their "Democratic" designation, Carolina conservatives embarked on a dangerous and delicate operation. Because of the black majority, a victory on white terms could come only through force and fraud, but extreme measures might still provoke federal intervention. If Democrats were to succeed, they had to overcome the dual challenge of Republican opposition and their own reckless, desperate nature.

With a voting minority, conservatives also knew that complete unity was vital. White solidarity came through a return to the South's great unifying factor, white supremacy.[1] Opinions not heard since the turbulent times of 1867 and 1868, except by the occasional Klansman, became a battle cry for conservatives. As 1876 opened, the *Rock Hill Grange* declared: "Let the last Southern State, one of the thirteen that declared herself free one hundred years ago, be again a white man's State."[2] The *Barnwell Sentinel* agreed, pledging "that the Fourth of July will find us armed and equipped for another great struggle even as our forefathers were an hundred years ago [sic]."[3] Alfred Brockenbrough Williams, a gun club member (and later author) who participated in at least one riot during 1876, wrote years later that "a few years more of the government of that kind . . . would make the Low County far worse than Haiti or Santo Domingo."[4] Matthew C. Butler, the former cooperationist who became a gun club commander in the military forces of redemption, asked "did not the mere fact of our migration to this land of freedom from the Mother Country presage the establishment of a pure white man's government? Did not the red man go to the wall before the superior race?" "The prime need for the body politic," Butler explained, "is to get to first principles & stick close to them; they will prove not only a check to degenerating tendencies of the times but a panacea for all of our ills."[5]

There was no dearth of support for Butler's "first principles." Speaking in March, A. M. Speights, the editor of the *Greenville News,* lectured that the "instincts of the white race" demand "that it will not be negroized, but will perish foot by foot, inch by inch, before it will consent to be mongrelized." "Let the men of the North of our own race know," Speights announced, "the solemn vow of Southern Society: WE WILL NOT HAVE THESE PEOPLE TO RULE OVER US!"[6] For Benjamin R. Tillman, it was a battle between "civilization" and "barbarism and the forces which were undermining the very foundations of our commonwealth." For Tillman and many like him, the white race represented civilization, since "the Creator made the Caucasian of a better clay than he made any of the colored people."[7] Carolinian Belton O'Neal Townsend concluded that "everyone thinks, and every child is trained up in the belief, that the negro is meant for the use of the white people, was brought here and thus should stay here for no other purpose." White Carolinians, Townsend claimed, believe that a black "should be ruled in all things political, social, and industrial by the white man, should be kept in his place, and decisively suppressed if he tries to put on airs."[8]

Past failures taught conservatives that raw sentiment and emotion were no substitutes for hard work and organization. The conservative press, local clubs, and state leaders began mobilizing the population after the judges' elections in December 1875, and these efforts intensified during the winter. The statewide "Democratic party" was in disarray, as conservatives had either abstained or been a weaker partner in the gubernatorial elections during Reconstruction. It was time, one Orangeburg citizen declared to the *Charleston News and Courier*, for "thorough organization, and a stubborn, persistent, uncompromising, unyielding, fight from now till next fall."[9] In fact, the designation "Democrat," dropped years earlier because of its negative associations, again became popular. There was "magic in the name of Democrat," one author commented, and "the union of the white people of the State is a prime necessity. Cost what it may, that must be had."[10]

The state Democratic executive committee reappeared as well after the December elections, and it quickly set out to mobilize the party. On January 6, committee chairman Alexander C. Haskell announced that "defeat cannot be borne" and "unity" and "discipline" were necessary to "ensure the prompt and efficient execution of [the committee's] policy when declared." He called for the creation of a new "political army" from the bottom up, organizing at the ward, precinct, township, and county levels.[11] Only careful preparation, Haskell warned, could "prevent South Carolina . . . from becoming as barbarous as Ashantee and as negro-ridden as San Domingo."[12]

In front of befuddled and anxious Republican eyes, "Organization the Watchword" became a reality. The *Spartanburg Herald* observed "a general uprising of the people who will no longer 'down [sic] at the bidding' of the corrupt majority." Bills were posted in Spartanburg calling on every man to "devote whatever of his time, energies, and means as may be necessary to redeem the State in the coming campaign."[13] The story was the same in Darlington, where a mass meeting called for "bolder and more vigorous measures than have hitherto been adopted to rescue the State from disgrace and misrule."[14] Large rallies were held in Greenville, Spartanburg, Newberry, Marion, Sumter, and Union.[15] The *Abbeville Medium* announced that "the people are thoroughly aroused on this subject and are determined to succeed by fair or foul means, the next campaign will be short, sharp, and decisive." If money and persuasion will not bring victory, one writer declared, then whites must "resort to another and more terrible appeal. The Democrats must carry the next election at every hazard."[16]

With organization proceeding, Democrats gathered on May 5 to nominate the ticket that they believed would redeem South Carolina.[17] But five months of preparation had not been enough, and delegates could not agree on a campaign strategy. The question was whether to run a "straight-out" ticket comprised wholly of Democrats or to open the ticket to renegade Republicans. "Straight-out" advocates, including Martin W. Gary and Matthew C. Butler, argued "the man who dares wins; not he who holds back." E. M. Murray agreed, stating there should be "no cringing and no more compromising with principle." But a small contingent of whites, including Johnson Hagood (yet another former Confederate general), sought to embrace moderate and bolting Republicans—perhaps even Chamberlain himself—arguing that black majority would snuff out any chances for a "straight-out" victory.[18]

Unable to reach a consensus, delegates decided to reconvene in a few months, when Democratic organization would be more complete. Both groups saw this situation as a victory: straight-outers hoped the postponement might increase their already considerable momentum, while cooperationists wanted to wait until after the Republican convention in September to nominate a ticket. Cooperationists planned to endorse Chamberlain if he were renominated. But the straight-outers had an ace-in-the-hole: the chairman of the state Democratic executive committee was responsible for calling the new convention; he was Alexander Haskell, an avowed straight-outer.[19]

Democratic mobilization continued after the convention adjourned, and news of meetings and the formation of clubs filled the newspapers.[20] There also appeared a fresh newspaper to carry these accounts, one whose existence testified to the importance and nature of the campaign. On May 1, 1876, the first issue of the *Charleston Journal of Commerce* rolled off the presses, a conservative paper meant to counterbalance the *News and Courier*, which many whites believed favored cooperation and Chamberlain. The chief editor of the *Journal* was none other than Robert Barnwell Rhett, Jr., and the paper promised to be as fire-eating as Carolinians had expected.[21]

Despite internal dissension, or perhaps because of it, Democratic whites were eager to display their advantages. One such occasion occurred on June 28, when Democrats and Republicans gathered in Charleston to celebrate the centennial of the battle of Ft. Moultrie. Governor Chamberlain attended the gala event, and dined with leading conservatives at Hibernian Hall; he sat to the left of the master of ceremonies, while Wade Hampton sat on the right. The governor was treated to an only slightly veiled display of Democratic force. Entertaining the crowds were various rifle and sabre clubs from the city and its environs, demonstrating their drills. This was the calm before the storm, for within a week such clubs would be instruments of terror, and within months Hampton and Chamberlain would be opposing commanders in the war over South Carolina.[22]

A week later, on July 4, 1876, while the country celebrated its centennial, a campaign characterized by propaganda, rhetoric, and organization gave way to a campaign based on bloodshed, force, and fear. In Aiken County, in the sleepy village of Hamburg on the Savannah River, began a chain of events which resulted in the solidification of white opinion and the triumph of the straight-out strategy. On July 4, Henry Getsen and Thomas Butler were passing through the nearly all-black town of Hamburg when a local militia company blocked the street. The captain, Doc Adams, was a former slave from Georgia who had served in the Union Army. Adams was openly hostile to the two men, but eventually the company opened and allowed the travelers to pass. Thomas Butler enlisted none other than local dignitary Matthew C. Butler (no relation to Thomas) to serve as his attorney, and filed suit against Adams for blocking a public highway. Adams countersued, charging the whites with interfering with a militia drill. After several postponed hearings, tensions came to a boil Saturday, July 8.[23]

Several hundred rifle club members appeared in town on Saturday morning, indicating that whites would have their justice one way or another. The trial justice, Prince Rivers, had escaped from South Carolina—and slavery—during the war and enlisted in the Union Army. Sensing trouble, he offered to collect the militia's guns and send them to Governor Chamberlain. Matthew C. Butler refused, stating that he alone would accept them. Seeking some security, Rivers asked if handing over the guns would guarantee the safety of the town; according to one witness, "his answer was no."[24] By mid-afternoon the whites were growing belligerent, so Rivers told the militiamen to lock themselves in the Sibley Building, an old brick warehouse; then the trial justice disappeared. Hundreds of whites took up positions around the warehouse and began firing into the building. Seeing that their small arms had little effect, they sent across the river to Augusta for a cannon. A few rounds from the cannon created a breech in one wall, and whites stormed inside. Some militiamen escaped by diving out windows and crawling out of the cellar; one was killed running out the back, but most others, between thirty and forty men, surrendered inside.[25]

Unfortunately for the captives, the whites were not yet finished. During the exchange around the Sibley Building, one white was killed by return fire from the militia. According to several witnesses who were hiding in the town, as well as participant Benjamin Ryan Tillman, gun clubs members were furious that a white lay dead but that only one black had been killed in the fight (although several were wounded). Consequently, club members selected six blacks from among their prisoners, lead them away, and shot them dead; Tillman was proud that he lent a pistol to one of the killers. The rest were then told to run, and as they bolted for the nearby woods, whites again opened fire—due compensation for earlier insults and a dead white. Reflecting on the evening's atrocities, Tillman said "we were all tired but more than satisfied with the result."[26]

A coroner's inquest lead to murder charges against many prominent local men, while nearly eighty others were charged with "aiding and abetting" in the murders. Over the next month, another local war hero-lawyer, Martin W. Gary, secured bail for all of the defendants; by October no one was in jail. Nor would they be in the future, for state Attorney General William Stone, and District Attorney David Corbin decided to postpone the case until after the election. The official reason was that due to the possibility of intimidation and retribution, on top of an already tense political environment, authorities decided that the delay was the safest course for the blacks involved. Although the dangers involved in holding a trial were certainly real, the fear of *losing* such an important case—and the damage it might do to the party in the middle of the campaign—may have also played a role in the decision to put off proceedings. Or this may have been an attempt to coax whites into abiding by the law by holding these prosecutions over their heads as some sort of "reward-or-punishment" device.[27]

Still, every possible motivation exposed the same problem: the government could not protect its citizens. Other Republican responses to the Hamburg massacre reiterated this sad fact. Only days after the killings, Representative Joseph B. Rainey was making the rounds in Washington, trying to get a pledge of assistance from the Grant administration.[28] U.S. Marshal R. B. Wallace, writing to the new attorney general, Alphonso Taft, claimed troops were necessary to assure blacks that "they were not to be abandoned to the swift destruction which was meted out to some of their friends and neighbors."[29] A few days later, Governor Chamberlain wrote to President Grant, warning him that "Hamburg is only the beginning" in the whites' drive for "the political subjugation and control of the State."[30]

Grant's enigmatic reply addressed directly the nature of power, the nature of government, and the relationship between the two in South Carolina. Although Grant promised the governor "every aid for which I can find law or constitutional power," the letter betrayed a growing impatience. Discussing his obligations as President, Grant explained that a "government that cannot give protection to the life, property, and all the guaranteed civil rights in this country . . . is insofar a failure. . . ." The veiled warning was probably not lost on Chamberlain. Grant continued on, sympathizing with the black population and fearing that "too long denial of the guaranteed rights is sure to lead to a revolution, a bloody revolution. . . ."[31] But as was the president speaking about blacks, or about the growing restlessness of the whites?

II

Striking while the iron was hot, the Democratic state central committee issued its call for a new convention to meet in Columbia. The committee aimed to disarm the few cooperationists who favored the "watch and wait" policy. Delegates would reconvene on August 15, well before the Republican convention scheduled for September, so there would be no opportunity to see if Republicans nominated Chamberlain again. But the timing of the call was important for other reasons. Chamberlain's reaction to the Hamburg outbreak—he blamed whites, called for troops, and then denied he had done so—inflamed white opinion and discredited those who sought an alliance. Furthermore, the lack of any substantive federal response and the postponement of legal action convinced moderate conservatives that force might work after all.[32] In the words of Alfred B. Williams, "the passion stirring event at Hamburg" made the straight-out policy "popular and possible."[33]

Democratic organization had continued across the state in July and early August, and newspaper accounts indicated that county conventions, clubs, and their voters overwhelmingly preferred the straight-out policy.[34] Richardson Miles claimed that "the people of the State are so sick at heart from the failure of every attempt that have hitherto been made—and so disgusted with the Republicans with whom they were forced to make alliances that they revolted against any coalition." A delegate to the new convention, Miles told his brother William Porcher Miles that although a gamble, any policy which "commands itself to the instincts and feelings of our people and which will *unite* them and enlist their enthusiasm and earnest support is better for us than the wisest policy which statesmanship can suggest which the people are unwilling to accept. . . ."[35] The cooperationists, fearing that an all-Democratic ticket could not succeed against a voting majority, did not collapse without a fight.[36] But the memories of failed alliances, the example of Mississippi, and the Republican response to Hamburg combined to make a powerful case. As Michael Perman has shown, Democrats now stressed their distinctiveness from, rather than similarity with, the Republicans; the focus would be on race, which was the uniting factor for whites.[37]

Democrats assembled in Columbia on August 15 and selected their ticket. The *Greenville News* announced that "a minority of white men, when united in a common purpose, never fails to drive from power a semi-barbarous majority." All that was missing, the paper declared, was "the apparition of some leader."[38] That leader was Wade Hampton III, member of one of South Carolina's oldest and most prestigious families, Confederate war hero, successful planter, and long-time opponent of Republican Reconstruction. More moderate than the Gary-Butler faction, Hampton made a back-handed effort to win black support and—perhaps wary of federal intervention—tried to control the violent tendencies of his fellow whites.[39] Still, he was a Carolina conservative, intent on redeeming his state. The *Nation* declared that Hampton was "neither a statesman nor a politician, nor a man of conciliatory disposition, nor any thing but a soldier and a Southern gentleman of the Old School, to who [sic] niggers, Yankees, schools, roads, free labor, and free speech are naturally almost as hateful as the Pope himself."[40]

Nominees for other positions were also former Confederate officers and native white conservatives. Delegates chose General William Dunlap Simpson to run for lieutenant governor, General James Conner (commander of the state's gun clubs during the campaign) for attorney general, and General Johnson Hagood for comptroller general.[41] B. Odell Duncan, a Carolina Democrat, wrote to Governor Chamberlain from Italy to comment on the convention's selections. Duncan regretted that the Democrats handed the campaign to "the most violent element of the party" and predicted "the triumph of violence, of oppression, and of the virtual disfranchisment of a race."[42]

Democratic unity forced Republican unity, and for the first time since 1868, the state Republican party held together in a gubernatorial campaign. At the September convention, the combination of the Democratic challenge and various back-room deals paved the way for Chamberlain's renomination. Included in the assorted deals was an agreement by Chamberlain to accept a leading rival, Robert B. Elliott, as his running mate. But Chamberlain's compromising with men of ill-repute cost him the last of his moderate conservative support, and even Francis W. Dawson returned humbly to the Democratic fold.[43] Immediately after the nomination, Chamberlain received a letter from Frank Arum, a trial justice, and John Gardner, the intendant of Edgefield. The letter offered congratulations and then turned solemn, the authors "hoping that you will live long enough [to see] . . . the expiration of the term. It would be idle words to express feelings, like Hope and wish of a Peaceful Administration, when we are on the very eve of war."[44]

"It Is in Every Sense a Military Campaign"

III

Yet as this "war" intensified, it became clear that Democratic warriors were not as unified as they wanted their enemies to believe. The difference lay in means, not ends. Both wings of the Carolina Democrats understood that force needed to be a central element of their campaign strategy—in order to overcome the black majority—but opinions differed on *how to use* that force. Wade Hampton advocated "bloodless coercion" with its displays of power, such as using demonstrations and parades to intimidate black voters. At the other end of the spectrum was Martin W. Gary, who had delivered his command over to a subordinate at the war's end, shouted "South Carolinians never surrender," and ridden off the field.[45] Gary led the most dangerous element in the Democratic party; their racist views and violent nature augured for a deadly campaign. Gary once proclaimed that "the glorious Palmetto has withered but not died, as it has been watered by tears of our women." "Should it become necessary," he warned, "it will be watered by the blood of the patriotic sons of South Carolina."[46]

Although not formally accepted as a campaign strategy, Gary's message was embraced by thousands of whites across the state who were tired of failure and submission. His plan, called "No. 1 Plan of the Campaign," listed thirty-three items necessary to winning the election. Many were rather mundane and obvious, such as making sure every Democrat was registered to vote. More telling were points left off from the public copies and circulated only in the privacy of Democratic club meetings. For instance, all clubs had to be armed and equipped—to the extent of having a supply wagon on hand, fully stocked, in case the club needed to be mobile or camp at a poll for a few days. Every Democrat had to "control" the vote of one black, "by intimidation, purchase, [or] keeping him away" from the polls. And do not bother arguing with blacks, Gary advised; just "treat them as to show them you are the superior race, and that their natural position is that of subordination to the white man." The Edgefield general even warned whites to "never threaten a man individually. If he deserves to be threatened, the necessities of the times require that he should die. A dead Radical is very harmless—a threatened Radical . . . is often very troublesome, sometimes dangerous, always vindictive."[47] Many South Carolinians agreed that physical intimidation was the most efficient means of influencing a voter. But organization was necessary, for a carefully planned murder—while alerting Republicans to their vulnerability—would not stir federal interest. One particular tactic popular during the 1876 campaign was the prearranged "scuffle." A group of Democrats would start a fight among themselves, and shots would be fired or knives drawn. When the smoke cleared, however, it was a Republican bystander or one who had been pulled into the brawl who lay dead.[48]

But Gary and his kind represented only one approach to the aim of carrying the election, and Democrats who were unwilling to murder had other tactics at their disposal. The boycott, for instance, was an agreement or resolution to not patronize any business run by a Republican. In Charleston, party officials posted the names of "Democratic butchers and stall-keepers," and local clubs resolved to use no others. Other towns followed suit, and other trades fell prey to white tactics; Alfred B. Williams recalled that "white men would walk rather than use a 'hack' drawn by a Republican or go unshaven rather than patronize a Republican barber."[49]

The "proscription" was a tactic conservatives had used before, in a way the reverse of the boycott. This was a refusal to sell goods, rent land, lend money, or even provide medical attention to Republicans. The Pond Bluff Democratic Club, resolving that "this is a white man's country and as such has to be ruled by the white men," declared that no member would "employ in any way directly or indirectly anyone who votes against us nor will we rent land or houses to them."[50] Scores of Democratic clubs drafted similar resolutions, some providing "certificates" to blacks who pledged to vote Democratic. If they presented their certificate, they were treated fairly; without one, whites would "refuse favors and help of all kinds."[51]

Nor were whites above purchasing votes to win back their state. Robert Wallace Shand admitted "intimidation and bribery" were the best ways of influencing black voters, and his club concentrated on the latter by collecting and selling old clothes and shoes and borrowing money from connections in New York. Shand boasted that his "area" had raised over one thousand dollars for the bribing of voters.[52] John Calhoun of Abbeville had to rely on his own resources: "I feel sure that three out of four of my freedmen will not vote," he asserted, "it will *cost me* something, but their voting might cost me more."[53]

Considering the range of pressures applied, it is not surprising to learn that some Republicans did indeed "cross Jordan" and vote the Democratic ticket. For most, however, the change was anything but voluntary. In Greenville, for example, blacks were "compelled to buy red shirts, declare themselves as Democrats, in order to save their lives [sic] and will be forced to vote the Democratic ticket. . . ." The marshal and trial justice claimed they were powerless to stop the intimidation, for "the Cavalry of this county is thoroughly organized and uniformed."[54] School Commissioner Joseph Clark observed similar activities in Lancaster County and reported that "nine colored men were forced to join a Democratic club last Saturday night; some being paid; others threatened." With violence and threats rampant and armed whites openly harassing Republicans, Clark described his county as "a perfect hell here on earth."[55]

What is surprising, given the brutal choices facing Republicans—especially black Republicans—was the small number of voters who did change sides. Alfred B. Williams recorded the existence of a few black Democratic clubs, and even some black rifle clubs. But clubs and members may have appeared to be more numerous than they were, for whites tried to reap political benefits by displaying blacks prominently at every rally. For instance, a Carolina newspaper claimed over two hundred mounted blacks were at an Edgefield parade, while a Northern reporter counted a mere nine. Another paper estimated three hundred black Democrats attended a Sumter meeting, but a visiting correspondent saw only thirteen.[56] At one rally a rifle club captain even admitted that "I do regret that our colored friends are not here in larger numbers."[57]

If Democrats could not make Republicans change their votes, they might at least keep them from voting at all. This was the mission of the chief agents of Democratic intimidation, the gun clubs. Rifle and sabre clubs had existed for years in the state and had already earned a reputation for brutality (to simplify matters, the generic phrase "gun club" will be used when referring to rifle clubs, sabre clubs, and other white paramilitary units). Following the Columbia convention, scores of new clubs appeared, most of them armed and many of them mounted. According to C. Irvine Walker of Charleston's Carolina Rifle Club, they were "the most powerful means by which the white men were enabled to quell negro [sic] and his carpetbag masters, and, regain the political control of the State."[58] Governor Chamberlain claimed that 240 gun clubs existed, with over 20,000 members, while Republican Senator John J. Patterson put the figure at 60,000.[59] Democrat Alexander Haskell later testified that there were "three or four hundred clubs in the State during the campaign—at least that number." Historians Francis Simkins and Robert Woody have estimated that at least 290 gun clubs were organized, with a membership of about 15,000 men.[60]

As with the Democrats' political reorganization, the speed of their military mobilization was frightening. In late August and early September, reports of the formation of rifle clubs filled conservative newspapers.[61] These were not haphazard gangs roaming the countryside; most had written constitutions, and all were under the ultimate command of General James Conner (who was also candidate for state attorney general). The clubs were divided into an "upper" command, under Colonel Samuel Pickens, and a "lower" one, under Major Theodore Barker, previously commander of the Carolina Rifle Club. The structure, according to

Richardson Miles, created a "very efficient force available in a moment."[62] The rifle clubs even adopted a uniform, another symbol of the organization and uniformity of purpose: the infamous "red shirt" of dyed red flannel, which became synonymous with Carolina rifle clubs in general.[63]

As the Democratic army grew, Republicans became more desperate. District Attorney David Corbin informed Attorney General Alphonso B. Taft that the Ku Klux Klan "was not, consequently broken up in these counties, or so punished as to destroy it." Corbin claimed "these Ku-Klux Klans have reorganized under the names of *rifle clubs* and have entered upon and intend to pursue the purposes and general plans of 1871 and 1872 of the old organizations."[64] U.S. Marshal R. B. Wallace wrote to Taft a week later, telling him that "combinations are rapidly forming . . . [which will] prevent the republicans of this and other counties from casting their full strength in the presidential election. . . ." According to Wallace, white leaders "openly declare that they intend to carry the coming election, and ostracize and threaten all leading men of the republican party." "I warn you," Wallace told his superior, "that there is certain danger ahead, and a liberal supply of U.S. Troops can alone prevent mobocracy and bloodshed."[65]

Considering the lack of federal response in other Southern states, most Republican officials realized that federal help was unlikely. As always, options were few. A well-organized, well-trained militia force did not exist; the black militia was poorly trained and even more poorly led. Nor did Governor Chamberlain try to create any auxiliary forces for the election. James P. Low, the state's chief constable of Charleston, suggested creating a "Special Force" that would "insure the preservation of the peace during the excitement likely to prevail here during the next three months." But the city's mayor, George Cunningham, opposed the idea on financial grounds, proposing instead that federal troops be called in should trouble occur; despite the unlikelihood of federal assistance, Chamberlain concurred.[66]

Instead, the administration opted for ill-conceived measures that bespoke its impotence. Lacking adequate time to prepare a security force, Chamberlain distributed state guns and ammunition in a haphazard manner to any Republican who asked. Some arms went to state officials, such as Henry E. Hendricks, Charleston's chief of police.[67] Many more, however, went to citizens' groups and Republican political clubs.[68] The *Charleston News and Courier* charged that at least 10,000 guns were in the hands of private individuals, many of whom belonged to "companies not organized as required by law."[69]

Although Democrats complained about the number of guns in Republican (and mostly black) hands, they neglected to comment on the surprising number of guns that seemed to disappear from the books. Republicans would badger the governor or the adjutant general for arms, only to have them intercepted en route. In one case, whites at a Newberry railroad depot opened a box marked "Agricultural Implements" and found a stack of Remington rifles (which they of course confiscated).[70] Guns earmarked for the Aiken County militia somehow found their way into white hands and were taken to Augusta for storage![71] In nearby Edgefield, Sheriff James Richardson awoke one morning to find that a band of men had locked his deputy in a cell and taken some two or three hundred militia guns from storage (this was an altogether too frequent occurrence in that county).[72]

While the rifle clubs were well armed—sometimes with Republicans' guns—some Democratic leaders were hesitant to risk the "Gary approach," choosing instead to walk a fine line between latent aggression and actual violence. With the explosion in the number of gun clubs and the Hamburg massacre, the *Charleston News and Courier* reprinted articles from outside South Carolina warning that violence could prove counterproductive. The *Richmond Dispatch* declared that such incidents "bode no good to the Democratic party." The *New York Herald* went further, stating that "these southern white madmen resolved to elect Hayes and Wheeler ... [since] one or two Hamburg riots will settle the business." The *News and Courier* added that "the Hamburg regulators are murderers in a double sense: They stabbed the State in the back, while killing their suppliant prisoners."[73]

With the conservative army growing and tensions running high, Wade Hampton and others tried to prevent bloodshed—and the reaction it might bring. Early in the campaign Johnson Hagood circulated a rumor that Hampton would quit if rifle clubs initiated violence. Alexander Haskell, chair of the state Democratic central committee, met often with county representatives, imploring them to avoid violence; such strength was for appearances only. The executive committee of Barnwell followed suit, declaring that "rioting before or at the polls, or race collisions brought about by the whites are deemed almost insane folly."[74] Even C. Irvine Walker of the Carolina Rifle Club agreed with the decision. Although "in a square fight the Whites could easily have cleaned them out," Walker believed it "an eminently wise policy" for the gun clubs "to avoid, if possible, any race trouble...."[75] The *Charleston Journal of Commerce* concurred, warning Democrats to "avoid being led into any collisions...."[76]

Hampton's policy of "bloodless coercion" relied on "presence" and the flexing of white muscle to intimidate Republicans. As with more violent methods, the gun clubs were at the center of Hampton's approach. One popular "bloodless" tactic was the "division of time." Democratic political and paramilitary clubs (often one and the same) would show up at a Republican speech or gathering, and demand that they receive equal time to address the audience. When Democrats were allowed to speak, they abused Republican leaders so badly that many stopped open campaigning. Yet refusal to give in would reflect badly on the Republican leaders, and result in an uproar.[77] This response, which Richardson Miles termed "hacking," involved the open abuse and discrediting of Republican leaders in front of their supporters. Rifle club members would gather by the hundreds—armed, mounted, and uniformed—and surround a Republican rally. The whites would create a commotion by shouting, riding, and firing weapons, often forcing the assembly to dissolve. Unless there was outright violence, the federal government could not interfere; as Miles suspected, the Republicans "cannot prevent our 'hacking' and discrediting process."[78] Democrat Alfred B. Williams stated the purpose of "hacking" was to "destroy confidence of the Negroes in their [leaders'] courage and their characters."[79] Even Governor Chamberlain could not deny this, for he admitted that the tactic "amounted to simply giving up the meeting to them; and you could not get quiet, peaceable Republicans to come out and expose themselves to such treatment after they had one or two experiences of it...."[80]

Beginning in late August and continuing until the election, Democrats harassed Republicans at nearly every meeting and gathering that they held. Early in the campaign Chamberlain personally canvassed the state, but after being humiliated at speeches in Edgefield, Newberry, and Abbeville, the governor ceased public speaking "because it was not considered safe...."[81] The depth of conservative white animosity, and their cold determination, was clear. At a rally at Strawberry Ferry just upriver from Charleston, Alfred B. Williams selected a black man—as all members of his gun club were told to do—and told him "you see this gun? It carries 16 balls and is loaded full. My orders are to stick to you all day and if any trouble is started here to shoot until you're dead, first thing; and I'm going to do it."[82] Thomas Pinckney Lowndes also attended, and used the same ferry as a black militia unit. He felt pity for "these American citizens of probably Baboon descent" who were "attempting to assert their rights to a citizenship which was no more theirs than that of the mule that ploughed their melon patch."[83] Most whites had no such pity, for marshals and Republicans reported that most whites were hostile, aggressive, and defiant; as Congressman A. S. Wallace said, "intimidation is the order of the day and terrorism reigns supreme...."[84]

While many rifle clubs were off harassing Republicans, others were appearing at Democratic rallies and parades. Public events were held all over the state, featuring speeches by revered Carolina cavaliers and exhibitions by rifle clubs; there is no record of violence or Republican interruptions at any Democratic assembly. The campaign opened in Columbia on August 16, with a torchlight parade that included over a thousand "cavalry" carrying transparencies that read "Carolina, Home of the White Man."[85] Some of the largest demonstrations—with thousands involved in the festivities—occurred at Edgefield and Yorkville.[86] Speakers in Yorkville drew parallels between the current campaign and the nearby battlefield of King's Mountain, "where white men of the same kind and blood and breed as were assembled at Yorkville to overthrow the alien struck the blow at Tories and invaders that assured the victory at Yorktown."[87]

Perhaps the most impressive element of the Democratic canvass was Wade Hampton's march across the state. Like some perverse reversal of Sherman's invasion over a decade earlier, Hampton's tour carried with it the same message: you are powerless against us, and we will do as we please. The tone of Hampton's trip across South Carolina was not that of a candidate or a challenger; rather, it resembled the triumphant procession of a conquering hero. Nothing better expressed the unity of sentiment, the depth of organization, and the sheer determination of white Carolinians than the march of Hampton and his entourage. Setting out from Abbeville in mid-September with a sendoff by three thousand mounted guards, Hampton passed into Newberry, Laurens, Greenville, Spartanburg, and along the North Carolina border through Marlboro, reaching Marion Court House by early October. Dozens of gun clubs and hundreds of men escorted him from stop to stop, and each town welcomed him with fanfare fit for a king.[88] By mid-October he had begun his trek back across the state, traveling through Sumter, across to Edgefield, then south to Barnwell and back east to Orangeburg.[89] When Hampton arrived in Sumter on October 16—as always, at the head of an army of rifle clubs—he found a white woman lying in the square, wearing a ribbon with "South Carolina" written across it. Hampton raised her off the ground in front of a crowd that broke into a frenzy. The scene was repeated over and over, sometimes with "justice" looking on, or with thirty-seven other women standing by, waiting to greet the risen state (the thirty seven representing other states).[90] At Georgetown the cavalry hero was met by banners saying "Let Carolina be Governed by Carolinians" and "See, Our Conquering Chieftan Comes."[91]

Hampton's procession ended with a spectacular entry into Charleston on October 31. James Conner, candidate for attorney general and overall commander of the state's gun clubs, had informed his wife of their progress along the way. "You can form no idea of the enthusiasm and excitement of the people," Conner wrote during their journey.[92] But he admitted lacking the words to describe the entry into Charleston, the second largest procession ever held in the city; only the funeral of John C. Calhoun was larger. The guest list at dinner was a Carolina "Who's Who": Hampton was joined by James Conner, William Dunlap Porter, Louis DeSaussure, and even John B. Gordon, along with various members from the Manigualt, Miles, and Simonton families.[93] Reflecting on the campaign thus far, Conner told his wife that "if we do not scare the darkies and astonish the Governor more than ever, I am a Dutchman."[94]

IV

Unfortunately, not all Democrats were content with dinners and parades. Many favored a more direct approach to redeeming their state, and even the influence of Hampton could not curb Democratic excesses. Reports of politically motivated violence began soon after the Democratic convention, when Martin W. Gary was at his most vocal. By the beginning of September, Governor Chamberlain was receiving detailed accounts of systematic attacks from the counties of Laurens, Edgefield, and Marlboro. "The Colored Citizens of Laurens" claimed that no one "dares to speak nor act with respect of his franchise privileges without being in extreme danger." Threats, the authors stated, "were being *put into execution* almost daily. No week passes without some of our people are either whiped, shot at by the night riders don't know that we can call them KKK but we are certain that they are Democratic desperadoes. . . ."[95] John Gardner, the intendant of Hamburg; George Wadell, the sheriff of Marlboro County; and Joseph Clark, a school superintendent in Lancaster—all requested U.S. troops to protect Republicans and help them enforce the law.[96]

With state officials powerless and federal forces standing neutral, Republican blacks became more desperate and more militant. A serious riot erupted in Charleston on September 6, one of the few such occurrences initiated by blacks.[97] In a remarkable display of discipline, whites did not stop the disturbance or retaliate. Both the police and the city's gun clubs assumed defensive postures but did not take an active part in suppressing the riot. Charleston's mayor, George Cunningham, and the rifle clubs' commander, Theodore Barker, came under sharp Democratic criticism for their inaction. But the decision was shrewd; in the "King Street riot," no one could accuse Democrats of killing Republicans. Barker replied to his critics that to use the rifle clubs "would have meant slaughter . . . [which] would have hardened the North against the entire South and South Carolina especially." Barker admitted that he had even been told to take his clubs to the upper wards and attack Republican clubs there. "I decided not to bring on this fight," Barker said, "... *but to postpone this encounter,* in order that, when made, it will be more effectual, and that more white men may have the opportunity . . . to engage in settlement of the issue. . . ."[98]

Whites did take precautions afterwards, and Charleston took on the appearance of an occupied city. Gun clubs posted artillery pieces at key locations throughout the city, mounted whites patrolled the streets at night, and a gunboat even patrolled the river "to prevent any influx of negroes from the outlying country." Rifle clubs slept in shifts, so that there were always men armed and ready. One club even ordered that "men not on duty at night must not take their clothes off, when they lie down at home."[99]

The "King Street riot" was uncommon because it reversed the usual role of agitator and victim; most violence was Democratic and white in origin. H. N. Bonney of Edgefield Court House declared that "all is not quiet in our hellish county" for the "Democrats are riding through the county striking terror in the hearts of Republicans."[100] From neighboring Barnwell County came the report that Democrats "intend to kill every leader in the Radical party—and they are going around our houses every night more or less, way laying us."[101] Another report from the same county described an attack on a black church that left one man dead; blacks were sleeping in the woods at night to avoid detection.[102] The situation was so bad along the southwestern counties that Henry W. Ravenel feared that "the excitement is now so high, that it would take but a trifle to produce a collision between the whites and blacks."[103] Fearing just such a collision, the War Department in late August moved several infantry units from Columbia to outlying regions. The new commander of the Department of the South, Brigadier General Thomas H. Ruger, moved his headquarters and the rest of his regiment, the Eighteenth Infantry, to Columbia in preparation for the campaign.[104]

Shrewd and pragmatic, Hampton again advised moderation and discretion to avoid arousing suspicion or angering the federal soldiers. In October, he told listeners that federal troops are "no longer our enemies but the best friends we have in the North, treat them kindly." "I am glad they have come," Hampton announced, "for they will recognize and sympathize with our efforts in behalf of republican freedom."[105] The *Army and Navy Journal* described a grand welcome received by troops as they entered Edgefield Court House; "if anything," the article read, the local whites "rather overdo the matter of enthusiasm." Troops saw through the ruse, for the *Journal* stated that "the soldiers are not as thoroughly assured as they might have wished to be as to the perfect sincerity of the demonstration. . . ."[106]

White sincerity received another blow after two blacks were accused of breaking into a house and robbing and beating an old woman inside. The incident—which was later proven false—took place in early September near Ellenton, along the border of Aiken and Barnwell Counties. When warrants went out for the arrest of two blacks, local militias gathered to protect the men from arrest. In response, white rifle clubs arrived from surrounding townships, and calls went out to nearby counties as well. According to Johnson Hagood, who commanded one of the clubs, nearly five hundred whites responded. For two days white gunmen scoured the region around Ellenton, playing a deadly cat-and-mouse game with the militiamen.[107]

The engagement approached its climax on September 19, at a place called Rouse's Bridge, a few miles outside of Ellenton. Over three hundred whites had trapped about a hundred militiamen in a wooded cul-de-sac. Around half past nine in the morning, just as whites were positioning for a final assault, Captain Thomas Lloyd arrived with a detachment of U.S. infantry. Lloyd reported "there was undoubted evidence of a well-digested plan of attack, which, if carried out would have resulted in the slaughter of nearly all the negroes in the place."[108] After making sure the militia and rifle clubs headed their separate ways, Lloyd and his men went to survey the damage in Ellenton, passing by dead blacks along the way. Although the infantry prevented a massacre, the final toll was still high; between thirty and fifty blacks had been murdered in two days, and three whites also lay dead. Simon Coker, a state representative from Barnwell, was among those killed; he had been shot in the head at point-blank range while on his knees praying.[109]

Knowing it would have no positive effect, the Governor Chamberlain did not even bother to declare martial law or call the state militia into service. Nor did he take the advice of concerned observers, such as E. H. Saltiel in Colorado Springs. After hearing of the Ellenton outrages, Saltiel—the publisher of the *Alabama State Gazette* before that state's redemption—recommended hiring one thousand whites from New York, "men not afraid of a brush," enlisting them in the state militia, declaring martial law, arresting the Democratic leaders, and court martialing them. "If found guilty," Saltiel said, "shoot or hang them without delay."[110] Chamberlain even received a letter from the Gatling Gun Company, suggesting he outfit his militia with their new machine-guns. "For the purpose of quelling riots," Edgar Welles, the company's secretary declared, ". . . these guns are especially suited."[111]

Believing that his forces were inadequate for such measures—and that such acts might only exacerbate the anarchy—Chamberlain chose another path. First he wrote an angry letter to Alexander Haskell. Democrats, the governor asserted, were to blame for the disturbances in the state, and accepting the notion that rifle clubs existed to uphold the law was akin to setting "kites to watch doves, or wolves to guard sheep."[112] A few days later, on October 7, the governor issued a proclamation to "forbid the existence of all said organizations or combinations of men, commonly known as 'Rifle Clubs.'" Chamberlain ordered all clubs disbanded, and made their existence illegal "in any place or under any circumstances in the State."[113]

Chamberlain intended that his action serve as a constitutional precursor for his bringing in the federal authorities. The besieged governor hoped that if he declared such organizations illegal, and they refused to disband, then the door would be open for federal intervention. Chamberlain wasted no time informing Washington of his plight: "Insurrection and domestic violence exist in various portions of the State," Chamberlain wrote to Grant, and "I am unable with any means at my command to suppress the same." Chamberlain called on the president, as chief executive, to "aid me in supressing [sic] said insurrection and domestic violence."[114] J. G. Winsmith, frequent correspondent to President Grant, went further. "Nothing but the declaration of martial law," Winsmith believed, ". . . and the exhibition of power and authority of the National Government can save South Carolina from a bloody revolution and the domination of Hampton and Gary and Butler." These men "have breathed nothing but rebellion since this campaign opened. It is in every sense a military campaign which they have been conducting."[115]

As Democrats happily pointed out—and many Republicans could not help but notice—the elected state authorities were unable to deal with internal problems of law and order. In a speech at Cheraw just after the Ellenton disorders, Wade Hampton remarked that "it seems to me that a Governor who cannot feel that his seat is secured by the confidence and affection of the people . . . would be untrue to himself . . . if he did not resign." Hampton's message was clear: no governor can long exist in power "unless he be sustained by the best sentiments of his people."[116] An editorial in the *Charleston Journal of Commerce* raised a similar point: "There can be no liberty where there is not self-government, and no free government without the consent of the governed."[117]

That message—that Chamberlain and the other elected Republican officials were not in control of the state—was brought home once again with violence. On October 15, Republicans met for a rally at the "Brick Church" just outside Cainhoy, a small town about thirty miles inland from Charleston. As was common at Republican meetings, at least two hundred Democrats attended. But Republicans, wary of any Democratic presence and by now familiar with Democratic tactics, had come fully armed, with several militia companies present. Democrats protested, so in order to avoid a confrontation, the militia stored their arms in several buildings nearby and settled in to hear the speeches.

It still remains a mystery as to what sparked the "Cainhoy riot." Some witnesses say a scuffle ensued between a Republican and a Democrat, while others contend that the whole event was preplanned by vengeful blacks. At some point during the speeches, a gun discharged, and blacks, fearing another massacre, ran for their weapons. Not surprisingly, whites had already seized some of the militia guns, and both groups began firing. Blacks had the better position and eventually drove many of the whites to the river, where they boarded the steamer *Pocosin*. The steamer left for Charleston and returned by evening with reinforcements from the Palmetto Guards and other rifle clubs (who had obviously ignored Chamberlain's proclamation). By the time they arrived, the battle was over and the militia had fled, leaving six dead whites and one of their own. As state Attorney General William Stone put it, "the negroes are learning the law of retaliation."[118] As in Charleston earlier, blacks were at least partially responsible for the bloodshed, but the significance remained: private citizens were killers, and private citizens were responsible for their own safety. The state government seemed a nonentity.

As Hampton had warned, the gun clubs had gone too far. Cainhoy and Ellenton, coming on top of a campaign already noted for its violence and political terrorism, convinced President Ulysses S. Grant that these were military forces engaged in violent operations, not political clubs trying to stir up votes. On October 17, citing the fact that "insurrection" and "domestic violence" existed in South Carolina, President Grant commanded all persons engaging in lawless activities to disperse to their homes within three days. The chief executive then ordered all available forces in the Division of the Atlantic to General Ruger in Columbia (Ruger's Department of the South was under the umbrella of the Division of the Atlantic, which had replaced the earlier Division of the South). Secretary of War James D. Cameron stated boldly that "it is the fixed purpose of the Government to carry out the spirit of the proclamation, and to sustain it by the military force of the General Government. . . ."[119]

A flurry of activity followed in the War Department. The army transferred men from the artillery schools at Fort Monroe, Virginia; recruiting posts in New York City; and posts in Rhode Island, Connecticut, Massachusetts, and as far away as Maine. The department even dredged up men from Forts Niagara and Ontario, all for duty in South Carolina. The entire Eighteenth Infantry was stationed in the state, along with companies from the First, Second, Third, and Fifth Artillery, and several companies of the Second Infantry. The total count came to 1,144 officers and men.[120] Chamberlain had won a small victory, and the state faced the election with more U.S. soldiers present than at any time since its readmission to the Union, including the period of the Ku Klux Klan operation.

By now, state conservatives were veterans at playing "cat-and-mouse" with authorities and adroitly sidestepped the president's proclamation ordering the disbandment of the clubs. As the Klan has done earlier, the gun clubs complied with the letter, rather than the spirit, of the law and adapted to the new conditions. James Conner told his wife that Chamberlain probably hoped whites would resist, "and he will be able to say to the President that the insurrection is too formidable." "But," Conner wrote, "we see the game and don't mean to play it to his hands."[121] Violence subsided briefly, and many of the gun clubs disbanded—or so it seemed. In Spartanburg, for instance, clubs disbanded to avoid providing "grist for the outrage mill," yet members agreed to remain "vigilant and active."[122] Matthew C. Butler openly declared that "if there are any rifle clubs, let them disband and re-organize themselves at once into *Democratic clubs, without arms.*" He added, "God will furnish them with arms" to defeat the Radicals. Just below his announcement in the *Herald* was an article that 370 guns had been stolen from the Edgefield jail (again!).[123]

Feigning compliance, many gun clubs changed nothing but their names. For instance, the "Columbia Flying Artillery" became the "Columbia Musical Club with Four Twelve Pounder Flutes."[124] The Allendale Rifle Club informed Chamberlain that it had been disbanded, but failed to tell him it now existed as the Allendale Mounted Baseball Club! There were mounted sewing circles, mounted dancing clubs, and even mounted church groups.[125]

With only such cosmetic changes, and despite the presence of over one thousand U.S. soldiers, violence continued as Democrats sought to pressure Republican voters and test administration will. Reports of attacks and requests for protection came in from Colleton, Clarendon, Chester, Spartanburg, and Aiken.[126] The fact that terrorism continued with additional troops in the state damaged morale even further. Republicans grew more desperate, and hopelessness and despair seeped into their correspondence. Not uncommon was the letter from an attorney in Greenville, in which he simply stated that "the object of the democrats is to keep them [blacks] away from meetings and away from the polls—I fear that if the election was to come off now that their labors in this district would not have been in vain."[127]

The campaign had, in fact, already demonstrated *who* was in control of South Carolina. The election served only to validate Hampton's authority. Chamberlain and the Republicans were ineffective both as leaders and protectors, and not even federal attention deflected the Democratic drive. The struggle for control of the state was nearly over, with conservatives poised for victory. This was a victory fifteen years in the making, and in the words of Carolinian Alvin Hart, "they don't intend for any thing to keep them from it."[128]

Notes

1. Historians still debate whether race was a pure issue in itself or the upper classes used the race issue to control and manipulate those more susceptible to the threats inherent in racial equality. Some excellent discussions on this topic include Otto H. Olsen, ed., *Reconstruction and Redemption in the South* (Baton Rouge: Louisiana State University Press, 1980), 8; Barbara J. Fields, "Ideology and Race in American History, in *Region, Race, and Reconstruction: Essays in Honor of C. Vann Woodward,* ed. J. Morgan Kousser and James M. McPherson (New York: Oxford University Press, 1982), 143–69; George M. Fredrickson, "Aristocracy and Democracy in the Southern Tradition," in *The Southern Enigma: Essays on Race, Class and Folk Culture,* ed. Walter J. Fraser and Winfred B. Moore, Jr. (Westport, Conn.: Greenwood Press, 1983), 102–3; James L. Roark, *Masters without Slaves: Southern Planters in the Civil War and Reconstruction* (New York: W. W. Norton, 1977), 192–95.

2. *Rock Hill Grange,* n.d.; quoted in the *Charleston News and Courier,* January 15, 1876.

3. *Barnwell Sentinel,* n.d.; quoted in the *Charleston News and Courier,* January 15, 1876.

4. Alfred Brockenbrough Williams, "Eyewitness to 1876," January 23, 1927, Alfred Brockenbrough Williams Scrapbook, South Caroliniana Library, University of South Carolina, Columbia, S.C. (hereafter SCL). Williams, who participated in the campaign of 1876 in South Carolina, wrote a series of articles commemorating the fiftieth anniversary of his state's Redemption. The dates accompanying these citations are the dates of the particular articles within the manuscript collection and do not refer to any particular historical events.

5. Matthew C. Butler, Matthew Calbraith Butler Papers, Special Collections Library Research Room, Perkins Library, Duke University, Durham, N.C.

6. Speech of A. M. Speights at Beaver Dam (Laurens County), March 18, 1876; printed in the *Spartanburg Herald,* April 5, 1876; emphasis in original.

7. Benjamin Ryan Tillman, "The Struggles of 1876," 8; quoted in Francis Butler Simkins, *The Tillman Movement in South Carolina* (Durham: Duke University Press, 1926), 39.

8. Belton O'Neal Townsend ("A South Carolinian"), "The Political Condition of South Carolina," *Atlantic Monthly* 39 (1877): 470.

9. *Charleston News and Courier,* January 6, 1876.

10. *Charleston News and Courier,* January 10, 1876.

11. Alexander C. Haskell, quoted in *Charleston News and Courier,* January 8, 1876. See also Walter Allen, *Governor Chamberlain's Administration in South*

Carolina: A Chapter of Reconstruction in the Southern States (New York: G. P. Putnam's Sons, 1888), 273.

12. *Charleston News and Courier,* January 10, 1876.
13. *Spartanburg Herald,* January 12, 1876.
14. *Charleston News and Courier,* January 14, 1876.
15. *Charleston News and Courier,* February 8, 10, 15, 1876; *Spartanburg Herald,* February 23, March 29, June 7, 1876.
16. *Abbeville Medium,* n.d.; quoted in the *Charleston News and Courier,* January 29, 1876.
17. For a list of delegates see John S. Reynolds, *Reconstruction in South Carolina, 1865–1877* (Columbia, S.C.: State Company, 1905), 340–43.
18. All quotes are taken from the *Charleston News and Courier,* May 6, 1876.
19. Michael Perman, *The Road to Redemption: Southern Politics, 1869–1879* (Chapel Hill: University of North Carolina Press, 1984), 168–69.
20. Allen, *Governor Chamberlain's Administration,* 399; *Charleston News and Courier,* June 23, 1876; *Spartanburg Herald,* June 21, 1876.
21. Evidently the only extant issues of the *Charleston Journal of Commerce* are in the book division of the South Caroliniana Library at the University of South Carolina. For this reason, my citations will include the location reference SCL. I wish to express my appreciation to the SCL staff, who spent an entire afternoon searching their holdings to find the elusive paper.
22. Irvine C. Walker, *Carolina Rifle Club, July 30, 1869,* in *Pamphlets: Reconstruction in South Carolina, Democratic and Republican, 1869–1880* (n.d., n.p.), 43; Richard Current, *Those Terrible Carpetbaggers* (New York: Oxford University Press, 1988), 348.
23. Williams, "Eyewitness to 1876," August 8, 1926, SCL; "Notebook on 1876," Martin Witherspoon Gary Papers, SCL; Eric Foner, *Reconstruction, 1863–1873: America's Unfinished Revolution* (New York: Harper and Row, 1988), 570, 572; Thomas Holt, *Black over White: Negro Political Leadership in South Carolina during Reconstruction* (Urbana: University of Illinois Press, 1977), 78–79.
24. See the entry for Reverend Paul Jefferson in "Notebook on 1876," Martin Witherspoon Gary Papers, SCL.
25. Benjamin Ryan Tillman, "Autobiography," 12–19, SCL; *Charleston News and Courier,* July 10, 1876; U.S. Senate, *"South Carolina in 1876": Testimony as to the Denial of the Elective Franchise in South Carolina at the Elections of 1875 and 1876,* 44th Cong., 2d sess., S. Doc. 48 (Serial 1727), 646–48 (hereafter "South Carolina in 1876"); "Notebook on 1876," Martin Witherspoon Gary Papers, SCL.
26. *Charleston News and Courier,* July 10 and 11, 1876; Tillman, "Autobiography," 12–24, SCL.
27. "Notebook on 1876," Martin Witherspoon Gary Papers, SCL; Williams, "Eyewitness to 1876," August 29, 1926, January 2, 9, 16, and 30, 1927, SCL; *Charleston News and Courier,* August 12, 1876; *Charleston Journal of Commerce,* September 12 and 13, 1876, SCL; William Stone to Daniel H. Chamberlain, September 6, 1876, in Box 14, Folder 23, Governor Chamberlain Papers,

South Carolina Department of Archives and History, Columbia, S.C. (hereafter SCDAH).

28. *Charleston Journal of Commerce,* July 21, 1876, SCL.

29. R. B. Wallace to Alphonso B. Taft, July 17, 1876, in Record Group 60, Microcopy 947, Reel 2, National Archives, Washington, D.C. (hereafter RG, MC, Reel, NA).

30. Daniel Chamberlain, quoted in Allen, *Governor Chamberlain's Administration,* 323.

31. Ulysses S. Grant to Daniel Chamberlain, July 26, 1876; quoted in the *Spartanburg Herald,* August 9, 1876. See also Allen, *Governor Chamberlain's Administration,* 325.

32. *Governor Chamberlain's Administration,* 331.

33. Williams, "Eyewitness to 1876," August 15, 1926, SCL.

34. For news on political mobilization and the growing support for a straight-out approach, see issues of the *Charleston News and Courier* for late July and early August, and Williams's "Eyewitness to 1876," accounts dated during August 1926.

35. Richardson Miles to William Porcher Miles, August 26, 1876, in Box 5, Folder 63, William Porcher Miles Papers, Southern Historical Collection, University of North Carolina, Chapel Hill, N.C. (hereafter SHC/UNC); emphasis in original.

36. Williams, "Eyewitness to 1876," September 5, 1926, SCL.

37. Perman, *The Road to Redemption,* 150–51, 170. See also Joel Williamson, *After Slavery: The Negro in South Carolina during Reconstruction, 1861–1877* (Chapel Hill: University of North Carolina Press, 1965), 353–55; Francis Butler Simkins and Robert Hilliard Woody, *South Carolina during Reconstruction* (Chapel Hill: University of North Carolina Press, 1932), 473; John A. Leland, *A Voice from South Carolina: Journal of a Reputed Ku-Klux* (Charleston, S.C.: Walker, Evans, and Cogswell, 1879), 135–36.

38. *Greenville News,* n.d.; quoted in the *Edgefield Advertiser,* August 10, 1876.

39. William Arthur Sheppard, *Red Shirts Remembered: Southern Brigadiers of the Reconstruction Period* (Atlanta: Ruralist Press, 1940), 122; Henry T. Thompson, *Ousting the Carpetbagger from South Carolina* (Columbia, S.C.: R. L. Bryan, 1926; New York: Negro Universities Press, 1969), 117.

40. *Nation,* n.d.; quoted in Allen, *Governor Chamberlain's Administration,* 337.

41. All candidates for high office had been general officers during the war, and with the exception of Conner, all would eventually be elected governor. See Williams, "Eyewitness to 1876," September 5, 1926, SCL.

42. B. Odell Duncan to Daniel Chamberlain, October 8, 1876; quoted in Allen, *Governor Chamberlain's Administration,* 420–21.

43. *Charleston News and Courier,* September 14, 1876; Current, *Those Terrible Carpetbaggers,* 353.

44. Frank Arum and John Gardner to Chamberlain, September 18, 1876, in Box 14, in Folder 34, Governor Chamberlain Papers, SCDAH.

45. *Cyclopedia of Eminent and Representative Men of the Carolinas of the Nineteenth Century*, vol. 1, *South Carolina* (Madison, Wisc.: Brant and Fuller, 1892; Spartanburg, S.C.: Reprint Company, 1972), 204.

46. Martin W. Gary, quoted in *Edgefield Advertiser*, October 19, 1876, in Folder 66, Martin Witherspoon Gary Papers, SCL.

47. Gary's "No. 1 Plan of the Campaign," quoted in Sheppard, *Red Shirts Remembered*, 47–50; Lawanda Cox and John H. Cox, eds., *Reconstruction, the Negro, and the New South* (Columbia: University of South Carolina Press, 1973), 302–9; Simkins and Woody, *South Carolina during Reconstruction*, 564–69.

48. Allen, *Governor Chamberlain's Administration*, 400–1; *New York Tribune*, October 14, 1876, quoted in Alrutheus Ambush Taylor, *The Negro in South Carolina during the Reconstruction* (Washington, D.C.: n.p., 1924; New York: AMS Press, 1971), 244–45.

49. Williams, "Eyewitness to 1876," November 7 and 28, 1926, SCL.

50. "Resolutions of the Pond Bluff Club," August 5, 1876, James Davis Trezevant Papers, SCL.

51. Williams, "Eyewitness to 1876," September 5, 1926, SCL.

52. Robert Wallace Shand Journal, 148–49, SCL.

53. John Calhoun, quoted in Williamson, *After Slavery*, 344; emphasis in original.

54. "Citizens of Greenville" to Daniel Chamberlain, October 25, 1876, in Box 15, Folder 15, Governor Chamberlain Papers, SCDAH.

55. Joseph Clark to A. S. Wallace, September 6, 1876, RG94, MC666, Reel 298, NA; reprinted in *Message from the President Transmitting Statements on the Use of the Army in Certain of the Southern States*, 44th Cong., 2d sess., H. Doc. 30 (Serial 1755), 56–57.

56. Williamson, *After Slavery*, 410–11.

57. Williams, "Eyewitness to 1876," October 5, 1926, SCL.

58. Walker, *Carolina Rifle Club*, in *Pamphlets: Reconstruction in South Carolina*, 18–19, SCL.

59. Williams, "Eyewitness to 1876," January 9, 1927, SCL.

60. Testimony of Alexander Haskell, "*South Carolina in 1876,*" 828; Simkins and Woody, *South Carolina during Reconstruction*, 501.

61. For a sampling of news concerning the formation of gun clubs, see *Charleston News and Courier*, August 31, 1876; *Spartanburg Herald*, October 4, 1876; Williams, "Eyewitness to 1876," August 29, September 26, 1926, SCL; *Charleston Journal of Commerce*, August 22, 1876, SCL; Records of the Black Oak Democratic Campaign Club, SCL.

62. Thompson, *Ousting the Carpetbagger*, 121; Walker, *Carolina Rifle Club*, in *Pamphlets: Reconstruction in South Carolina*, 53; Richardson Miles to William Porcher Miles, August 26, 1876, in Box 5, Folder 63, William Porcher Miles Papers, SHC/UNC.

63. *Charleston News and Courier*, September 6, 1876. There are various stories about the origin of the "red shirt," but most claim it was designed to mock Senator Oliver Morton's "waving the bloody shirt." Allan Millett and Michael Les Benedict have suggested to the author that whites may have been alluding to

Garibaldi's Red Shirts in the Italian conflict a few years earlier. The originator is even more of a mystery, but while Alfred Williams claims it first appeared in Newberry, the best evidence points toward Aiken and posits its genesis in the Sweetwater Sabre Club, after the Hamburg riot. See Williams, "Eyewitness to 1876," November 14, 1926, SCL; clipping of article entitled "Red Shirt Revolution" (no source, but dated 1911), located in Scrapbook, in Conway, Black, and Davis Family Papers, SCL.

64. David Corbin to Alphonso B. Taft, August 21, 1876, RG60, MC947, Reel 2, NA; emphasis in original. Reprinted in *Message from the President Transmitting Statements,* 44th Cong., 2d sess., H. Doc. 30 (Serial 1755), 96–97.

65. R. B. Wallace to Taft, August 25, 1876, RG60, MC947, Reel 2, NA.

66. James P. Low to Daniel Chamberlain, September 7, 1876, in Box 14, Folder 25, and September 12, 1876, in Box 14, Folder 30, Governor Chamberlain Papers, SCDAH.

67. H. E. Hendricks to Chamberlain, September 12, 1876, in Box 14, Folder 30, Governor Chamberlain Papers, SCDAH.

68. For examples of the haphazard distribution of guns, see D. R. Edwards to Chamberlain, October 12, 1876, in Box 15, Folder 9, and James G. Varn to Chamberlain, September 20, 1876, in Box 14, Folder 35, Governor Chamberlain Papers, SCDAH.

69. *Charleston News and Courier,* October 11, 1876.

70. *Charleston Journal of Commerce,* August 16, 1876, SCL; Williams, "Eyewitness to 1876," September 5, 1926, SCL.

71. Frank Arum, trial justice, Aiken County, to Daniel Chamberlain, September 8, 1876, in Box 14, Folder 27, Governor Chamberlain Papers, SCDAH.

72. James Richardson to Chamberlain, October 11, 1876, in Box 15, Folder 9, and Richardson to Chamberlain, September 14, 1876, in Box 15, Folder 10, Governor Chamberlain Papers, SCDAH; *Spartanburg Herald,* October 18, 1876.

73. *Richmond Dispatch,* n.d., and *New York Herald,* n.d.; quoted in the *Charleston News and Courier,* July 13, 1876.

74. "South Carolina in 1876," 537, 985.

75. Walker, *Carolina Rifle Club,* in *Pamphlets: Reconstruction in South Carolina,* 69.

76. *Charleston Journal of Commerce,* August 31, 1876, SCL.

77. Robert Wallace Shand Journal, 149–50, SCL.

78. Richardson Miles to William Porcher Miles, August 26, 1876, in Box 5, Folder 63, William Porcher Miles Papers, SHC/UNC.

79. Williams, "Eyewitness to 1876," August 29, 1926, SCL.

80. Daniel Chamberlain, quoted in *"South Carolina in 1876,"* 24.

81. For details on the meetings, see the *Edgefield Advertiser,* August 17, 1876; *Charleston News and Courier,* August 14 and 15, 1876; Sheppard, *Red Shirts Remembered,* 94–108; Williams, "Eyewitness to 1876," August 29 and September 12, 1926, SCL.

82. Williams, "Eyewitness to 1876," October 3, 1926, SCL.

83. Thomas Pinckney Lowndes, "Reminiscences," 118–19, in Box 2, Folder 21, William Lowndes Papers, SHC/UNC.

84. A. S. Wallace to Secretary of War J. D. Cameron, October 12, 1876, RG94, MC666, Reel 298, NA. For other complaints about gun clubs and the need for federal assistance, see James Strain to Daniel Chamberlain, September 7, 1876, in Box 14, Folder 25, SCDAH, and R. A. Cummings to Chamberlain, October 20, 1876, in Box 15, Folder 12, Governor Chamberlain Papers, SCDAH.

85. Lizzie Geiger to William Leaphart, August 15, 1876, Folder 2, Lizzie Geiger Papers, SCL; *Spartanburg Herald,* August 23, 1876.

86. *Charleston News and Courier,* October 17, 1876.

87. Williams, "Eyewitness to 1876," January 2, 1927, SCL.

88. *Charleston News and Courier,* September 18, October 2 and 3, 1876.

89. *Charleston News and Courier,* October 20, 1876; Williams, "Eyewitness to 1876," January 16, 1927, SCL.

90. "Eyewitness to 1876," January 2, 1927.

91. "Eyewitness to 1876," February 6, 1927.

92. James Conner to "Wife," October 10, 1876, in Box 6, Hampton Family Papers, SCL.

93. Conner to "Wife," October 10, 1876.

94. Conner to "Wife," October 31, 1876.

95. "Colored Citizens of Laurens" to Daniel Chamberlain, August 22, 1876, in Box 14, Folder 8, Governor Chamberlain Papers, SCDAH; emphasis in original.

96. John Gardner to Chamberlain, August 25, 1876, in Box 14, Folder 10, and George Wadell to Chamberlain, September 4, 1876, in Box 14, Folder 2, Governor Chamberlain Papers, SCDAH; Joseph Clark to Congressman A. S. Wallace, September 6, 1876, RG60, MC947, Reel 2, NA.

97. Williams, "Eyewitness to 1876," October 10, 1926, SCL; *Charleston News and Courier,* September 7, 1876; *Spartanburg Herald,* September 13, 1876.

98. Theodore Barker, quoted in *Charleston Journal of Commerce,* September 8, 1876; emphasis in original.

99. Walker, *Carolina Rifle Club,* in *Pamphlets: Reconstruction in South Carolina,* 60–61, 64, 67.

100. H. N. Bonney to Daniel Chamberlain, September 7, 1876, in Box 14, Folder 25, Governor Chamberlain Papers, SCDAH.

101. "Republicans of Midway [Barnwell County]" to Daniel Chamberlain, September 20, 1876, in Box 14, Folder 35, Governor Chamberlain Papers, SCDAH.

102. "Colored Citizens of Blacksville" to Chamberlain, September 28, 1876, Box 14, Folder 40, Governor Chamberlain Papers, SCDAH.

103. Arney Robinson Childs, ed., *The Private Journal of Henry William Ravenel, 1859–1887* (Columbia: University of South Carolina Press, 1947), 381.

104. *Annual Report of the Secretary of War for 1876,* 44th Cong., 2d sess., H. Doc. 1, pt. 2 (Serial 1742), 81–82; General William T. Sherman to General Winfield S. Hancock, August 17, 1876, RG94, MC666, Reel 298, NA.

105. Wade Hampton, quoted in Harry Wilcox Pfanz, "Soldiering in the South during the Reconstruction Period, 1865–1877" (Ph.D. diss., Ohio State University, 1958), 553.

106. *Army and Navy Journal,* November 4, 1876, 200.

107. *Charleston Journal of Commerce,* September 27, October 14, and December 5, 1876, SCL; *Charleston News and Courier,* October 3, 1876.

108. Captain Thomas Lloyd to the assistant adjutant general, Department of the South, September 21, 1876; printed in *Message from the President Transmitting Statements,* 44th Cong., 2d sess., H. Doc. 30 (Serial 1755), 62–63.

109. Lloyd to the assistant adjutant general, September 21, 1876; *Charleston Journal of Commerce,* September 18 and 27, 1876, SCL; David Corbin to Alphonso B. Taft, October 6, 1876, RG60, MC947, Reel 3, NA; Allen, *Governor Chamberlain's Administration,* 413.

110. E. H. Saltiel to Daniel Chamberlain, September 30, 1876, in Box 14, Folder 41, Governor Chamberlain Papers, SCDAH.

111. Edgar Welles to Chamberlain, September 23, 1876, in Box 14, Folder 36, Governor Chamberlain Papers, SCDAH.

112. Chamberlain to Alexander C. Haskell, October 4, 1876; quoted in Allen, *Governor Chamberlain's Administration,* 385–87.

113. Chamberlain, "Proclamation re Military Clubs" October 7, 1876, in Box 15, Folder 4, Governor Chamberlain Papers, SCDAH; *A Vindication of the People of South Carolina,* n.p., n.d., in *Pamphlets: Reconstruction in South Carolina Democratic and Republican, 1869–1880,* n.p., n.d., 1; *Spartanburg Herald,* October 11, 1876.

114. Chamberlain to Ulysses S. Grant, October 11, 1876, RG60, MC947, Reel 3, NA.

115. J. G. Winsmith to Grant, October 14, 1876, printed in *Message from the President Transmitting Statements,* 44th Cong., 2d sess., H. Doc. 30 (Serial 1755), 104.

116. Wade Hampton, quoted in *Charleston Journal of Commerce,* September 29, 1876.

117. *Charleston Journal of Commerce,* October 4, 1876.

118. See William Stone to Alphonso B. Taft, October 21, 1876, RG60, MC947, Reel 3, NA—from which letter this summary of the incident at Cainhoy is drawn. For other accounts of the riot, see Marshal R. B. Wallace to Taft, October 18, 1876, RG60, MC947, Reel 3, NA (also printed in *Message from the President Transmitting Statements,* 44th Cong., 2d sess., H. Doc. 30 [Serial 1755], 104–10); *Charleston News and Courier,* October 17, 19, and 20, 1876; Williams, "Eyewitness to 1876," December 25, 1926, SCL; *Spartanburg Herald,* October 25, 1876; and *Charleston Journal of Commerce,* October 17, 18, 19, and 20, 1876. A good narrative of the event is in Melinda Meeks Hennessey, "Racial Violence during Reconstruction: The 1876 Riots in Charleston and Cainhoy," *South Carolina Historical Magazine* 86 (April 1985): 100–12.

119. James D. Cameron, quoted in *Charleston News and Courier,* October 18, 1876; *Army and Navy Journal,* October 21, 1876, 163; *A Vindication of the People of South Carolina,* in *Pamphlets: Reconstruction in South Carolina,* 7, SCL.

120. The breakdown was as follows: 185 men of the First Artillery (at Columbia), 96 men of the Second Artillery (various towns), 153 men of the Third

Artillery (various towns), 159 men of the Fifth Artillery (various towns), 181 men of the Second Infantry (concentrated in Edgefield and Aiken counties), and 370 men of the Eighteenth Infantry. Taken together, U.S. troops were in Columbia, Lancaster, Marion, Blackville, Charleston, Summerville, Aiken, Edgefield, Yorkville, Abbeville, Newberry, Allendale, and Laurens. See *Annual Report of the Secretary of War for 1876,* 61–63, 68; and *Message from the President Transmitting Statements,* 44th Cong., 2d sess., H. Doc. 30 (Serial 1755), 20–21.

121. James Conner to "Wife," October 10, 1876, in Box 6, Hampton Family Papers, SCL.

122. *Spartanburg Herald,* October 18, 1876.

123. Matthew C. Butler, quoted in *Spartanburg Herald,* October 18, 1876.

124. *Columbia Union Herald,* November 8, 1876.

125. See assorted reports in Box 15, Folders 10 and 12, Governor Chamberlain Papers, SCDAH; and Williams, "Eyewitness to 1876," December 12, 1926, SCL.

126. Some examples of last-minute calls for troops in the Governor Chamberlain Papers, SCDAH, are: J. Henry Barnwell to Chamberlain, October 21, 1876 (Box 15, Folder 12); Joseph Galluchat to Chamberlain, October 23, 1876 (Box 15, Folder 14); T. M. Graham to Chamberlain, October 30, 1876 (Box 15, Folder 17); "Citizens of Aiken County" to Chamberlain, October 30, 1876 (Box 15, Folder 17); A. C. Merrick (auditor) and other local officials of Spartanburg County to Chamberlain, October 30, 1876 (Box 15, Folder 18).

127. A. Bly to Chamberlain, September 19, 1876, in Box 14, Folder 35, Governor Chamberlain Papers, SCDAH.

128. Alvin Hart to Daniel Augustus Tompkins, October 24, 1876, in Folder 5, Daniel Augustus Tompkins Papers, SHC/UNC.

CHAPTER NINE

THE REVOLUTION OF '76

[It was] for us a struggle for Republican government & for emancipation from negro and alien rule: God help the right!

> Henry William Ravenel, *Private Journal*

Sixteen years ago this Union of equal States was practically destroyed by a proclamation calling for seventy-five thousand troops to coerce the Seceded States. To-day the use of the bayonet in the formation of a State Legislature is but the last act in the drama then begun.

> *Charleston News and Courier,* December 6, 1876

I

The revolution that had begun in December of 1860 came to its close a decade and a half later, when white South Carolinians finally won the right to regulate their own society. Despite a Republican voting majority, the gubernatorial election of 1876 was close enough to be contested, a fact demonstrating how effective the Democratic campaign had been. But Republicans refused to back down, refused to acknowledge that they had lost the war for control of South Carolina. But the struggle finally came to an end in the city where it had begun: in Columbia in April of 1877, the last Republican governor capitulated.

The Democratic campaign was a model of a popular uprising, even in terms of modern revolutionary theory. When Eqbal Ahmad's "insurgency recipe" is applied to the straight-out movement, the campaign indeed appears destined for success from the very start. Ahmad posits seven factors necessary for a successful revolution or insurgency: (1) mass support among the population; (2) a well-structured focus on politics and political goals; (3) the "moral alienation of the masses from the existing government"; (4) the existence of problems and causes arising out of social change, rather than simply a creation of the revolutionaries; (5) a concentration on "outadministering" rather than outfighting the enemy, for a successful revolution must be *constructive* as well as *destructive*; (6) the *selective* use of terrorism; and (7) an external sanctuary, which is important for psychological support, not necessarily military or political aid.[1] With the possible exception of the seventh point (unless one considers the moral support of the other Southern states or even Northern interests), Democrats appeared to understand well the demands of a successful insurgency.

The Democrats' growing sense of optimism was evident in the weeks immediately prior to the election. The *Charleston Journal of Commerce* even tweaked the federal government's nose about recent decisions in the *Slaughterhouse* and *Cruikshank* cases: "We beg leave to remind United States Marshals, likewise Deputy Marshals and other Federal officials in the South," an editor wrote, of the Supreme Court's "declaring the enforcement act unconstitutional and defining the manner in which federal soldiers may be called upon—that is through the State governments." The editor advised federal officials "to ponder these things carefully. . . ."[2] Democrats were well aware of the constitutional limitations governing federal soldiers and the meager power of federal marshals. In the words of Alfred B. Williams, whites "had burned their bridges and could not be scared. Facing a 30,000 negro majority, hostile state and federal government, a promised horde of troops, election machinery in hostile and even criminal hands, some hundreds of deputy marshals could add little to the obstacles to be overcome. . . ."[3]

Yet it seemed Republicans faced the more severe obstacles, beginning with the Democrat's potent and unified display of force, a force which neither the state government nor the black population could combat. Unlike the situation in other elections, there would be no "truce" at election time. The odd combination of desperation and optimism—coupled with a brittle trust in the neutrality of the federal government—drove conservative whites to keep up their coercive tactics right to the end. One poll manager, E. Jonathan Nelson, promised Governor Chamberlain: "I shall do my part without fears of intimidation. I shall die to [*sic*] the polls—in the defense of the Republican Party—once we allow the Democrats in the

State to get in power, then we will see a Second Georgia. What right has a colored man in Georgia today? None whatever, but on the other hand treated like a dog." But Nelson's loyalty and political insight could not deter the Democratic onslaught, and he worried about other managers in the face of "a mass of deception—force, imposition, fraud."[4]

Soldiers' reports confirmed state officials' fears. In Aiken County, a detachment of infantry stumbled across a rifle club chasing a Republican speaker, and the troops felt compelled to interpose themselves between the two. Soldiers finally caught "Mr. Palmer" and escorted him to a waiting train. One officer admitted, "I sincerely believe that the intention was to assassinate him."[5] Another officer discovered that a trainload of whites had come from Georgia "to help redeem the State." He also reported a great deal of rifle club activity the night before the election, with men riding and shooting in the black districts.[6]

Democrats did not discard their strong-arm tactics when election day arrived on November 8. Many polls were quiet, and some officers reported that blacks voted freely and whites behaved themselves.[7] At other polls, however, conservatives opted for "bloodless coercion" in a last-minute effort to carry the day. At one poll in Edgefield, armed horsemen surrounded the cabin, allegedly to prevent more than ten voters from approaching at a given time; the effect on blacks was obvious, and many stayed away. A nearby poll also had mounted men who blocked the staircase leading to the window holding the ballot box.[8] Captain William Falck found the same situation at the Shains Hill poll in Edgefield, where state officers even refused to question voters' eligibility (many of whom Falck suspected were from out-of-state) because they feared retaliation.[9]

At other polls, Democrats eschewed caution and attacked Republicans directly. At Calhoun Mills in Abbeville, Lieutenant Frank Barnhart of the Eighteenth Infantry, a commander of black troops in the Civil War, drove off a band of whites who had attacked the marshal, only to find them at another poll, armed and ready; as long as he was present, they remained peaceful, so the lieutenant could neither act nor leave.[10] In Greenville, poll supervisors had built a fence to control the influx of voters, but whites tore it down and rushed the box. They set up their own "Police Force" to guard the box, but it admitted whites only! Soldiers arrived and with fixed bayonets managed to cut a path to the box; they then assembled around it to prevent the "Police Force" from returning.[11] Troops arrived after a shooting at the Macedonia Church poll in Edgefield, and the commanding officer had "not the slightest doubt that scores of negroes would have been killed and wounded" had the army not appeared. Even so, Captain E. R. Kellogg reported, *"several hundred negroes were not able to cast their votes."*[12] At Robbins Precinct in Barnwell, whites shot at the depot housing the ballot box, driving off voters and managers. Deputy marshal Lawrence Mimms ran to a nearby poll to get soldiers but was told by an officer that the troops could not be moved. When Mimms returned to the depot, the ballot box was gone![13]

Nor could soldiers and state authorities counter the many manifestations of Democratic fraud. The manager of one poll, John Sheppard (who later authored a book on the campaign), made sure to read the oath and rules to each voter individually—a tactic which caused a long wait and allowed only a few votes to be cast.[14] An English observer of the election described the use of "gossamer" paper for tickets, whereby several sheets were folded inside a single ticket which was then shaken as it was placed into the ballot box. This motion forced loose the inner "tickets" so that a single voter might deposit a dozen or more votes. This trick may explain why some counties—in particular Edgefield and Laurens—had more Democratic votes than total registered voters.[15] Another explanation for the large Democratic turnout is the presence of men from Georgia and North Carolina: Lewis Cass Carpenter, having become an agent for the U.S. Department of Revenue, informed President Grant that some rail lines had offered rates reduced by fifty percent for trips from neighboring states into South Carolina.[16] Historians Francis Butler Simkins and Robert Hilliard Woody claim that under-age voting was also rampant and that some whites even boasted of having voted eighteen or twenty times at different polls. Managers were either sympathetic to the conservatives or too frightened to stop the abuses.[17]

Democrats also capitalized on black illiteracy to garner votes. Secret Democratic presses printed thousands of ballots that carried the heading "UNION REPUBLICAN TICKET" but listed only Democratic candidates! Some tickets had a single name that blacks might recognize, such as a well-known local official, but most of the candidates for state offices—and especially that of governor—would be Democrats. James Canton, the manager of a poll in Chester, reported finding these ballots, and Laura M. Towne noted their use on the Sea Islands; she wrote in her dairy that "Mr. Judd" confiscated over a hundred of them at his poll alone.[18]

The worst election day incident, however, took place in Charleston, a city that had already seen serious rioting. About midday, several dozen black Republicans had gathered outside the courthouse, waiting for election news. When the preliminary word came that the Republican Hayes/Chamberlain ticket had won, the crowd—which had begun moving down the street in the direction of the offices of the *News and Courier,* perhaps hoping for confirmation—came across a large group of Democrats, and a scuffle began. Whites started shooting into the crowd of blacks, forcing them to retreat down other streets. Infuriated rather than intimidated, the blacks began gathering whatever weapons could be found, picking up rocks, bricks, sticks, and breaking off fence rails.

The whites had quickly dispersed, but Mayor George Cunningham summoned soldiers to help break up the black mob. By early afternoon General Henry Hunt had arranged his artillery companies—backed by police and the city's "disbanded" rifle clubs—around the perimeter of the rioting mob. The rioters were in control of several city blocks and were looting businesses and attacking whites who unwittingly came into reach. Hunt's soldiers, firing into the air and brandishing bayonets, eventually squeezed the crowd into a stretch of Broad Street, where they laid down their makeshift weapons. By evening, when the last rioter had dispersed, two whites were dead and eleven wounded; the black casualty count was one dead and ten wounded.[19]

Tempers did not subside overnight, and General Hunt received word early on November 9 that more trouble was brewing. Hunt learned that the city's blacks had not appeared for work at the wharves and warehouses; they had, in fact, seized control of the courthouse. Even worse, white gun clubs were already in their armories, preparing for action. Several tense hours followed, until Hunt finally got the go-ahead from General Thomas Ruger, commanding the Department of the South from Columbia, to "do what is necessary to preserve the peace." These men knew that state resources were ineffectual to the point of nonexistence. General Hunt proceeded to take control of the city away from the Democratic mayor, who Hunt believed was in cahoots with conservatives and was trying to use the army and the rifle clubs to destroy the black Republican clubs. Hunt had his men escort the blacks out of the courthouse, ordered James Conner to disperse his rifle clubs, set up day and night military patrols throughout the city, and even forbade gatherings large enough to block the city's sidewalks.[20]

II

Fickle Fate, weighing the election returns, could not decide who should take control of South Carolina. On one hand was the formidable effort put forth by Democrats, on the other the courage and loyalty of Republican voters. The problem lay with a dispute over vote counts, which not only threw the state into chaos but also disrupted the electoral count and thereby the presidential election. Carolina whites, however, paid little attention to the national arena, even though the election of Samuel Tilden might have meant automatic redemption. Instead, as during the campaign itself, state Democrats followed their hearts and focused entirely on securing a victory for Wade Hampton.

Initially, vote counts received in Columbia indicated that Democrats had taken control of the General Assembly by a slim margin, and that Wade Hampton had been elected by a vote of 92,261 to 91,127.[21] Then the county commissioners for Edgefield and Laurens reported that fraud had occurred during the election; in both of those counties, Democrats received more votes than there were voters. Officials also uncovered serious abuses in the voting for governor, a situation which meant (according to the state constitution) that the General Assembly would choose the governor. The question then became what was to be done about the disputed counties: including the returns would create a Democratic House of Representatives, while discarding them (on account of fraud) would mean a Republican majority.

Adding to the confusion was a dispute over *who* was legally responsible for deciding the validity of the county returns. The State Board of Canvassers believed itself to be responsible, for a statute charged the board with tabulating the votes and declaring the highest vote-getter to have been elected. Democrats opposed this solution, as Republican members dominated the board, three of whom—Francis Cardozo, Henry Hayne, and T. C. Dunn—were up for reelection.[22] Another law, however, stated that the General Assembly judged the validity of its members. Democrats supported this solution, for if a few legislators could be swayed to allow the contested members in (from Edgefield and Laurens), then the Democrats would hold a majority and elect Hampton.[23]

Both parties maneuvered to control the assembly and thereby elect their candidate. The State Board of Canvassers, ignoring protests charging a lack of jurisdiction, began its deliberations during the second week of November.[24] Conservative Daniel Augustus Tompkins wrote to his fiancee in New York that the Republicans planned to "steal the election," and William Young was "afraid that our people would be swindled out of their victory."[25] In response, Democrats took their case to the state supreme court; one of the Grimball daughters asked cynically, "what chance can Brains and Justice do in this country against Grant and his bayonets?"[26] Yet even though all justices were Republicans, the court decided unanimously that the board could not invalidate the elections. The board only tabulated the votes; the decision on members was to be left to the legislature. The court then issued writs of preemptory mandamus to the board, ordering it to issue certificates of election to the disputed candidates. Board members refused, declared the county elections invalid, and adjourned. Infuriated, the supreme court retaliated by charging the commissioners with contempt and ordered the arrest of the board members. Republicans countered, and judge Hugh L. Bond of the U.S. Circuit Court ordered the prisoners released. Bond's objectivity was questionable; during this Columbia term, he was staying at the home of his good friend Daniel H. Chamberlain.[27]

Perhaps finally sensing the precarious nature of his position, Chamberlain acted swiftly. Lacking any capable armed force, he took advantage of confusion among army officers in Columbia, duping two companies of infantry into taking up positions *inside* the statehouse. The governor provided officers with keys, and when legislators arrived on the morning of November 28, they found soldiers already inside. Under orders from Chamberlain—who was still governor until the next inauguration—the soldiers admitted only men who were holding certificates from the secretary of state or the State Board. The candidates from Edgefield and Laurens, although holding certificates from the supreme court, were turned away (when General Thomas Ruger learned of the army's role, he immediately ordered the soldiers out of the statehouse).[28]

When news of the exclusion became public, Columbia erupted in indignation. Hundreds of residents seething with anger—among them several rifle clubs—surrounded the statehouse, protesting the "barefaced usurpation" which had bid "defiance to the highest tribunal of the State."[29] Crowds forced some soldiers to retreat into the building, leaving two infantry companies preparing to defend the legislature from the steps. Having offices in another wing of the capitol building, Governor Chamberlain and General Ruger watched the spectacle with growing anxiety. They finally decided on an ironic but eminently practical course of action. Ruger, with Chamberlain's consent, sent an officer to find Wade Hampton with the request that *he* disperse the crowd. Hampton arrived and once again demonstrated who really ruled in South Carolina. After a few words delivered by him from the statehouse steps, the people reluctantly drifted back to their homes and armories. Hampton, not Chamberlain or Ruger, was responsible for restoring calm, and just as easily Hampton could have started a bloodbath.[30]

After the crowd dispersed, the remaining Democrats, joined by one Republican, voluntarily left the hall where the House of Representatives was meeting. Democratic members calculated that their withdrawal would prevent a quorum, so the House would be unable to function, thus unable to elect a governor. The remaining Republicans, however, never swayed from their assertion that the two county elections were void, and this reduced the total number of House members. Although a complete House of Representatives would total 124 members, the invalidation of the two counties yielded 116 members. Since the remaining Republicans numbered 59 (54 blacks and 5 whites), Republicans considered this a quorum.[31]

No novices to political chicanery, Democrats organized their own House of Representatives in Carolina Hall. With a total enrollment of 65, the "Wallace House," named for the speaker (and former confederate general) William Henry Wallace, claimed to be the constitutional body, since it did comprise a quorum if the full House was specified at 124 members. The Republican House, or the "Mackey House" for its Speaker E. W. M. Mackey, still presided in the statehouse and proclaimed that the rival body was illegal and unconstitutional.[32]

The two Houses did not stay separate for long. On November 30, only a day after the Wallace House organized, Alexander Haskell and James L. Orr (son of the former Republican governor James L. Orr) led a group of Democrats over to the capitol building. Haskell, Orr, and others had been legitimately elected—in the eyes of the Republicans—and the sergeant-at-arms allowed them to enter. As they passed inside, the remaining Democratic members, including those from Edgefield and Laurens, rushed the doors, caught the guards by surprise, and surged into the assembly hall. In the words of one witness, "there was one sharp decisive struggle, and all was over, although at one time it seemed that bloodshed was imminent." Each party claimed control and ordered the other to submit; by evening, rival Houses were still in competition, only now they occupied the same floor.[33]

Republican Speaker Mackey immediately requested assistance from General Ruger. Initially, it appeared as though federal soldiers would intervene and oust Wallace's Democratic invaders; Democrats might have finally crossed the line and drawn down federal wrath. Acting on his own, Ruger acceded to Mackey's request, and notified Wallace that the Edgefield and Laurens representatives must leave by noon on December 1. The commander implied that military action might be necessary if the men had not departed the hall.[34] (Ruger admitted to the secretary of war, however, that there was "no question" of the legitimacy of the disputed representatives.)[35] Encouraged by this news, Speaker Mackey called for a vote on the governor to take place at one o'clock, *after* the Democrats had left.[36]

Republican mirth was short-lived, however, for Washington quickly clamped down on any questionable exercise of military authority. Attorney General Taft informed Chamberlain that "the President does not think that the exigency has arisen that justifies affirmative action on his part...." Taft implored Chamberlain to use state forces for the execution of state laws; only if Democrats resisted such forces might federal action be appropriate.[37] Secretary of War James D. Cameron quickly sent a message to Ruger, countermanding the general's earlier decision. Cameron told the general that the governor must use his own resources to "purge the legislature," and only "if he is resisted in this it will become your duty to enforce his authority."[38] The next day, December 3, President Grant followed with his own warning to Ruger. The election dilemma was a state problem, the lame-duck president reminded Ruger: "to be plain, I want to avoid anything like an unlawful use of the military. . . ."[39]

Left to their own devices, state Republicans, watching their position weaken with each passing day, gambled that a clever ruse might secure control of the statehouse. In early December, rumors spread of a plan to use hired thugs and the black Hunki-Dory clubs to forcibly remove Democrats from the hall. Reports circulated that "constables" were already lurking in the building, sleeping in committee rooms or posing as spectators and maintenance personnel.[40] At first it appeared the bluff backfired; Hampton called for reinforcements, and scores of armed men flocked to the capital to defend their victory. Messengers woke rifle club member Robert Wallace Shand, and he hurriedly boarded a waiting train, which was to stop at depots along the way to pick up other Democratic "troops." Shand recalled that "there was a little army on hand" when he reached Columbia, and John Sheppard estimated that three thousand men arrived within a day.[41]

Oddly enough, the Republican plan worked, and Democratic legislators left the hall on December 4. They did not capitulate, however, and merely reconvened their House of Representatives in Carolina Hall (it must be noted that this confusion related to the House only; the Senate did not divide, and sat by passively watching). Their reasons for abandoning the statehouse are unclear, especially since a significant number of experienced, armed conservatives were on hand. After the close call with Ruger, perhaps Democrats were eager to avoid an outbreak that might alter the neutrality of the federal government. Or, although black Republicans were no match for white Democrats in a gunfight, whites may have feared that blacks might resort to arson, which would have wreaked unimaginable damage. Whatever the reasons for the Democrats' departure, the fact remained that the paramilitary forces at Hampton's immediate command had grown considerably; their presence signified that although Republicans might score some minor "victories," their position was as tenuous as ever.[42]

Once again in control of the statehouse, Speaker Mackey called for a tabulation of the votes (without the Edgefield and Laurens members), and the body elected Daniel H. Chamberlain governor. Chamberlain was sworn in on December 6, by a probate judge whose term had expired nearly a month earlier.[43] The same day, however, the state supreme court ruled that the "Mackey House" was the legal House of Representatives, and the Democrats responded by holding an election of their own. It is possible that their retreat from the statehouse occurred in preparation for this election. On December 14, the Mackey House—declaring a quorum—proclaimed Wade Hampton governor by a margin of 1,134 votes. The oath of office was delivered by none other than Judge Thomas Jefferson Mackey, former Republican and uncle of opposing Speaker E. W. M. Mackey; Judge Mackey had defected to the Democrats during the campaign of 1876.[44]

The election of Hampton was another blow to Chamberlain's nearly nonexistent authority. But Republicans could make no move against Hampton—the mythical "thugs" were nowhere to be found—because the capital was now garrisoned by his gun clubs. Support for Chamberlain waned as citizens tired of the confusion and anxiety—and the embarrassing performance by Republicans. William J. Balentine summed up the situation when he asked Chamberlain "is it not revolutionary for persons to attempt to exercise the functions of governor, legislators, and other state offices without authority? Have you not, as Governor, authority to command such revolutionists to desist and to return to their homes?" "As an American," Balentine continued, "I am tired of this mexican style of government, and hope that a way will be soon found to put a stop to it."[45]

III

No one wanted an end to the confusion more than South Carolina whites and Wade Hampton. A victory years in the making was almost theirs, and it was up to the chosen savior, Wade Hampton, to reach out and take it.

After first issuing a formal call for Chamberlain to step aside—Chamberlain refused—Hampton set out to convince Republicans of the hopelessness of their situation.[46] He dispatched letters to presidential contenders Rutherford B. Hayes and Samuel Tilden, describing the "profound peace" that existed throughout South Carolina and informing them that all courts were functioning and no resistance to law had occurred. But do not confuse peace with passivity, Hampton warned, for "the people of this State are not wanting either in the spirit or means to maintain their rights of citizenship against the usurpers' power...."[47]

Unlike the Republicans, Hampton had the means to back up his bluster. As conservatives had demonstrated throughout Reconstruction, their arsenal reached far beyond the weapons of violence; once again, whites turned to bloodless tactics backed by the all-too-real threat of force. Bolstered by the presence of the gun-club army, the Democratic House passed a resolution allowing Hampton, as governor, to issue a special call for taxes (this was done by resolution as the unified Senate would not concur in passing a levy). Hampton called on citizens to pay one-tenth of their previous year's taxes, the amount to be deducted from their dues once the Democrats formally controlled the government. The money, however, must be paid only to men named by Hampton; he told whites to ignore completely the regular state tax collectors.[48]

Whites greeted the "Starve Them Out" policy with unbridled enthusiasm.[49] During the latter half of December and into the new year, the call of "Pay No Taxes!" rang throughout county meetings and township gatherings. "Disregard the Usurpers" read one *News and Courier* headline, while the *Spartanburg Herald* used the patriotic cry "Millions for defense, but not a cent for tribute."[50] The *Herald* warned readers that anyone paying Republican collectors would be "giving aid and comfort to the enemy," and such funds would not be credited once the Democrats were in power.[51]

As with many conservative tactics, the "starve them out" policy had its foundation in the shortcomings of Reconstruction. The black-and-carpetbag government lacked the two elements which are necessary for stable rule: legitimacy in the eyes of many of its citizens, and a monopoly on violence. In addition, whites were still the primary holders of capital and property, and regardless of black numbers, the state government could not function without white money. Without the power of compulsion, which the Republicans did not have, neither court rulings nor legislative acts could bring in white money. As early as January 17, the editor of the *Spartanburg Herald* projected that "the Chamberlain Government is bound to fall to pieces ere long if the tax-payers will only hold out in their determination not to pay a cent of taxes for its support."[52] By early March, Hampton's call had raised between $120,000 and $135,000, while three separate appeals by Republicans had accomplished little.[53]

Hampton's control over the state's finances—a by-product of his control over the white population—doomed the state Republican party. Even President Grant recognized that Chamberlain's position was untenable. Grant told a *New York Tribune* reporter that "the whole army of the United States would be inadequate to enforce the authority of Governor Chamberlain. The people of that State resolved not to resort to violence, but adopted a mode of procedure much more formidable and effective than any armed demonstration. Unless Governor Chamberlain can compel the collection of taxes, it will be utterly useless for him to expect to maintain his authority for any length of time."[54] The *News and Courier* rejoiced over Grant's observation and added that "the true and highest test of authority under a popular government is the power to levy and collect taxes. The argument of the purse is more convincing than the logic of the sword."⁵⁵ Everyone understood, however, that it was the sword that allowed the argument of the purse to have such an impact.

Nonetheless, Grant was in an awkward position. The lame-duck president kept watch over the South while waiting to pass along the dilemma to a successor. But just as Democratic fraud and intimidation had thrown the state election into chaos, they also wreaked havoc with the presidential election. South Carolina was one of three states (along with Florida and Louisiana) whose electoral votes were under dispute because of charges of Democratic abuses. Like the gubernatorial election, the presidential race was close, although Democrat Samuel Tilden had a lead in the electoral college; Tilden needed only one electoral vote to win, while Republican Rutherford B. Hayes required all the contested votes—there were nineteen—to carry the election.⁵⁶

South Carolina conservatives concentrated on their revenue battle rather than on the political maneuverings taking place around Washington in the winter of 1877. As they had done in the campaign, Carolinians were hedging their bets. On the surface, whites appeared to be throwing caution to the wind by concentrating on their state race instead of pushing for Tilden and probable redemption. But by focusing on South Carolina, conservatives were assuring themselves of home rule; if Tilden won, he would in all probability recognize the Hampton government, while if Hayes won, the Hampton government would be so entrenched that its removal would be impossible without large-scale federal intervention. State Democrats hoped that a fait accompli—the government in the hands of Democrats, backed by an impressive paramilitary organization, the obvious support of the white population, and a sympathetic North—would prove too much for whoever became chief executive.

The upshot of the deliberations, negotiations, and manipulations was the election—by special commission—of Republican Rutherford B. Hayes as president of the United States. Hayes's inauguration on March 4, 1877, offered a spark of hope to the dying embers of the South Carolina Republican party.⁵⁷ But more astute Republicans realized the war was already lost. So too did Hayes, who soon dispelled myths that he had come to deliver Republicans in the South. On March 10, the new president met with a delegation of blacks from South Carolina, including Francis Cardozo and Congressmen Joseph Rainey, Richard Cain, and Robert Smalls. In no uncertain terms Hayes told the delegation that "the use of the military forces in civil affairs was repugnant to the genius of American institutions, and should be dispersed with if possible."⁵⁸

Hoping to reach a peaceful solution, the new president invited both Chamberlain and Hampton to Washington for private consultations. After conferring separately with Hayes, both politicians returned to South Carolina and quickly put into writing, for the president, the substance of their oral arguments. Judging by their letters, Hayes had already made his decision. Chamberlain sent the president a letter opposing the removal of troops from the capital and detailing the grim future of blacks in South Carolina. Hampton, on the other hand, offered Hayes what the president sought: promises to preserve the peace, protect the lives and property of all citizens, and support civil rights in the courts. (Allegedly, in their meeting, Hayes had asked Hampton what would happen if he recognized Chamberlain as governor. According to one source, Hampton replied, "the first thing would be that every [Republican] tax-collector in the State would be hanged in twenty-four hours.")[59]

On April 2, President Hayes yielded to the only reasonable course of action. At a cabinet meeting that evening, Hayes and his advisors discussed their alternatives and agreed that removing the troops from statehouse in Columbia represented the most practical solution. On April 3, Hayes notified the new secretary of war, George W. McCrary, that "there does not now exist in that State such domestic violence as is contemplated by the Constitution as the grounds upon which the military power of the national Government may be invoked for the defense of the State." The president ordered that all troops on duty in Columbia be removed and returned to their previous encampments, which were just outside the city limits. McCrary informed General William T. Sherman of the order and told him to execute it at noon on April 10.[60]

Historians continue to debate the decision to leave Southern Republicans to their fate.[61] Was some "bargain" involving the troops tied to Hayes's desire to curry favor with the white South? Were economic considerations more important than political ones? Perhaps the growing intolerance for an activist government, especially among the Northern business elite, helped Hayes decide. Still, most historians recognize the limited use of any "compromise" in 1877, for Reconstruction had already begun its final chapter long before that winter. C. Vann Woodward admits that—regardless of the political and economic deals—Republicans would have given up the South as lost.[62] "Indeed," agrees Eric Foner, "the abandonment of Reconstruction was as much a cause of the crisis of 1876–1877 as a consequence."[63]

Credit must go to South Carolina whites, who did their best—meaning at times their worst—to guarantee the redemption of their state. Through organization, cunning, fraud, and outright force, state conservatives had created a situation that left both state and federal Republicans devoid of alternatives. White Carolinians had given a conservative federal government no choice but to allow white home rule, and powerless state

Republicans had to acquiesce. When news of the troop removal arrived, state officers, among them Robert Elliott and Francis Cardozo, advised Chamberlain to "discontinue the struggle for the occupancy of the Gubernatorial Chair."[64]

Daniel H. Chamberlain was alone in his office when church bells tolled noon on April 10. He knew without looking that the soldiers had begun leaving the statehouse for their camp. The embattled governor sat and addressed a letter to the black and white Republicans of South Carolina, saying that today "the Government of the United States abandons you, deliberately withdraws from you its support, with full knowledge that the lawful Government of the State will be speedily overthrown." The federal government had forsaken "the lawful State Government to a struggle with insurrectionary forces too powerful to be resisted." The lesson, which Chamberlain and fellow Republicans had finally come to understand, was that "if a majority of the people of a State are unable by physical force to maintain their rights, they must be left to political servitude." At last accepting that authority is meaningless without the power to compel and the power to protect, Chamberlain ceased to assert his position as governor of South Carolina.[65]

For South Carolina—and perhaps for the nation—the era of the Civil War ended at noon on April 11, 1877, when Wade Hampton's private secretary entered the office of the executive secretary. There he met Chamberlain's assistant, a Mr. Babbitt, who delivered up to him the great seal of the state and various office keys. Conservative white Carolinians finally held the talismans of authority; the power they had wielded illegally was now legal, legitimate, official. After handing over the reins of command, Babbitt put on his coat and hat, bowed, and left the office.[66] Reconstruction, and, in effect, the Civil War, had finally come to a close.

Notes

1. Eqbal Ahmad, "Revolutionary Warfare and Counterinsurgency," in *Guerrilla Strategies: An Historical Anthology from the Long March to Afghanistan*, ed. Gérard Chaliand (Berkeley: University of California Press, 1982), 245–46; emphasis added.

2. *Charleston Journal of Commerce*, August 30, 1876, South Caroliniana Library, University of South Carolina, Columbia, S.C. (hereafter SCL).

3. Alfred B. Williams, "Eyewitness to 1876," October 26, 1926, South Caroliniana Library, University of South Carolina, Columbia, S.C. (hereafter SCL).

4. E. Jonathan Nelson to Daniel H. Chamberlain, November 6, 1876, in Box 15, Folder 24, Governor Chamberlain Papers, South Carolina Department of Archives and History, Columbia, S.C. (hereafter SCDAH).

5. Lieutenant Henry Cathay to the assistant adjutant general, Department of the South, November 12, 1876, in Record Group 94, Microcopy 666, Reel 300, National Archives, Washington, D.C. (hereafter RG, MC, Reel, NA).

6. Lieutenant [first name illegible] Harkind to the post adjutant, Aiken, November 9, 1876, RG94, MC666, Reel 300, NA.

7. For a number of such reports, see Major C. L. Best (of the First Artillery) to the assistant adjutant general, Department of the South, November 9, 1876, RG94, MC666, Reel 300, NA—a document which includes the observations of several other officers in addition to Best's own.

8. Captain [first name illegible] to the post adjutant, Edgefield, November 7, 1876, RG94, MC666, Reel 300, NA.

9. Captain William Falck to the post adjutant, Edgefield, November 10, 1876, RG94, MC666, Reel 300, NA.

10. Lieutenant Frank Barnhart to Captain [no first name given] Lloyd, November 9, 1876, RG94, MC666, Reel 300, NA.

11. Captain H. C. Croh to the assistant adjutant general, Department of the South, November 10, 1876, RG94, MC666, Reel 300, NA.

12. Captain E. R. Kellogg to the post adjutant, Edgefield, November 8, 1876, RG94, MC666, Reel 300, NA; emphasis in original.

13. Reported in U.S. Senate, *"South Carolina in 1876": Testimony as to the Denial of the Elective Franchise in South Carolina at the Elections of 1875 and 1876*, 44th Cong., 2d sess., S. Doc. 48 (Serial 1727), 743–46 (hereafter "South Carolina in 1876").

14. William Arthur Sheppard, *Red Shirts Remembered: Southern Brigadiers of the Reconstruction Period* (Atlanta: Ruralist Press, 1940), 153–56; *Edgefield Advertiser*, November 20, 1876.

15. Sir George Campbell, *White and Black: The Outcome of a Visit to the United States* (New York: n.p., 1879), 180–87, quoted in Lawanda Cox and John H. Cox, eds., *Reconstruction, the Negro, and the New South* (Columbia: University of South Carolina Press, 1973), 312; Melinda Meeks Hennessey, "Racial Violence during Reconstruction: The 1876 Riots in Charleston and Cainhoy," *South Carolina Historical Magazine* 86 (April 1985): 110.

16. Lewis Cass Carpenter to Ulysses S. Grant, November 23, 1876, in *Message from the President Transmitting Statements*, 44th Cong., 2d sess., H. Doc. 30 (Serial 1755), 111.

17. Francis Butler Simkins and Robert Hilliard Woody, *South Carolina during Reconstruction* (Chapel Hill: University of North Carolina Press, 1932), 515.

18. Testimony of James Canton, "South Carolina in 1876," 715. Several of these fraudulent ballots have been preserved and can be found in Box 6, Folder "December 1876–September 1877," Hampton Family Papers, SCL; Rupert Sargent Holland, ed., *Letters and Diary of Laura M. Towne, Written from the Sea Islands of South Carolina, 1862–1884* (Cambridge: Riverside Press, 1912; New York: Negro Universities Press, 1969), 255.

19. Colonel (Brevet General) Henry J. Hunt to the assistant adjutant general, Department of the South, November 27, 1876, RG94, MC666, Reel 300, NA

(printed also in *Army and Navy Journal,* January 20, 1877, 373–74); *Charleston News and Courier,* November 9, 1876; Irvine C. Walker, *Carolina Rifle Club, July 30, 1869,* in *Pamphlets: Reconstruction in South Carolina, Democratic and Republican, 1869–1880* (n.d., n.p.), 71–74. Perhaps the most vivid and detailed description of the riot is in D. E. Huger-Smith, *A Charlestonian's Recollections, 1846–1913* (Charleston, S.C.: Walker, Evans, and Cogswell, 1950), 152–57.

20. Henry J. Hunt to the assistant adjutant general, Department of the South, November 27, 1876, RG94, MC666, Reel 300, NA; also printed in *Army and Navy Journal,* January 20, 1877, 373–74.

21. *Spartanburg Herald,* January 10, 1877.

22. Simkins and Woody, *South Carolina during Reconstruction,* 515.

23. *South Carolina during Reconstruction,* 516–18.

24. *South Carolina during Reconstruction,* 519–20.

25. Daniel Augustus Tompkins to "Hal" (Harriet Bingham), December 7, 1876, in Box 1, Daniel Augustus Tompkins Papers, and William B. Young to "Aunt," November 18, 1876, in Box 5, William Dunlap Simpson Papers, Special Collections Library Research Room, Perkins Library, Duke University, Durham, N.C.

26. [Daughter of James B. Grimball] to Grimball, November 23, 1876, in Folder 33, Grimball Family Papers, Southern Historical Collection, University of North Carolina, Chapel Hill, N.C. (hereafter SHC/UNC).

27. General Thomas Ruger to General William T. Sherman, December 1, 1876, RG94, MC666, Reel 299, NA; Henry T. Thompson, *Ousting the Carpetbagger from South Carolina* (Columbia, S.C.: R. L. Bryan, 1926; New York: Negro Universities Press, 1969), 136–37; Simkins and Woody, *South Carolina during Reconstruction,* 522.

28. Ruger to Sherman, December 1, 1876, RG94, MC666, Reel 299, NA.

29. *Army and Navy Journal,* December 2, 1876, 265.

30. *Charleston News and Courier,* December 2, 1876; *Army and Navy Journal,* December 2, 1876, 265; Thompson, *Ousting the Carpetbagger,* 140; George C. Rable, *But There Was No Peace: The Role of Violence in the Politics of Reconstruction* (Athens: University of Georgia Press, 1984), 184.

31. *Charleston News and Courier,* November 29, 1876.

32. Arney Robinson Childs, ed., *The Private Journal of Henry William Ravenel, 1859–1887* (Columbia: University of South Carolina Press, 1947), 387; Thompson, *Ousting the Carpetbagger,* 172; Simkins and Woody, *South Carolina during Reconstruction,* 527; Walter Allen, *Governor Chamberlain's Administration in South Carolina: A Chapter of Reconstruction in the Southern States* (New York: G. P. Putnam's Sons, 1888), 428–79.

33. *Charleston News and Courier,* December 1, 1876; Thompson, *Ousting the Carpetbagger,* 144–49.

34. *Spartanburg Herald,* December 6, 1876.

35. General Thomas Ruger to Secretary of War James D. Cameron, November 30, 1876, RG94, MC666, Reel 299, NA.

36. *Charleston News and Courier,* December 1, 1876.

37. Alphonso B. Taft to Daniel Chamberlain, December 1, 1876, in *Message from the President Transmitting Statements*, 44th Cong., 2d sess., H. Doc. 30 (Serial 1755), 36–37.

38. James D. Cameron to Thomas Ruger, December 2, 1876, RG94, MC666, Reel 299, NA.

39. Ulysses S. Grant to Ruger, December 3, 1876, in *Message from the President Transmitting Statements*, 44th Cong., 2d sess., H. Doc. 30, (Serial 1755), 37–38.

40. *Charleston News and Courier*, December 4, 1876.

41. Robert Wallace Shand Journal, 152, SCL; Sheppard, *Red Shirts Remembered*, 175.

42. *Press and Banner*, December 5, 1876; Sheppard, *Red Shirts Remembered*, 177.

43. *Charleston News and Courier*, December 8, 1876; Thompson, *Ousting the Carpetbagger*, 151; Sheppard, *Red Shirts Remembered*, 184.

44. Thompson, *Ousting the Carpetbagger*, 152; *Spartanburg Herald*, December 20, 1876.

45. William J. Balentine to Daniel Chamberlain, December 16, 1876, in Box 15, Folder 45, Governor Chamberlain Papers, SCDAH.

46. *Spartanburg Herald*, January 3, 1877.

47. *Charleston News and Courier*, December 30, 1876.

48. Simkins and Woody, *South Carolina during Reconstruction*, 535; Thompson, *Ousting the Carpetbagger*, 156. The idea to use taxation as a weapon did not originate in 1876. Since whites contributed a majority of the revenue, A. P. Aldrich had advocated the idea as early as 1871, and former governor Benjamin F. Perry called on fellow whites to refuse to pay taxes in 1872. See the *Edgefield Advertiser*, April 1, November 23, 1871, and February 29, August 15, November 23, 1872.

49. *Charleston News and Courier*, December 16, 1876.

50. *Charleston News and Courier*, December 18, 1876; *Spartanburg Herald*, January 3, 1877.

51. *Spartanburg Herald*, January 3, 1877.

52. *Spartanburg Herald*, January 17, 1877.

53. Robert Wallace Shand Journal, 154, SCL; Simkins and Woody, *South Carolina during Reconstruction*, 535; Thompson, *Ousting the Carpetbagger*, 157.

54. Ulysses S. Grant, in *New York Tribune*, February 18, 1877; quoted in the *Charleston News and Courier*, February 20, 1877, and in the *Spartanburg Herald*, February 28, 1877.

55. *Charleston News and Courier*, February 20, 1877.

56. Peggy Lamson, *The Glorious Failure: Black Congressman Robert Brown Elliott and the Reconstruction in South Carolina* (New York: W. W. Norton, 1973), 250–51.

57. *Charleston News and Courier*, March 5, 1877.

58. *Charleston News and Courier*, March 12, 1877.

59. *Charleston News and Courier*, April 4, 1877; Simkins and Woody, *South Carolina during Reconstruction*, 540–541; Williams, "Eyewitness to 1876," March 13, 1927, SCL.

60. *Charleston News and Courier,* April 4, 1877; *Spartanburg Herald,* April 11, 1877; General Winfield S. Hancock to William T. Sherman, April 9, 1877, RG94, MC666, Reel 300, NA; *Army and Navy Journal,* April 7, 1877, 554.

61. A great deal of literature exists on the drama surrounding the election of 1876 and the alleged "Compromise of 1877." All inquiries must begin with C. Vann Woodward's *Reunion and Reaction: The Compromise of 1877 and the End of Reconstruction* (Boston: Little, Brown, 1951). From there the debate increases in intensity and intellectual fervor, with Allan Peskin's "Was There a Compromise of 1877?" *Journal of American History* 60 (1973): 63–75; and C. Vann Woodward's reply, "Yes, There Was a Compromise of 1877," *Journal of American History* 60 (1973): 215–23. For another interpretation see the excellent article by Michael Les Benedict, "Southern Democrats in the Crisis of 1876–1877: A Reconsideration of *Reunion and Reaction,*" *Journal of Southern History* 46 (1980): 489–524. A solid overview of the entire historiography of the question can be found in Vincent P. DeSantis, "Rutherford B. Hayes and the Removal of the Troops and the End of Reconstruction," in *Region, Race, and Reconstruction: Essays in Honor of C. Vann Woodward,* ed. J. Morgan Kousser and James M. McPherson (New York: Oxford University Press, 1982), 417–50.

62. Woodward, *Reunion and Reaction,* 204–15.

63. Eric Foner, *Reconstruction: America's Unfinished Revolution 1863–1877* (New York: Harper and Row, 1988), 582.

64. *Spartanburg Herald,* April 18, 1877.

65. General Thomas Ruger to the assistant adjutant general, Division of the Atlantic, April 10, 1877, RG94, MC666, Reel 300, NA; Daniel H. Chamberlain, in *Spartanburg Herald,* April 18, 1877.

66. *Spartanburg Herald,* April 18, 1877.

CONCLUSION

> ... I think the time will come, if we ever have a white man's civil government again, when they will be more slaves than they ever were.
> William Gregorie, June 4, 1868, Gregorie-Elliott Family Papers, University of North Carolina, Chapel Hill

I

An era of conflict and crisis, begun when white South Carolinians violently rejected the Union, ended when white South Carolinians ousted their last Republican governor of the nineteenth century. It is fitting that Daniel Chamberlain stepped down in April, for that month is replete with dates significant to the Civil War—the bombardment and surrender of Ft. Sumter, the surrenders of Lee and Johnston, the assassination of Lincoln. Gathered outside the statehouse in Columbia, Wade Hampton and his Red Shirts delivered the climactic blow that ended Reconstruction in South Carolina and shattered the promises created by Union victory.

Now holding power in name as well as in fact, whites set out to safeguard their position and reinstitute the checks and balances that would form the basis of their own program of reconstruction. Power formerly based on force and intimidation could now be backed by legal statute and political manipulation. In the months following Hayes's removal of the troops from the capitol grounds, Democratic leaders used a mixture of loopholes and strong-arm tactics to oust and force resignations from Republican legislators.[1] By the fall session the Democratic party controlled both the House and the Senate, and the judiciary soon followed. Within a year, one death and various fraud investigations transformed an all-Republican supreme court into an all-Democratic one.[2] The General Assembly also converted the circuit courts into a bastion of conservatism; by 1878, five of the six Republican judges had been removed, giving the Democrats seven of the eight judgeships.[3]

Conservatives also investigated the Republican party in an attempt to discredit Republicans and portray Democrats as righteous reformers. Among those indicted for corruption were Daniel Chamberlain, John J. Patterson, Niles G. Parker, Francis Cardozo, Robert Smalls, and Richard Carpenter. State courts convicted a few men, but Democrats dropped most charges when the Justice Department agreed to close the books on its investigations into election violations during the 1876 campaign.[4]

But just as with secession nearly a generation earlier, the political act of assuming power was only a means to an end. Whites now proceeded to secure that end, building a new South Carolina upon the revered traditions of the old. After punishing the past and securing the present, Redeemers focused on the future, to insure the fruits of their victory. In 1877 and 1878, the General Assembly revised the state's election laws, amended the poll supervising codes, and redrew many voting precincts. In some cases, blacks had to walk twenty miles to the nearest poll. The "eight-box law" soon followed, eliminating the full ticket and forcing voters to place individual ballots in boxes designated for particular offices. Often Democrats placed ballot boxes inside a room and admitted only one voter at a time; Democrats claimed this measure would eliminate fraud, but it was really designed to take advantage of black illiteracy. None of this came as a surprise to South Carolinian Belton O'Neal Townsend, who declared in 1877 that "Negro citizenship rests solely on the very insecure support of United States bayonets." Townsend predicted that "whenever they dare, the whites in the Southern States will disfranchise the negro outright and by law; and in the mean time while they will, in States they control, practically disfranchise him."[5]

The Democratic onslaught devastated an already bruised-and-battered Republican party. Republicans did not even offer a gubernatorial candidate in 1878. A drastic decline in the black vote bore witness to the sense of hopelessness brought on by Democratic fraud and intimidation. Reflecting on the Republican's dismal showing in the 1886 election, the *Charleston News and Courier* openly admitted that such defeats were due to "white mastery" of the black voter.[6] The trend only grew worse; while Republicans cast nearly 92,000 votes in 1876, the Republican count for the election of 1888 was just 13,740.[7] In 1895, Conservatives would revise the constitution to provide for the outright disfranchisement of most blacks, but their ad hoc measures of the 1870s were already adequate to insure white rule.

Intent on a South Carolina "as it was," Democrats swept away the legislation that had raised white taxes while providing black benefits.[8] The legislature cut funding to the state hospital and asylum, and repealed Republican legislation that allowed poll taxes to fund public schools.

Conclusion

Education went back into the hands of private academies and military and denominational schools, as had been the case during the antebellum period.[9] The legislature even lowered the detested land taxes, showing the continued influence of the old planters.

In a similar way, whites turned to legislation to guarantee their supremacy in labor relations. What had been enforced by illegal bands and private action now became the responsibility of the state. The "black codes" of 1865 had provided a sampling of white intentions toward blacks, and Redemption allowed whites to reinstate economic subjugation unmolested. In the late 1870s and early 1880s, the legislature altered lien laws, provided legal enforcement for landowners, and formally limited black economic opportunities.[10] In 1880, a measure made oral contracts legally binding, favored the planter in all disputes, and declared breach of contract a criminal offense equivalent to fraud. Another law provided that laborers indebted to planters—common under the prevalent crop-sharing system—could be held on the plantation to work off the debt.[11] Isaac Seabrook DuBose exaggerated only slightly when he said that "southerners of the old regime are still the advisors, the benefactors, and to some extent the supporters of multitudes of negroes...." According to DuBose, "one frequently hears the old words 'boss' and 'massa' coming from their lips with a strange fidelity to the old relations."[12]

II

To be sure, conservative victory was incomplete. The restructuring that followed Redemption occurred within the bounds proscribed by the new amendments to the U.S. Constitution and the state's own 1868 constitution (eventually this would prove too limiting and would be swept away by the constitutional convention of 1895). Slavery was abolished, and the power relationship central to that system would never again exist in the United States. Blacks had become citizens with civil and political rights (at least for males), and their gains—including the opportunity to vote (at least nominally), the ownership of property, the legitimacy of black marriage, and the right to sue—were truly revolutionary. In *practice*, however, it was the counterrevolution that guided the South for the next hundred years.

Although the South's losses—the changes, in effect—were significant, to focus on these is to examine the issue in reverse. The North did not begin the Civil War; the South, led by South Carolina, began the conflict with the hope of protecting its white supremacist slave society from the destructive designs of the Republican party and its Northern sympathizers. South Carolina sought to be *self-regulating*, left alone to set its racial policy, its economic goals, its political agenda. By 1860, many state conservatives became convinced that continuance in the Union meant regulation, supervision, dependence, even race war. If power slipped from state hands to federal ones, a Republican-dominated government could destroy slavery, white supremacy in all walks of life, and the noble American traditions of federalism and decentralization.

The Civil War began when South Carolina sought a conventional military solution to this threat. Appomattox ended the dream of independence, but there were other ways to create a white supremacist society with a reasonable degree of autonomy. From 1865 to 1877, Carolina whites struggled to achieve this, first through legal means (during the provisional government) and later through a variety of campaigns designed to weaken, and even topple, the Republican government.

So while the *why* of the war for South Carolina is rather routine in terms of military history—the struggle for political dominance in order to institute a desired social or political program—it is the *how* of this war which is truly interesting. For in this state, during a period of alleged peace, citizens were at war, and the attempts to classify that war as "crime" ignored the aims, intensity, methods, and organization of the competing forces. State whites were armed, trained, disciplined, even uniformed (be it in a white cotton bed-sheet or a red flannel shirt), and directed toward a singular political goal by their commanders—the same men who had led them during the Civil War. Paramilitary bands intimidated and outfought the state militia, and evaded and frustrated federal soldiers. Even the intervention of the federal government at various points—most significantly in 1871—failed to suppress hostility or curb resistance. At the same time, conservatives used methods beyond the federal government's reach, such as economic extortion and fraud. By 1876, the various elements in this conflict had merged into a unified, coherent thrust against the Republican government. This was insurrection, rebellion, even revolution, begun as a disjointed and disorganized effort to hamper Reconstruction programs and evolving into a deliberate, coherent drive that succeeded in removing a government. Taking its cue from other states recently redeemed, South Carolina's conservatives struck for native white control and white supremacy, sweeping Republicans from power through an awesome display of unity, force, and organization.

Certainly a great many other factors influenced the outcome of Reconstruction, but state conservatives deserve the lion's share of the credit—or blame—for its failure. Scholars will continue to argue about why Reconstruction failed, why Southern Republican governments were so unstable, and how conservatives managed to regain control. While dis-

CONCLUSION

cussions about constitutional conservatism, traditions of federalism, Northern apathy, and Republican corruption are useful in explaining the weaknesses of Reconstruction, its failure must be ultimately attributed to Southern white hostility. None of these factors, and perhaps not even all in combination, would have brought down Reconstruction if an opposing force with an viable alternate program had not existed. Judicial and legislative conservatism weakened Reconstruction only because they hampered the government's ability to contend with the opposition and enforce civil and political rights. Similarly, Northern disillusionment and disinterest came in the wake of continued resistance; a successful, stable Southern Republican party might have contributed significantly to the national party and national economy as a whole. No such stability existed, for conservative opposition precluded peace and resulted in what can only be termed "war weariness" in the North.

In the end, Reconstruction did not fail; it was defeated. The prize—control of the Palmetto State, and the South itself—went to native whites, who were more determined to take it than Republicans were to keep it. Wade Hampton's Red Shirts represented the culmination of a decade of preparation, planning, adaptation, experimentation, and mobilization, until whites faced head-on the state and federal governments in a risky game of brinkmanship. Years of anger and bloodletting had shown that Carolinians did not bluff; Republicans backed down, knowing that opposition would result only in further bloodshed, not in lasting peace.

So after fifteen years of fighting, peace finally came to South Carolina. But unlike the peace of Appomattox, this settlement was on South Carolina's terms. From 1877 onward, white South Carolinians guided the racial, economic, and political affairs of their state. In a small way they achieved their independence and regained some of what had been lost through secession. Whites had fulfilled their state motto—"While I breathe, I hope"—a motto that had been guiding them for over a decade. State blacks would now look to that motto, and continue to do so for the next century.

Notes

1. *Charleston News and Courier,* April 25, June 1, November 28, 1877; William J. Cooper, Jr., *The Conservative Regime: South Carolina, 1877–1890* (Baltimore: Johns Hopkins University Press, 1968), 25; Alrutheus Ambush Taylor, *The Negro in South Carolina during the Reconstruction* (Washington, D.C.: n.p., 1924; New York: AMS Press, 1971), 290–92.
2. Taylor, *The Negro in South Carolina,* 262.
3. *Charleston News and Courier,* February 14, 1878; Cooper, *The Conservative Regime,* 26–27.

4. Francis Butler Simkins and Robert Hilliard Woody, *South Carolina during Reconstruction* (Chapel Hill: University of North Carolina Press, 1932), 542–43.

5. Belton O'Neal Townsend ("A South Carolinian"), "The Political Condition of South Carolina," *Atlantic Monthly* 39 (1877): 191.

6. *Charleston News and Courier,* December 26, 1890.

7. Claude Hunter Nolen, "The Aftermath of Slavery: Southern Attitudes toward Negroes, 1865–1900" (Ph.D. diss., University of Texas, 1963), 147.

8. Francis Butler Simkins, *The Tillman Movement in South Carolina* (Durham: Duke University Press, 1926), 16–22, 70–102.

9. Orville Vernon Burton, *In My Father's House Are Many Mansions: Family and Community in Edgefield, South Carolina* (Chapel Hill: University of North Carolina Press, 1985), 254.

10. Orville Vernon Burton, "Race and Reconstruction in Edgefield County, South Carolina," *Journal of Social History* 12 (Fall 1978): 45.

11. Glennon Graham, "From Slavery to Serfdom: Rural Black Agriculturalists in South Carolina, 1865–1900" (Ph.D. diss., Northwestern University Press, 1982), 114, 117.

12. Isaac Seabrook DuBose, "Before and After or the Relations of the Races at the South," 31, Issac Seabrook DuBose Papers, South Caroliniana Library, University of South Carolina, Columbia, S.C.

BIBLIOGRAPHY

I. Primary Sources

A. ARCHIVES AND COLLECTIONS

National Archives, Washington, D.C. (NA)

Letters Sent by the Department of Justice: General and Miscellaneous, 1818–1904. Microcopy 699. General Records of the Department of Justice. Record Group 60.

Letters Sent by the Department of Justice: Instructions to U.S. Attorneys and Marshals. Microcopy 701. General Records of the Department of Justice. Record Group 60.

Letters Received by the Office of the Attorney General. Microcopy 947. General Records of the Department of Justice. Record Group 60.

Letters Sent by the Office of the Adjutant General, Main Series, 1800–1890. Microcopy 565. Records of the AdjutantGeneral's Office, 1780–1917. Record Group 94.

Returns from U. S. Military Posts, 1800–1916. Microcopy 617. Records of the Adjutant General's Office, 1780–1917. Record Group 94.

Returns from Regular Army Infantry Regiments, 1821–1916. Microcopy 665. Records of the Adjutant General's Office, 1780–1917. Record Group 94.

Letters Received by the Office of the Adjutant General (Main Series), 1871–1880. Microcopy 666. Records of the Adjutant General's Office, 1780–1917. Record Group 94.

Index to Letters Sent by the Secretary of War Regarding Military Affairs, 1871–1889. Microcopy 420. Letters Sent by the Secretary of War. Record Group 107.

Telegrams Collected by the Secretary of War, 1861–1882. Microcopy 473. Letters Sent by the Secretary of War. Record Group 107.

Returns from Regular Army Cavalry Regiments, 1833–1916. Microcopy 744. Records of the United States Regular ArmyMobile Units, 1821–1942. Record Group 391.

Library of Congress, Washington, D.C. (LC)

Winfield S. Harvey Diary, Edward Settle Godfrey Papers.

BIBLIOGRAPHY

Alderman Library, University of Virginia, Charlottesville, Virginia (UVA)
Amos Tappan Akerman Letterbooks

Ohio Historical Society, Columbus, Ohio (OHS)
Robert K. Scott Papers

South Carolina Department of Archives and History, Columbia, South Carolina (SCDAH)
Records of the Office of the Adjutant and Inspector General
Chief Constables' Letterbooks
Governor Daniel H. Chamberlain Papers
Military Affairs File (part of the "Green Series")
Governor Franklin J. Moses, Jr., Papers
Governor Robert K. Scott Papers

South Caroliniana Library, University of South Carolina, Columbia, South Carolina (SCL)
David Wyatt Aiken Papers
Records of the Black Oak Democratic Campaign Club
Bratton Family Papers
Mary Davis Brown Diaries
The Charleston Journal of Commerce
Conway, Black, and Davis Family Papers
D. T. Crosby Papers
Edward Crosland Papers
Elias Horry Deas Papers
Records of the Democratic Club of Liberty Hill
Records of the Democratic Club of Ward No. 4, Chalreston
Issac Seabrook DuBose Papers
Martin W. Gary Papers
Records of the Georgetown Rifle Guards Club
Louis Gervais Papers
Hampton Family Papers
Joshua H. Hudson Papers
Frederick Jackson Letters
Janney-Leaphart Family Papers
Iredell Jones Papers
Ellison Summerfield Keitt Collection
J. J. McIver Papers
Charles Cotesworth Pinckney, Jr. Papers
Richard Realf Papers
Reconstruction Scrapbook
Mrs. Edward LeRoy Reeves Papers
Records of the Richland Democratic Club
Records of the Governor's Guards/Richland Rifle Club
Records of the Sally Rifles Club
Robert Wallace Shand Journal

BIBLIOGRAPHY

J. Y. Simons Papers
William Dunlap Simpson Papers
Edward M. Stoeber Papers
Benjamin Ryan Tillman, "Autobiography"
James Davis Trezevant Account Book
Alfred Brockenbrough Williams "Eyewitness to 1876 "Scrapbook
Benjamin Stuart Williams Papers
Williams-Chestnut-Manning Papers

    Southern Historical Collection, University of North Carolina, Chapel Hill, North Carolina (SHC/UNC)

Boykin Family Papers
John Hamilton Cornish Papers
DeCaradeuc Family Papers
William Porcher DuBose, "Reminiscences"
Habersham Elliott Papers
Gregorie-Elliott Papers
David Gavin Diary
David Golightly Harris Journal
Hannibal A. Johnson Papers
Emma LeConte Diary
Lipscomb Family Papers
William Lowndes Papers
James L. Orr and W. Patterson Papers
Christopher Gustavus Memminger Papers
William Porcher Miles Papers
James S. Milling Papers
Benjamin F. Perry Papers
Phillips-Myers Papers
Elizabeth Rankin Papers
Ravenel Family Papers
Martha Schofield Diaries
Springs Family Papers
George Coffin Taylor Papers
Daniel Augustus Tompkins Papers
Trenholm Family Papers
William Henry Trescot Papers
Wallace-Gage Papers
Benjamin Cudworth Yancey Papers

    Special Collections Library Research Room, Duke University, Durham, North Carolina (SCLRR)

Eglantine Agours Papers
James Chaplin Beecher, "Diary and Memorandum Book"
Eli Whitney Bonney Papers
Matthew Calbraith Butler Papers

Armistead L. Burt Papers
Horatio R. Cook Memorandum Book
Francis W. Dawson Papers
Henry William and Wilmot Gibbes DeSaussure Papers
Thomas Rhett Smith Elliott Papers
Eliza (Borden) Fludd Papers
Sarah Ely Journal, George Gage Collection
Martin W. Gary Papers
Wade Hampton Papers
Paul Hamilton Hayne Papers
J. C. Hemphill Scrapbook
Nickels J. Holmes Papers
Iredell Jones Papers
Daniel W. Jordan Papers
Allan MacFarlan Papers
Thomas Jefferson McKie Papers
Joseph Warren Waldo Marshall Papers (Ann Elizabeth Marshall, "Reminiscences")
James L. Orr Papers
Lalla Pelot Papers
Benjamin Franklin Perry Papers
Francis Wilkinson Pickens Papers
Octavius Theodore Porcher Papers
Robert A. Pringle Papers
Daniel Edgar Sickles Papers
William Dunlap Simpson Papers
D. A. Tompkins Papers
William Henry Trescot Papers
George McCottry Witherspoon Papers
Josephus Woodruff Diary

B. ESSAYS AND SPEECHES

Speech of the Honorable D.T. Corbin, U.S. District Attorney for So. Ca. N.p., n.d. In *Collected Pamphlets including Preston, John Smith Address delivered before the Survivors' Association of South Carolina, November 10, 1870*. Bound by L.F. Youmans, n.d.

Speech of Hon. Samuel Shellabarger, In House, on April 6, 1871, on Enforcement of the Fourteenth Amendment. N.p., n.d. In volume 6, *J. Warren Keifer Collection of Speeches and Pamphlets.* 6 Vols. N.p., n.d.

Speech of the Honorable J. J. Wright at Liberty Hall, Charleston, S.C., May 31, 1872. Columbia: South Carolina Republican Printing Company, 1872. In *Pamphlets: Reconstruction in South Carolina, Democratic and Republican 1869–1880.* N.p., n.d.

C. PERIODICALS

Abbeville Medium
The Army and Navy Journal

BIBLIOGRAPHY

Charleston Courier
Charleston News
Charleston News and Courier
Columbia Daily Union
Edgefield Advertiser
Fairfield Herald
Spartanburg Herald
Yorkville Enquirer

D. GOVERNMENT PUBLICATIONS

The War of the Rebellion: A Compilation of the Official Records of the Union and Confederate Armies. 70 vols. Washington, D.C.: Government Printing Office, 1880–1901.

United States Circuit Court. *Proceedings in the Ku-Klux Trials at Columbia, South Carolina, November Term, 1871.* Republican Printing 1872; New York: Negro Universities Press, 1969.

U.S. Congress. Joint Select Committee to Inquire into the Condition of Affairs in the Late Insurrectionary States.*Testimony Taken by the Joint Select Committee to Inquire into the Condition of Affairs in the Late Insurrectionary States (The Ku-Klux Conspiracy).* Volumes III, IV, V. Washington, D.C.: Government Printing Office, 1872; New York: AMS Press, 1968.

——. *Report of the Joint Committee on Reconstruction at the First Session of the Thirty-Ninth Congress.* Washington, D.C.: Government Printing Office, 1866.

——. *The Public Statutes at Large of the United States of America, 1789–1983.* 107 vols. Boston: Charles Co. Little and James Brown, 1845–1993.

——. House. *Message of the President of the United States and Accompanying Documents. . . . Including the Annual Report of the Secretary of War for 1866.* 39th Cong., 2nd sess., H. Doc. 1, Serial 1285.

——. House. *The Murder of Union Soldiers.* 39th Cong., 2nd sess., H. Rept. 23, Serial 1305.

——. House. *Message of the President of the United States and Accompanying Documents. . . . Including the Annual Report of the Secretary of War for 1867.* 40th Cong., 2nd sess., H. Doc. 1, Serial 1324.

——. House. *Message of the President of the United States and Accompanying Documents. . . . Including the Annual Report of the Secretary of War for 1868.* 40th Cong., 3rd sess., H. Doc. 1, Serial 1367.

——. House. *Letter from the Secretary of War Transmitting Reports of Commanders of Military Departments South, Relative to Persons Turned Over for Trial to Civil Authorities.* 40th Cong., 3rd sess., H. Doc. 102, Serial 1381.

——. House. *Additional Papers in the Case of Wallace vs. Simpson.* 41st Cong., 1st sess., H. Doc. 17, Serial 1402.

——. House. *Papers in the Case of S. L. Hoge vs. J. P. Reed.* 41st Cong., 1st sess., H. Rept. 3, Serial 1403.

——. House. *Papers in the Case of A. S. Wallace vs. W. D. Simpson.* 41st Cong., 1st sess., H. Rept. 5, Serial 1403.

———. House. *Papers in the Case of S. L. Hoge vs. J. P. Reed.* 41st Cong., 1st sess., H. Rept. 6, Serial 1403.

———. House. *Papers in the Case of A. S. Wallace vs. W. D. Simpson.* 41st Cong., 1st sess., H. Rept. 7, Serial 1403.

———. House. *Additional Papers in the Case of Hoge vs. Reed.* 41st Cong., 1st sess., H. Doc. 18, Serial 1403.

———. House. *Message of the President of the United States and Accompanying Documents. . . . Including the Annual Report of the Secretary of War for 1869.* 41st Cong., 2nd sess., H. Doc. 1, Serial 1412.

———. House. *Letter of the Secretary of War Concerning Officers on Duty in the Southern States.* 41st Cong., 2ndsess., H. Doc. 211, Serial 1418.

———. House. *Additional Papers in the Case of Wallace vs. Simpson.* 41st Cong., 2nd sess., H. Doc. 17, Serial 1431.

———. Senate. *Letter of the Secretary of War Communicating a Copy of a Letter of the Governor of South Carolina Relative to Outrages Committed upon Citizens of the United States Resident in that State.* 41st Cong., 3rd sess., S. Doc. 28, Serial 1440.

———. House. *Message of the President of the United States and Accompanying Documents. . . . Including the Annual Report of the Secretary of War for 1870.* 41st Cong., 3rd sess., H. Doc. 1, Serial 1446.

———. House. *Annual Report of the Attorney General for 1870.* 41st Cong., 3rd sess., H. Doc. 90, Serial 1454.

———. Senate. *Resolution of the Senate of the United States.* 42nd Cong., 1st sess., S. Doc. 16, Serial 1467.

———. House. *Message from the President of the United States Relative to the Condition of Affairs in the South.* 42nd Cong., 1st sess., H. Doc. 14, Serial 1471.

———. Senate. *Report of the Joint Select Committee to Inquire into the Condition of the Late Insurrectionary States.* 42nd Cong., 2nd sess., S. Repts. 6–7, Serial 1483.

———. House. *Message of the President of the United States and Accompanying Documents. . . . Including the Annual Report of the Secretary of War for 1871.* 42nd Cong., 2nd sess., H. Doc. 1, Serial 1503.

———. House. *Annual Report of the Attorney General for 1871.* 42nd Cong., 2nd sess., H. Doc. 55, Serial 1510.

———. House. *Message from the President of the United States in Answer to a Resolution of 25 January Last Relative to the Lawlessness in Insurrectionary States.* 42 Cong., 2nd sess., H. Doc. 268, Serial 1515.

———. House. *Papers in the Case of Christopher C. Bowen vs. Robert C. DeLarge.* 42nd Cong., 2nd sess., H. Doc. 37, Serial 1525.

———. House. *Papers in the Case of Issac G. McKissick vs. A. S. Wallace.* 42nd Cong., 2nd sess., H. Doc. 48, Serial 1525.

———. House of Representatives. *Joint Resolution of the Legislature of South Carolina, Asking that the Federal Troops Be Not Removed from that State.* 42 Cong., 2nd sess., H. Doc. 160, Serial 1526.

Bibliography

―――. Senate. *Annual Report of the Attorney General for 1872.* 42nd Cong., 3rd sess., S. Doc. 32, Serial 1545.

―――. Senate. *Resolution of the Legislature of South Carolina, Remonstrating against the Withdrawal of the United States Troops from that State.* 42nd Cong., 3rd sess., S. Doc. 81, Serial 1546.

―――. House. *Message of the President of the United States and Accompanying Documents. . . . Including the Annual Report of the Secretary of War for 1872.* 42nd Cong., 3rd sess., H. Doc. 1, Serial 1558.

―――. House. *Message of the President of the United States and Accompanying Documents. . . . Including the Annual Report of the Secretary of War for 1873.* 43rd Cong., 1st sess., H. Doc. 1, Serial 1597.

―――. House. *Annual Report of the Attorney General for 1873.* 43rd Cong., 1st sess., H. Doc. 6, Serial 1606.

―――. House. *Resolutions of the Legislature of South Carolina Regarding the Civil Rights Bill.* 43rd Cong., 1st sess., H. Doc. 25, Serial 1617.

―――. House. *Resolutions of the Legislature of South Carolina Regarding the Civil Rights Bill.* 43rd Cong., 1st sess., H. Doc. 111, Serial 1618.

―――. House. *Message of the President of the United States and Accompanying Documents. . . . Including the Annual Report of the Secretary of War for 1874.* 43rd Cong., 2nd sess., H. Doc. 1, Serial 1635.

―――. House. *Annual Report of the Attorney General for 1874.* 43rd Cong., 2nd sess., H. Doc. 7, Serial 1638.

―――. House. *Message of the President of the United States and Accompanying Documents. . . . Including the Annual Report of the Secretary of War.* 44th Cong., 1st sess., H. Doc. 1, Serial 1674.

―――. House. *Annual Report of the Attorney General for 1875.* 44th Cong., 1st sess., H. Doc. 14, Serial 1686.

―――. Senate. *"South Carolina in 1876": Testimony as to the Denial of the Elective Franchise in South Carolina at the Elections of 1875 and 1876.* 44th Cong., 2nd sess., S. Doc. 48, Serials 1727–1729.

―――. House. *Message of the President of the United States and Accompanying Documents. . . . Including the Annual Report of the Secretary of War for 1876.* 44th Cong., 2nd sess., H. Doc. 1, Serial 1742.

―――. House. *Annual Report of the Attorney General for 1876.* 44th Cong., 2nd sess., H. Doc. 20, Serial 1751.

―――. House. *Message from the President Transmitting Statements on the Use of the Army in Certain of the Southern States, in Response to a Resolution of the House of Representatives.* 44th Cong., 2nd sess., H. Doc. 30, Serial 1755.

―――. House. *Message of the President of the United States and Accompanying Documents. . . . Including the Annual Report of the Secretary of War for 1877.* 45th Cong., 2nd sess., H. Doc. 1, Serial 1794.

―――. House. *Annual Report of the Attorney General for 1877.* 45th Cong., 2nd sess., H. Doc. 7, Serial 1802.

―――. House. *Annual Report of the Attorney General for 1878.* 45th Cong., 3rd sess., H. Doc. 7, Serial 1852.

E. CONTEMPORARY WORKS

Ames, Mary. *From a New England Woman's Diary in Dixie in 1865*. N.p.: 1906; New York: Negro Universities Press, 1969.

Andrews, Sidney. *The South since the War*. Boston: Ticknor and Fields, 1866; New York: The Arno Press, 1969.

Bleser, Carol K., ed. *The Hammonds of Redcliffe*. New York: Oxford University Press, 1981.

———. *Secret and Sacred: The Diaries of James Henry Hammond, a Southern Slaveholder*. New York: Oxford University Press, 1988.

Cauthen, Charles E., ed. *The Family Letters of Three Wade Hamptons, 1782–1901*. Columbia: University of South Carolina Press, 1953.

Childs, Arney Robinson, ed. *The Private Journal of Henry William Ravenel, 1859–1887*. Columbia: University of South Carolina Press, 1947.

Constitutional Convention of the State of South Carolina. *Journal of the Convention of the People of South Carolina, held at Columbia, S.C., September 1865*. Columbia: Julian A. Shelby, 1865.

Constitution and Rules of the Richland Rifle Club, Columbia, S.C. Columbia, S.C.: Williams Sloane, 1874.

DeForest, John William. *A Union Officer in the Reconstruction*. Edited by James H. Croushore and David M. Potter. New Haven: Yale University Press, 1948.

Holland, Rupert Sargent, ed. *Letters and Diary of Laura M. Towne, Written from the Sea Islands of South Carolina, 1862-1884*. Cambridge: Riverside Press, 1912; New York: Negro Universities Press, 1969.

Huger-Smith, D.E. *A Charlestonian's Recollections, 1846-1913*. Charleston, S.C.: Walker, Evans, and Cogswell Company, 1950.

Kendrick, Benjamin B. *The Journal of the Joint Committee of Fifteen on Reconstruction*. New York: n.p., n.d; New York: Negro Universities Press, 1969.

King, Edward. *The Great South*. Hartford, Conn.: American Publishing, 1875; New York: The Arno Press, 1969.

Leland, John A. *A Voice from South Carolina: Journal of a Reputed Ku Klux*. Charleston, S.C.: Walker, Evans, and Cogswell Company, 1879.

Lester, J. C. and D. L. Wilson. *The Ku Klux Klan: Its Origin, Growth, and Disbandment*. N.p.: 1884; New York: Da Capo Press, 1973.

Meats, Stephen, and Edwin Arnold, eds. *The Writings of Benjamin F. Perry*, 2. vols. Vol 1: *Essays, Public Letters and Speeches*. Spartanburg, S.C.: The Reprint Company, Publishers, 1980.

Moore, John Hammond, ed. *The Juhl Letters to the Charleston Courier: A View of the South, 1865–1871*. Athens: University of Georgia Press, 1974.

Proceedings of the Constitutional Convention of S.C. held at Charleston, S.C., begun January 14 and ending March 17, 1868. N.p., n.d.

Proceedings of the Taxpayers' Convention of South Carolina held in Columbia 9–12 May 1871. Charleston, S.C.: Edward Perry, 1871.

Reid, Whitelaw. *After the War: A Tour of the Southern States, 1865–1866*. Cincinnati: Moore, Wilstach and Baldwin, 1866; New York: Harper and Row, 1965.

Report on the Condition of the South [Accompanied by the Report of Carl Schurz]. Washington, D.C.: Government Printing Office, 1865; New York: The Arno Press, 1969.

South Carolina General Assembly. *Report of the Joint Investigating Committee on Public Frauds and the Election of John J. Patterson to the U.S. Senate,* 9 Vols. Columbia, S.C.: Calvo and Patton, 1878.

———. *Reports and Resolutions of the General Assembly of the State of South Carolina Passed at the Annual Session of 1865.* Columbia: Julian A. Shelby, 1865. In *Acts and Resolutions of the General Assembly of the State of South Carolina, Session of 1864–1865.* Columbia: Julian A. Shelby, 1866.

Townsend, Belton O'Neal ("A South Carolinian"). "The Political Condition of South Carolina." *The Atlantic Monthly* 39 (1877), 177–194.

———. "South Carolina Morals." *The Atlantic Monthly* 39 (1877), 467–475.

Trowbridge, John T. *The South: A Tour of its Battlefields and Ruined Cities.* Hartford, Conn.: L. Stebbins, 1866; New York: The Arno Press, 1969.

"Truth" [author]. *Statement of Dr. Bratton's Case being an Explanation of the Ku-Klux Prosecutions in the Southern States.* London, Ontario: "Free Press" Steam Book and Job Printing Co., 1872.

A Vindication of the People of South Carolina. N.p., n.d. In *Pamphlets: Reconstruction in South Carolina, Democratic and Republican 1869–1880.* N.p., n.d.

Walker, C. Irvine. *Carolina Rifle Club, Charleston, S.C., July 30, 1869.* N.p., n.d. In *Pamphlets: Reconstruction in South Carolina, Democratic and Republican 1869–1880.* N.p., n.d.

Whiting, William. *War Powers under the Constitution of the United States.* Boston: Lee and Shepard, Publishers, 1871.

Williams, Alfred Brockenbrough. *Hampton and his Red Shirts: South Carolina's Deliverance in 1876.* 2nd ed. Charleston, S.C.: Walker, Evans, and Cogswell, 1935.

Woodward, C. Vann, ed. *Mary Chesnut's Civil War.* New Haven: Yale University Press, 1981.

II. Secondary Sources

A. Books

Abbott, Martin. *The Freedmen's Bureau in South Carolina, 1865–1872.* Chapel Hill: University of North Carolina Press, 1967.

Allen, Walter. *Governor Chamberlain's Administration in South Carolina: A Chapter of Reconstruction in the Southern States.* New York: G. P. Putnam's Sons, 1888.

Anderson, Eric, and Alfred A. Moss, eds. *The Facts of Reconstruction: Essays in Honor of John Hope Franklin.* Baton Rouge: Louisiana State University Press, 1991.

Ayers, Edward L. *Vengeance and Justice: Crime and Punishment in the 19th-Century American South.* New York: Oxford University Press, 1984.
Ballantine, Henry Winthrop. *Unconstitutional Claims of Military Authority.* Chicago: Hale-Crossley, 1915.
Belknap, Michael R. *Federal Law and Southern Order: Racial Violence and Constitutional Conflict in the Post-Brown South.* Athens: University of Georgia Press, 1987.
Benedict, Michael Les. *A Compromise of Principle: Congressional Republicans and Reconstruction, 1863-1869.* New York: W.W. Norton, 1974.
———. *The Fruits of Victory: Alternatives in Restoring the Union, 1865–1877.* 2nd ed. Lanham, Md.: University Press of America, 1986.
Bleser, Carol K. *The Promised Land: The History of the South Carolina Land Commission, 1869–1890.* Columbia: University of South Carolina Press, 1969.
Brown, Richard Maxwell. *Strain of Violence: Historical Studies of American Violence and Vigilantism.* New York: Oxford University Press, 1975.
Bruce, Dickson D., Jr. *Violence and Culture in the Antebellum South.* Austin: University of Texas Press, 1979.
Burton, Orville Vernon. *In My Father's House are Many Mansions: Family and Community in Edgefield, South Carolina.* Chapel Hill: University of North Carolina Press, 1985.
Burton, Orville Vernon, and Robert C. McMath, Jr., eds. *Class, Conflict, and Consensus: Antebellum Southern Community Studies.* Westport, Conn.: Greenwood Press, 1982.
Carter, Dan T. *When the War Was Over: The Failure of Self-Reconstruction in the South, 1865–1867.* Baton Rouge:Louisiana State University Press, 1985.
Cauthen, Charles Edward. *South Carolina Goes to War: 1860–1865.* Chapel Hill: University of North Carolina Press, 1950.
Chaliand, Gerard, ed. *Guerrilla Strategies: An Historical Anthology from the Long March to Afghanistan.* Berkeley: University of California Press, 1982.
Chalmers, David M. *Hooded Americanism: The History of the Ku Klux Klan.* New York: Franklin Watts, 1965.
Channing, Steven A. *Crisis of Fear: Secession in South Carolina.* New York: Simon and Schuster, 1970.
Clark, E. Culpepper. *Francis Warrington Dawson and the Politics of Restoration: South Carolina, 1874–1889.* Tuscaloosa: University of Alabama Press, 1980.
Cooper, William J., Jr. *The Conservative Regime: South Carolina, 1877–1890.* Baltimore: John Hopkins University Press, 1968.
Coulter, E. Merton. *The South during Reconstruction.* Baton Rouge: Louisiana State University Press, 1947.
Cox, Lawanda, and John H. Cox, eds. *Reconstruction, the Negro, and the New South.* Columbia: University of South Carolina Press, 1973.
Current, Richard. *Those Terrible Carpetbaggers.* New York: Oxford University Press, 1988.
Cyclopedia of Eminent and Representative Men of the Carolinas of the Nineteenth Century. Vol. 1, *South Carolina.* Madison, Wisc.: Brant and Fuller, 1892;

Spartanburg, S.C.: Reprint Company, 1972.
Elkins, Stanley, and Eric McKitrick, eds. *The Hofstadter Aegis: A Memorial.* New York: Alfred A. Knopf, 1974.
Escott, Paul. *After Secession: Jefferson Davis and the Failure of Confederate Nationalism.* Baton Rouge: Louisiana State University Press, 1978.
Faust, Drew Gilpin. *The Creation of Confederate Nationalism: Ideology and Identity in the Civil War South.* Baton Rouge: Louisiana State University Press, 1988.
Fitzgerald, Michael W. *The Union League Movement in the Deep South: Politics and Agricultural Change during Reconstruction.* Baton Rouge: Louisiana State University Press, 1989.
Foner, Eric. *Nothing but Freedom: Emancipation and Its Legacy.* Baton Rouge: Louisiana State University Press, 1983.
———. *Politics and Ideology in the Age of the Civil War.* New York: Oxford University Press, 1980.
———. *Reconstruction, 1863-1877: America's Unfinished Revolution.* New York: Harper and Row, 1988.
Ford, Lacy K. *Origins of Southern Radicalism: The South Carolina Upcountry, 1800-1860.* New York: Oxford University Press, 1988.
Foster, Gaines M. *Ghosts of the Confederacy: Defeat, the Lost Cause, and the Emergence of the New South, 1865-1913.* New York: Oxford University Press, 1987.
Franklin, John Hope. *Reconstruction: After the Civil War.* Chicago: University of Chicago Press, 1961.
Fraser, Walter J. *Charleston! Charleston! The History of a Southern City.* Columbia: University of South Carolina Press, 1989.
Fraser, Walter J., and Winfred B. Moore, eds. *The Southern Enigma: Essays on Race, Class, and Folk Culture.* Westport, Conn.: Greenwood Press, 1983.
Fredrickson, George M. *The Black Image in the White Mind: The Debate on Afro-American Character and Destiny, 1817-1914.* New York: Harper and Row, 1971.
Freehling, William W. *The Road to Disunion: Secessionists at Bay, 1776-1854.* New York: Oxford University Press, 1990.
The General Service Schools. *Military Aid to the Civil Power.* Leavenworth, Kansas: The General Service Schools Press, 1925.
Gillette, William. *Retreat from Reconstruction: 1869-1879.* Baton Rouge: Louisiana State University Press, 1979.
Glenn, Garrard. *The Army and the Law.* New York: Columbia University Press, 1918.
Gregorie, Anne King. *History of Sumter County, South Carolina.* Sumter: Library Board of Sumter County, 1954.
Hall, Kermit L., and James W. Ely, eds. *An Uncertain Tradition: Constitutionalism and the History of the South.* Athens: University of Georgia Press, 1989.
Henry, H. M. *Police Control of the Slave in South Carolina.* N.p., 1914; New York: Negro Universities Press, 1968.

Holt, Thomas. *Black over White: Negro Political Leadership in South Carolina during Reconstruction.* Urbana: University of Illinois Press, 1977.

Jordan, Winthrop D. *White over Black: American Attitudes toward the Negro, 1550–1812.* Chapel Hill: University of North Carolina Press, 1968.

Kaczorowski, Robert J. *The Nationalization of Civil Rights: Constitutional Theory and Practice in a Racist Society 1866-1883.* New York: Garland, 1987.

———. *The Politics of Judicial Interpretation: The Federal Courts, Department of Justice and Civil Rights, 1866–1876.* New York: Oceana Publications, Inc., 1985.

Kousser, J. Morgan, and James M. McPherson, eds. *Region, Race, and Reconstruction: Essays in Honor of C. Vann Woodward.* New York: Oxford University Press, 1982.

Lamson, Peggy. *The Glorious Failure: Black Congressman Robert Brown Elliott and Reconstruction in South Carolina.* New York: W. W. Norton, 1973.

Landrum, J. B. O. *History of Spartanburg County.* Atlanta: Franklin Printing and Publishing, 1900.

Leemhuis, Roger P. *James L. Orr and the Sectional Conflict.* Washington, D.C.: The University Press of America, Inc., 1979.

McFeely, William S. *Grant: A Biography.* New York: W. W. Norton, 1981.

———. *Yankee Stepfather: General O.O. Howard and the Freedmen.* New York: W. W. Norton, 1968.

McKitrick, Eric L. *Andrew Johnson and Reconstruction.* Chicago: University of Chicago Press, 1960.

McPherson, James M. *Ordeal by Fire: The Civil War and Reconstruction.* New York: Alfred A. Knopf, Inc., 1982.

———. *The Struggle for Equality: Abolitionists and the Negro in the Civil War and Reconstruction.* Princeton: Princeton University Press, 1964.

Marshall, Burke. *Federalism and Civil Rights.* New York: Columbia University Press, 1964.

Maslowski, Peter. *Treason Must Be Made Odious: Military Occupation and Wartime Reconstruction in Nashville, Tennessee, 1862–1865.* Millwood, N.Y.: KTO Press, 1978.

Nieman, Donald G. *To Set the Law in Motion: The Freedmen's Bureau and the Legal Rights of Blacks 1865–1868.* Millwood,N.Y.: KTO Press, 1979.

Oakes, James. *The Ruling Race: A History of American Slaveholders.* New York: Vintage Books, 1983.

Olsen, Otto, ed. *Reconstruction and Redemption in the South.* Baton Rouge: Louisiana State University Press, 1980.

Owens, Harry P., and James J. Cooke, eds. *The Old South and the Crucible of War.* Jackson: University Press of Mississippi, 1983.

Paret, Peter, ed. *Makers of Modern Strategy: From Machiavelli to the Nuclear Age.* Princeton: Princeton University Press, 1986.

Perman, Michael. *Reunion without Compromise: The South and Reconstruction, 1865–1868.* New York: Cambridge UniversityPress, 1973.

———. *The Road to Redemption: Southern Politics, 1869–1879.* Chapel Hill:

University of North Carolina Press, 1984.
Potter, David M. *Division and the Stresses of Reunion, 1845-1876*. Glenview, Ill.: Scott, Foresman, 1973.
Rabinowitz, Howard, ed. *Southern Black Leaders of the Reconstruction Era*. Urbana: University of Illinois Press, 1982.
Rable, George C. *But There Was No Peace: The Role of Violence in the Politics of Reconstruction*. Athens: University of Georgia Press, 1984.
Rankin, Robert S. *When Civil Law Fails: Martial Law and its Legal Basis in the United States*. Durham: Duke University Press, 1939.
Reynolds, John S. *Reconstruction in South Carolina, 1865-1877*. Columbia, S.C.: The State Company, 1905.
Rich, Bennett Milton. *The Presidents and Civil Disorder*. Washington, D.C.: The Brookings Institution, 1941.
Roark, James L. *Masters without Slaves: Southern Planters in the Civil War and Reconstruction*. New York: W. W. Norton, 1977.
Rogers, George C. *The History of Georgetown County, South Carolina*. Columbia: University of South Carolina Press, 1970.
Rose, Willie Lee Nichols. *Rehearsal for Reconstruction: The Port Royal Experiment*. Indianapolis: Bobbs-Merrill, 1964.
Schultz, Harold S. *Nationalism and Sectionalism in South Carolina, 1852-1860: A Study of the Movement for Southern Independence*. Durham: Duke University Press, 1955.
Sefton, James E. *The United States Army and Reconstruction, 1865-1877*. Baton Rouge: Louisiana State University Press, 1967.
Shapiro, Herbert. *White Violence and Black Response: From Reconstruction to Montgomery*. Amherst: University of Massachusetts Press, 1988.
Sheppard, William Arthur. *Red Shirts Remembered: Southern Brigadiers of the Reconstruction Period*. Atlanta: Ruralist Press, Inc., 1940.
Simkins, Francis Butler. *Pitchfork Ben Tillman: South Carolinian*. Baton Rouge: Louisiana State University Press, 1944.
Simkins, Francis Butler, and Robert Hilliard Woody. *South Carolina During Reconstruction*. Chapel Hill: University of North Carolina Press, 1932.
Simpson, Brooks Donahue. *"Let Us Have Peace:" Ulysses S. Grant and the Politics of War and Reconstruction*. Chapel Hill: University of North Carolina Press, 1991.
Singletary, Otis A. *Negro Militia and Reconstruction*. Austin: University of Texas Press, 1957.
Summers, Mark U. *Railroads, Reconstruction, and the Gospel of Prosperity: Aid under the Radical Republicans, 1865-1877*. Princeton: Princeton University Press, 1984.
Swinney, Everette. *Suppressing the Ku Klux Klan: The Enforcement of the Reconstruction Amendments 1870-1877*. New York: Garland, 1987.
Taylor, Alrutheus Ambush. *The Negro in South Carolina during Reconstruction*. New York: AMS Press, 1971.
Thompson, Henry T. *Ousting the Carpetbagger from South Carolina*. New York: Negro Universities Press, 1926.

Trelease, Allen W. *White Terror: The Ku Klux Klan Conspiracy and Southern Reconstruction.* New York: Harper and Row, 1971.
Wallace, David Duncan. *South Carolina: A Short History.* Columbia: University of South Carolina Press, 1951.
Wikramanayake, Marina. *A World in Shadow: The Free Black in Antebellum South Carolina.* Columbia: University of South Carolina Press, 1973.
Williams, Jack Kenny. *Vogues in Villainy: Crime and Retribution in Ante-Bellum South Carolina.* 2nd ed. Columbia: University of South Carolina Press, 1959.
Williamson, Joel. *After Slavery: The Negro in South Carolina During Reconstruction, 1861–1877.* Chapel Hill: University of North Carolina Press, 1965.
Wilson, Theodore Brantner. *The Black Codes of the South.* Tuscaloosa: University of Alabama Press, 1965.
Woodward, C. Vann. *Origins of the New South: 1877-1913.* Baton Rouge: Louisiana State University Press, 1951.
———. *Reunion and Reaction: The Compromise of 1877 and the End of Reconstruction.* Boston: Little, Brown, 1966.
Wyatt-Brown, Bertram. *Southern Honor: Ethics and Behavior in the Old South.* New York: Oxford University Press, 1982.

B. Articles and Essays

Benedict, Michael Les. "Equality and Expediency in the Reconstruction Era: A Review Essay." *Civil War History* 23 (December 1977): 322–335.
———. "Preserving the Constitution: The Conservative Basis of Radical Reconstruction." *The Journal of American History* 61 (June 1974): 65–90.
———. "Southern Democrats in the Crisis of 1876–1877: A Reconsideration of *Reunion and Reaction.*" *Journal of Southern History* 46 (November 1980): 489–524.
Burton, Orville Vernon. "Race and Reconstruction: Edgefield County, South Carolina." *Journal of Social History* 12 (Fall 1978): 31–56.
Curry, Richard O. "The Civil War and Reconstruction, 1865–1877: A Critical Overview of Recent Trends and Interpretations." *Civil War History* 20 (September 1974): 215–238.
Foner, Eric. "Reconstruction Revisited." *Reviews in American History* 10 (December 1982): 82–100.
Hennessey, Melinda Meeks. "Racial Violence during Reconstruction: The 1876 Riots in Charleston and Cainhoy." *South Carolina Historical Magazine* 86 (April 1985): 100–112.
Hackney, Sheldon. "Southern Violence." *American Historical Review* 74 (1969): 906–925.
Kaczorowski, Robert J. "To Begin the Nation Anew: Congress, Citizenship, and Civil Rights after the Civil War." *American Historical Review* 92 (February 1987): 45–68.
Landon, Fred. "The Kidnapping of Dr. Rufus Bratton." *Journal of Negro History* 10 (July 1925): 330–334.
McPherson, James M. "Redemption or Counterrevolution? The South in the 1870s." *Reviews in American History* 13 (December1985): 545–550.

Maltz, Earl. "Reconstruction without Revolution: Republican Civil Rights Theory in the Era of the Fourteenth Amendment." *Houston Law Review* 24 (March 1987): 221–279.
Meier, August. "An Epitaph for the Writing of Reconstruction History?" *Reviews in American History* 9 (March 1981): 82–87.
Post, Louis F. "A Carpetbagger in South Carolina." *Journal of Negro History* 10 (January 1925): 10–79.
Shapiro, Herbert. "Afro-American Responses to Race Violence during Reconstruction." *Science and Society* 36 (Summer 1972):158–170.
———. "The Ku Klux Klan during Reconstruction: The South Carolina Episode." *Journal of Negro History* 49 (1964): 34–55.
Simkins, Francis B. "The Ku Klux Klan in South Carolina." *Journal of Negro History* 12 (1927): 606–647.
Singletary, Otis A. "The Negro Militia during Radical Reconstruction." *Military Affairs* 19 (Winter 1955): 177–186.
Stagg, J. C. A. "The Problem of Klan Violence: The South Carolina Up-Country, 1868–1871." *Journal of American Studies* 8 (December 1974): 303–318.
Swinney, Everette. "Enforcing the Fifteenth Amendment, 1870–1877." *Journal of Southern History* 28 (May 1962): 203–218.
Weisberger, Bernard A. "The Dark and Bloody Ground of Reconstruction Historiography." *Journal of Southern History* 25 (November 1959): 427–447.
Wiecek, William M. "The Great Writ and Reconstruction: The Habeas Corpus Act of 1867." *Journal of Southern History* 36 (November 1970): 531–548.

C. Theses and Dissertations

Ford, Lacy K. "One Southern Profile: Modernization and the Development of White Terror in York County, 1856–1876." Unpublished Master's thesis, University of South Carolina, 1976.
Graham, Glennon. "From Slavery to Serfdom: Rural Black Agriculturalists in South Carolina, 1865–1900." Unpublished Ph.D. diss., Northwestern University, 1982.
Greenberg, Kenneth. "The Second American Revolution: South Carolina Politics, Society, and Secession, 1776–1860." Unpublished Ph.D. diss., University of Wisconsin, 1976.
Jones, Norrece Thomas. "Control Mechanisms in South Carolina Slave Society, 1800–1865." Unpublished Ph.D. diss., Northwestern University, 1981.
Kirkland, John Robert. "Federal Troops in the South Atlantic States during Reconstruction, 1865–1877." Unpublished Ph.D. diss., University of North Carolina, 1968.
Loftus, Robert Drew. "Federal Protection of the Freedmen in South Carolina: 1871." Unpublished Master's thesis, The American University, 1968.
Neal, Diane. "Benjamin Ryan Tillman: The South Carolina Years, 1847–1894." Unpublished Ph.D. diss., Kent State University, 1976.
Nolen, Claude Hunter. "Aftermath of Slavery: Southern Attitudes toward Negroes 1865–1900." Unpublished Ph.D. diss., University of Texas, 1963.

Pfanz, Harry Wilcox. "Soldiering in the South during the Reconstruction Period: 1865–1877." Unpublished Ph.D. diss., Ohio State University, 1958.

Pope, Ida Waller. "Violence as a Political Force in the Reconstruction South." Unpublished Ph.D. diss., University of Southwestern Louisiana, 1982.

Saville, Julie. "A Measure of Freedom: From Slave to Wage Laborer in South Carolina, 1860–1868." Unpublished Ph.D. diss., Yale University, 1986.

Silvestro, Clement Mario. "None but Patriots: The Union League in the Civil War and Reconstruction." Unpublished Ph.D. diss., University of Wisconsin, 1959.

Thompson, Michael Edwin. "Blacks, Carpetbaggers, and Scalawags: A Study of the Membership of the South Carolina Legislature, 1868–1870." Unpublished Ph.D. diss., Washington State University, 1975.

Williams, Lou Faulkner. "The Great South Carolina Ku Klux Klan Trials, 1871–1872." Unpublished Ph.D. diss., University of Florida, 1991.

Wolfe, Allis. "Women Who Dared: Northern Teachers of the Southern Freedmen, 1862–1872." Unpublished Ph.D. diss., City University of New York, 1982.

Woody, Robert Hilliard. "The South Carolina Reform Movements of 1870 and 1872." Unpublished Master's thesis, Duke University, 1928.

INDEX

Abbeville, 19
Abbeville County, 30, 62, 73; armed bands in, 80, 107; black militia in, 79; Democratic clubs in, 73; and Hampton's march, 173; Ku Klux Klan in, 58; political violence in, 53; Republican rally at,172; U.S. Army intervenes in, 190; violence in, 190
Abbeville Medium, 161
Abney, Joseph, 52
Abstention, and the 1872 election, 137
Adams, Doc, 163
Agricultural clubs, 139
Ahmad, Eqbal, 49; and the campaign of 1876 as a popular revolution, 189
Aiken, 16, 50
Aiken County, armed bands in, 190; black militia in, 163; 171; 1876 election in, 190; riot in, 163; violence in, 179
Aiken Journal, 126
Akerman, Amos T., 98, 102, 105, 106, 118, 120; becomes attorney general, 81; and the Columbia trials, 100; and court backlog, 101; and extradiction of Klansmen, 102; resignation of, 102, 103; selective prosecutions, 99
Alabama State Gazette, 176
Albany Penitentiary, convicted Klansmen in, 102, 122

Aldrich, A. P., 14, 35, 40, 49, 151–53
Allendale Mounted Baseball Club, 179
Allendale Rifle Club, 179
American Metallic Ammunition Manufacturing Company, 75
American Revolution, 138, 160
Ames, Adelbert, 13; as governor of Mississippi, 149, 150
Ames, Mary, 19
Amnesty, 12, 77; 1872 congressional act, 120
Amnesty and Pardon, proclamation of, 11
Anderson, J. M., 37
Anderson, J. W., 79
Anderson, John, intervenes during election, 146
Anderson, Robert, raises flag in Charleston, 1
Anderson County, 62; black soldiers in, 19; violence toward blacks in, 19
Andrews, Sidney, 12, 16–19
Appomattox Court House, 1, 47, 51, 210
Arkansas, 94; Klan fugitives in, 102, 119
Army and Navy Journal, and troops in South Carolina, 175
Army Appropriations Act, 38
Arrests, during the "crackdown" of 1871, 98, 99, 104; under the habeas corpus suspension, 98, 99
Arum, Frank, 166

229

INDEX

Ashantee, 161
Assassination, 5, 57; and the 1868 presidential election, 54; attempted, 53; of Abraham Lincoln, 1, 5, 206; of B. F. Randolph, 60
Atlanta (Ga.), 103
Atlantic Monthly, 135, 147
Atlantic, Division of, 178
Augusta (Ga.), 30, 53; and the Hamburg Massacre, 163; white munitions at, 171
Avery, James W., 120; escapes the "crackdown" of 1871, 102
Ayers, Edward, 56

Babbitt, Mr., 201
Bailey, T. P., 124
Balentine, William J., 197
Baltimore (Md.), Democratic national convention at, 124; Hampton speech at, 127
Barker, Theodore, 169; and the King Street Riot, 174, 175
Barnhart, Frank, 190
Barnwell County, 171; 1876 election in, 190–91; and Hampton's march, 173; hostility toward freedmen's school at, 31; violence in, 175
Barnwell Sentinel, 160
Beaufort County, black militia in, 141
Beecher, James, 18
Belknap, William W., 144; shifts troops in South Carolina, 148, 149
Benedict, Michael Les, 3, 72, 96
Black, Tim, 90
Black Codes, 15, 16, 28, 208; and the Civil Rights Act, 32; in South Carolina, 33
Black and Tan Convention, 49, 50
Blacks, and the 1870 election, 76; accused of crimes in Ellenton, 175; arming of, 59, 74, 75, 80, 140, 141, 170; and Charleston riot of election day 1876, 192; conservative attitudes toward, 41, 127; and the constitution of 1865, 13; and the constitution of 1868, 48; and economic coercion, 52, 145; economic difficulties of, 17, 29, 208; enfranchisement of, 3, 37–39, 47–49, 79; fail to support the Union Reform Party, 78; in the General Assembly, 72; illiteracy of, 191, 207; as jurors, 73; and the justice system, 33, 35; and King Street Riot, 174; and Klan assaults, 61, 72; inferiority of, 37, 51, 160, 161, 172; intimidation of, 167, 169, 174, 178; landlessness of, 17; and military courts, 33; and the militia, 74, 75, 79, 80, 89, 140, 163; Northern, hired by South Carolina conservatives, 78; opposition to suffrage of, 37, 51, 52, 63, 166, 207; political rights of, 3; protection for, 29, 32, 81, 164, 179; Reconstruction gains of, 208; shun the Democratic Party, 129; and restrictions under the Black Codes, 15; as soldiers in South Carolina, 19, 20; in South Carolina, 13, and the "straight-out" policy, 162; and tax-supported education, 151; targets of gun clubs, 142, 148; and the Union Reform Party, 76, 77; 15, 17, 33; in the U.S. Army, 19, 20, 143, 163, 190; violence toward, 18–20, 30, 34, 53, 57, 78, 89–91, 106, 142, 163, 164, 167, 175, 190
"Black Thursday" judges, 151, 161; and conservative reaction, 152, 153
Blair, Francis P. Jr., 51
"Bloodless coercion" and "hacking," 172; and the 1876 campaign, 167; on election day 1876, 190; policy of Hampton, 167
Board of Trade of Columbia, 140
Bond, Hugh L., 194
Bonham, M. L., 59
Bonney, H. N., 175

230

Bonsall, James, 78, 79
Boozer, Lemuel, 49
Boston (Mass.), 13, 127
Bowen, Christopher C., 54, 125, 142; bolts the Republican Party, 82
Bowers, Claude, 3
Boycott, Democratic tactic in 1876, 168
Bratton, J. Rufus, escapes the "crackdown" of 1871, 102; extradiction of, 119, 120
Brinkley, M. L., 33
Brisbane, B. L., 144, 145
Brown, Mary Davis, 99
Bullock, Richard, 139
Bureau of Refugees, Freedmen, and Abandoned Lands, 30, 34, 49, 52–54; courts of, 33; diminishing role of, 50; and education, 31, 125; inadequacies of, 29, 30; investigation by, 30; and the Ku Klux Klan, 58; labor contracts of, 17, 29; opposition to schools of, 31; in South Carolina, 11, 17–19; in the South, 29; unconstitutionality of, 51
Burgess, John, 3
Burt, Armistead, 15, 28, 40, 52, 100
Burton, Orville Vernon, 4
Bushwackers, 106, 138; in Newberry County, 30
Butler, Andrew Pickens, and the Sweetwater Sabre Club, 139
Butler, Benjamin R., 145
Butler, Matthew C., 77, 100, 138, 160, 163, 166, 177; and the 1870 election, 77; response to Grant's proclamation on gun clubs, 179; and "Second Ned Tennant Riot," 148; and "straight-outism," 162; supports Greeley in 1872, 124; and the Union Reform Party, 77
Butler, Thomas, 163

Cain, Lawrence, 142
Cain, Richard, 76, 199

Cainhoy, riot at, 177, 178
Calhoun, John C., funeral of, 174
Calhoun, John, 168
Calhoun Mills, U.S. Army intervenes at, 190
Cameron, James D., 178; denies request for troops in the 1876 election crisis, 195
Campaign of 1876, 197; and "bloodless coercion," 167; and Democratic organization, 163; and Democratic divisions, 160, 167; and division of time, 172; and Gary's "No. 1 Plan of the Campaign," 167; gun clubs in, 164, 170; and "hacking," 172; and Hampton's march, 173; and Justice Department investigations, 207; as a popular uprising, 189; violence in, 163, 168, 174–78, 189; and white man's government, 160
Canada, and the kidnapping of Bratton, 120
Canby, Edward R. S., 53, 54
Canton, James, reports fraud in 1876, 191
Cape Cod (Mass.), 127
Cardozo, Francis L., 48, 49, 142, 199, 201; and the State Board of Canvassers in 1876, 193; indicted for corruption, 207
Carolina Hall, "Wallace House" in, 196; establishment of "Wallace House" in, 195
Carolina Rifle Club, 74, 138, 169, 171
Carolina Spartan, 95
Carpenter, Lewis Cass, 140, 141; and fraud at the 1876 election, 191
Carpenter, Richard B., 77, 82, 126; bolts the party in 1870, 76; indicted for corruption, 207
Carpetbaggers, 3, 47, 53, 150, 153, 147, 198; at the constitutional convention, 48; in the state government, 72

INDEX

Carter, Dan T., 3, 16
Carter, Eugene, 34
Cartersville (Ga.), 103
Chamberlain, Daniel H., 54, 135, 142, 143, 145, 148, 150, 151, 153, 162, 163, 165, 166, 169, 174, 179, 189, 191, 194; and the 1876 election crisis, 194, 195, 197; appeals for federal help, 148, 164, 196; and the "Black Thursday" judges, 152; and conflict with state Republicans, 151, 152; and conservatives' tax manuever in 1876, 198; challenged by Hampton to resign, 177, 197; elected governor in 1874, 146; indicted for corruption, 207; leaves governorship, 201, 206; proclamation ordering gun clubs to disband, 178; reelected governor by Republican House, 196; renominated for governor in 1876, 166; requests federal government repress violence, 177; and response to Ellenton riot, 176; seeks Hampton's help in calming crowds, 194; and success of "hacking," 172; tackles Republican corruption, 151; visits Hayes, 199, 200; wins nomination for governor in 1874, 143
Charleston, 19, 50, 53, 192; 1876 election day riot in, 191, 192; armed bands in, 175; arming of blacks in, 75; constitutional convention in, 48; and Fort Moultrie celebration, 162; and Hampton's march, 173; and the King Street Riot, 174; gun clubs in, 139, 175; Independent Republican convention of 1874, 144; Klan trials in, 101, 119, 122; U.S. Army in, 1, 128, 141, 192
Charleston County, 82
Charleston Courier, 33
Charleston Daily News, 58

Charleston Daily Republican, 136
Charleston Journal of Commerce, 171, 177, 189; appears in 1876, 162
Charleston Mercury, 40, 42
Charleston News and Courier, 128, 137, 143, 151, 153, 161, 162, 170, 188, 191, 198, 199, 207; and the "Black Thursday" judges, 153
Cheraw, 17; Hampton speech at, 177
Chesnut, James, 40
Chester Conservative Clan, 57
Chester Reporter, 129
Chester County, 34, 81; armed bands in, 89, 91; arrests in, 99; black militia in, 79, 93; fraud in during 1876, 191; guns in, 79; suspension of habeas corpus in, 98; violence in, 19, 179
Chesterfield County, 34; suspension of habeas corpus in, 98
Childs, L. D., 60
Citizen's Party, 78; in the 1870 election, 76
Civil Rights Act, 33, 95; Johnson veto of, 32; and state courts, 33
Civil Rights Bill of 1872, 120
Civil rights, and blacks, 208; dwindling concern for, 147, 148
Civil War, 1, 206; and continuity with Reconstruction, 4; end of, 201; Northern victory in, 1, 6; origins of, 208, 209; and slavery, 4
Civil-military relations, and the 1876 election crisis, 195, 196; and the 1876 election crisis in South Carolina, 199; breech of, 149; Hayes's views on, 199
Clarendon County, movement against violence in, 95; political violence in, 53; violence in, 179
Clark, Joseph, 168, 169, 174
Clinton, riot in, 80, 81
Clubs, conservative. *See* Gun clubs
Cochran, John, 58
Cochran, Mrs. John, 58

232

Coker, Simon, murder of, 176
Colleton County, violence in, 179
Collier, Thomas, 5
"Colonel Williams," 31
Columbia, 16, 50, 78, 80, 91; 1867 conservative convention at, 40; 1868 state Democratic convention in, 52; 1874 conservative convention at, 144; 1874 Republican state convention in, 143; 1876 Democratic state convention in, 165, 166; and 1876 campaign opening, 173; Board of Trade of, 140; capitulation of Chamberlain in, 188; congressional committee at, 97; gun clubs in, 139; Klan trials at, 99, 100, 105, 122; and the meeting of the Conservative Executive Committee in 1872, 126; and public reaction against soldiers in the statehouse, 194; U.S. Army at, 128; withdrawal of troops from, 200
Columbia Daily Union, 136, 140
Columbia Flying Artillery, 179
Columbia Musical Club with Four Twelve Pounder Flutes, 179
Columbia Phoenix, 40, 107
Columbia Union-Herald, 136
Confederates, amnesty for, 123; disfranchisement of, 2
Confederate States of America, and slavery, 4; and the arming of slaves, 4; army of, 77; defeat of, 10; goals of, 4
Confiscation of Southern property, rejection of, 17; opposition to, 123
Congress, 48, 51, 54, 63; and the backlog of Enforcement Act cases, 101; conservatism of, 96; investigation by, 56, 61, 97, 145; and Democratic control, 147; and the 1866 elections, 36; and the elections of 1872, 126; and the Joint Committee on Reconstruction, 32; and the Ku Klux Klan, 56; overrides Johnson vetoes, 32; and passage of the Military Reconstruction Act, 38; passes the Army Appropriations Act, 38; passes the Enforcement Act, 81; passes the Tenure of Office Act, 38; passes the Third Enforcement (Ku Klux) Act, 96; and the readmission of South Carolina, 16; Reconstruction program of, 2, 3, 32, 36, 38; refusal to seat South Carolina congressmen, 21, 28; refusal to seat Southern representatives, 32; and the removal of troops from South Carolina, 128; and Southern state militias, 74; and struggle with Johnson, 11, 21, 28, 32, 38; terminates the suspension of the writ of habeas corpus, 120–22; as viewed by "revisionists" 3; and waning enthusiasm for civil rights enforcement, 120
Conkling, Roscoe, 38
Conley, Benjamin, 103
Connecticut, 178; Democratic gains in, 147
Conner, James, 143, 144, 152, 153, 174; commands state's gun clubs, 169, 169; comments on Hampton's march in 1876, 173; and Grant's proclamation on gun clubs, 179; ordered to disperse gun clubs in Charleston, 192; and the Union Reform Party, 77; wife of, 174
Conservatives, and the 1868 presidential election, 53, 54; and the 1870 election, 75, 78, 88; and the 1874 election, 135, 137; assume power in South Carolina, 206; and abstention in the 1872 election, 127; and alliance with "Independent" Republicans, 144; and alliance with reform Republicans, 75, 76, 78; and arms shipments, 53, 54; concentrate on state election in 1876, 199; and fraud in

233

the 1874 election, 146; and fraud in the 1876 election, 191; and response to black militia, 74, 79, 89, 91, 139, 140, 141, 142, 148, 163, 164; and support for Chamberlain, 150; and the "Black Thursday" judges, 152; and the Citizen's Party, 76; and the Columbia Klan trials, 100; and the defeat of 1870, 83; and the formation of gun clubs, 138; and the issue of race, 129, 130, 160, 165; and the Ku Klux Klan, 61; and the Liberal Republican movement, 123, 124; leave the state House, 196; and the meaning of the 1874 elections, 147; meet with Governor Scott, 92; opposition to black suffrage by, 39; opposition to constitutional convention by, 39; racial attitudes of, 137, 138, 160, 161, 172, 207, 208; reconstruction plan of, 11–13; response to Grant's proclamation on gun clubs, 179; return to use of "Democratic" label, 160, 161; revise state constitution, 207; revise voting laws after Reconstruction, 207. *See also* Democratic Party

Constabulary, 74. *See also* Police

Constitution, convention for, 13; of 1868, 48–50, 57, 208; under the provisional government, 13; revision of in 1895, 207, 208

Constitution, U.S., 51, 61, 200, 208; and the Ku Klux Klan, 58

Constitutional conservatism, 210

Constitutionalist, 137

Constitution of 1865, 13; amendments to, 14; and emancipation, 14; and secession, 13

Contracts, and black labor, 17; and the Freedmen's Bureau, 17, 18

Convention, constitutional, 11, 13; of 1867, 40, 41; of 1868, 47–49; Democratic national of 1872, 124; Democratic state of 1872, 137; Democratic state of 1876 reconvened, 165, 166, 169; Democratic state of 1876, 162; of "Independent Republicans," 144; under Johnson's plan, 11; under the Military Reconstruction Act, 38, 39; opposition to in South Carolina, 39; Republican state of 1872, 125; Republican state of 1874, 142, 143; Republican state of 1876, 162, 166; in South Carolina, 13, 39; of state conservatives in 1874, 144; Taxpayer's, 137

Cooperationists, 130; and the 1876 campaign, 162, 165; opposition to in 1876, 165. *See also* Union Reform Party

Corbin, David T., 58, 94, 98, 101, 102, 105, 107, 119, 121, 125, 129; and the Columbia trials, 100; doubts Klan's destruction, 106; and the "Hamburg Massacre," 164; and the proliferation of gun clubs, 170; requests extra court terms, 121; and "selective prosecutions," 99

Cornish, Andrew, 41

Corruption, and conservative reaction, 136; and South Carolina Republicans, 136, 142, 148, 207, 210; and the gubernatorial election of 1874, 142; and the Republican schism in 1874, 143

Couch, Darius, 35

Councils of safety, 89

Courts, backlog of Enforcement Act cases in, 101, 119; civil, 13, 33, 34, 90, 121; and the Civil Rights Act, 32, 33; Democratic control of, 206; and election of the "Black Thursday" judges, 152, 159, 161; federal, 32, 33, 100, 101, 119, 194; fraud in, 73; inadequacy of, 101; and the Ku Klux Klan, 100,

121; military, 33, 34; and need for additional terms, 101; suspension of, 96; white control of, 34, 35, 73
"Crackdown" of 1871, 98, 99, 102, 108, 118, 119, 209; and court backlog, 101; and escape of leading Klansmen, 102; failure of, 102–104, 107, 121; historical interpretations of, 103; pardons for those convicted in, 129; problems with, 108; and resulting backlog, 100
Crosland, Edward, 71
"Crossing Jordan," 168
Cunningham, George, 170; and Charleston riot on election day 1876, 192; and the King Street Riot, 174

Dahomey, 127
Dakota, Department of, 122
Dana, Richard Henry, 10, 96
Darlington County, 34; armed blacks in, 59; mobilizes for the 1876 campaign, 161
Davis, Jefferson, and Southern independence, 4
Davis, John C., 151
Davis, John, 48
Davis, Mary Brown, 102
Davis, W. W., 107
Dawson, Francis W., 137, 143, 153; ceases supporting Chamberlain, 166; supports Chamberlain, 151
Dayton (Ohio), 98
DeCaradeuc, James, 14
DeForest, John W., 29
DeKnight, M., 53, 58
Delany, Martin, 144, 147
Democratic Party, 167; 1876 state convention, 162; and the 1870 election, 79; and the 1872 elections, 124, 126; and arms shipments, 79; and the black militia, 79; and the convention of 1868, 49; and dearth of black constituents, 169; and defeat in 1868, 63, 71; and the "division of time" in 1876, 172; divisions in during 1876, 167; and fraud in the 1868 presidential election, 62; and fraud in the 1876 election, 191; and Gary's "No. 1 Plan of the Campaign," 167; and intimidation during the campaign of 1876, 167; and the Ku Klux Klan, 57, 60; and the Liberal Republican movement, 124; maneuvering during the 1876 election crisis, 193, 195; need for organization in 1876, 161; and the "New Departure," 124; paramilitary mobilization of, 169, 170, 189; and remonstrance to Congress, 48; revises voting laws, 207; in South Carolina, 10; state executive committee of, 60, 161, 165; and "straight-outism" in 1876, 165; and tactic of "hacking" in 1876, 172; and tax manuever during the 1876 election crisis, 198; and usage of name in South Carolina, 161. *See also* Conservatives
Department of Revenue, 191
Depression of 1873, 147
DeSaussure, Louis, 174
DeSaussure, William, 40
DeSaussure, Wilmot, 77
Detroit (Mich.), 120
Devereux, John, 30, 34
Dill, Solomon Washington, assassination of, 54
Division of time, 171, 172
Dred Scott v. Sanford, 100
DuBose, Isaac Seabrook, 208
DuBose, William Porcher, 59
Duncan, B. Odell, 166
Dunn, T. C., 193
Dunning, William, 3

Edgefield County, 30, 52, 73, 81, 128, 166; 1874 election day violence,

146; 1876 election day violence, 190; armed bands in, 142, 190; black Democrats in, 169; black militia in, 141, 148; courts in, 73; Democratic club of, 52; disputed delegates from, 193–96; Freedmen's Bureau in, 18; gun clubs in, 139, 148; and Hampton's march, 173; hostility toward freedmen's school at, 31; Ku Klux Klan in, 72; militia guns confiscated from, 171; and Ned Tennant Riots, 141; riot in, 142, 148; violence in, 18, 141, 142, 174, 175; white militia in, 20

Edgefield Advertiser, 10, 14, 48, 51, 58, 129, 130

Edgefield Court House, 145; confiscation of militia guns at, 148, 179; courts in, 73; Democratic rally at, 173; storage of militia guns at, 142; U.S. Army at, 141, 175

Edie, John R., 53

Edisto Island, guerrillas on, 19

Edmunds, George, 119

Education, blacks and, 31; conservative opposition to, 31, 48; and the Redeemers, 207, 208; tax-supported, 151

Eight-box law, 207

Eighteenth Infantry, 34, 89, 92, 93, 128, 146, 190; and the campaign of 1876, 175, 178

Eighth Infantry, 51

Elections, of 1866, 35, 36, 38; of 1867 in South Carolina, 41; of 1868 in South Carolina, 47, 50, 58; of 1868 (presidential), 51, 52, 58–63, 71, 72, 74; of 1870, 75, 76, 78, 79, 81, 82, 88; of 1872, 123–27; of 1874, 135, 136, 138, 140, 142, 144, 147, 148; of 1876, 152, 153, 161, 162, 167, 170, 172, 179, 188, 190, 192, 197, 199, 207; of 1888, 207; and 1877 special commission, 200; of the "Black Thursday" judges, 161; disputed, 194; fraud in, 146, 191, 190, 193; and the Republican bolt of 1872, 125; violence in, 189, 190, 191, 192; and white immigration in 1874, 137

Electoral votes, contested in 1876, 199

Ellenton, riot at, 176, 178

Elliott, Robert Brown, 76, 78, 166, 201; distrusts the Union Reform Party, 77

Emancipation, 11; and the constitution of 1865, 14

Enforcement Act, 81, 95, 97; cases pending under, 122; cases thrown out, 128; and the Columbia Klan trials, 100, 101, 105; and crimes committed during the 1874 election, 146; and mild punishment in the Klan trials, 101; unconstitutionality of, 189

Enforcement, retreat from, 127

Escott, Paul, 4

Evans, W. McKee, 108

Extradition of Klan fugitives, 119–20

Fairfield County, black militia in, 79; suspension of habeas corpus in, 98

Fairfield Herald, 48, 127

Faust, Drew Gilpin, 4

Federalism, 210; and the Fifteenth Amendment, 72

Fereter, John, 73

Fifteenth Amendment, conservative nature of, 72; and the Democratic Party, 124; ratification of, 72

Fifth Artillery, and the campaign of 1876, 178

First Artillery, and the campaign of 1876, 178

First Ned Tennant Riot, 141, 142, 145

Fish, Hamilton, 120

Fitzgerald, Michael, 57

Fleming, Julius, 29, 33, 35, 41, 42

Florida, and the 1876 electoral dispute, 199
Fludd, Eliza, 17
Flynn, Charles, 56
Folger, O. C., 82
Foner, Eric, 16, 36, 57, 77, 103, 147, 200
Fort Monroe (Va.), 178
Fort Niagara (N.Y.), 178
Fort Sumter, bombardment of, 206; U.S. flag raised at, 1
Fourteenth Amendment, 32, 36, 40; and black suffrage, 36; and the Democratic Party, 124; ratification of, 37; South Carolina's rejection of, 37; Southern attitudes toward, 36–38
France, revolution in, 60
Franklin, John Hope, 3
Fraud, and the 1870 election, 78; and the 1876 election, 160, 161, 168, 191, 193, 199; as a conservative tactic in 1874, 146; and the defeat of Reconstruction in South Carolina, 200
Freedmen's Bureau Act, 32; Johnson's veto of, 32; revised version, 32
Fries Rebellion, 96
Fugitives, amnesty for, 128

Gaines, Tilman R., 137
Gardner, John, 166, 174
Garlington, A. C., 33
Gary, Martin W., 20, 52, 145, 166, 168, 174, 177; and the 1874 election, 137, 138; in the Civil War, 167; and the Hamburg Massacre, 164; and his "No.1 Plan of the Campaign," 167, 171; and immigration, 137; on race, 137; and "straight-outism," 162
Gatling Gun Company, and violence during the campaign of 1876, 176
General Assembly of South Carolina, 14, 37, 54, 71, 72, 137; and army intervention, 196; and election of the "Black Thursday" judges, 152; and the elections of 1868, 50; and the selection of governor in 1876, 193; corruption in, 125; creates National Guard Service of South Carolina (militia), 74; petition against removal of federal soldiers, 106, 107; and the reorganization of the black militia, 140; Republicans removed from, 206; resolution regarding the removal of federal soldiers, 127; revises election laws, 207; and the state militia, 20; supports "Sheridan's purge" in Louisiana, 149
General Orders No. 15, dissolution of military courts under, 34
General Orders No. 100, 96
Georgetown (village), riot in, 141
Georgetown Rifle Guards Club, 139
Georgetown Rifles, 139
Georgia, 81, 163; and federal policy of nonintervention, 149; Georgians voting in the 1876 election, 191; gun clubs in, 149; Klan fugitives in, 102; Ku Klux Klan in, 56; after Redemption, 190; violence against Republicans in, 149
Germany, immigrants from, 137
Getsen, Henry, 163
Ghislen, George, 53
Gile, George W., 34
Gillette, William, 3, 63, 108, 147
Gillmore, Quincy A., 13, 16
Gist, Joseph, 91
Gleaves, Richard H., 125; and the 1874 election, 144
Glover's plantation, 141
Gordon, John B., 174
Government, provisional, 209
Grant, Ulysses S., 3, 38, 62, 63, 90–92, 95, 96, 138, 145, 152, 178, 193; and the 1868 election, 60; and the 1872 elections, 124; and the 1874 elections, 147; appeals for enforcement legislation, 95;

237

and civil rights enforcement in the South, 103; and the congressional investigation, 98; corruption in the administration of, 123; and the "crackdown" in South Carolina, 88, 98, 108; and federal policy of nonintervention, 150, 164, 165, 174, 189, 195, 196, 198; and Hampton's call for taxes in 1876, 199; and lawlessness in South Carolina, 88; and Louisiana difficulties, 149; and the kidnapping of Bratton, 120; and the Liberal Republican movement, 123; May 3 proclamation of, 97, 106; and the Mississippi election of 1875, 150; petitions to, 164, 177; proclamation on "insurrection," October 17, 1876, 178; reelected in 1872, 127; and the "Reform Republicans" in South Carolina, 125; and the removal of troops from South Carolina, 128; and the South Carolina gubernatorial election of 1874, 143; suspends the writ of habeas corpus, 104; and use of troops in the 1876 election crisis, 196

"Grasp of War," 10, 96

Great Britain, 160

Greeley, Horace, and the Democratic Party in 1872, 124; defeat in 1872, 126; as Liberal Republican candidate, 123

Green, Henry D., 48

Green, John T., 146, 147; as "Independent" Republican nominee for governor, 144

Greenville County, 30, 128, 168, 179; 1876 election in, 190; and Hampton's march, 173; mobilizes for the 1876 campaign, 161; U.S. Army intervention in, 190

Greenville Court House, violence toward blacks at, 30

Greenville News, 160, 166

Gregorie, William, 206

Grimball daughters, 193

Guerrilla warfare, 49; Klan violence as, 108

Guffin, Lew, 73

Gun clubs, 138, 140, 145, 159, 160, 163, 166, 177; and the 1874 election, 144; and the 1876 campaign, 159, 164, 169, 170, 178, 179, 190; ; and the 1876 election crisis, 194, 196, 199; and altercations with black militia, 139, 141, 142, 148, 163, 164, 171, 172, 176–78; black, 169; and Chamberlain's proclamation ordering their dissolution, 177; in Charleston, 153; and Charleston riot on election day 1876, 192; demonstration at Fort Moultrie celebration, 162, 163; and division of time, 172; in Edgefield County, 139; estimated enrollment in, 169; formation of, 138, 139; in Georgia, 149; and Grant's proclamation ordering their dissolution, 178, 179; and the Hamburg Massacre, 163, 164; and Hampton's march, 173; and the King Street Riot, 174, 175; occupy Columbia, 196, 197; and the political mobilization of the Democratic Party, 139; and social functions, 139, 140; structure of, 139; and tactic of "hacking," 172; uniform of, 170

Guns, confiscation of by whites, 89, 171; distribution of by Republicans prior to 1876 election, 170; for the black militia, 75; purchase of by Scott administration, 59, 75; theft of, 179; white supply of, 79, 80, 139, 171

Habeas corpus, congressional termination of the suspension of, 120, 121; expiration of suspension, 122; and the Ku Klux Act, 96;

suspension of, 98, 100, 102, 104, 106, 120
"Hacking," 172
Hagood, Johnson, 166, 171; and the Ellenton riot, 176; opposes a "straight-out" ticket in 1876, 162
Haiti, 160
Halleck, Henry W., 73, 81, 90; opposes military intervention, 73, 74, 81
Hamburg, request for troops by intendant of, 174
Hamburg Massacre, and appeals for federal intervention, 164; Chamberlain's response, 165; and execution of blacks, 164; judicial proceedings following, 164; and negative effect of Northern opinion, 171; and "straight-outism," 163, 165
Hampton, Wade, 40, 100, 127, 162, 163, 174, 177–79, 193, 196, 199, 206, 210; and 1868 proclamation, 60; and 1876 campaign march, 173; asks Chamberlain to resign, 197; assumes governorship, 201; and black voters, 166; calls for taxes, 198; critical of Freedmen's Bureau, 17; disperses crowd in Columbia, 194; and the disputed election of 1876, 193; heads the "straight-out" ticket in 1876, 166; and the Ku Klux Klan, 60; nominated for governor in 1865, 14; opposes violence in 1876, 171; and opposition to 1867 convention, 40; and the policy of "bloodless coercion," 167, 171; promotes abstention in the election of 1872, 124; and the Union Reform Party, 77; unable to control Democratic excesses in 1876, 174; and U.S. troops in South Carolina, 175; views on black soldiers, 19; visits Hayes, 199, 200
Harris, W. P., 62

Hart, Alvin, 180
Harvey, Winfield S., 105, 106
Haskell, Alexander C., 61, 161, 162, 169, 176; leads takeover of "Mackey House," 195; urges conservatives avoid violence in 1876, 171
Hatch, John, 13
Hayes, Rutherford B., 171, 191, 199, 200; contacted by Hampton, 197; and the contested election in South Carolina, 200; elected president by commission, 199; and nonintervention in the South, 199–201, 206; orders removal of troops from statehouse, 200, 206
Haymond, John, 74, 75
Hayne, Henry, 129, 130; on the State Board of Canvassers in 1876, 193
Hayne, James H., nominee for lieutenant governor in 1872, 125
Hayne, Paul Hamilton, 136
Heath, William, 143, 145
Hemphill, Robert H., 93
Henderson, James, 62
Hendricks, Henry E., 170
Hennessey, Melinda Meeks, 4
Hibernian Hall, Fort Moultrie celebration at, 162; gun club demonstration at, 162; rally to protest the "Black Thursday" judges, 152
Hoge, S. L., 60, 63
Holmes, Nickels, 37
Hopkinson, James, 18
Horry County, 153
House of Representatives (South Carolina), Democrats withdraw from, 194; and the disputed vote counts in 1876, 193; divides during the 1876 election crisis, 197. *See also* General Assembly of South Carolina
Howard Amendment, 32. *See also* Fourteenth Amendment
Howard, Oliver O., 18, 29, 30, 34,

52, 53, 58; and Freedmen's Bureau schools, 31
Hubbard, John B., 59, 60, 78–82, 90
Huger, Alfred, 40
Huger-Smith, D. E., 139
Hunki-Dory clubs, and the 1876 election crisis, 196

Immigration, as a strategy for restoring white rule, 137
Impeachment, of Chamberlain, 152; of President Johnson, 100; of Scott, 125
Independent Republicans, and the 1874 election, 146
Indiana, Democratic gains in, 147
Indians, and fighting in the West, 122

Jackson, Frederick, 13
Jackson, J. A., 79
Jails, in antebellum South Carolina, 55
Jamaica, uprising in, 20
Johnson, Andrew, 2, 4, 13, 14, 17, 19, 29, 33, 38, 42, 47, 77; and the 1866 election, 35; and congressional opposition, 32; and the Fourteenth Amendment, 37; impeachment of, 100, 103; and leniency of Reconstruction program, 11; and the National Union Party, 35, 36; Northern opposition to, 28; proclamation declaring Civil War over, 32, 33; and provisional governments, 12; Reconstruction program of, 3, 11, 12, 21, 28, 39; second proclamation ending the Civil War, 33, 34; and the struggle with Congress, 11, 35, 38; "Swing around the Circle," 36; vetoes Civil Rights Act, 32; vetoes Freedmen's Bureau Act, 32
Johnson, H. A., 17
Johnson, Reverdy, as defense counsel at the Columbia Klan trials, 100
Johnson, W. R., 19

Johnston, Joseph E., surrender of, 1, 206
Joint Committee on Reconstruction, 100
Joint Select Commitee to Inquire into Conditions of Affairs in the Late Insurrectionary States, 56 97, creation of, 96; Report of, 104. *See also* Ku Klux Klan Report
Jones, A. O., 136
Jones, Cadawaller, 20
Jones, Iredell, 54, 57
Judd, Mr., confiscates counterfeit ballots in 1876, 191
"Juhl." *See* Fleming, Julius
"July" (former confederate soldier), 19
Justice. *See* Courts
Justice Department, 81, 98, 100, 102; and the campaign of 1876, 207; retreats from enforcement, 128, 129; and the U.S. Army, 98, 118, 119

Kaczorowski, Robert, 103
Keitt, Ellison S., 52
Kellogg, E. R., 190
Kershaw, James, 77, 138, 143, 144
Kershaw County, political violence in, 53
King, Edward, 136
King's Mountain, battle of, 173
Kingstree, 20
King Street Riot, 175
Kinyon, Richard, 62
Ku Klux Act, 96, 98, 100, 106; and the Columbia trials, 105; and the habeas corpus, 96; passage of, 96
Ku Klux Klan, 62, 73, 74, 78, 88, 90, 93, 97, 104, 107, 108, 123, 137–39, 144, 145, 174; and the 1868 presidential election, 58, 59; appearance in South Carolina, 55–57; an arm of the Democratic Party, 57, 58; arrests of, 98, 99, 101, 102, 104, 122; cases sus-

pended, 128; and class conflict, 56; clemency toward, 122, 129; and the "crackdown" of 1871, 125, 179; defense counsel for, 100; evades federal intervention, 102, 104, 119, 120; extradiction of, 119; in Georgia, 56; as a guerrilla movement, 57; inactivity of, 103, 105–7; investigated by Merrill, 94; and labor control, 56; membership of, 101, 102; and a movement against violence, 95; and Northern public opinion, 103; origins of, 55; political nature of, 56–58; reappearance of, 107, 118, 121, 128; and Republican resignations, 92; in South Carolina, 55, 56; surrender of members, 99, 102; targets Republicans, 57, 59, 72, 90, 91, 107; trial of, 100, 101, 104, 119, 122, 145; in Union County, 90; and the Union Leagues, 57; and Unionville assault, 91; and white supremacy, 160

Labor, contract system, 18, 29; and contract violations by whites, 29; interference with, 30; postwar situation, 17, 18, 29; restrictions under the Black Codes, 16; role of violence in, 29; and weaknesses of the Freedmen's Bureau, 29; white control of, 17, 18, 29, 52, 53
Laissez-faire, 123; and opposition to intervention in the South, 149
Lancaster County, political violence in, 53; suspension of habeas corpus in, 98
Lane, S. E., 128
"Largent" (former confederate soldier), 19
Laurens County, 51, 62, 89, 107, 119; armed bands in, 30, 79, 80, 89, 174; arrests in, 99, 119; black militia in, 79, 80; disputed delegates from, 193, 195, 196;

flight of Klansmen from, 119; and Hampton's march, 173; Klan activity in, 107; martial law in, 89; reappearance of Klan in, 106; riot in, 80, 119, 122; suspension of habeas corpus in, 98; violence in during 1876, 174; War Department investigation at, 30, 31
Laurens Court House, 61
Laurensville, 80; riot in, 88, 89, 119
Laurensville Herald, 119
Lawton, William, 54
Leahy, James, 78, 90
Leahy, Matthew, 142; intervenes in Edgefield riot, 141
LeConte, Emma, 11
Lee, Robert E., surrender of, 1, 206
Legislature of South Carolina. *See* General Assembly of South Carolina
Leighton, William, 31
Leland, John A., 122
Lester, J. C., 57
Lexington Court House, freedmen's school at, 31
Liberal Republican movement, 123; and the 1872 election, 123, 126; and Greeley, 123; and South Carolina conservatives, 123
Lieber, Francis, 96
Lieber's Code (General Orders No. 100), 96
Lincoln, Abraham, assassination of, 1, 206; calls for volunteers, 96
Lipscomb, Edward, 73, 93
Lloyd, Thomas, intervenes in Ellenton riot, 176
Logan, John, 38
Louisiana, and the 1876 electoral dispute, 199; legislature of, 149
Low, James P., wants "Special Force" for 1876 election, 170
Lowell (Mass.), 59
Lowndes, Thomas Pinckney, 41, 47, 72, 172
Loyalty oath, 11, 13

INDEX

Lyle, J. Banks, escapes the "crackdown" of 1871, 102

Machiavelli, Niccolò, 77
Mackey, E. W. M., 196, 197; speaker of Republican state House of Representatives, 195
Mackey, Thomas Jefferson, 54, 59, 142, 197; alleged corruption of, 76
Mackey House, claims legitimacy as House of Representatives, 195; elects Hampton governor in 1876, 197; as legal House of Representatives, 196
Magrath, Andrew, 143
Magrath, Thomas, 124
Maine, 178
Manigault, Edward, 102
Manigualt family, 174
Mann, E. L., 79
Marion County, 153; mobilizes for the 1876 campaign, 161; suspension of habeas corpus in, 98
Marlboro County, and Hampton's march, 173; violence in during 1876, 174
Marshall, Ann Eliza, 102
Marshals, U.S., during elections, 146, 164, 172, 191; legal restraints upon, 189; and the proclamation of May 3 (1871), 97; and the use of federal troops, 61, 81
Martial law, 89, 92, 95–97, 176; in South Carolina, 60
Martin, James, assassination of, 54
Martin, W. E., 40
Maryland, Klan fugitives in, 102
Massachusetts, 150, 178
McCrary, George W., 200
McDaniel, Harry, 61
McKie, Joshua, 145, 146
McKissick, Isaac, 82
McKitrick, Eric, 3
Meade, George G., 50, 51, 60, 61
Meigs Patent Arms, 59
Memphremagog, 127

Merrill, Lewis, 94, 95, 97, 98, 101, 107, 119–21; and catalog of Klan outrages, 105; doubts Klan's destruction, 106; and flight of Klan, 102; and the federal "crackdown," 99; investigates the Klan, 94; opposes Williams's selective prosecutions, 121
Miles family, 174
Miles, Richardson, 165, 170; and "hacking," 172
Miles, William Porcher, 77, 165
Military District of Western South Carolina, 13
Military Reconstruction Act, 38, 41, 50, 51, 103; becomes law, 38; and black suffrage, 39; conservative opposition to, 40; and creation of the Second Military District, 38; Johnson's veto of, 38; requirements for readmission under, 38; and Southern state militias, 74; unconstitutionality of, 61
Military rule, as preferable to black suffrage, 40, 41
Militia, and the 1870 election, 79; and altercations with gun clubs, 141, 142, 148, 163, 176, 177; arming of, 75; black, 56, 74, 75, 79, 82, 89–91, 93, 139, 140, 163, 172, 176, 209; creation of under the Scott administration, 74; disbanding of by governor, 93, 106, 148; disbanding of, under the Reconstruction Acts, 38; expansion of (black), 79; and the formation of the South Carolina Klan, 56; and the Hamburg Massacre, 163, 164; inadequacies of, 170; under the provisional government, 13; reforms in, 151; reorganization of in 1874, 140; white, 13, 20, 74; and white violence, 89, 141, 142, 172
Milling, David, 33
Mimms, Lawrence, 191

Missionary Herald, 76
Mississippi, 13, 98, 165; and the 1875 election, 149; impact on South Carolina, 150; Klan fugitives in, 102; riots in, 149; "White Man's Party" in, 149
Missouri, 94
Mitchell, Robert Hayes, 101
Montell, F. M., 19
Morris, J. M., 60
Moses, Franklin J., 75, 128, 139, 142; elected governor, 126, 127; elected judge, 152, 153; and the gubernatorial election of 1872, 125; and the reorganization of the militia, 140, 141; and Republican corruption, 136
Mullaly, John, 40
Murray, E. M., 162

Nance, Lee, assassination of, 54
Nation, The, 93, 94; and Hampton as a gubernatorial candidate in 1876, 166
National Guard Service of South Carolina, 74. *See also* militia
National Union Party, 35
Natter, George, 78
Nelson, E. Jonathan, 189, 190
New Departure, 77
New Hampshire, Democratic gains in, 147
New Orleans, riot at, 35
New York Evening Post, 99
New York Herald, 171
New York Tribune, 36, 123, 198; New York, 168, 178; hiring of men from, 176
Newberry County, 90, 119; armed bands in, 30, 78, 80; arrests in, 99, 119; guns in, 79, 171; and Hampton's march, 173; Klan activity in, 107; martial law in, 89; mobilizes for the 1876 campaign, 161; suspension of habeas corpus in, 98; U.S. Army in, 128; War Department investigation at, 30
Newberry College, 62
Night patrols, 106
Nuckles, Samuel, 62
No.1 Plan of the Campaign, damaging to the Democratic cause, 171; issued by Gary, 167; opposition to among Democrats, 171
North Carolina, 81, 173; voters from, at the 1876 election, 191

Oconee County, 62
Ohio, and Reconstruction, 72; Democratic gains in, 147; state printing system in, 136
Olsen, Otto, 4, 57
Ontario (Canada), Klan fugitives in, 102, 120
Orangeburg County, and Hampton's march, 173; Democratic club in, 53
Orangeburg Times, 126
Oregon, 103
Orr, James L., 13, 50; advises rejection of the Fourteenth Amendment, 37; and the gubernatorial election of 1872, 125; leads takeover of "Mackey House," 195; and the National Union Party, 35; and nomination for governor, 14

Pagan, James, 53, 54
Palmer, Mr., chased by gun club, 190
Palmetto Guards, 178
Palmetto Sabre Club, 139
Papacy, Southern attitudes toward, 166
Paramilitary forces. *See* gun clubs
Pardon, of Klansmen, 120
Pardons, Johnson's granting of, 11
Parker, Niles G., 125; indicted for corruption, 207
Patronage, and the black militia, 74, 93, 140
Patterson, John J., 76, 144, 169; indicted for corruption, 207

Pease, G. W., 18
Pennsylvania, Klan fugitives in, 102
Pennsylvanians, in South Carolina, 1
"People's War," definition of, 5
Perman, Michael, 3, 4, 39, 151
Peronneau, Miss, 59; and the campaign of 1876, 165
Perry, Benjamin Franklin, 12–14, 20, 33, 37; and the 1874 election, 136, 137; and the Fourteenth Amendment, 36; opposes 1867 convention, 40; and the presidential election of 1868, 53; proclamation of, 12; supports Greeley in 1872, 124
Philadelphia (Pa.), National Union Convention at, 35
Phillips, Wendell, 21
Pickens County, 82
Pickens, Samuel, 169
Picksley, John, 18
Piedmont, Ku Klux Klan concentrated in, 138
Pierrepont, Edwards, replaces Williams as attorney general, 150
Pillsbury, Gilbert, 75
Pilsbury, Amos, 122
Plataea, battle of, 61
Pleasants, M. F., 11
Pocosin, 178
Police, 59; and the King Street Riot, 174; in antebellum South Carolina, 55; inadequacy of, 59, 73
Political clubs; and black Democrats, 169, 186; Democratic, 139, 140, 167, 168; and division of time, 172; and Hampton's march, 173; and the policy of proscriptions, 168; receive guns, 170; Republican, 170
Pond Bluff Democratic Club, 168
Pond, C. H., 75
Poole, R. C., 63
Pope, Ida Waller, 56
Porcher, Louise, 28
Port Royal, 144

Porter, Judd, 62
Porter, William Dunlap, 49, 137, 138, 174
Posse comitatus, and the U.S. Army, 81
Post, Louis, 99
Pressley, B. C., 152, 153
Pringle, Robert A., 19
Printing, and Republican corruption, 136
Proclamation of Amnesty and Pardon, 11
Proclamation, by Chamberlain, ordering gun clubs to disband, 177; by Grant, on "insurrection" in South Carolina, 179; of May 3 by Grant, 97, 106
Proscriptions, in the campaign of 1876, 168; in the election of 1874, 145
Provisional government, in South Carolina, 4, 12
Provost courts. *See* courts, military
Purvis, Henry, 140, 141

Rable, George, 4, 51, 57, 147
race, as an election issue, 129, 137, 138, 165
race war, 36, 59, 79, 80; and the 1874 election, 140; white fears of, 20
Railroads, offer cheap rates into South Carolina for the 1876 election, 191
Rainey, Joseph B., 164, 199
Randolph, B. F., assassination of, 54, 57, 60
Ransier, Alonzo J., 82, 92
Ravenel, Henry W., 11, 19, 20, 36, 41, 59; and the campaign of 1876, 175, 188
Readmission, of South Carolina, 15, 50; of the Southern states, 28, 74, 96
Realf, Richard, 76
Reconstruction, and the 1874 elections, 147, 148; congressional program of, 2, 21, 32, 38, 72;

conservative plan of, 12, 15, 16, 21; and conservatives' victory in South Carolina, 200; and the continuity with the Civil War, 52; defeated by conservatives, 206, 209; and failure to restructure the Southern economy, 198; and federal enforcement, 83, 88; historiography of, 2, 3; Joint Committee on, 18, 28, 32, 100; and the Liberal Republican movement, 123; and Ohio, 72; opposition to, 4; and the presidential election of 1868, 51; presidential program of, 2, 11, 28; slave patrols during, 55

Red Shirts, 170, 206, 210. *See also* Gun clubs

Redeemers, 3, 207; and the campaign of 1876, 159; economic policies of, 208

Redemption, 135; impact on blacks, 207, 208; and the Liberal Republican movement, 123

Reed, J. P., 63

reformers, 76; in the 1870 election, 75; and the Union Reform (Citizen's) Party, 76

Reform Republicans, and the Democratic Party, 126; and the 1872 election, 125, 126

Regulators, 18, 107

Reid, Whitelaw, 21

Reister, John, 91

Reno, Marcus A., 106

Republican Party, 15, 56, 103; and the 1866 elections, 36; and the 1868 convention, 49; and the 1868 presidential election, 54, 61; and the 1870 election, 82, 88; and the 1874 election, 136, 143; abused by division of time in 1876 campaign, 172; and alliance with moderate conservatives, 75; appeals to Washington, 140, 170, 177; applies to Grant for aid, 92; and the black electorate, 38; blacks in, 3; and the bolt of 1872, 125; and the Citizen's Party, 76; collapse of in the South, 3, 4; and conflict with Chamberlain, 151; and control of the General Assembly, 50; corruption in, 3, 123; corruption in (in South Carolina), 58, 71, 75–78, 82, 125, 126, 135, 136, 142, 143, 148, 151, 207, 210; and the "crackdown" of 1871, 104; damaged by the failure of federal intervention, 108; economic deficiencies of in South Carolina, 198; fraud by, 82; and Gary's "No. 1 Plan of the Campaign," 167; in Georgia, 103; and Hampton's call for taxes, 198; inability to govern South Carolina, 128, 135, 148, 164, 174, 177, 178, 197; intimidation of, 81, 82, 90, 107, 128, 140, 145, 148, 164, 167, 169–71, 174, 178, 179, 189; investigations into by conservatives, 207; lack of legitimacy of in South Carolina, 49; and the Liberal Republican schism, 123; loses control of Congress in 1874, 147; maneuvering during the 1876 election crisis, 193, 196; Reconstruction program of, 32, 36, 38; resignations of, 92, 93; ruptures in, 71, 75–77, 118, 125, 142–44, 148, 150, 159; state convention of in 1872, 125; takes control of Congress and the presidency, 63, 71; and slavery, 208, 209; in the South, 3, 103; in South Carolina, 2, 5, 47, 130; as a target of the Ku Klux Klan, 55, 56, 58, 59, 73, 107; and unity for the 1876 campaign, 166; violence toward, 54, 89, 90

Restoration, of South Carolina, 12. *See also* Readmission

Rhett, Edmund, 15

Rhett, Robert Barnwell, Jr., 162

INDEX

Rhode Island, 178
Richardson, James, 171
Richland Rifles, 139
Richmond Dispatch, 171
Ridge Spring, riot in, 141
Riot, at Cainhoy, 177, 178; at Laurens, 122; in Charleston on election day 1876, 191, 192; King Street Riot, 174
Rivers, Prince, trial justice at Hamburg, 163
Roberts Breech-Loading Company, 75
Robertson, W. R., 80
Robespierre, Maximilien, 60
Rock Hill Grange, 160
Rock Hill, 20, 62, 90
Rose, Edward M., 90
Rouse's Bridge, and the Ellenton riot, 176
Ruger, Thomas H., 175, 178, 194; and the 1876 election crisis, 196; and Charleston riot, 192; moves to Columbia for the campaign of 1876, 175; restrained during the 1876 election crisis, 196
Runkle, Benjamin, 34

St. Helena, 20
Sally Rifles, 139
Saltiel, E. H., 176
Santo Domingo, 160, 161
Savannah River, 19, 81, 163
Sawrey, Robert, 72
Saxton, Rufus, 18, 29
Scalawags, 53, 72, 153; in the state government, 50
Schofield, John, 60; as new secretary of war, 50
Schofield, Martha, 72
Schurz, Carl, 12, 16, 19
Scoffin, John, 75
Scott, John, 97
Scott, Robert K., 51, 53, 58, 59, 61, 63, 72, 73, 76, 81, 82, 90, 94, 120, 143; and the 1870 election, 76; and the 1872 election, 125; and the appointment of trial justices, 73; assassination plot against, 54; as assistant bureau commissioner, 31, 35, 52; and the black militia, 74; and the "crackdown" on the Klan, 98; declares martial law, 89; disbands black militia, 91, 93; elected governor, 50; as gubernatorial candidate, 49; and martial law, 60; meets with leading conservatives, 93, 94; and militia patronage, 74; and party corruption, 125, 136; reelected governor, 82; requests federal assistance, 90–92; and the second black militia, 140; second inaugural address of, 82, 83; and the Union Reform Party, 78
Sea Islands, 1, 31; and fraud in 1876 election, 191
Secession, 4, 51, 188, 207; and the provisional government, 13; repeal of, 14; required repudiation of, 11; in South Carolina, 6, 12, 13; of South Carolina, 1, 206, 209
Second Artillery, and the campaign of 1876, 178
Second Enforcement Act, 95
Second Infantry, and the campaign of 1876, 178
Second Military District, 38, 50
Second Ned Tennant Riot, 148
Secret Service, investigations by, 102; and the kidnapping of Bratton, 120
Sefton, James, 103
Selective prosecutions, 99, 121; Merrill's opposition to, 121
Senate (South Carolina), 142; and the 1876 election crisis, 196; refuses tax levy, 198
Seventh Cavalry, 92–95, 105, 106; withdrawal of, 122, 127
Seymour, Horatio, 51, 62
Shand, Robert Wallace, 91, 102, 146, 168, 196; on the campaign of 1876, 159

Shapiro, Herbert, 48, 103
Sheppard, John, 191, 196
Sheridan, Philip H., 145, 149
Sherman, John, 38
Sherman, William T., 92; and march through South Carolina, 88, 173; removes troops from South Carolina, 128; removes troops from the statehouse, 200
Shofner, Jerrell, 3
Shorey, Henry, 30
Shy, John, 5
Sickles, Daniel E. 38
Simkins, Francis B., 49, 169; on fraud in the 1876 election, 191
Simonton, family, 174
Simpson, Brooks, 3
Simpson, William Dunlap, 166
Simpson, William, 63
Slaughterhouse cases, 189
Slave patrols, 55; in antebellum South Carolina, 18; postwar reappearance of, 18
Slavery, abolition of, 208; defense of, 4; end of, 2; protection of, 209; and the provisional government, 13; in South Carolina, 5, 12
Smalls, Robert, 199; indicted for corruption, 207
South, Department of the, 60, 90, 175, 178, 192
South, Division of the, 73, 81, 90, 97, 178
South Carolina College, 96
South Carolina University, 129, 130
South Carolinian, 129
"South Carolinian, A." *See* Townsend, Belton O'Neal
Spartanburg County, 63, 90, 93, 119, 145, 153; armed bands in, 80; arrests in, 99; black militia in, 79; gun clubs in, 179; and Hampton's march, 173; martial law in, 89; mobilizes for the 1876 campaign, 161; movement against violence in, 95; suspension of habeas corpus in, 98; violence in, 179
Spartanburg Herald, 149, 153, 161, 179, 198; and the 1875 election in Mississippi, 150
Spartanburg Village, congressional investigation at, 97; Ku Klux Klan in, 58; U.S. Army at, 106
Speights, A. M., 160
Springs, A. B., 15, 54, 80
Springs, N. L., 15
Springs, Richard Clark, 58
Stagg, J. C. A., 56
Stanbery, Henry, as defense counsel at the Columbia Klan trials, 100
State Board of Canvassers, and the disputed election of 1868, 194; and the disputed vote count in 1876, 193
Stevens, Mat, 90
Stevens, Thaddeus, 38
Stevenson, Job, 97
Stone, William, 53, 164; and the Cainhoy riot, 178
"Straight-out" ticket, arguments for, in 1876, 162; and the Hamburg Massacre, 165; unifies state Republicans, 166; wins support of state Democrats, 166
Strawberry Ferry, Republican rally at, 172
Stuart, Johnson, assassination of, 54
Suffrage, black, 36; federal protection of, 81; and the Fifteenth Amendment, 72; and the Fourteenth Amendment, 36; legal limitations on black exercise of, 207; qualifications for, 72
Sumner, Charles, 38, 120
Sumter County, 34, 73; black Democrats in, 169; and Hampton's march, 173; mobilizes for the 1876 campaign, 161; movement against violence in, 95
Supplementary Reconstruction Act, duties of the U.S. Army under, 39
Supreme Court of South Carolina,

and the 1876 election dispute, 193; denies jurisdiction to State Board of Canvassers, 193; orders arrest of State Board of Canvassers, 194; Republicans ousted from, 206; supports "Mackey House," 196
Supreme Court, U.S., 96, 148, 189;
Swails, S. A., 78
Sweetwater Sabre Club, 139
Swing around the Circle, 36

Taft, Alphonso, 164, 170; and federal policy of nonintervention, 195
Taft, William, 82
Taxes, Democratic reduction of, 208; Hampton's call in 1876, 198, 199; reduction of by Democrats, 207
Taxpayers' Convention, 137
tax unions, 137, 145
Taylor, Joe Gray, 3
Tennant, Ned, 139, 141, 142, 145, 146, 148
Tennessee, and the Ku Klux Klan, 55
Tenure of Office Act, 38, 103
Terry, Alfred H., 90, 97
"Texas Brown" (former confederate soldier), 19, 31
Texas, excluded from Johnson's first peace proclamation, 34
Thermopylae, battle of, 82
Third Artillery, 93; and the campaign of 1876, 178
Third Enforcement Act. *See* Ku Klux Act
Third Military District, 50
Thirteenth Amendment, 32, 50
Thompson, Henry, 56
Tilden, Samuel, 199; and the electoral vote controversy, 192; Hampton contacts, 197
Tillman, Benjamin R., 148, 160; and the 1874 election, 146; and the Hamburg Massacre, 163, 164
Tolbert, William, 54, 57
Tomlinson, Reuben, 54, 126; as gubernatorial candidate in 1872, 125

Tompkins, Daniel Augustus, 193
Torbell, Felix, 89
Towne, Laura M., 1, 20; reports fraud in 1876, 191
Townsend, Belton O'Neal ("A South Carolinian"), 55, 56, 135, 147, 160, 161, 207; and the 1874 election, 147
Townsend, Edward, 97
Trelease, Allen, 4, 57, 81, 103
Trenholm, George, 143
Trenholm, W. L., 63
Trescot, William, 72
Trial justices, 73
Trials, of Ku Klux Klan, 99, 100, 145
Trowbridge, John T., 12
Trumbull, Lyman, 38
Tucker, W. W., 71
Tullock, Thomas, 60
Tuxbury, G. E., 61

U.S. Army, 106, 107; and the 1868 presidential election, 61; and the 1874 election, 146; blacks in, 19, 20; and civil law, 73, 93, 94, 97; and conservatives' tax manuever in 1876, 198; cooperates with Justice Department, 98, 118, 119, 121; and the "crackdown" of 1871, 118; duties under the Military Reconstruction Act, 38; duties under the Supplementary Reconstruction Act, 39; and the Enforcement Act, 81; intervenes in Charleston riot, 192; intervenes in Edgefield, 141; intervenes in Ellenton riot, 176; intervention of, 60, 90, 97, 142, 190; and intervention in Louisiana, 149; and the Ku Klux Klan, 58, 60, 94, 95, 97, 103; opposition of conservatives to, 12; petition against removal of, 106; and provisional government, 13; refuses to intervene, 141; removal from civil affairs, 50; removal of, from statehouse, 200, 201, 206;

requests for, 90, 91, 170, 174; restraints upon, 148; in South Carolina, 1, 11–13, 17–19, 30, 33, 34, 51, 53, 60, 61, 92–94; in South Carolina for the campaign of 1876, 175, 178, 179; in statehouse during 1876 election dispute, 194, 196; and withdrawal from South Carolina, 122, 127, 138; in York County, 105, 106; withdraws from South Carolina

U.S. v. Cruikshank, 189

Union County, 59, 61, 62, 79, 119; armed bands in, 80; arrests in, 99; black militia in, 79, 93; Klan in, 90, 91; martial law in, 89; mobilizes for the 1876 campaign, 161; suspension of habeas corpus in, 98; violence in, 91

Union Leagues, 54, 57, 59

Union Reform Party, 71, 78, 100, 124, 126; and the 1870 election, 77; and alliance with reform Republicans, 77; convention of, 76, 78; defeat of, 82; fraud by, 82; replaces Citizen's Party, 76

Unionists, in South Carolina, 12, 13, 19; violence toward, 19

Unionville, 93; congressional investigation at, 97; Klan assault upon, 90, 91 *Unionville Times*, 79

Van Trump, Philadelph, 97

Vigilantism, in South Carolina, 16; South Carolina tradition of, 55; in Southern history, 55

Violence, and the 1868 presidential election, 53, 54, 58–61, 72; and the 1870 election, 75, 78–82; and the 1874 election, 141, 142, 145, 146; and the 1876 campaign, 161, 163, 167, 168, 175; conservative monopoly on in South Carolina, 198; in the defeat of Reconstruction, 210; failure of, 159; and Gary's "No.1 Plan of the Campaign," 167; influences Grant in 1874, 143; overwhelms Republican state government, 128, 170, 177, 178; and political goals, 51; and the second black militia, 141; in the South, 3, 4, 32, 95, 145; in South Carolina, 2, 5, 18, 30, 34, 60, 72, 81, 83, 89, 107, 128, 135, 141, 148; as a tool of labor control, 18, 30; toward blacks, 30, 32, 34, 72, 163, 164, 176; toward Unionists, 32

Virginia, Klan fugitives in, 102
Von Clausewitz, Carl, 5

Wadell, George, 174
Walhalla, 62; Ku Klux Klan in, 58
Walker, C. Irvine, 138, 169, 171
Wall, Henry, 128
Wall, O. S. B., 18
Wallace, A. S., 58, 63, 82, 172
Wallace, David Duncan, 56
Wallace House, established as state House of Representatives, 195; passes tax levy, 198
Wallace, R. B., 164, 170
Wallace, Robert M., 140, 145
Wallace, William Henry, speaker of Democratic state House of Representatives, 195
War Department, 12, 17, 50, 96, 98; and administrative changes following readmission, 50; and civil rights enforcement, 121; investigation by, 30, 31; and military courts, 33; Militia Bureau of, 75; sends troops into South Carolina, 175, 178; withdraws troops from South Carolina, 122
Wardlaw, David, 15
Watson, John, 61
Weatherly, T. C., 37
Welles, Edgar, 176
Wells, D. T., 51
West Point, 94

INDEX

Wharton, J. P., 79
Wharton, Vernon, 3
Wheeler Compromise, 149
Wheeler, William A., 171
Whipper, William J., 125; elected judge, 152, 153
Whiskey Rebellion, 96
White leagues, 145
White Line politics, 151; and the 1874 election, 137, 138
White supremacy, and the 1876 campaign, 160; and the Civil War, 208, 209; and the Ku Klux Klan, 57; unifies whites, 160
White, H. R., 92
Whiting, William, 12
Whittemore, B. F., 53, 78, 125
Wilkes, Jim, 91
Wilkins, Martin, 36
Williams, Alfred B., 160, 168, 169, 189; attends Republican rally, 172; and "hacking," 172; and the Hamburg Massacre, 165
Williams, George, 106, 119–21, 129, 140, 145, 148, 150; attempts to move troops into South Carolina, 144; clemency toward Klansmen, 122; and retreat from civil rights enforcement, 128; succeeds Akerman as attorney general, 102, 103
Williams, Jim, 101
Williams, John, 18
Williams, Lou Faulkner, 4, 55, 56
Williamson, Joel, 3, 51, 103
Wilson, D. L., 57
Wilson, Henry, 80, 81

Winnsboro County, riot in, 146
Winsmith, J. G., 145; requests federal intervention, 177
Witherspoon, Isaac, 80
Woodruff, Josephus, 142, 143
Woodward, C. Vann, and the Compromise of 1877, 200
Woodward, Charles, 37
Woody, Robert H., 49, 169; on fraud in the 1876 election, 191
Wright, James, 37
Wright, Jonathan J., and the Union Reform Party, 78
Wyatt-Brown, Bertram, 55, 56

Yale University, 90
Yocum, Benjamin, 74, 79, 89
York County, 62, 119; arrests in, 99; black militia in, 79, 93; Ku Klux Klan in, 61, 90, 94, 105; local movement against lawlessness in, 95; Seventh Cavalry in, 94; suspension of habeas corpus in, 98, 102
Yorktown, 173
Yorkville, 93, 98, 99, 120; congressional investigation at, 97; Democratic rally at, 173; local movement against lawlessness in, 94; Seventh Cavalry at, 94, 128; surrender of Klan at, 99
Yorkville Enquirer, 58, 94, 95
Young, Amie, 72
Young, William, 193

Zeigler, G. H., 30

www.ingramcontent.com/pod-product-compliance
Lightning Source LLC
Chambersburg PA
CBHW031347230426
43670CB00006B/456